'Rowlands is right that me
ography. He is also right th
their methods and what fol
place, *The Metaphysics of*
der, and I heartily endorse … plea for an authentic plurality, for allowing a multiplicity of metaphysical frameworks to operate freely within our discipline.'

Dale C. Allison, Jr., Richard J. Dearborn Professor of New Testament, Princeton Theological Seminary

'In this ambitious and very well-researched book, Jonathan Rowlands goes where most New Testament scholars fear to tread: the metaphysics of historical research. The study should challenge scholars to examine their own commitments, and to scrutinise those of others, when making judgements about how best to understand the historical figure of Jesus.'

Jonathan C. P. Birch, Lecturer in Theology and Religious Studies, University of Glasgow

'In this stimulating book Jonathan Rowlands uncovers what he terms the secular metaphysics undergirding modern historical Jesus research, arguing that the monopoly of such a perspective has had a deleterious effect upon the field. While accepting the need for such a perspective, Rowlands argues the case for a plurality of metaphysical frameworks within such historical enquiry, including an avowedly theological one. In what is a striking work of "meta-criticism," Rowlands, who displays an enviable literacy in philosophy and theology as well as New Testament studies, lays bare the often-unstated assumptions of a scholarly industry, while in suggestive mode, proposing a new, but complementary, Christian historiography. Whether in agreement or in disagreement, all those who read this book will learn much and ponder even more.'

James Carleton Paget, Reader in New Testament Studies, Faculty of Divinity, University of Cambridge

'Rowlands' book is a long overdue methodological intervention in Historical Jesus scholarship. He articulates and provides carefully argued and cogent reasons to think thoughts I have often had, however inchoately. His "From Reimarus to Wright" may prove a watershed contribution to the intellectual inquiry into the central subject of our discipline. Certainly, though not always easy, his challenge should be faced by all serious historical Jesus scholarship.'

Crispin Fletcher-Louis, Visiting Research Fellow, University of Gloucestershire

'Rowlands' *The Metaphysics of Historical Jesus Research* has the audacity to combine two things biblical scholars and historians have consistently kept apart: historiography and metaphysics. After demonstrating that every historical investigation is shaped by metaphysical presuppositions, he concludes that the methodological neutrality sought by historical Jesus studies has been an impossible goal. Instead, all three quests for the historical Jesus have been beholden to secular metaphysical assumptions. To remedy this rejection of a Christian worldview, Rowlands offers the beginnings of a Christian historiography based on a series of metaphysical commitments centered on the historical reality of Jesus's resurrection. Rowlands adds his voice to a growing chorus of biblical scholars and theologians who are rejecting historiography as it is currently practiced and pushing for more specifically Christian approaches. This book is a most welcome addition to that project and worth a thorough exploration.'

Seth Heringer, Assistant Professor of Theology and Scripture, Toccoa Falls College

'Calling the guild of historical Jesus scholars to examine the metaphysical presuppositions of their endeavors, Rowlands' work is an arresting and exhilarating intellectual journey. Exposing the secular underpinnings of historical Jesus research, Rowlands presents a compelling vision of how historical research into the New Testament can be more capacious and hospitable of theological worldviews. This work will be valued by historical Jesus researchers, and all those who seek to bring together biblical reasoning with theological reasoning.'

Angus Paddison, Acting Deputy Vice-Chancellor and Reader in Theology, University of Winchester

'This is an extremely impressive, lucidly argued and articulated, clarion call. Rowlands doesn't hide behind obfuscation or couch his important claims in inaccessible sophistry, but with enviable clarity maintains a simple yet important argument: historical Jesus scholarship has proceeded under the banner of an often unarticulated secular metaphysical substructure. This is so not only for the Hector Avalos' of this world, but also for purported Christian/evangelical treatments as proffered by N.T. Wright. Rowlands seeks to scrutinize the metaphysical underpinning of historiographical practices in this important book, and sheds light on an area often left in the dark. It is without question that he is absolutely correct in his contention that the assessment of historical plausibility, cause and effect and such like are not metaphysically neutral, and he is absolutely correct that faith in the risen Jesus raises fascinating questions at the moment prior to historiography, namely metaphysics. But this is no theological triumphalism! Rowlands wants both/and, so this is a welcome contribution to scholarly discourse, and sits proudly next to other recent treatments such as those penned by Sam Adams and Seth Heringer. What makes this work particularly important is its focus on "historical Jesus" scholarship as well as its astonishing clarity. I heartily endorse this volume and hope that it will deservedly stimulate important discussion in the years to come.'

Chris Tilling, Head of Research and Senior Lecturer in New Testament Studies, St. Mellitus College

‘Rowlands’ study patiently and insightfully surfaces fundamental questions about the ways in which real, operative, yet regularly unreflective metaphysical commitments orient and channel our exercise of historical imagination, judgment and insight in the study of fundament questions of Christian origins. By calling upon historians of early Christianity to acknowledge the need to make explicit, scrutinize, and dispute over these very commitments, he properly invites a better, self-critical and more sophisticated understanding and practice of the discipline of history in biblical studies.’

Philip G. Ziegler, Chair in Christian
Dogmatics, University of Aberdeen

The Metaphysics of Historical Jesus Research

In this book, Jonathan Rowlands interrogates the theological and philosophical foundations of the 'Quest' for the historical Jesus, from Reimarus to the present day, culminating in a call for greater metaphysical transparency and diversity in the discipline.

This multidisciplinary approach to historical Jesus research, drawing on historiography, sociology, philosophy, and theology, makes a significant and original contribution to the field. Part I outlines the implicit role of metaphysical presuppositions in historical methodology by examining the concept of a historiographical worldview. Part II provides an overview of the 'Quest' for the historical Jesus, demonstrating that the disparate historiographical worldviews operative in the 'Quest' evidence a particular shared characteristic, in that they might accurately be described as 'secular.' Rowlands' study concludes with a call for a greater plurality and openness regarding the philosophical and theological presuppositions at work in historical Jesus research.

The Metaphysics of Historical Jesus Research is of interest to students and scholars working on New Testament studies and historical Jesus research.

Jonathan Rowlands is Graduate Tutor and Lecturer in Theology at St. Mellitus College, UK. This is his first monograph and he has had articles published in *Novum Testamentum*, *Journal of Theological Interpretation*, and *Journal of Pentecostal Theology*.

The Metaphysics of Historical Jesus Research

A Prolegomenon to a Future Quest for the Historical Jesus

Jonathan Rowlands

LONDON AND NEW YORK

First published 2023
by Routledge
4 Park Square, Milton Park, Abingdon, Oxon OX14 4RN

and by Routledge
605 Third Avenue, New York, NY 10158

Routledge is an imprint of the Taylor & Francis Group, an informa business

British Library Cataloguing-in-Publication Data
A catalogue record for this book is available from the British Library

ISBN: 978-1-032-33282-6 (hbk)
ISBN: 978-1-032-33283-3 (pbk)
ISBN: 978-1-003-31895-8 (ebk)

DOI: 10.4324/b23077

Typeset in Times New Roman
by Deanta Global Publishing Services, Chennai, India

Jo, whose love and support are more integral to this book than the pages upon which it is written.

Contents

Preface xii
List of Abbreviations xiv

PART I
Worldviews and Historiographical Decision-Making 1

1 Theology and History, Then and Now 3

2 Defining Metaphysics 30

3 The Concept of a Worldview 50

4 Worldviews and Historiographical Decision-Making 71

5 Characterising Secular Scholarship 95

PART II
Worldviews and Historical Jesus Research 115

6 Metaphysics and the First 'Quest' 117

7 Metaphysics and the Second 'Quest' 133

8 Metaphysics and the Third 'Quest' 146

9 Metaphysics and N.T. Wright 166

10 Expanding the Boundaries of Historical Jesus Research 190

Bibliography 219
Author Index 252
Subject Index 255

Preface

This study is a revised version of my doctoral thesis, completed in the Department of Theology and Religious Studies at the University of Nottingham and supervised by Prof. Roland Deines and Dr. Conor Cunningham. This thesis was funded by the award of the Sir Francis Hill Postgraduate Scholarship at the University of Nottingham. I could only undertake my doctoral research due to this scholarship, and I am grateful to the University of Nottingham for this award.

There are many people to whom I owe a significant debt of gratitude in completing this thesis. I am inevitably unable to thank everyone who deserves it, for which I apologise. However, a few people deserve to be singled out for their efforts in helping me bring this thesis to completion. That I have been able to submit it is due in large parts to these people and their loving support.

Thanks are due, first and foremost, to my wonderful wife, Jo. She has been unwavering in her support of me throughout the duration of my doctorate, emotionally, spiritually, financially, and practically. For me to put into words how much she means to me, and how incredible she has been over these past few years, this book would be at least twice the length it is. She has done more for me than I could possibly say here, and I will forever be grateful for her, and her unending love. This book is dedicated to her; indeed, it could only be dedicated to her.

Chapter 9 is a revised version of my earlier article: Jonathan Rowlands, 'The Theological Lineage of N. T. Wright's Historical Method,' *Journal of Theological Interpretation* 16.1 (2022), 110–31. I am grateful to Julie Ann Lambert and Penn State University Press for permission to reuse this material here.

I also wish to thank my supervisors at the University of Nottingham, Prof. Roland Deines and Dr. Conor Cunningham. Prof. Deines, especially, has always read my work in extraordinary detail and has gone beyond what is required of him to develop me as a scholar and a person, beyond merely helping me gain a qualification. This has been true despite us working in different countries for much of my PhD.

Thanks are also due to my parents, Angela and Yam. They have always encouraged me in my desire to pursue postgraduate study, and they have been unquestioning in their support of my choice to do so. I'm still not sure I have grasped how much they have helped me to get to this point, and I'm not sure I ever will.

My thesis was examined by Dr. Angus Paddison and Prof. Thomas O'Loughlin, and I am immensely grateful to both of them for the gracious yet incisive manner in which they probed my argument in my viva. To have two scholars such as these discuss one's work in the detail they did is an immense privilege that I am grateful to have received. I am also grateful to them for encouraging me to pursue the publication of my thesis, and for their advice on this matter, too.

Amy Davis-Poynter and Marcia Adams at Routledge have been a complete joy to work with throughout the entire publication process, as has Jayanthi Chander, Project Manager of the book. This book is far better for all of the careful and tireless work they have put into it.

I am also grateful to the faculty in the department of Theology and Religious Studies at the University of Nottingham. Besides my supervisors, several individuals have been a source of support, joy, (helpful) challenge, and encouragement. They are Prof. Carly Crouch, Prof. Alison Milbank, Dr. Tim Murray, Prof. Simon Oliver, Dr. Sara Parks, Dr. Peter Watts, and Dr. Mark Wreford. Mark Wreford and Tim Murray both kindly read the thesis closely and offered very constructive feedback; it is far stronger due to their advice.

Finally, I wish to thank my colleagues at St. Mellitus College, East Midlands, Sam Baker, Phoebe Chevassut, Geri Coates, David Emerton, Ali Hogger-Gadsby, David Hughes, Alex Irving, Alison Jones, Steve and Andrea Lees, Jitesh Patel, Sharon Prentis, Grant Walton, and Anna Westin. I joined St. Mellitus as I was in the final stages of writing up my thesis, perhaps the most stressful juncture of my PhD. They were a constant source of encouragement and prayer during this time and made the process that bit more bearable. I am also grateful to the rest of the team in the St. Mellitus family, who made me feel so welcome, and to David Emerton, Alex Irving, Steve Smith, Chris Tilling, and Jane Williams, in particular, for helpful conversations about my thesis and getting it published. Finally, I wish to thank our wonderful current MA students at St. Mellitus College, East Midlands: Simon Bentley, Angelika Bocchetti, Daniele Bocchetti, Jake Hyatt, Maria Jukes, Richard Knowles, John Lees-Robinson, Danny Marshall, Erin Pickersgill, Tors Ramsey, James Roe, Ian Sweeney, and Rob Wood. While recently working through N.T. Wright's *History and Eschatology* with them, their charitable yet incisive engagement with the text (and with my reading of the text) helped me to sharpen and clarify many of my thoughts on the matters discussed in this study, for which I remain immensely grateful.

Soli Deo Gloria

Nottingham, March 2022

Abbreviations

Abbreviations in this study follow *The SBL Handbook of Style: For Biblical Studies and Related Disciplines* 2nd edn (Atlanta, GA: SBL, 2014). Abbreviations not found there are listed below.

ASR	*American Sociological Review*
HNTR	William Baird, *History of New Testament Research*, 3 vols (Minneapolis, MN: Fortress, 1992–2013)
HSHJ	Tom Holmén and Stanley Porter (eds), *Handbook for the Study of the Historical Jesus*, 4 vols (Leiden: Brill, 2011)
IJPS	*International Journal of Philosophical Studies*
JM	*Journal of Management*
JP	*Journal of Philosophy*
JPE	*Journal of Political Economy*
JR	*The Journal of Religion*
JSHJ	*Journal for the Study of the Historical Jesus*
JSL	*Journal of Symbolic Logic*
JSS	*Journal of Semitic Studies*
JSSR	*Journal for the Scientific Study of Religion*
JTI	*Journal of Theological Interpretation*
JVG	N. T. Wright, *Jesus and the Victory of God* (London: SPCK, 1996)
KSA	Friedrich Nietzsche, *Sämtliche Werke: Kritische Studienausgabe in 15 Bänden*, ed. Giorgio Colli and Mazzino Montinari (Berlin: de Gruyter, 1980)
NTHIP	Werner Georg Kümmel, *The New Testament: The History of the Investigation of its Problems* trans. S. McLean Gilmour and Howard C. Kee (London: SCM, 1973)
NTPG	N. T. Wright, *The New Testament and the People of God* (London: SPCK, 1992)
PFG	N. T. Wright, *Paul and the Faithfulness of God* (London: SPCK, 2013)
PhilSci	*Philosophy of Science*
PP	*Philosophical Perspectives*

PPQ	*Pacific Philosophical Quarterly*
PQ	*Philosophical Quarterly*
PRS	*Perspectives in Religious Studies*
PT	*Philosophical Topics*
RP	*Research in Phenomenology*
RSG	N. T. Wright, *The Resurrection of the Son of God* (London: 2003)
Soc. Forces	*Social Forces*
SR	*Sociology of Religion*
TLP	Ludwig Wittgenstein, *Tractatus Logico-Philosophicus* (London: Kegan Paul, 1922)
UM	Friedrich Nietzsche, *Untimely Meditations*, ed. Daniel Breazeale, trans. R. J. Hollingdale (Cambridge: Cambridge University, 1997)
WP	Friedrich Nietzsche, *The Will to Power: An Attempted Transvaluation of All Values*, 3rd edn, trans. Anthony M. Ludovici (London: T. N. Foulis, 1914)

Part I

Worldviews and Historiographical Decision-Making

1 Theology and History, Then and Now

1.1 Introduction

Metaphysics is prior to historiography. And there can be no value-neutral system or framework of metaphysics from which a methodological consensus about historical enquiry may proceed. It is the central thesis of this study that these two claims form intractable problems for the discipline of historical Jesus research and, moreover, that these problems ought not to be 'solved' (as though that were possible), but embraced, if the discipline is to advance in any meaningful sense. Only by embracing our fundamental philosophical and theological biases—and not by the impossible task of trying to overcome them—can the field truly progress.

In this study I examine the metaphysical presuppositions operative within modern academic historical Jesus research. The discipline has not sufficiently reflected upon its metaphysical foundations, and I argue it operates within a series of metaphysical frameworks one might accurately label 'secular.' My concern is to probe one aspect of the relationship between faith and history, not in terms of historically informed faith, but in terms of faith-informed historiography. I am concerned with the question, 'is it reasonable to construct an academic historical method that presumes belief in God as a given, or even as axiomatic for a full account of the past?' I argue secular metaphysical presuppositions influence historical judgement and observe this influence by employing the category of worldview in relation to historical decision-making. This observation invites us to examine the metaphysical presuppositions at work within modern academic historical Jesus research, which one may observe as adhering to a totalising secular metaphysical presupposition not to allow religious perspectives to contribute to the historical task. I conclude by claiming this observation should encourage the discipline to allow a greater plurality of metaphysical frameworks within the field, although the construction of historical-critical methods based upon alternative metaphysical frameworks is necessarily reserved for a future project rather than developed fully here.

Elisabeth Schüssler Fiorenza speaks of the need for 'exploration of the contemporary presuppositions and frameworks of exegetical-historical and theological work that govern historical Jesus research,' in a manner that 'seeks to

DOI: 10.4324/b23077-2

expose the contesting interests and theoretical frameworks that determine the re-constructions of the historical Jesus and their implications for contemporary communities of faith.'[1] In what follows, I seek to take up this call by examining the presence within these frameworks of certain particular metaphysical presuppositions that guide, influence, and govern the boundaries of historical Jesus research. In many ways, therefore, this present study shares affinities with Hart's recent meta-critique of Pauline studies, which also seeks to highlight foundational assumptions upon which that particular discipline is predicated to encourage scholars within the field to reflect upon the (often implicit) preconditions posited for academically acceptable study of Paul.[2] In what follows here I undertake a similar task with particular reference to the 'Quest(s)' for the historical Jesus.

From the very beginnings of the early Jesus movement, there have been attempts to apprehend the 'historical Jesus,' in some sense. By this, I mean (1) there has always been some concern to understand and preserve truths about the historical Jesus, and (2) the historical reality of what Jesus said and did (or, at least, what the New Testament writers *thought* Jesus said and did) played a vital role in informing the subsequent theological reflections of the early Church. Of course, this does not preclude the possibility the New Testament writers consciously *created* narratives they attempt to present as historical. Even if this is the case in certain instances, this still suggests claims about the historical Jesus carried weight among the primary readership of the New Testament. Concerns about the historical Jesus may not be *the* central concern of the New Testament, but they certainly were *a* central concern.

One may observe this sensibility not only in the work of the four evangelists—who ground their gospels in Jesus' life and teaching—but in the New Testament epistles also. The author of Hebrews, for example, presents Jesus' ministry as congruent with the work of a High Priest, but faces a historical problem: 'it is evident that our Lord was descended from Judah, and in connection with that tribe Moses said nothing about priests' (Heb. 7.14). If the author wishes to develop a high priestly Christology, the historical data available to the author prevents him from doing so in a conventional manner. The author's commitment to preserving what he believes to be a historical truth concerning Jesus' genealogy leads the author to claim Jesus is 'a priest forever, *according to the order of Melchizedek*' (Heb. 7.17; cf. 5.6, 10; 6.20; 7.1, 10, 11, 15). While the connection to Melchizedek becomes a vital part of the author's Christology, this claim is at least partly born from an acknowledgement of the lineage of the historical Jesus. If the author of Hebrews and his audience were disinterested in the historical reality of Jesus' life, such theological manoeuvres would be unnecessary. In other words, a concern about the historical Jesus informs the author's theology.[3]

Historical claims about Jesus are also present in the most fundamental NT statements of faith. In 1 Cor. 15.17 Paul warns, 'if Christ has not been raised, your faith is in vain and you are still in your sins.' This statement is bound up with questions of the historical Jesus; it rests upon the claim that God in some sense interacted with the world of human affairs to raise Jesus from the dead. The plural ταῖς ἁμαρτίαις suggests Paul's focus is on individual infringements of divine law perpetrated by human agents, that the claim has in its sights the lives of historical, concrete individuals.[4] This frames the soteriological elements of Jesus' ministry not only ontologically, whereby he has freed humankind from bondage to sin (sin here conceived of as a unified power, or force), but also as exerting a real, tangible impact upon the human realm.

Paul writes as though it is reasonable to base his proclamations about Christ upon historical claims. He operates within a cultural milieu wherein divine agency is not easily divorced from historiography. Ancient historians operated with 'reserved objectivity,' Deines notes, whereby miraculous events were discussed in such a manner that allowed for the possibility of divine agency.[5] Josephus, for example, would often conclude such discussions by stating: 'concerning such matters, let each one judge as is pleasing to him' (e.g., *Ant.* 1.108). The NT writers composed their texts in a cultural setting that allowed the incorporation of theological presuppositions concerning divine agency into their historiographical claims. If those outside the faith disputed the apparently miraculous claims of the early Christians, it was not because such things did not or could not have happened, but that the Christians happened to be wrong in this instance. In Matt. 28.11–15, the evangelist combats a 'widely circulated' (v. 15) Jewish polemic against the Christian claims about Jesus' resurrection. Rather than God raising Jesus from the dead, these Jews claimed Jesus' disciples stole his body. The need to offer counter evidence against Jesus' resurrection suggests that such a historical claim was, in the first instance, reasonable in this particular cultural and historical context. There is no need to polemicise against something one's broader milieu views as impossible. For the NT writers—and their cultural counterparts—divine agency was a reasonable component of historiography.

In contrast, modern academic historical Jesus research approaches the historical figure of Jesus in a manner that precludes the possibility that religious perspectives may contribute to the discipline. Bultmann famously declared that 'people cannot use electric lights and radios … and at the same time believe in the spirit and wonder world [*Geister-und Wunderwelt*] of the New Testament.'[6] Post-Enlightenment developments and the pursuit of scientific accounts of the universe encourage historians to conduct their research along similar lines. The foundational observation that underpins Bultmann's demythologising programme is the recognition that secular and Christian accounts of reality are incompatible, an observation forcefully echoed to differing effect by the likes of Taylor and Milbank.[7] More importantly, it is a claim with implications for historical Jesus research.

In cultures, pervasive in many modern societies, which highlight the epistemological value of science and reason as much as (or even more than) theology and faith, one may no longer uncritically take divine or spiritual agency as a 'given' in historiographical methodology. In its place, attempts have been made to posit a neutral framework for historiography, one whereby all participants may approach the past with parity. The present study enquires as to the success of these endeavours within historical Jesus research in particular.

1.2 The State of the Question

There has been a revitalised interest in the theological interpretation of scripture in recent years.[8] Paddison notes:

> In response to a biblical studies guild that at its margins, and sometimes at its core, has wanted to distance study of the Bible from questions provoked by the patterns of Christian living, the movement that has become known as "theological interpretation of Scripture" has made clear and concerted efforts to rejuvenate the relationship between thinking biblically and thinking theologically.[9]

Elsewhere I have argued theological interpretation might renew (and re-secure) the discipline of New Testament studies as a whole.[10] However, regardless of this emerging sensibility, biblical scholars and historians have devoted less attention to issues of theological approaches to *historiography*, and there remain those who question the legitimacy of theologically motivated scholarship broadly construed.[11] This is not to say the issue has been entirely neglected; several scholars have reflected in depth upon the relationship between history and theology broadly construed, or, in some cases, historical Jesus research and Christian theology specifically. This list of scholars, below, is necessarily incomplete; there are many more works contributing to this discussion I cannot discuss here.[12] However, I hope what follows serves as an overview of the question at hand, of the nature of the proper relationship between Christian theology and historiography. By giving the brief overview that I do here, I hope that the contribution of my own study to this ongoing conversation, outlined in detail below, can more clearly be drawn into focus.

1.2.1 Martin Kähler

One of the first scholars to offer a meta-critique of post-Enlightenment approaches to the historical Jesus from a theological perspective was Martin Kähler. In this respect, one may trace concerns about the relationship between historical Jesus research and Christian theology to the publication of Kähler's *Der sogenannte historische Jesus und der geschichtliche, biblische Christus*.[13] Kähler rejected attempts to study Jesus as though he were simply another man in antiquity, claiming insufficient evidence: 'the New Testament presentations were not written for the purpose of describing how Jesus developed' (51).[14] These historians, Kähler claims, neglect 'the special nature of the problem and the peculiar claims of Scripture' (46) namely, that Jesus was not simply one man among others, but was 'the revelation of the invisible God' (58). Thus, for Kähler, historical-critical approaches to Jesus can never reveal the truth encapsulated by his life and teaching, that it is 'inadvisable and indeed impossible … to reach a Christian understanding of Jesus when one deviates from the *total* biblical proclamation about him—his life as well as its significance' (68, emphasis in original). Thus—and this is the crucial point—there can be no equivocation of the historical Jesus with the theological Christ. 'The risen Lord,' Kähler writes, 'is not the historical Jesus *behind* the Gospels, but the Christ of the apostolic preaching, of the *whole* New Testament' (65, emphasis original). In other words, the historical Jesus is not the real Jesus. Rather:

> The real Christ, that is, the Christ who has exercised an influence in history, with whom the great witnesses of faith have been in communion—while striving, apprehending, triumphing, and proclaiming—*this real Christ is the Christ who is preached.* The Christ who is preached, however, is precisely the Christ of faith.
>
> (66, emphasis original)

But herein lies the problem with Kähler's work: the 'preached Christ,' the kerygma, lacks any normative historical framework by which it resists abuse and misinterpretation. Ebeling writes:

> If the person to whom the kerygma refers is in no way concretely definable in his historicity, if the reference of the kerygma to Jesus consists exclusively in assertions for whose understanding Jesus himself is irrelevant, as merely a cipher that is accidental and in itself says nothing, then the kerygma—if it could be kerygma at all—would be pure myth.[15]

Beyond concerns about the ahistorical nature of Kähler's kerygma, I wish briefly to note another objection. While Kähler's work is concerned primarily with the ability of historical Jesus studies to inform Christian theology, Kähler neglects to countenance the notion that Christian theology might impact upon one's reconstruction of the historical Jesus. In other words, for Kähler, the task of the historian is only ever one that is guided by secular presuppositions and metaphysics, although he of course does not state the matter in these terms. This claim will be substantiated in more detail in Chapter 6 (§4) of this study, but suffice it to say here that, while Kähler's rupture between the Jesus of history and the Christ of faith highlighted crucial distinctions between methodological approaches in historiography and theology, his proposed solution, his emphasis on the proclaimed Christ, perpetuates the very issues raised in the first place and results in an amorphous Christ whose proclamation can simultaneously mean anything and nothing.

1.2.2 Ernst Troeltsch

Shortly after the publication of Kähler's provocative essay came Ernst Troeltsch's 'Über historische und dogmatische Methode in der Theologie' in 1898,[16] in which Troeltsch sought to rebuff criticisms that he was a 'historical relativist,' while simultaneously demonstrating the superiority of the Christian religion.[17] Troeltsch distinguished between theologically motivated historiography (that proceeds from 'the old authoritarian concept of revelation') and the apparently a-theological and 'genuine historical scholarship of the present' (12–3). Only this new scholarship provides reliable forms of knowledge, such that the 'old' approach to history is no longer viable: this new scholarship 'represents a complete revolution in our patterns of thought vis-à-vis antiquity and the Middle Ages' (16).

But this poses a problem for Troeltsch, insofar as the superiority of Christianity cannot be demonstrated with recourse to this new scholarship. As he wrote elsewhere, 'history is no place for "absolute religions" or "absolute personalities." Such terms are self-contradictory.'[18] The result of this is a sharp distinction between historical and theological methodology in Troeltsch's thought; one must either approach Jesus historically *or* theologically, there can be no confluence between the two methods. To discuss historical issues of incarnation, resurrection, transfiguration, or the miraculous, is to operate in a manner that 'vitiates and distorts the methodology of secular history in various ways' (23).

This point is crucial for the possibility of theological historiography, because Troeltsch makes clear that a purely historical project is one that resists theological influence throughout. As he himself writes:

> once employed, the inner logic of the [historical] method drives us forward; and all the counter-measures essayed by the theologians to neutralize its effects or to confine them to some limited area have failed, despite eager efforts to demonstrate their validity.
>
> (18)

To be clear, then, Troeltsch's approach to history is a thoroughly totalising one; at no point can theology be allowed to speak into the issue of the historical Jesus. 'Give the historical method an inch,' he writes, 'and it will take a mile. From a strictly orthodox standpoint, therefore, it seems to bear a certain similarity with the devil' (16).[19] Or, as he puts it elsewhere, 'once applied to the scientific study of the Bible and church history, the historical method acts as a leaven, transforming everything and ultimately exploding the very form of earlier theological methods' (12).

As with my reading of Kähler, my critique of Troeltsch's position centres around the metaphysical presuppositions operative in his approaches to historiography, which will be spelled out in more detail in Chapter 6 (§5). Suffice it to say for now that, for Troeltsch, history and historiography are terms laden with secular metaphysical presuppositions. However, as I seek to make clear in this study, there can be no metaphysics—including secular metaphysics—that does not impinge upon theology. Troeltsch was one of the first to reflect in depth on the nature and possibility of theology and history coexisting; he rightfully remains a key figure in this debate.

Troeltsch's position appears to have softened in later years, when he would write:

> Total exclusion of religious faith from scientific work is only a possibility for those who for special reasons have killed or let die their notion of religion.

> Those in whom religion continues to live ... will always be convinced that the different sources of knowledge must somehow coincide and harmonise.[20]

This notwithstanding, his earlier distinction between theological and historical methods greatly influenced historical Jesus research and New Testament studies in the 20th century.[21] And yet, Troeltsch's early position is no longer tenable, as I seek to demonstrate in this study. Instead, I hope to demonstrate that a confluence of theological and historical methodology is not only possible, but unavoidable.

1.2.3 George M. Marsden

Following the important groundwork set by Kähler and Troeltsch, the 20th century saw little in the way of reflection upon the interaction of theology and history on the part of Jesus historians. Heikki Räisänen, for example, went as far as to suggest that NT theologies have uncritically mixed historical and theological concerns to such a degree that the entire task of writing NT theologies ought to be abandoned. He suggests replacing it with either a historical reconstruction of early Christian belief in the context of second temple Judaism, or critical reflection upon the NT and its influence, but not both together. He calls for scholars not to mix these two tasks, and encourages them to include their theological results, if any, 'in a concluding section of the historical work, or in an appendix following the historical account.'[22] However, following the turn of the 21st century, several scholars began again to reflect upon the proper relationship of history and theology. One such figure is George Marsden, an American historian concerned with the intersection between Christianity and American culture, most famous for his biographical work on Jonathan Edwards.[23]

In 1994, Marsden published *The Soul of the American University* which contrasted the Protestant roots of American higher education with the (then-)present culture within American universities which considers religious perspectives inappropriate frameworks for academic research.[24] His aim is to trace the manner in which American higher education rejected its Protestant roots so that non-belief became the established default framework for academic enquiry. In a 'Concluding Unscientific Postscript,' Marsden argues that Christian perspectives should no longer be viewed as inferior or inappropriate frameworks for academic enquiry. Instead, this systematic undervaluing of Christian scholarship contrasts the foundational ideals of academia. He argues there is no reason to exclude religious perspectives from the academy, and that 'exclusivist naturalism is unsubstantiated and unfalsifiable.'[25] Reviewers of *The Soul of the American University*, while praising Marsden's monograph as an 'historical work of extremely high quality,'[26] questioned Marsden's calls for religiously inclusive scholarship. Some questioned how appropriate it was for Marsden to conduct research from an explicitly religious perspective. As one reviewer put it, 'there is a certain incongruity in the sixteen page [postscript] tail wagging an over-400-page dog.'[27]

Conscious of these reservations, Marsden later outlined his argument in more detail in *The Outrageous Idea of Christian Scholarship*.[28] Therein, he begins by claiming 'many of the most prominent academics ... are unable to produce a compelling basis for preferring one set of principles over another ... Others, probably most academics, do not even try to deal with first principles' (3). Thus, Marsden posits:

> Mainstream American higher education should be more open to explicit discussion of the relationship of religious faith to learning. Scholars who have religious faith should be reflecting on the intellectual implications of that faith and bringing that faith into the mainstream of intellectual life. Although scholars of no faith or of other faiths may strongly disagree on the issues involved, all should participate on equal terms in academic dialogue.
>
> (3–4)

He begins (14–24) by recapping the historical arguments made in *The Soul of the American University*, focussing on the claim that post-Enlightenment efforts to undermine religious hegemony in higher education resulted in naturalism *replacing* Protestant Christianity as the gatekeeper of academic acceptability. The academy replaced one form of hegemonic scholarship for another, rather than promoting a genuine pluralism and, as a result, the desire for 'tolerance' proved fruitless. In its place, academia is characterised by 'silence' where faith-informed perspectives are concerned (26–7). Marsden notes double standards concerning faith in academia, observing that there have been 'other intellectual trends, long present in western thought but widespread since the 1960s, which have pilloried 'the Enlightenment project' and claims to simple empirical standards for truth' (26), while a post-Enlightenment preference for 'science' over 'faith' remains the *de facto* default position for academics. Postmodern historiographical approaches by the likes of Foucault,[29] White,[30] Lyotard,[31] and Rorty[32] have highlighted the dangers of allowing a dominant, totalising historiographical approach. Similarly, the post-structuralism of Derrida[33] and the reader-response approach of the likes of Iser[34] and Fish[35] have argued for the plurality of textual meanings. When it comes to alternative narratives regarding the past, faith-informed perspectives are not considered academically acceptable, Marsden argues. He claims the academy's denial of faith-perspectives as acceptable scholarly narratives is upheld by appeal to so-called indisputable works of scholarship, including Ayer's *Language, Truth, and Logic*,[36] and Kuhn's *Structure of Scientific Revolutions*,[37] both of which are appealed to in the course of denying faith-informed narratives (27), as is an arbitrary distinction between 'church' and 'state' (41).

Marsden claims faith-informed perspectives should be welcomed by other scholars if these perspectives are submitted to the same rules of the academy as everyone else: they are, after all, not writing for the church (45, 56): 'what may be appropriate to a church gathering may not be appropriate to an academic gathering' (56). Since academia proceeds from Protestant Christian presuppositions, in practice such a change may be imperceptible anyway (50–51). However, Marsden is unclear as to what these 'rules' consist of, or whether they persist from the early 'Christian' form of the University.

Next, Marsden devotes a great deal of time (59–100) demonstrating Christian scholarship will positively impact scholarship more broadly, including a discussion on pneumatology and historiography (94–6). He claims properly formulated pneumatology involves the claim that 'God's spirit is actively working in history' (94). This should prompt Christian historians to be cautious when reconstructing the past. He writes:

> Christians have often confused the belief *that* the Holy Spirit is working in history and in our lives with the ability to tell precisely *how* the Spirit works ... [But] the Holy Spirit works in mysterious ways. When we as Christians look at history, or study any human activity, we are dealing with a perplexing mix of divine and human agencies that is impossible to sort out.
>
> (95, emphases original)

Thus, Marsden's main contribution to historiography is not new or improved methods, but a more pronounced sense of intellectual humility. 'If scholars saw themselves in such a role,' Marsden writes, 'they would not necessarily become more competent map-readers, but it might have a commendable impact on their *attitude* towards their scholarship' (96, emphasis in original). Marsden concludes by advocating for more explicitly Christian higher education communities (101–11), including Christian research institutions. Such communities, he argues, only flourish if they commit exclusively to employing believers and cultivating spiritual growth alongside academic formation.

Marsden's work is valuable for two reasons. First, the historical groundwork Marsden lays in *The Soul of the American University* highlights the enmeshment of (at least some forms of) religious belief and (at least some forms of) academic enquiry, the latter emerging from the former. Second, Marsden is right to call for an *expansion* of notions of academic acceptability, not for religious perspectives to replace those of non-belief, but rather their coexisting within academia (a point I reinforce here).

However, some facets of Marsden's argument limit its usefulness for Jesus historians. First, his work addresses American higher education, and it is not clear that one should or even could transfer his findings to other contexts universally. Second, the American higher education system's origins in Protestant Christianity does not *de facto* demand religious perspectives continue to be viewed as academically acceptable. Marsden fails to justify this historical conservatism. Third, Marsden's discussion about pneumatology and historiography is of limited use. It fails to provide the proper groundwork upon which Christian historians may make a meaningful (and different) impact upon scholarship. Although right (theologically speaking) to note the mysterious activity of the Spirit in history, the intellectual humility for which Marsden advocates serves as a constrained role for the Christian historian. While intellectual humility is certainly a hallmark of Christian scholarship,[38] Marsden's Christian historian has little constructive to offer as an alternative to the dominant 'secular' modes of academic discourse, except occasionally reminding others there may be more to the past than meets the eye. This posits Christian historians as guards against totalising accounts of the past, rather than someone themselves able to contribute to these accounts in a meaningfully different and distinctively Christian manner. Although Marsden's work on American higher education and Christian scholarship is of great value, it fails to convince regarding the need for a plurality of historiographies within modern academic historical Jesus research in particular.

1.2.4 Murray Rae

While primarily a Christian theologian, Murray Rae's 2005 *History and Hermeneutics*[39] explicitly touches upon issues central to historical Jesus methodology. It is a shame, then, that his work has received little attention from New Testament scholars in general, and Jesus historians in particular. Rae claims contemporary biblical hermeneutics and historical-critical methodology are constructed upon problematic metaphysical assumptions about the nature of history, assumptions he seeks to counter by positing a theological account of history. In his own words:

> [This] is not a forcing together of what should properly be kept apart, but an enquiry into the realities of God and of history and of their concurrence in Jesus Christ. Such an enquiry arises from and becomes in turn a prelude to the reading of the Christian bible. The refusal to think theology and history together has been the cause of many hermeneutical false turns during the past hundred years or so, beginning about the time that Descartes revived the ancient belief of the philosophers that the realms of history and of eternal truth were mutually exclusive.
>
> (1)

He argues that Modernity rejects the possibility that history might disclose truth, and instead views truth and meaning as the product of rational analysis, prompting a view of history which means that 'theology and history have been torn apart, especially so in biblical studies' (4). The result of this divorce—to use Rae's term—is twofold: first, theologians seek to protect their discipline 'from the alleged vagaries of history,' and second, historians seek to protect their craft from 'the allegedly ephemeral and speculative claims of theology' (4). Crucially, Rae observes that 'both strategies are premised on the conviction that history and divine action are mutually exclusive categories and that it is improper, therefore, at least in academic circles, to speak of God's participation in the unfolding nexus of historical life' (4).

However, the two approaches to the relationship between history and theology arise from philosophical and theological assumptions not always properly articulated. Theological rejection of historiography 'has its roots, as is well known, in the metaphysics of classical Greek philosophy' (5), notably platonic notions of the world as a mere shadow of eternal truth. These notions are then exacerbated by Descartes and, subsequently, Spinoza, who stress the fallibility of the senses, and the impossibility of ascertaining truth through historical enquiry. Historiographical rejection of theology, on the other hand, begins within the English Deists, whose thoughts are taken up and popularised by Reimarus, Lessing and, subsequently, numerous key historians both within the 'Quest' and without (9–17).[40]

Having surveyed numerous works on the relationship between history and theology (22–48), Rae concludes that 'what is needed, therefore, is a theological account of what history is' (48). Rae correctly asserts that a theology of history can only be thought of in tandem with a doctrine of creation,[41] and so undertakes a scriptural discussion of the doctrine of creation which is, to my mind, somewhat deficient. He discusses the conception(s) of creation in the Hebrew Bible (49–63, esp. 54–61) but does not engage in any depth with relevant passages in the NT about Christ's role in creation, of which there any many.[42] For example, the protological statements about Christ in Col. 1.15–20 are not discussed, save for a passing mention (59). This is even more surprising given Rae's statement that he has 'set out from certain theological convictions about the self-revelation of God' (45) which, presumably, include convictions about God's self-revelation in the person of Jesus of Nazareth? Where Rae's work is more helpful is in his insistence that 'the resurrection is not simply the centre of Christian faith; it is also the centre and goal of creation and thus of history itself' (77),[43] and in his emphasis on the setting of the Church as the proper place for the interpretation of Scripture (131–52).

Perhaps more problematic than his incomplete discussion of the relevant biblical texts, Rae's work suffers from a lack of justification. The only warrant Rae offers for his project is that previous attempts to think theology and history together—here Rae names Kähler, Bultmann, Barth, Käsemann, Cullmann, Pannenberg, Frei, and Wright (22–48)—are misguided, or inefficient. However, what of those who reject the very notion of theology and history being thought together at all? Or of the likes of Avalos, who would advocate for all confessional interests to be removed from biblical studies entirely?[44] On the more fundamental issue of whether theological historiography should be permissible at all, Rae has less to say. Thus, regardless of whether one agrees with Rae's argument—and I do find myself in agreement with much of it—a justification for approaching this question is required if his thoughts are to have wider impact.

Moreover, Rae's argument—regardless of its merit—suffers from its brevity. He himself acknowledges this, noting:

> This book could, and probably should, have been a much bigger one. There is a vast amount of literature that bears upon the topic that I have not engaged with. The book would no doubt be a better one had I done so. As it stands, however, the book sets forth a simple proposal that has merit, or not, regardless of how otherwise it might have been stated through more extensive engagement with the literature.
>
> (3)

Similarly, Briggs rightly notes that 'those who disagree with the diagnosis will, I fear, find it easy to suggest that the interaction with actual biblical scholarship here is dated and on the superficial side.'[45] Thus, while I find myself in agreement with

Rae's claims, there is still the need for a fuller treatment of the issue. Moreover, while Rae's work has much of benefit for historical Jesus scholarship, the manner in which he presents it means, unfortunately, that there is little obvious reason for the discipline to interact with it in its present form.

1.2.5 Joseph Ratzinger

Joseph Ratzinger's book *Jesus of Nazareth*[46] provoked 'a helpful and necessary discussion within New Testament scholarship,'[47] about the foundational presuppositions operative within historical Jesus research.[48] Responses have been mixed: one group of scholars responded positively[49] while Crossley questions 'how certain contributors believe that overtly reading orthodox Christian theology into the historical Jesus is somehow intellectually sophisticated, refreshing or innovative (or, indeed, accurate).'[50] Others damned with faint praise: the highest compliment Johnson could muster was that 'the book does no harm to its subject,'[51] while Morgan describes it as 'a work of religious apologetics by a senior churchman and fine theologian who is not a biblical specialist but not ignorant of biblical scholarship either.'[52]

Ratzinger's primary contribution is found in his opening reflection on the relationship between the Jesus of history and the Christ of faith; I am not concerned with *what* Ratzinger says about Jesus, but what he says about *how* we should approach the historical Jesus. Operating within the Roman Catholic tradition, Ratzinger acknowledges an intellectual debt to Schnackenburg's work on the historical Jesus,[53] itself only made possible by the 1943 encyclical *Divino Afflante Spiritu* which first permitted Catholic scholars to engage text-critical and historical-critical approaches. So important was the encyclical that Brown described it as the 'Magna Carta for biblical progress.'[54] Ratzinger takes *Divino Afflante Spiritu*—along with two other Vatican documents[55]—as the basis for constructing a method which aims to 'go beyond Schnackenburg' to reconnect the real and the historical Jesus (xiv). In so doing, Ratzinger acknowledges history's importance for faith: 'the *factum historicum* (historical fact) is not an interchangeable symbolic cipher for biblical faith, but the foundation on which it stands: *Et incarnatus est*—when we say these words, we acknowledge God's actual entry into real history' (xv). What he describes here may be labelled a theologically sensitive historiography.

However, as he continues, Ratzinger ultimately falls short of his goal. Ratzinger stresses the limitations of the historical-critical method, recognising that 'it does not exhaust the interpretive task for someone who sees the biblical writings as a single corpus of Holy Scripture inspired by God' (xvi). One significant part of this interpretive task is canonical exegesis, the reading of one biblical text considering other biblical texts (xviii–xx). Ratzinger notes:

> In these words from the past, we can discern the question concerning their meaning for today; a voice greater than man's echoes in Scripture's human words; the individual writings [*Schriften*] of the Bible point somehow to the living process that shapes the one Scripture [*Schrift*]. (xviii)

These hermeneutical and exegetical musings are important because they impact Ratzinger's attempt to portray the historical Jesus: 'they govern my interpretation of the figure of Jesus in the New Testament ... the main implication of this for my portrayal of Jesus is that I trust the Gospels' (xxi). In other words, Ratzinger is a self-professed maximalist when it comes to the biblical texts, their continuing theological and spiritual potency serving as evidence of their historical reliability. However, despite Ratzinger's commitment to the theological content of the gospels, he writes:

> I wanted to try to portray the Jesus of the Gospels as the real, 'historical' Jesus in the strict sense of the word. I am convinced, and I hope the reader will be, too, that this figure is much more logical and, historically speaking, much more intelligible than the reconstructions we have been presented with in the last couple of decades. I believe that this Jesus—the Jesus of the Gospels—is a historically plausible and convincing figure. (xxii)

This theologically sensitive *hermeneutics* is the also the key to his *historical* method. He cites Christological developments between Jesus' death, and the Christological hymn of Philippians 2.6–11 (dated to 'twenty or so years after Jesus' death'), as evidence that theological claims about Jesus are also true of the 'historical' Jesus (xxii–xxiii). How can one explain the rapid rise of early Christianity and its increasingly complex theology and Christology, if these claims are not based in historical truth?[56] And yet he concludes: 'to believe that, as man, he was truly God, and that he communicated his divinity veiled in parables, yet with increasing clarity, exceeds the scope of the historical method' (xxiii). Despite claiming that theological presuppositions serve as the key to his historical method, he also claims these presuppositions themselves lie beyond the realm of historiography, a tension left unresolved by Ratzinger.

I do have objections to Ratzinger's argument, despite remaining largely sympathetic to the aims (and overall conclusions) of his work. Ratzinger correctly claims that 'if history, if facticity in this sense, is an essential dimension of Christian faith, then faith must expose itself to the historical method—indeed, faith itself demands this' (xv). But is the inverse not also true? Should faith not be a check against unfettered secular historicism? It seems to me that Ratzinger is not describing faith-informed historiography, as he intimates, but history-informed faith. The latter remains a vital component of the Christian life since historical claims about Jesus comprise fundamental beliefs within early Christianity. However, this is not my focus in this study (and not the stated aim of his own project, either): I am concerned with whether such faith-statements can (perhaps *should*) exert any methodological influence upon those historians who assent to them.

Besides this, his concluding admission that the theological foundation of his method is beyond the scope of historical apprehension undermines his project. Ratzinger continues to refer to 'history' and 'historiography' in a sense that is decidedly secular. That is, in a sense that precludes religious metaphysics from contributing to the historical task.[57] Despite his theologically sensitive hermeneutic, and the historical method he draws from it, as long as Ratzinger operates with a model of history that cannot assess theological claims about the person of Jesus, his project will not be able—on a very fundamental level of first order logic—to (re-)unite the 'historical' Jesus with the 'real' Jesus.

1.2.6 Roland Deines

Next, I highlight Roland Deines and his 2013 collection of essays *Acts of God in History*, essays—most previously published elsewhere[58]—that seek to 'touch upon the question of God acting in this world and the possibility of experiencing him, in some way' (x). The most important contribution of this volume (as far as present purposes are concerned) is the text of Deines' 2009 Tyndale New Testament Lecture, entitled 'God's Role in History as a Methodological Problem for Exegesis,' which addresses the issue of theologically sensitive historiography. He begins with two problems with contemporary biblical studies. First, academic approaches to the Bible take place within a secular ideological framework that does not allow for belief in divine agency to be a constituent part of one's method (3–6). Instead, to conform to secular standards of academic acceptability, scholars must proceed from the starting point that God does not act in historical affairs. Second, there is a problematic dichotomy between faith and historical method (6–9). The former is viewed as subjective, individualistic, and (therefore) irrelevant for critical scholarship, while the latter is an objective (or at least *more* objective), scientific approach, by which scholars may participate in critical discussions about the past. To counteract this, Deines proposes a historical-critical method taking as its starting point the conviction that:

> It is plausible, reasonable, and worthwhile to write history based on the assumption that God acted, is acting and will act in the lives of individuals, as well as in larger social bodies like families, the Church, the people of Israel, in particular, and perhaps within other peoples *qua* peoples as well. (21)

Deines does not offer such a method in his essay—given constraints of space—but outlines six criteria such a method must fulfil (24–6). It must be: (1) critical, (2) coherent, (3) rational, (4) describable, (5) comprehensive, and (6) pluralistic (i.e., tolerant of other methods).

Deines' contribution to a theologically sensitive historiography is, by his own admission, 'a work in progress' (20), and his opening essay (helpfully) raises more questions than answers. My thesis is largely consonant with Deines' contribution and my argument is similar to his contention that academic biblical studies operate within a secular ideology. Moreover, I agree with Deines' second assertion, that theologically sensitive historiographies are the most effective means of bypassing an unhelpful faith-historiography dichotomy present within the discipline of biblical studies. However, where Deines' essay (and the original lecture before it) is forced to conform to constraints of space, I hope that this study might argue this point in a sustained manner, albeit with some points of divergence from Deines' thought.

In particular, the six criteria that Deines posits as vital to any proposed Christian historiography are rather theologically underwhelming. Certainly, they are the hallmarks of good historiography, but there is nothing distinctly or authentically *Christian* about these criteria. In other words, one need not be a Christian to agree on the importance of these criteria for historiography. To be clear, it is not Deines' aim to describe the contours of an authentically Christian historiography; Deines simply outlines those characteristics that any historiography must possess if it is to retain academic acceptability and maintain scholarly standards. Regardless, one wonders if Deines might not offer more constructive suggestions concerning the possibility of particularly and distinctively Christian historiography?

In this regard, it is telling that Deines posits these criteria as 'some first elements of such a critical methodology that allows for consideration of transempirical realities' (24). Such terminology of 'transempirical realities' here is unhelpful in its lack of particularity. Different faith traditions maintain different and competing conceptions of what constitutes 'transempirical realities' (often even within their respective traditions!), such that to speak of 'transempirical realities' without specific reference to which particular conception of 'transempirical realities' is envisioned, lacks utility. One does not needs a 'catch-all' historiography that might stand open to the possibility of 'transempirical realities' broadly construed, as though there were universal assent regarding what this constitutes. In other words, it will not do to replace one methodology which reject 'transempirical realities' with another that is open to them. Rather, the discipline must be open to a plurality of methodological approaches from scholars of a variety of traditions that incorporates the activities of 'transempirical realities' *as this is understood by scholars' respective traditions*. Again, Deines' criteria are, to my mind, a helpful lowest common denominator, or bare minimum that any historical method (secular, Christian, or otherwise) must attend to, if it is to be considered academically permissible. However, this does not go far enough insofar as *Christian* historiography is concerned, and one can say much more about what characteristics a distinctively and authentically *Christian* historiography must possess in addition to these initial criteria. Indeed, it is precisely this task I seek to undertake in the final chapter of this present work.

1.2.7 Seth Heringer

Finally, Seth Heringer stands as the most recent scholar—to my knowledge—to offer a sustained discussion on the relationship between theology and history. In a 2014 article, Heringer issues a call 'to develop a fully integrated account of history which does not straddle the line between history and theology. This account cannot be afraid of prejudices, realising that scripture itself is biased and is best read in relation to that bias.'[59] This is a task he has subsequently taken up in his monograph *Uniting History and Theology*.[60] He begins by re-reading

German historicism as exemplified by the work of Troeltsch (discussed above) and Leopold von Ranke. For Heringer:

> It is impossible to understand the state of modern historiography without comprehending its roots in German historicism. Many of the practices and theories used today come directly from Ranke and his push for scientific exactness in historiography. The same can be said for Troeltsch and biblical studies, for the trench he dug between history and theology by distinguishing between the dogmatic and historical methods has broadened into the wide ditch that exists today. (30)

But, Heringer claims, these figures have been greatly misunderstood. Later interpreters of Ranke have focussed solely on his *wissenschaftliche* and naturalist approach to historiography, at the expense of his overtly idealist and aesthetic approaches he discusses elsewhere (11–9). Similarly, the totality of Troeltsch's thought is too often ignored when scholars evaluate only his early essay 'Über historische und dogmatische Methode in der Theologie'; when his later work is considered too, it becomes clear that Troeltsch, too, is not merely a naturalist, but an idealist (19–28). When Ranke and Troeltsch are recovered as idealist figures first and foremost, one may read them as important forerunners to a possible Christian historiography, insofar as they conceive of 'a world of ideals that acted similarly to the world of the divine' (28). Thus, later historiographical theory is misguided in its appeal to Ranke and Troeltsch to ground its methodology in naturalism.

He then proceeds to examine the work of four later figures—Frei, Kähler, Pannenberg, and Wright—who seek to unify theology and history, while retaining a naturalist approach to the historical method (here predicated upon the misinformed reading of Ranke and Troeltsch just discussed). Heringer argues that all four thinkers ultimately fail in this task, since they are unable to identify the naturalist presuppositions at the heart of the historical-critical method that preclude such a unification. Thus, Frei tries to circumvent the problem altogether, 'making a modern attempt to section off the Bible from the criticism of the historical method' (51); Kähler 'rejects history as the foundation of Christian faith and replaces it with an experience of the risen Christ' (58); Pannenberg seeks to make modern theology appealing to Rankean historiography and, as such, 'relinquished much to keep theology within the boundaries of public knowledge, but the more he gave, the more history and science took' (74); finally, Wright's critical realist efforts to build upon the historical-critical method 'is so loaded with baggage of the Enlightenment that it is unredeemable' (89).[61] Thus, these four thinkers evince the need for 'an alternative' to the historical-critical method 'that reclaims a boldly Christian understanding of the past' (92).

Next, Heringer seeks to demonstrate that historiographical discourse outside of biblical studies has already moved beyond Rankean approaches to the past so prevalent within the discipline. To substantiate this claim, he discusses the contributions of Arthur Danto (107–11), Roland Barthes (111–4), Hayden White

(115–30), and Frank Ankersmit (130–52). According to Heringer, these historians have shown that 'the Rankean tradition fails in its beginning, middle, and end' (153) and claims that Rankean approaches to historiography remain prevalent within biblical studies only because 'ignoring these problems is easier than trying to overcome them. To continue the tradition that is currently practiced does not require a wholesale rethinking of historical theory' (154).

Finally, Heringer offers five 'cairns' that might 'mark the way forward for the construction of an intentionally Christian historical method' (179). First, it must be a two-level process that seeks to account for events and narratives (179–86). Second, Christian historiography must recognise that no account of the past can ever be 'neutral' or 'objective' (186–95). Third, Christian historiography must take note of the intractable connection between the past and the present, and even the future (195–201). Fourth, theological aesthetics may serve as a source for the construction of historiographical criteria (202–8). And finally, fifth, Christian historians are encouraged to be bold about the contents of their faith and its ability to speak into matters of the past (208–10).

There is much to commend about Heringer's work. His Idealist retrieval of Ranke and Troeltsch is a much-needed antidote to contemporary readings of these figures that shows that historiography has never been a purely naturalistic discipline. Moreover, he is entirely correct to suggest that Frei, Kähler, Pannenberg, and Wright are all incapable of uniting history and theology because they do not recognise that the dominant historical-critical method is inherently incompatible with Christian theological discourse of any kind. Heringer has also convincingly demonstrated that biblical studies (and historical Jesus research) persists with historiographical models that are viewed as outdated and unsustainable by those outside the discipline. Finally, his five helpful suggestions (or 'cairns') for the shape of potential Christian historiography seem, to my mind, to be the result of sober-minded reflection.

However, I do think Heringer could make clearer the connection between his premises and his conclusion. Even if it is granted that modern historiography has its roots in German idealism as much as German naturalism, and even if it is granted that subsequent historians have mistakenly predicated their work upon idealist approaches to the past, this still does not demand the guild should therefore be open to theologically motivated historiographies. It seems to me to be perfectly possible to argue, despite the idealist origins of Rankean historiography, that a naturalist approach to the past should be the preferred stance within historical Jesus research. In other words, it is entirely possible and reasonable to agree with all Heringer's premises but still reject his conclusion. Although I agree with Heringer's argument, I do not think he has sufficiently justified either (1) the need for theologically motivated historiography, or (2) the academic legitimacy of such an endeavour.

1.2.8 Conclusion

It is possible to divide these interlocutors into two groups. On the one hand, the first group recognises the need to reflect upon the relationship of history and theology, but ultimately assent to a view of historiography that is decidedly secular. This would include Kähler, Troeltsch, and Ratzinger. Despite the differences in thought between these three thinkers, each is unable to reconcile historical Jesus research to Christian theology because of their failure to resist a secular approach to the historical task and, subsequently, their commitment to an epistemological framework for historical knowledge that is fundamentally incompatible with the epistemological processes of Christian theology. In other words, by adopting a secular approach to history, these three thinkers guarantee—whether consciously or not—that they cannot simultaneously operate in both a historical and a theological mode (at least, on a very fundamental logical level).

On the other hand, the second group of thinkers—Marsden, Rae, Deines, and Heringer—correctly identify the need for integration between history and theology, that theological historiography might be an academically possible (even desirable) endeavour. However, even within this group, there is more that can and must be said. If we follow Marsden's work, for example, we might suggest that theological historiography is characterised largely by impotence; that his work does not offer a method itself, or even a prolegomenon to a method, but merely calls for theologically motivated intellectual humility among Christian historians. Rae's work is too brief to be convincing to those not already predisposed to agree with his argument and offers little in the way of justification for his project. Deines's work correctly and convincingly advocates for theologically motivated historiography, but one wonders what is uniquely 'Christian' about the contours of his proposed historiography. Finally, Heringer helpfully highlights the way important interlocutors on the issue have been misread by subsequent generations but does not, to my mind, offer a justification for theologically motivated historiography that will appeal to all.

In short, I suggest none of these forerunners has fully outlined or diagnosed the core of the problem, namely, that historiography is always already governed and influenced by metaphysics, and that only by explicating our (often implicit) metaphysical frameworks can Christian theology and historical Jesus research finally, and genuinely, be reunited. Marsden, Rae, Deines, and Heringer do, at various points, highlight issues with the metaphysical foundation of the post-Enlightenment 'Quest' for the historical Jesus. However, there remains, to my mind, a need for this foundation to be examined in more depth, and for the implications of such an examination to be spelled out more clearly. In other words, what is needed is a recognition that metaphysics—and only metaphysics—can offer a meaningful comment on the proper relationship between the historical Jesus and the Christ of faith. This study seeks to remedy this by addressing the issue head-on.

1.3 Overview of This Study

Clearly, given the brief foregoing survey, this study is not the first to think about metaphysical presuppositions in historical Jesus research. Rather, my aim in what follows is to contribute to, and build upon, this ongoing and vital conversation.

In the present study I examine the metaphysical presuppositions that influence modern academic historical Jesus research. I enquire on a fundamental level how one accrues historical knowledge, and how historians make judgements regarding the evidence before them. My argument is that modern academic historical research operates within a 'secular' metaphysical framework, where I define secularism in terms of the decline of the authority of religious perspectives to contribute to public life (Chapter 5). This argument is substantiated by examining the role of worldviews within historiographical decision-making in general (Chapter 4), and historical Jesus research in particular (Chapters 6–9).

In what follows I do not take issue with secularism itself, or its suitability as a historiographical framework; I do not wish to suggest that secularism is the root of all contemporary theological and historiographical ills. Instead, I argue secular reasoning is not a metaphysically neutral system of thought, and any discipline displaying a totalising adherence to secular metaphysics at the expense of other frameworks will be constrained by what is possible within a secular metaphysics. More than anything, in this study I seek not to be unduly negative of scholars preceding me. I hope to demonstrate the importance of a lightly held conception of academic acceptability within historical Jesus research; I claim the discipline benefits when other perspectives are *added* to it, not that any perspectives ought to be *subtracted* from it. I am here advocating for the academic legitimacy of other metaphysical frameworks within which historical-critical methods may be constructed, including (but not limited to) a Christian metaphysical framework that is neither mastered by other frameworks, nor seeks to master other frameworks. This is consonance here with Tonstad's recent call for a 'non-defensive' model of theological studies with secular universities, a model that acknowledges (and indeed embraces) the perceived foolishness unique to theology in a secular context.[62] As such, I seek not to be prescriptive about what other Jesus historians should or should not do, but to make the case for what is to be gained by ascribing academic permissibility to a greater number of metaphysical frameworks upon which historiographical methods might be constructed.

This study comprises two main sections. In Part I, following this introduction, I lay a technical foundation regarding the concept of worldviews and the characteristics of secular scholarship (Chapters 2–5). In Part II, I apply this to the 'Quest' for the historical Jesus (Chapters 6–9), before offering some concluding remarks (in Chapter 10).

In Chapters 2 and 3, I define two terms fundamental to my argument: 'metaphysics' and 'worldview.' I begin with metaphysics, which is defined practically by examining five focal points of metaphysical philosophy and key debates therein. They are (1) ontology, (2) identity, (3) space and time, (4) causation, and (5) modality. In so doing, I define metaphysics as *the study of reality, including all its constituent parts and how they relate.* Then, in Chapter 3—'The Concept of a Worldview'—I trace the term 'worldview' back to Kant and chart the development of the concept in the western philosophical tradition. These two chapters culminate in a definition of a worldview as a set of metaphysical presuppositions taken for granted when apprehending the external world.

In 'Worldview and Historiographical Decision-Making'—the fourth chapter of the study—I examine the nature of historical plausibility and the role of worldviews in assessing historical data. I claim the degree to which one designates historical data plausible is correlated to the degree to which that data coheres with one's historiographical worldview (the worldview adopted to assess historical data, distinct from one's worldview *per se*). To substantiate this, I engage with Bayesian reasoning, a mathematical process for measuring probabilities employed by some New Testament scholars, as a test case for how one might measure historical plausibility. I demonstrate that Bayesian reasoning also relies upon one's historiographical worldview, and will claim it is not possible to undertake historical analysis without implicitly adopting a historiographical worldview and filtering one's judgements through that worldview.

Chapter 5 is entitled 'Characterising Secular Scholarship.' Therein I discuss the characteristics a work of scholarship must exhibit before one may describe it as secular, engaging with three sociological theories of secularisation. The first account of secularisation posits the phenomenon as the decline in religious *participation*, the second as the decline of religious *authority* and the third as a self-limiting supply minded *economic* process. I argue one may describe works of scholarship as secular if they refuse to allow religious metaphysics the authority to contribute to academic enquiry, even as just one option within pluralistic academic contexts. Thus, we may describe the quest as secular if it evidences a tendency to preclude religious metaphysical presuppositions from contributing to the methods within the discipline.

These four chapters thus comprise a technical foundation upon which I determine the extent to which modern academic historical Jesus research may be described as 'secular,' an endeavour taken up in the second part of this study. The sixth, seventh, and eighth chapters assume a macro approach to the issue, with Chapter 9 offering a complementary micro approach. The combination of the broad overview of secular metaphysical trends within the three 'quests,'[63] as well as detailed engagement with one of its participants—N.T. Wright—support my claim that modern academic historical Jesus research is a secular discipline. (My reasons for choosing Wright may be found at the start of this chapter). Through surveying the quest in these terms, I claim it is possible to perceive a secular metaphysical framework within which the entire 'Quest' for the historical Jesus has operated.

Following this is a concluding chapter, wherein I discuss how the discipline might move beyond this metaphysical lacuna by operating with a more inclusive conception of academic acceptability. This involves allowing a greater plurality of metaphysical frameworks within historical enquiry, rather than prioritising secular frameworks at the expense of others. I stress here from the outset that I reject notions of *replacing* secular metaphysics with another totalising framework. I do not argue for the priority of one metaphysical framework or historiographical worldview within historical Jesus research. Rather, I call for a plurality of frameworks to operate concurrently. I am not seeking to police the boundaries of academic acceptability within the quest, but to appeal to the discipline to expand those borders, to view the historiographical worldview of the other with a greater sense of charity rather than imposing secular standards of acceptability upon it.

This overview leads naturally into the question of how best to categorise such a work. While I do indeed draw heavily upon other disciplines throughout this study, it is not a *contribution* to any of them *per se*. Sociologists, philosophers, and theologians will find little 'new' in the pages that follow. Rather, what I seek to accomplish in this study is to demonstrate that the work *already done* in these disciplines has clear and important implications for New Testament studies broadly construed, and historical Jesus research in particular, and to begin to explore these implications in earnest. Thus, while my sustained engagement with the insights of the other disciplines is apparent, I hope it is equally clear that this engagement is done to advance an argument that is (properly construed) a contribution to New Testament studies and historical Jesus research, namely that there is always already a philosophical and theological foundation from which any work of biblical scholarship and/or historical Jesus research proceeds.

James Crossey has recently issued a clarion call for the 'Next Quest' for the historical Jesus, outlining 'what will be a more expansive and open Quest than what we are used to.'[64] While he rightly identifies that 'now is the time to reconstruct and reinvigorate the Quest for the Historical Jesus,' Crossley's envisioned 'New Quest' fails to recognise and grapple with the underlying reason for previous quests faltering in the first place. It is because the 'Quest' for the historical Jesus has operated with a metaphysically and theologically myopic view of history, a view which has only permitted a narrow spectrum of voices and perspectives to contribute to the discussion. As such, Crossley's 'New Quest' can only be taken as 'expansive and open' within the context of an already narrow framework of what is and is not metaphysically permissible within historical Jesus research. What is needed is not a re-positioning of the discipline to ask new questions within the old, narrow, pre-established confines of what is considered academic historiography. Rather, nothing less than a thoroughgoing meta-critique of the discipline is needed at present, one that enquires on a fundamental level as to the current metaphysical foundation of the discipline and posits a future wherein this metaphysical foundation *itself* might be expanded. This study seeks to contribute to this vital meta-critical task.

Writing in conversation with historical Muḥammad scholarship, Berg and Rollens call for the removal of theological presuppositions from the study of the historical Jesus, writing that Jesus historians 'whether religious or not, are also often overtly or covertly theological in their methodological framework.'[65] While I agree with Berg and Rollens's claim that theological presuppositions permeate the discipline in frequently implicit, and occasionally insipid ways, in what follows I instead argue that such presuppositions should not (and indeed, *cannot*) be expunged from the historiographical task. Rather, I argue that these presuppositions should be made *more* explicit, not less, that they may be critically interacted with to foster a greater level of metaphysical and theological diversity within the discipline. I expect some readers will not be convinced of this point upfront. Understandably so: the purpose of this monograph is to address these readers in particular. It is for this reason that I return to this discussion in the conclusion of this study, with the foundation for such a claim having been laid. As I hope will become clear during the course of this study, historical Jesus scholarship can either choose to explicate or obfuscate its theological and metaphysical foundation(s), but it cannot remove these foundations altogether. To re-categorise works such as this present study beyond the boundaries of 'mainstream' biblical studies or historical Jesus research because it is *explicitly* theological is tacitly to legitimise (and thus uncritically to empower) works that are *implicitly* theological.

1.4 Conclusion

In this introduction I sketched an overview of this study and surveyed numerous previous attempts to engage with theologically sensitive historiography, highlighting my own contribution. Paddison is right to highlight 'how tightly policed by secular presumptions academic pluralism is.'[66] In this study I examine the metaphysical presuppositions within historical Jesus research. This is traced effectively by understanding the role of historiographical worldviews with the discipline. In what follows, I substantiate this notion, and draw out the implications this may have for approaching Jesus as a historical figure. With the introductory material concluded, I turn to the main substance of my argument.

Notes

1 Elisabeth Schüssler Fiorenza, 'Jesus and the Politics of Interpretation', *HTR* 90.4 (1997), 343–58 (44).
2 Patrick Hart, *A Prolegomenon to the Study of Paul* (SMTSR 15; Leiden: Brill, 2020).
3 See, further, Marie E. Isaacs, *Sacred Space: An Approach to the Theology of the Epistle to the Hebrews*, JSNTSup 73 (Sheffield: JSOT, 1992), 54–55; Albert Vanhoye, *The Letter to the Hebrews: A New Commentary* (Mahwah, NJ: Paulist Press, 2015), 122–23; David M. Moffitt, '"If Another Priest Arises": Jesus' Resurrection and the High Priestly Christology of Hebrews', in *The Letter to the Hebrews: Critical Readings*, ed. Scott D. Mackie (London: T&T Clark, 2018), 124–35 (esp. 131–32), originally idem, '"If Another Priest Arises": Jesus' Resurrection and the High Priestly Christology of Hebrews', in *A Cloud of Witnesses: The Theology of Hebrews in Its Ancient Context*, ed. Richard Bauckham et al. (London: T&T Clark, 2008), 68–79.
4 The plural 'sins' in Paul is discussed in Simon Gathercole, *Defending Substitution: An Essay on Atonement in Paul* (Grand Rapids, MI: Baker Academic, 2015), 48–50; idem, '"Sins" in Paul', *NTS* 64.2 (2018), 143–61. Richard H. Bell, however, argues that the plural here is evidence of Semitic influence upon Paul's language. See his forthcoming essay 'The Resurrection Appearances in 1 Corinthians 15', in *Epiphanies of the Divine in the Septuagint and the New Testament: International Symposium of the Corpus Judaeo-Hellenisticum Novi Testamenti, 14–17 May 2015, Nottingham,* ed. Roland Deines and Mark Wreford (Tübingen: Mohr Siebeck, forthcoming).
5 See the discussion in Roland Deines, *Acts of God in History: Studies towards Recovering a Theological Historiography*, ed. Christoph Ochs and Peter Watts, WUNT 317 (Tübingen: Mohr Siebeck, 2013), 1.
6 Rudolf Bultmann, *The New Testament and Mythology and Other Basic Writings*, trans. Schubert Miles Ogden (Philadelphia, PA: Fortress, 1984), 4.

7 For example, Charles Taylor, *A Secular Age* (Cambridge, MA: Belknap Press, 2007); John Milbank, *Theology and Social Theory: Beyond Secular Reason*, 2nd ed. (Oxford: Blackwell, 2006); idem, *Beyond Secular Order: The Representation of Being and the Representation of the People*, Illuminations: Theory and Religion (Oxford: Blackwell, 2013). The work of Taylor and Milbank (along with Milbank's 'Radical Orthodoxy' movement more generally) will be discussed in the final chapter of this study.

8 See, for example, Zondervan's 'Scripture and Hermeneutics Series' published between 2000–2008, and *Journal of Theological Interpretation*, first published in 2007.

9 Angus Paddison, 'Theological Interpretation and the Bible as Public Text', *JTI* 8.2 (2014), 175–92 (175).

10 Jonathan Rowlands, 'Reception History, Theological Interpretation, and the Future of New Testament Studies', *JTI* 13.2 (2019), 147–67. A similar argument is also made by C. Kavin Rowe, 'What if it Were True? Why Study the New Testament', *NTS* 68.2 (2022), 144–55. Whereas I argue the discipline would benefit from theological interpretation being incorporated into New Testament studies (broadly construed) *alongside* alternative approaches, Rowe (if I read him accurately) seems to go further than this, suggesting New Testament studies at large ought to be reframed as "read[ing] for truth … require[ing] us to take the NT seriously as the possibility of 'God's question to us'" (155).

11 I refer here particularly to the late Hector Avalos, who rues the (apparently) confessional nature of biblical scholarship: "the only mission of biblical studies should be to end biblical studies as we know it." See Hector Avalos, *The End of Biblical Studies* (Amherst, NY: Prometheus Books, 2007), 1, 341.

12 Two recent works are worth highlighting. First is Austin Stevenson, 'The Self-Understanding of Jesus: A Metaphysical Reading of Historical Jesus Studies', *Scottish Journal of Theology* 72.3 (2019), 291–307. Stevenson's article is a distillation of his doctoral research on the same topic, and I find myself generally in agreement with his arguments. He claims "the various 'quests' for the historical Jesus have largely operated with an understanding of history hindered by a severely constricted range of divine and human possibilities" (291), and that "this restricted sphere of possibilities remains intact among much Jesus scholarship today" (292). His solution to this problem is to explicate the underlying metaphysical presuppositions that dictate these 'restrictions': "to introduce a metaphysical grammar into this discussion is not to de-historicise it, but to recognise that it is *already inherently metaphysical*, only confusedly so" (307, emphasis original). Despite my affinity for Stevenson's work, I await the completion (and hopefully publication) of his doctoral thesis, rather than engaging in depth with this article here.

Second is Craig G. Bartholomew, *The God Who Acts in History: The Significance of Sinai* (Grand Rapids, MI: Eerdmans, 2019). The aim of Bartholomew's work is to demonstrate the reasonableness of assuming that God acted in history in the Sinai event. While he engages in much methodological and philosophical ground-clearing to make this claim, as I understand his work, he does not apply his arguments to historical Jesus research. A further scholar concerned with the interaction of theology and historiography is N.T. Wright. He is not engaged in this chapter due to my detailed engagement in the penultimate chapter of this monograph.

13 This first appeared as Martin Kähler, *Der sogenannte historische Jesus und der geschichtliche biblische Christus* (Munich: Kaiser, 1892), and was published in English as Martin Kähler, *The So-Called Historical Jesus and the Historical Biblical Christ*, ed. & trans. Carl E. Braaten (Philadelphia, PA: Fortress, 1964). There is unfortunately no English translation in print at the time of writing; the current standard German edition is Martin Kähler, *Der sogenannte historische Jesus und der geschichtliche biblische Christus* (Berlin: Berlin University, 2013). In what follows, quotations are taken from the 1964 English translation, hereafter referred to as *SCHJ*. Throughout this section, to avoid an excessive number of footnotes, I place page numbers in the main body of the text itself.

14 Here Kähler aims his criticism towards those who sought to write a 'life' of Jesus (hence the comment about Jesus's development). Additionally, Rae notes similar thoughts expressed by Kierkegaard: "Christendom has taken the liberty of construing the whole thing altogether historically, of beginning with letting [Christ] be dead." See Søren Kierkegaard, *Practice in Christianity*, ed. & trans. Howard V. Hong and Edna H. Hong (Princeton, NJ: Princeton University, 1991), 107. Cf., Murray A. Rae, *History and Hermeneutics* (London: T&T Clark, 2005), 22; idem, 'The Forgetfulness of Historical-Talkative Remembrance in Kierkegaard's "Practice in Christianity"', in *International Kierkegaard Commentary: Practice in Christianity*, ed. Robert L. Perkins (Macon, GA: Mercer University, 2004), 69–94.

15 Gerhard Ebeling, *Theology and Proclamation: A Discussion with Rudolf Bultmann*, ed. John Riches (London: Collins, 1966), 64. Here, of course, one cannot mention the broader notions of proclamation and kerygma without referring to Bultmann and his influence upon later thought. Bultmann will be critiqued in more detail in Chapter 7 (§3) of the present study.

16 The essay first appeared in response to Friedrich Niebergall, 'Über Die Absolutheit Des Christentums', *Studien Des Rheinischen Predigervereins*, 4 (1898) and was subsequently revised reprinted as Ernst Troeltsch, *Zur religiösen Lage, Religionsphilosophie und Ethik*, Gesammelte Schriften II (Tübingen: J.C.B. Mohr [Paul Siebeck], 1913). The text of the original essay is now available as *Ernst Troeltsch Lesebuch: Ausgewählte Texte*, ed. Friedemann Voigt, UTB 2452 (Tübingen: Mohr Siebeck, 2003). Here, all quotes are taken from the English translation: Ernst Troeltsch, 'Historical and Dogmatic Method in Theology', in *Religion in History*, ed. J.L. Adams and W.F. Bense (Minneapolis, MN: Fortress Press, 1991), 11–32 (translated from the 1913 text).

17 The historical context is outlined in Hans-Georg Drescher, *Ernst Troeltsch: Leben und Werk* (Göttingen: Vandenhoeck & Ruprecht, 1991), 160–66.

18 Ernst Troeltsch, *The Absoluteness of Christianity and the History of Religions*, trans. David Reid, 2nd ed. (Louisville, KY: Westminster John Knox, 2005), 78.

19 As Deines notes (*Acts of God in History*, 12 n.32), the phrase about similarity with the devil is not in Troeltsch's original essay. Instead, this reads: "Wer ihr den kleinen Finger gegeben hat, wird von ihr [i.e., the historical method] so energisch ergriffen, dass er ihr die ganze Hand geben muss" (Voigt, *Troeltsch Lesebuch*, 7). When reprinted in 1913, this became "Wer ihr den kleinen Finger gegeben hat, der muß ihr auch die ganze Hand geben. Daher scheint sie auch von einem echt orthodoxen Standpunkt aus eine Art Ähnlichkeit mit dem Teufel zu haben" (Troeltsch, *Zur religiösen Lage*, 734).

20 Ernst Troeltsch, 'Half a Century of Theology: A Review', in *Writings on Theology and Religion*, ed. Robert Morgan and Michael Pye (London: Duckworth, 1977), 53–81 (57). The essay was originally published as Ernst Troeltsch, 'Rückblick auf ein halbes Jahrhundert der theologischen Wissenschaft', *Zeitschrift für die Wissenschaftliche Theologie* 51 (1909), 97–135.

21 Heikki Räisänen, *Beyond New Testament Theology: A Story and a Programme*, 2nd ed. (London: SCM, 2000), 204.

22 One possible exception is Martin Hengel, and especially his short series of theses on the issue in 'Historische Methoden und theologische Auslegung des Neuen Testaments', *KuD* 19 (1973), 85–90, now available in Martin Hengel, *Studien zum Urchristentum*, Kleine Schriften VI, ed. Claus-Jürgen Thornton (WUNT 234; Tübingen: Mohr Siebeck, 2008), 9–104; ET: 'Historical Methods and the Theological Interpretation of the New Testament', in *Acts and the History of Earliest Christianity*, trans. John Bowen (London: SCM, 1979), 127–36. I do not engage with Hengel here because, while he is critical of Troeltsch, he offers no alternative.

23 George M. Marsden, *Jonathan Edwards: A Life* (New Haven, CT: Yale University, 2003); idem, *A Short Life of Jonathan Edwards* (Grand Rapids, MI: Eerdmans, 2008).

24 George M. Marsden, *The Soul of the American University: From Protestant Establishment to Established Nonbelief* (New York: Oxford University, 1994).
25 Ibid., 430.
26 David J. O'Brien, 'Review: *The Soul of the American University: From Protestant Establishment to Established Nonbelief* by George M. Marsden', *The Catholic Historical Review* 82.2 (1996), 305–7 (305); cf. Robert L. Johnson, 'Review: *The Soul of the American University: From Protestant Establishment to Established Nonbelief* by George M. Marsden', *ThTo* 52.3 (1995), 430–32.
27 Bruce Kuklick, 'Review: George M. Marsden, *The Soul of the American University: From Protestant Establishment to Established Nonbelief*', *Method and Theory in the Study of Religion* 8.1 (1996), 79–84.
28 George M. Marsden, *The Outrageous Idea of Christian Scholarship* (New York: Oxford University Press, 1998).
29 Michel Foucault, *Folie et déraison: Histoire de la folie à l'âge classique* (Paris: Plon, 1961); idem, *Naissance de la clinique* (Paris: PUF, 1963); idem, *L'archéologie du savoir* (Paris: Gallimard, 1969).
30 Hayden White, *Metahistory: The Historical Imagination in Nineteenth-Century Europe* (Baltimore, MD: John Hopkins University, 1973); idem, *Tropics of Discourse: Essays in Cultural Criticism* (Baltimore, MD: John Hopkins, 1978).
31 Jean-François Lyotard, *La condition postmoderne: rapport sur le savoir* (Paris: Minuit, 1979); ET: *The Post-Modern Condition: A Report on Knowledge*, trans. Geoff Bennington and Brian Massumi (Manchester: Manchester University, 1984).
32 Richard Rorty, *Philosophy and the Mirror of Nature* (Princeton, NJ: Princeton University, 1979).
33 Jacques Derrida, *La Voix et le Phénomène* (Paris: PUF, 1967); idem, *De la grammatologie* (Paris: Minuit, 1967); idem, *L'écriture et la différence* (Paris: Seuil, 1967).
34 Wolfgang Iser, *The Implied Reader: Patterns of Communication in Prose Fiction from Bunyan to Beckett* (London: John Hopkins University, 1974); idem, *The Act of Reading: A Theory of Aesthetic Response* (London: Routledge and Kegan Paul, 1978); idem, 'Interaction between Text and Reader', in *The Reader in the Text: Essays on Audience and Interpretation*, ed. Susan R. Suleiman and Inge Crosman (Princeton, NJ: Princeton University, 1980), 106–19.
35 Stanley Fish, *Is There a Text in This Class? The Authority of Interpretive Communities* (Cambridge, MA: Harvard University, 1980); idem, *Doing What Comes Naturally: Change, Rhetoric and the Practice of Theory in Literary and Legal Studies* (Oxford: Clarendon, 1989).
36 A.J. Ayer, *Language, Truth, and Logic* (Oxford: Oxford University, 1936).
37 Thomas S. Kuhn, *The Structure of Scientific Revolutions*, International Encyclopaedia of Unified Science (Chicago, IL: University of Chicago, 1962).
38 As, for example, MacAskill has recently argued. See Grant MacAskill, 'Christian Scriptures and the Formation of Intellectual Humility', *Journal of Psychology and Theology* 46.4 (2018), 243–52; idem, *The New Testament and Intellectual Humility* (Oxford: Oxford University, 2019).
39 Rae, *History and Hermeneutics*.
40 The role of the English Deists and their influence upon the first quest for the historical Jesus are discussed in Chapter 6 (especially §2).
41 It is beyond the scope of this study to outline such matters here. Rather, this study may be read as a justification for that project, which I hope to write at a later date.
42 To be clear, the third chapter of Rae's work—'Creation and Promise'—seeks to demonstrate the importance of a "biblical conception of history [i.e., the past itself]" (62) for hermeneutics. However, the "biblical conception of history" is lacking in engagement with the relevant biblical texts themselves, as noted above. This is a shame, given there are ample texts worthy of discussion in this regard. See, for example, Sean M.

McDonough, *Christ as Creator: Origins of a New Testament Doctrine* (Oxford: Oxford University, 2009).

43 This will be discussed in more detail in relation to the work of N.T. Wright in Chapter 9 of this study.

44 Cf., Avalos, *End of Biblical Studies*. To be clear, Avalos' work was published *after* Rae's. My point is merely that the justification for Rae's work is not self-evident, and some would question such a project should have any bearing on the workings of biblical scholars and Jesus historians.

45 Richard S. Briggs, '*History and Hermeneutics*. By Murray A. Rae', *HeyJ* 50.1 (2008), 123–24 (123).

46 Joseph Ratzinger, *Jesus of Nazareth: From the Baptism in the Jordan to the Transfiguration* (London: Bloomsbury, 2007).

47 Deines, *Acts of God*, 17.

48 See Adrian Pabst and Angus Paddison (eds.), *The Pope and Jesus of Nazareth: Christ, Scripture and the Church* (London: SCM, 2009). Deines' contribution (199–232) was expanded and published as Roland Deines, 'Can the "Real" Jesus Be Identified with the Historical Jesus? A Review of the Pope's Challenge to Biblical Scholarship and the Various Reactions It Provoked', *Didaskalia* 39.1 (2009), 11–46, now available in idem, *Acts of God*, 351–406.

49 Cf. Pabst and Paddison (eds.), *The Pope and Jesus of Nazareth.*

50 James G. Crossley, 'Review of *The Pope and Jesus of Nazareth: Christ, Scripture and the Church*, Edited by Adrian Pabst and Angus Paddison', *Relegere* 1.1 (2011), 188–95 (190).

51 Luke Timothy Johnson, 'Review of Joseph Ratzinger, *Jesus of Nazareth: From the Baptism in the Jordan to the Transfiguration*', *Modern Theology* 24.2 (2008), 318–20 (320).

52 Robert Morgan, 'Pope Benedict's Jesus: Joseph Ratzinger/Pope Benedict XVI, *Jesus of Nazareth*', *ExpTim* 119.6 (2008), 282–83 (282).

53 Rudolf Schnackenburg, *Jesus in the Gospels: A Biblical Christology*, trans. O. C. Dean Jr. (Louisville, KY: Westminster John Knox, 1995).

54 Raymond E. Brown, 'Church Pronouncements', in *The New Jerome Biblical Commentary*, ed. Raymond E. Brown, Joseph A. Fitzmyer, and Roland E. Murphy (Englewood Cliffs, NJ: Prentice-Hall, 1993), 1167.

55 1993's *The Interpretation of the Bible in their Church*, and 2001's *The Jewish People and Their Sacred Scriptures in the Christian Bible.*

56 So also Martin Hengel, *The Son of God: The Origin of Christology and the History of Jewish Hellenistic Religion* (Philadelphia, PA: Fortress, 1976); Larry W. Hurtado, *One God, One Lord: Early Christian Devotion and Ancient Jewish Monotheism* (London: SCM, 1988); idem, *Lord Jesus Christ: Devotion to Jesus in Earliest Christianity* (Grand Rapids, MI: Eerdmans, 2003); idem, *How on Earth Did Jesus Become a God? Historical Questions about Earliest Devotion to Jesus* (Grand Rapids, MI: Eerdmans, 2005).

57 The term 'secular' and its cognates are discussed in Chapter 5 of this study.

58 As an aside, note the comments on the issue of 'republication' highlighted in Paul Foster, 'Book Review: Collected Writings of Roland Deines: C. Ochs and P. Watts (Eds), Roland Deines - *Acts of God in History*', *ExpTim* 126.5 (2015), 255, although much of Deines's work was reprinted here in English for the first time.

59 Seth Heringer, 'Forgetting the Power of Leaven: The Historical Method in Recent New Testament Theology', *SJT* 67.1 (2014), 85–104 (103).

60 Seth Heringer, *Uniting History and Theology: A Theological Critique of the Historical Method* (Lanham, MD: Lexington/Fortress, 2018). Some of Heringer's earlier article is reprinted in Chapter 1 of this book.

61 Again, I deal with Wright's methodology myself in Chapter 9 of this study.

62 Linn Marie Tonstad, '(Un)wise Theologians: Systematic Theology in the University', *IJST* 22.4 (2020), 494–511.

63 I am aware of the problems with the traditional three-stage structure of the quest but employ the terminology here for the sake of clarity. See my comments at the start of Chapter 6.

64 James Crossley, 'The Next Quest for the Historical Jesus', *JSHJ* 19.3 (2021), 261–64 (264).

65 Herbert Berg and Sarah Rollens, 'The Historical Muḥammad and the Historical Jesus: A Comparison of Scholarly Reinventions and Reinterpretations', *Studies in Religion* 37.2 (2008), 271–92 (272).

66 Angus Paddison, *Scripture: A Very Theological Proposal* (London: T&T Clark, 2013), 123.

2 Defining Metaphysics

2.1 Introduction

In the next four chapters of this study, I set a technical foundation that facilitates examination of the metaphysical presuppositions operative in modern academic historical Jesus research. This study is concerned with the ways in which one makes historical claims about Jesus. This therefore necessitates discussion about how historical decisions are made more generally, without specific recourse to the historical Jesus *per se*. The concept of historiographical worldviews is helpful in conceptualising how these decisions are made, and I argue the category of worldview and its role in historiographical decision-making is helpful for conceptualising the influence of metaphysical presuppositions upon modern academic historical Jesus research. Therefore, in Chapter 3, I introduce the category of worldview, before applying it to historical decision-making in Chapter 4. However, since the term 'worldview' will be defined in relation to the term 'metaphysics', I will begin in this chapter by explaining what I mean when I speak of metaphysics.

As with the term 'worldview' itself, 'metaphysics' is used almost ubiquitously, and occasionally without clarity. Before I define worldview, therefore, I will briefly define metaphysics. Stated simply, 'metaphysics is concerned with the foundations of reality.'[1] However, whilst this may be the case, I wish to define metaphysics with a greater degree of specificity, not least because the term will carry a considerable amount of weight as my argument progresses. As Hart notes, defining metaphysics is an arduous task, 'not because it is particularly rich in meanings, but because it is a word to which neither any stable, nor any useful, meaning can be assigned.'[2] This is because, like worldview, its meaning is more often than not intuited or implied rather than outlined. Etymologically, the term 'metaphysics' derives from μετά ('after, beyond') and φυσικά ('physics'), suggesting we might understand metaphysics as the study of those phenomena that in some sense lie 'beyond' the physical world. But this, too, lacks a certain degree of specificity and, as we shall see, might encourage one to overlook some issues that have classically come under the auspices of metaphysics.

In his famous treatise Τα Μετά Τα Φυσικά, Aristotle does not use the term 'metaphysics,' instead referring to his subject matter as 'first philosophy,' 'the

DOI: 10.4324/b23077-3

study of being, *qua* being,' or simply 'wisdom' or 'theology.'[3] Moreover, metaphysical concerns within the western philosophical tradition can be traced back beyond Aristotle to Plato before him. Indeed, Aristotle's relationship to the Platonic corpus has been the focus of much scholarship within Aristotelian studies. Most scholars follow either Jaeger or Owen on the matter. The former viewed Aristotle as a keen disciple of Plato who gradually became disillusioned with his master's work during his lifetime;[4] the latter claims Aristotle was a critic of Plato who gradually came to accept and integrate aspects of his thought into his own.[5]

Etymological considerations aside, the most helpful way to understand the content and aims of metaphysical discourse is to observe it in practice, to discuss some of the key moments in the history of the field, and the common touchstones for debate. I do not outline a complete history of metaphysical philosophy but discuss five central concerns of metaphysical philosophy, and the central problems therein. These problems, I suggest, comprise the five 'pillars' of metaphysics. They are (1) ontology, (2) identity and the possibility of change, (3) space and time, (4) causality, and (5) modality. I aim not to 'solve' these problems nor outline my own 'stance' on any of them. Instead, by highlighting these key debates within metaphysics, the reader should gain a glimpse into the kaleidoscopic whirlpool of debates and issues to which I refer when I employ the term 'metaphysics' throughout the rest of my study.

By approaching the topic in this manner, I hope that the meaning given to the term 'metaphysics' in this study, which will become increasingly important as it progresses, will become clear. Having discussed each of these five 'pillars' of metaphysical philosophy, I will then be placed to define what I mean by metaphysics, before offering a quick overview of some rejections of metaphysics, and their bearing for the present study.

2.2 Ontology

Ontology, often considered the core of metaphysical philosophy, is the study of being, becoming, and existence. Stated simply, it is 'the study of what there is.'[6] As Inwagen notes, 'ontology is a very old subject, but "ontology" is a relatively new word.'[7] Since it is the central concern of metaphysics, in which all other metaphysical issues find their source, I commit more detail to ontology than to the four other 'pillars' of metaphysical discourse.

Since the 20th century, perhaps no metaphysician has impacted the field of ontology as much as W.V.O. Quine, whose 1948 essay 'On What There Is,' remains a classic text on the subject. Even if Quinean ontology has not received universal assent,[8] his work remains one of the most influential approaches to the topic and may now be described as 'mainstream metaphysics,'[9] despite facing occasional 'dismissivism' from followers of Carnap who view such questions as largely pointless.[10] This is true to the extent that Quine has been credited with 'single-handedly' establishing the field of ontology,[11] with Quinean ontology having been described as the 'dominant view of how to achieve results in ontology,'[12] and metaphysics a 'central Quinean majority, amid a smattering of Carnapian dissidents.'[13] Quine himself describes ontology thus:

> A curious thing about the ontological problem is its simplicity. It can be put in three Anglo-Saxon monosyllables: 'What is there?' It can be answered, moreover, in a word—'Everything'—and everyone will accept this answer as true. However, this is merely to say that there is what there is. There remains room for disagreement over cases; and so the issue has stayed alive down the centuries.[14]

In other words, one of the concerns of ontology is to give an account of everything that *is*: what can be said to exist. More formally, this is known as establishing one's *ontological commitments* (i.e., the beings in whose existence one is obligated to believe, given the premises about reality she or he accepts as true).

However, ontology is concerned with more than ascertaining which things exist. It is also concerned with related issues such as the problem of non-existent beings, and the relationships between beings. Regarding the former, Quine is again a helpful conversation partner. He takes the example of Pegasus, and the statement 'Pegasus does not exist.' For this statement to be true—and presumably all would agree it is true—it must be *meaningful*; for the statement to be meaningful, every part of the statement must possess meaning. Therefore, the name 'Pegasus' must (logically) refer to something: one appears to have an ontological commitment to Pegasus, if only on a formal logical level. As Quine notes:

> Non-being must in some sense be. Otherwise what is there that there is not? … Thus, take Pegasus. If Pegasus *were* not … we should not be talking about anything when we use the word; therefore it would be nonsense to say even that Pegasus is not. Thinking to show thus that the denial of Pegasus cannot be coherently maintained, [one] concludes that Pegasus is.[15]

Furthermore, it is not sufficient to say that Pegasus is a 'possible' being that lacks the 'actuality' of existence, since this reduces existence to a predicate: something that is simply possessed by certain beings.[16] This equation of being with existence has become a foundational presupposition with meta-ontology. Accordingly, Inwagen has built upon Quine's work to produce a list of five theses[17] that represent the foundations of ontology.[18] (The fourth and fifth theses will not be discussed here. These two theses require discussion of the use of paraphrase, first order logic, and verification principles not conducive to the broader purpose of defining metaphysics.) The first three of Quine's theses are as follows:

Thesis 1: Being is not an activity. Despite 'being' being a verb (grammatically speaking), being is not something one *does*, as one might run, write, or speak.

Thesis 2: Being is the same as existence. There is no such thing as something that *is* but does not *exist*. Equally, there is no such thing as something that *exists* but *is not*.

Thesis 3: Existence is univocal. All things that exist, share the same *kind* of existence. I exist in the same way the chair I am sitting on exists, for example.[19]

The potential relationship between ontology and historical Jesus research is clear and multivalent. First and foremost, historiographical methodology—not least when concerned with the historical Jesus—*necessarily* concerns itself with establishing ontological commitments. For example, does one posit the existence of God, or not? Does this God act in history? Does one incorporate divine agency into one's methods, or not? However one decides to answer these questions, here the historian has begun to engage in ontology and metaphysics, even if only on an uncritical level. Note, too, that a decision to proceed *as though* God were not an agent in history is still to make a metaphysical, ontological claim, even if the historian themselves privately believes in God and divine agency. What is decisive here is not the personal beliefs of particular historians, but the manner in which these beliefs are (or are not) incorporated into historical methodology. And here there can be no neutral position: a reserved non-incorporation of divine agency into the historical method is tantamount to a rejection of the possibility of divine agency.

But it is not only in the case of God and divine agency that Jesus historians must clarify their ontological commitments. The New Testament narratives are awash with spirits (Holy or otherwise), demons, and other 'transempirical realities,' to borrow a phrase from Anthony Thiselton.[20] Here Jesus historians are again confronted with a metaphysical choice regarding their ontological commitments: does one attempt to incorporate these realities into one's historical reconstruction or preclude the possibility of transempirical agents acting in history? And as with the issue of divine agency, there can be no neutral position on the matter. For example, simultaneously to affirm the possibility of transempirical agency, but claim they lie beyond the borders of historiographical apprehension is tacitly to reject their existence insofar as the practicable, historiographical outworking of a particular metaphysical presupposition is concerned; it is to take a metaphysical stance that rejects this possibility, when writing in historiographical mode.

To be clear, at no point in this study do I wish to prescribe ontological commitments to anyone in the discipline. Nor do I wish to argue that one set of metaphysical claims is inherently 'better' than another. Rather, I wish to demonstrate that metaphysics is an unavoidable part of the historiographical task, and to call for a greater degree of metaphysical reflection within the discipline. In the case of ontology, it is incumbent upon Jesus historians to outline their ontological commitments as part of their historiographical methodology and, in so doing, to acknowledge their participation in metaphysical discourse.

To summarise, ontology is one of the fundamental sub-concerns of metaphysics, and comprises questions about the nature of being, including attempts to identify what might be said to exist, and how these things relate to one another. This relates most clearly to historical Jesus research with regards to ontological commitments and historiographical methodology. To reconstruct the life of the historical Jesus involves, in practice, either acknowledging or rejecting the existence of transempirical realities and the divine, and their role(s) as agents in history. To engage in these issues is concurrently to engage in the ontological branch of metaphysical philosophy.

2.3 Identity and Change

The second of the five key concerns of metaphysics is the nature of identity and the possibility of change. Stated simply, questions of identity ask what it means for something to be the same as itself. Often questions of identity are expressed temporally. For example, am I the same person I was ten years ago? If I am, what is it about me that means I am the same person? Related to these questions is the problem of change. How many constituent parts of an object must be replaced or removed before the object is no longer itself? If I take a four-legged, blue table, add a leg and paint it red, is it the same table? One of the most famous thought experiments concerned with these issues is the 'ship of Theseus' problem expounded by Heraclitus, Plato, and (later) Plutarch in the 1st century CE. Plutarch describes the problem thus:

> The ship on which Theseus sailed with the youths and returned in safety, the thirty-oared galley, was preserved by the Athenians down to the time of Demetrius Phalereus. They took away the old timbers from time to time, and put new and sound ones in their place, so that the vessel became a standing illustration for the philosophers in the mooted question of growth, some declared that it remained the same, others that it was not the same vessel.[21]

The problem of identity is such a fundamental one that it is often difficult to directly express within the confines of human language. As Hawthorne notes, 'the concept of identity is so basic to our conceptual scheme that it is hopeless to analyse it in terms of more basic concepts.'[22]

Despite this, Leibniz—one of the most influential figures in this field—advanced the 'Indiscernibility of Identicals,' also known as Leibniz's Law (although, as Feldman notes, one finds 'little to support the view that Leibniz stated [this] most fundamental logical law concerning the concept of identity'[23]). This law may be expressed formally (as a mathematical proof[24]) but, in its most simple form may be understood as follows: *object A and object B are identical to one another if every predicate possessed by object A is also possessed by object B, and* vice versa. If two things possess all the same attributes as one another, they are identical. Whilst this sounds uncontroversial, its application has led to a great variety of unusual arguments and conclusions,[25] such that the use of Leibniz's Law is not without its detractors.[26] Regardless of its use and abuse, Leibniz's Law serves as a useful example of one of the central concerns of metaphysical philosophy: identity, and the possibility of change.

Of the five primary concerns of metaphysics, identity is perhaps the least immediately relatable to historical Jesus research. One might reasonably object that Jesus historians all agree that the subject of the discipline is the historical figure of Jesus of Nazareth, even if the precise metaphysical and/or historical nature of his identity and personhood remains contested. Despite this, there are insights the discipline can glean from metaphysical discourse on identity and change. For example, it is important for Jesus historians to think more deeply about the metaphysics of change in relation to the historical Jesus. Jesus' life and teaching are frequently presented as a unified, unchanging whole. But once it is acknowledged that the possibility that Jesus' teaching and personality may have changed over time, and a more thoroughly delineated metaphysics of identity and change will be a vital first step in that endeavour.

This is perhaps even more true of an explicitly Christian historiography which seeks to uphold the immutability of Jesus, insofar as he is the second person of the immutable Trinity. For example, in Phil. 2.9 we read of Jesus that ἐχαρ ίσατο αὐτῷ τὸ ὄνομα τὸ ὑπὲρ πᾶν ὄνομα, the Tetragrammaton, following his obedient death (cf. 2.8). There is also, I think, evidence to suggest the synoptic evangelists—our most important sources for the historical Jesus—equate Jesus of Nazareth with the person of YHWH, in some sense.[27] (How) should Christian historians reconcile this claim about the historical Jesus with the theological claim that Ἰησοῦς Χριστὸς ἐχθὲς καὶ σήμερον ὁ αὐτός, καὶ εἰς τοὺς αἰῶνας (Heb. 13.8)?

There are theological and historical implications, not only for Jesus' equivocation with YHWH, but with his very divinity too, particularly with reference to debates about adoptionist Christolgies. For example, if at Jesus' baptism, the heavenly pronouncement σὺ εἶ ὁ υἱός μου (Mark 1.11; cf. Matt. 3.17; Luke 3.22; Heb. 1.5) marks Jesus' adoption as divine Son,[28] then this must be fundamentally grounded in a metaphysics of identity and change. In short, claims about the historical Jesus, and the earliest forms of Christological speculation must be grounded in a metaphysical understanding on identity and the nature of change, not least when these two spheres intersect.

Issues of identity and change are, properly understood, metaphysical issues. With regards to historical Jesus research, this means that any attempts to describe changes over the lifetime of the historical Jesus or attempts to discuss the possible of change within Jesus *qua* the second person of the Trinity, must properly be grounded in a thorough metaphysical understanding of these issues.

2.4 Space and Time

Third, metaphysical philosophers are concerned with the notions of space and time. As Graham Nerlich writes, 'space and time held a central place in metaphysics from its beginnings in Plato. It is easy to see why. Everything real is somewhere, sometime.'[29] I have already highlighted the fact that questions of identity are often linked with those of time, in particular (am I the same person I was when I began writing this book?). Beyond this, these concerns involve attempting to answer questions such as the following: can space and time be said to exist independently from our conception of them? Do they exist independently of one another? Does time only flow forward, and why?

Perhaps the most famous discussion regarding the metaphysics of space is that which has come to be known as the Leibniz-Clarke correspondence.[30] This comprised a series of letters exchanged between Gottfried Wilhelm Leibniz and Samuel Clarke, a fervent supporter of the work of Isaac Newton. Therein, Clarke defends Newton's view of space as a thing in and of itself that exists regardless of our experience of it (the 'absolute theory of space'), whereas Leibniz posited a 'relational' theory of space, whereby space is best understood merely as one aspect of the relationship between two or more things. Leibniz's approach suggests that space is not a thing that exists independently of anything else (as Clarke/Newton) suggested, but that it only exists in the relation to observing subjects. This view is similar to the position Kant would later advocate, wherein space is merely a framework we employ to structure our experiences of the external world.[31]

Similar debates also occur regarding the nature of time. Common sense seems to dictate that past events should be afforded a different metaphysical quality to future events. One has memories of past events: I remember graduating from university, getting married, and so on. I am convinced these things 'happened' in some sense. But my future is less certain. I may know what I *wish* to happen in my future, but they have not happened yet, and indeed may never happen at all. They instinctively seem to be less 'real' than the events of my past.

However, there is no intrinsic reason that my *experience* of reality ought to dictate my ontological commitments. Why should the reality of events be governed by my experiences of them? In other words, just because I have not experienced my future, does not *de facto* mean it is not 'real.' Accordingly, some philosophers[32] (*presentists*) contend that only the present may truly be said to be 'real,' whilst others[33] (*eternalists* or *four-dimensionalists*[34]) contend that the past, present, and future all comprise reality.[35] Others still[36] (adherents of the *growing block theory*) contend that past and present objects exist, but future ones do not.

The relation of the metaphysics of space and time to historical Jesus research should be clear: every claim about the historical Jesus invokes specificities of time and place. To say the historical Jesus did something is to say this action happened at a specific time and in a specific place. This may seem trite, or so obvious as to be vacuous, but the importance of reflecting on the metaphysics of time has perhaps never before been so important for biblical studies and historical Jesus research, given the recent 'temporal turn' in these (and related) disciplines.[37]

If nothing else, even on a purely textual level, it is important to acknowledge that our sources for the historical Jesus do not operate within a post-Newtonian metaphysics of time and space, as Simon Oliver has noted.[38] For example, Ma'afu Palu reads Mark 1.15 temporally in relation to the restoration of Israel[39] and, if this saying is authentic to the historical Jesus, we should recognise the likely metaphysical 'otherness' of Jesus' saying here: time is likely not conceived of as we might conceive of it today. This is perhaps most pertinent for historical reconstructions that stress the apocalyptic nature of Jesus' ministry, which will benefit from more thorough metaphysical reflection upon the nature of time and space.[40]

Beyond saying whether something exists, and its relationship to other things that exist, metaphysics is therefore also concerned with providing an account of *when* and *where* these things exist. Thus, to make claims that appeal to categories of space and time is to encroach, to some degree, on the field of metaphysics.

2.5 Causality

The fourth 'pillar' of metaphysical philosophy concerns causation. David Hume famously called causation the 'cement of the universe'[41] and debates concerning causality may be traced back to the very origins of western philosophical discourse, as far back as Aristotle, and Plato before him.[42] Stated most simply, causation refers to the process by which something contributes to the emergence of another thing.

Metaphysicians discuss different types of cause, be it *final* or *teleological* causes, or *efficient* causes. *Final/teleological causes* convey the ultimate purpose or goal of an activity or object. For example, the final/teleological cause of building a radiator may be to heat my home; the final/teleological cause of me going to a restaurant may be to spend time with my wife, or to eat dinner. *Efficient causes* are concerned with identifying what has brought something into existence. For example, the efficient cause of a broken window may be that I have accidentally kicked a ball at that window. In addition to these two types of causes, Aristotle identified a further two causal categories: (1) *material causes*, the presence of a material from which an object has emerged (e.g., a knife is made of steel), and (2) *formal causes*, the form (or shape) that contributes to a thing's properties or functions (e.g., a knife's sharpness causes it to be a knife).[43]

One of the most pervasive models of causality still employed by modern metaphysicians is that expounded by Hume. It is from the Humean account of causality that most modern metaphysicians begin their treatment of the issue. Tooley suggests modern metaphysical accounts of causation may be divided into four approaches—(1) direct realism, (2) Humean reductionism, (3) non-Humean reduction, and (4) indirect (or, theoretical) realism—each of which takes important cues from Hume's initial account of causation.[44] Hume's empiricist approach to philosophy—which holds that one can only obtain knowledge of the world through our experience of it—became problematic when assessing more ineffable concepts such as causation. Accordingly, Hume famously outlined three criteria for discerning a causal relationship, whilst retaining his staunchly empiricist approach:[45]

1. The cause and effect must be contiguous in space and time.
2. The cause must be before the effect (temporally speaking).
3. There must be a constant, unbroken connection between the cause and effect.

However, over against discussions regarding causal relationships, the very nature of causes themselves has also been the subject of debate. Increasing numbers of metaphysicians are advancing the notion that causes are best understood as a sub-category of 'event.' The category of 'event' is a relatively recent locus of philosophical discourse: Simons notes that there was no entry for 'event' in the

1967 *Encyclopedia of Philosophy*.[46] Since then, however, the category of 'event' has been the focus of studies by the likes of Badiou,[47] Žižek,[48] and Kirkeby,[49] amongst others. These important works attempt to reframe 'causes,' not at things in themselves, but as types of event, events being 'happenings' that may, or may not, contain some causal element to them. In introducing the category of event into this discourse, it therefore becomes possible to speak of events in the life of the historical Jesus beyond the restrictive linearity of cause/effect, to speak of events apart from any apparent causes to more closely apprehend the event itself.

As with other historiographical disciplines, historical Jesus research is interested in cause and effect. This includes, but is not limited to, the cause(s) of the apparent or so-called 'miraculous' events alleged to have happened in Jesus' life, the cause(s) of Jesus' dispute with Jewish and Roman authorities and his subsequent crucifixion, and the cause(s) of belief in his resurrection from the dead. However, a thorough metaphysical framework for approaching causation in the life of the historical Jesus has yet to be attempted with the discipline. Indeed, before even this task can be undertaken, it is necessary to reflect on whether causes or events should be the focus of the historian's attention. Are causes a 'thing' in and of themselves, or merely a sub-category of the more fundamental category of 'event'? Whilst no mean feat in itself, once this question is answered there next comes the issue of how one identifies causes and/or events in the life of the historical Jesus. In other words, delineating a comprehensive metaphysical understanding of the nature of causes and/or events will be central to delineating a comprehensive, and metaphysically astute reconstruction of the life and teaching of the historical Jesus.

More detailed reflection on the nature of causes, effects, and events is surely needed with regards to the so-called miraculous elements of Jesus' life and teaching. Much of the discipline still subscribes—explicitly or tacitly—to a decidedly Humean notion of causality, not least with regards to the possibility of miracles.[50] Indeed, although I cannot outline a thorough methodology here, a theologically sensitive Christian historiography would do well to delineate a detailed understanding of the relationship between Nature and Grace.[51] Even Keener's well-intentioned language of 'extranormal causation'[52] with regards to miracles too closely resembles Humean notions of 'the supernatural' and 'miraculous' where the divine interrupts the mundane 'vertically, from above,' as it were. This conception of the relationship between Nature and Grace is a particularly modern theological development—and therefore an anachronism with regards to the New Testament and historical Jesus—that might be overcome by a theologically sensitive Christian historiographical method that properly takes into account a correct notion of the intermingling of the divine and the mundane.

All this is to say that causality (and the issues it raises) remains a deeply contentious issue amongst metaphysicians. What is important for the present purposes, however, is recognition of the fact that, when one speaks of or makes assumptions regarding the nature of causation, such claims are, properly understood, metaphysical claims. Stated differently, it is impossible to speak of causes or events in the life of the historical Jesus without straying into the territory of metaphysical philosophy, even if this is done at an implicit and uncritical level. I have suggested that one area where this might be of particular benefit is in relation to the apparently miraculous elements of Jesus' life and teaching, where a refusal to repeat uncritically the modern affinity of a Grace/Nature divide would enable a more coherent approach to these elements.

2.6 Modality

The final area of metaphysics I highlight is *modality*. Stated most simply, modal claims are philosophical statements that involve possibilities. They express facts about what is possible, impossible, necessary, and contingent (which here means neither necessary, nor impossible). Within the field of modality are two discreet sub-concerns of the discipline: modal logic and modal realism.

Modal logic is a branch of formal logic that seeks to account for statements of necessity and contingency. It suggests that statements lie not only within a binary distinction between 'true' and 'false,' but that there are different 'modes' of truth and falsity also, hence the term 'modal logic'. As Theodore Sider summarises, 'logic begins but does not end with the study of truth and falsity. Within truth there are the *modes* of truth, ways of being true: necessary truth and contingent truth … falsity has modes as well.'[53]

One may observe intimations of what would later become formal modal logic in the philosophy of Aristotle, and particularly his work *Prior Analytics*.[54] Modern modal logic was inaugurated by Clarence Irving Lewis, whose 1910 Harvard doctoral thesis paved the way for its introduction into formal logic.[55] Many of the ideas Lewis advanced in this thesis would later be distilled and represented in his 1918 monograph,[56] and a co-authored work published in 1932 entitled *Symbolic Logic*,[57] which would later come to be recognised as 'the first comprehensive treatment of systems of strict implication (or indeed of systems of modal logic at all).'[58]

Amongst others, Lewis' work would later be advanced in the mid-1940s by Barcan[59]—who proposed the first axiomatic systems to quantify modal logic—and Prior[60] in the mid-1950s, who introduced elements of temporality into the field of modal logic (e.g., including claims that something will be true *in the future*). Following these advancements, one may understand the field of modal logic as assessing metaphysical statements including the mode of truth (or falsity) to which they appeal.

In contrast to modal logic, modal realism—as the name suggests—deals with the possible constituent parts of reality itself. It is concerned, first and foremost, with the issue of possible worlds, a notion given its genesis by Leibniz, whose work I have already discussed regarding identity, and space and time, above. Leibniz introduced the notion of possible worlds as a logical category for evaluating necessity. Leibniz suggests conceiving of the actual or real world as one world within an infinitely large set of logically possible worlds. Accordingly, Leibniz claimed that a proposition is 'necessary' only if it is true in every possible world; it is 'possible' if it is true in at least one of the possible worlds. (This position has since come to be known as the Leibnizian biconditional). Thus, the modality of all propositions is correlated to the number of possible worlds within which a proposition might be said to be 'true.'

More recently, discussions concerning possible worlds has intensified following the work of David Lewis who defended modal realism in his important 1986 monograph, *On the Plurality of Worlds*.[61] Lewis claims that possible worlds are just as concrete[62]—or real—as the world in which we find ourselves. These 'concrete' possible worlds have no spatial, temporal, or causal relationship to one another and cannot be reduced to anything more fundamental than themselves: they are entities independent from us and the world which we perceive as 'actual.'

As Sider notes, 'for most of us this is too much to take,'[63] and certainly, we might now feel far from anything considered useful to the realm of historical Jesus research. Despite this, Lewis suggests modal realism is a reasonable position because 'the hypothesis is serviceable, and that is a reason to think that it is true.'[64] Modal logic itself, predicated upon the Leibnizian biconditional, demands that we uphold the existence of possible worlds if we are to speak meaningfully about *possibilia* at all: 'if we want the theoretical benefits that talk of *possibilia* brings, the most straightforward way to gain honest title to them is to accept such talk as the literal truth.'[65]

Certainly, regarding historical Jesus research, much of the historian's task enters into the realm of modal metaphysics. Claims made about the historical Jesus stand (at least implicitly) upon a scale of probabilities rather than certainties. Few, if any, Jesus historians would be willing to ascribe certainty to any aspects of their historical reconstruction(s). And yet a detailed metaphysical outworking of the nature of possibility and probability is seldom offered, if at all. By this I am not referring to detailed discussion about criteria or method, but a detailed discussion about the nature of probability in its most essential form: what makes statement X probable, or not? This question will be discussed again in Chapter 4 but suffice it to say for now that it is impossible to deal with possibilities and probabilities, as Jesus historians must necessarily do, without concurrently engaging metaphysics, even if only tacitly.

Regardless of the modal realism debate, the most important point here, concerning the concepts of worldviews and their role in historiographical decision-making at least, is that when one makes claims (or even assumptions) about what is *possible*, one concurrently ventures into the field of modality and, thus, metaphysics itself. This is highly significant for historical Jesus research not least because (as we shall see in Chapter 4) historiography is inescapably dependent upon notions of plausibility and possibility and, therefore, upon modality.

2.7 Conclusion

Before moving on to discussing the concept of worldview in the next chapter, however, I will pause and discuss the various rejections of metaphysics that have been offered from within the western philosophical tradition. It is worth briefly noting here some of the more influential of these objections and why they have no bearing on the present study.

Such objections can be traced back to as early as 1620 when Francis Bacon published his philosophical treatise *Novum Organum Scientiarum*.[66] Therein Bacon rejected scholastic metaphysics, derived from syllogistic deduction, as pure speculation and proceeded to outline what he considered to be a more robust philosophical framework built solely upon logic, making Bacon one of the early forefathers of the scientific method.

In 1748, David Hume famously offered a fierce critique of metaphysical philosophy. Like Bacon, Hume objected to the fact that metaphysics sought to go beyond mathematical and scientific forms of knowledge, which he considered the only reasonable epistemological tools. He writes:

> If we take in our hand any volume; of divinity or school metaphysics, for instance; let us ask, *Does it contain any abstract reasoning concerning quantity or number?* No. *Does it contain any experimental reasoning concerning matter of fact and existence?* No. Commit it then to the flames: for it can contain nothing but sophistry and illusion.[67]

Immanuel Kant would later reiterate the basic sentiment of Hume's objection, albeit in a softer form which did not outright preclude the possibility of synthetic *a priori* knowledge as sharply as did Hume.[68]

In the 20th century famous rejections of metaphysics came from Ludwig Wittgenstein as well as members of the Vienna Circle, A.J. Ayer and Rudolf Carnap. The central thesis of Wittgenstein's hugely influential work *Tractatis Logico-Philosophicus*[69]—the only book published before his death in 1951—has been described as a 'fruitful ambiguity.'[70] This is best evidenced by the two competing readings of *TLP*.

The traditional view holds that *TLP* attempts to make speculative metaphysical claims about the relationship between language and reality.[71] The revisionist view holds that *TLP* seeks to demonstrate that such assertions are necessarily nonsensical in nature.[72] The growing tendency towards the latter reading is primarily birthed out of the fact that the metaphysical reading seems to make *TLP* internally problematic. In *TLP*, Wittgenstein notes that metaphysics can only be shown or observed, not spoken about, and that it is impossible to even engage with such philosophical questions:

> Most of the propositions and questions to be found in philosophical works are not false [*falsch*] but nonsensical [*unsinnig*]. Consequently we cannot give any answer to questions of this kind, but can only point out that they are nonsensical [*unsinnig*]. Most of the propositions and questions of philosophers arise from our failure to understand the logic of our language.[73]

If this is the case, then under the metaphysical reading of *TLP*, Wittgenstein would seem to repudiate the very possibility of making such metaphysical claims. This is why Bertrand Russell—a proponent of the metaphysical reading of *TLP*—uneasily acknowledges that 'Mr. Wittgenstein manages to say a good deal about what cannot be said.'[74] The options appear, then, to be that *TLP* is a self-contradictory metaphysical treatise, or a treatise on the impossibility of enunciating metaphysical propositions. Either way, *TLP* only served to problematise the possibility of metaphysics.

Finally, Vienna Circle members A.J. Ayer and Rudolf Carnap sought to amalgamate the positions of Hume and Wittgenstein to present their own critique of metaphysics.[75] Ayer and Carnap followed Hume's experimental approach to philosophy, holding the view that metaphysical claims are demonstrably unverifiable; 'experimental' here carrying the sense of a scientific experiment, i.e., hypothesis verification. Because of this they conclude along the lines of Wittgenstein, who asserted that, whilst metaphysical claims are not 'false' (*falsch*) *per se*, the impossibility of verifying them renders them meaningless or nonsensical (*unsinnig*), and so beyond the realms of philosophical apprehension.

What effect, then, do these objections have on the present study? One might suggest, with Loux and Zimmerman, that apparently anti-metaphysical philosophical frameworks remain 'thoroughly metaphysical in [their] orientation,' and 'no less metaphysical than the views they sought to undermine.'[76] This highlights the broader point made in the following chapter: metaphysical claims, regardless of their *epistemological* legitimacy, are unavoidable in *historiographical* work. In other words, *even if* metaphysical philosophy is a zero-sum game (and I am not suggesting this is the case), it is a game in which all historians unavoidably participate as an irrevocable dimension of the historiographical task.

Revising his previous assessment of Barth as an anti-metaphysical theologian, Bruce McCormack has recently written that 'ontology (of whatever sort) always reflects a series of metaphysical commitments … if Barth was doing "ontology" (and he was), then he too was engaged in a form of metaphysical reflection.'[77] It is my contention that metaphysical presuppositions are a precondition of historiographical writing such that, even for those who would do away with metaphysics on epistemological grounds, such a move naïvely overlooks the practical realities of historiography. If it can be substantiated that metaphysical presuppositions are operative in historical Jesus research (regardless of intent, and regardless of the content of these metaphysical presuppositions), then epistemological rejections of metaphysics will contain no bearing on my argument. The category of worldview, and its role in historiographical decision-making (discussed in Chapter 4) provides this substantiation.

The five 'pillars' of metaphysics, as outlined above, provide a kaleidoscopic, sideways glimpse at the answer to the question, 'what is metaphysics?' At the heart of metaphysics lies ontology, the concern for identifying what there is, or one's *ontological commitments*. From this ultimate concern emerges the other key concerns of metaphysics, relating to identity (and the possibility of change), space and time, causation, and modality.

If one were to summarise these concerns into a condensed definition of metaphysics, one may state that metaphysics is *the study of the essential nature of reality and all its constituent parts, including how they relate to one another*. This is the definition of metaphysics that I will carry forward into my discussion about 'worldviews.' When, therefore, I claim worldviews are comprised of metaphysical presuppositions, I mean they are comprised of claims about (1) *what* exists, (2) the *identity* of what exists, (3) *where* and *when* things exist, (4) the *causal relationships* between what exists, and (5) what is *possible* and *probable*.

Moreover, I have argued that attempts to reject the possibility of metaphysics have no bearing upon the matter at hand. This is because there can be no historical claim that does not tacitly make assumptions about the nature of ontology, identity, space, time, causation, and modality. *Even if* anti-metaphysical philosophers are right to suggest that metaphysics is purely unverifiable speculation, my point is that metaphysics is simply unavoidable insofar as historiography is concerned. *Even if* metaphysics is unscientific and subjective, my point is that it is an intractable part of the historian's task. There can be no historiography without metaphysics, a point I will substantiate in detail in Chapter 4.

Having defined in some detail the term 'metaphysics' and its cognates, I am now positioned to define the term 'worldview.' It is to this task I turn my attention in the next chapter.

Notes

1 David Manley, 'Introduction: A Guided Tour of Metametaphysics', in *Metametaphysics: New Essays on the Foundations of Ontology*, ed. David Chalmers, David Manley, and Ryan Wasserman (Oxford: Clarendon, 2009), 1–37 (1).
2 David Bentley Hart, *The Beauty of the Infinite: The Aesthetics of Christian Truth* (Grand Rapids, MI: Eerdmans, 2003), 8.
3 At least one interpreter understands the pursuit of 'oneness' to be central to Aristotle's concerns in the *Metaphysics*. See Adam Crager, 'Three Ones and Aristotle's *Metaphysics*', *Metaphysics* 1.1 (2018), 110–34.
4 Werner Wilhelm Jaeger, *Studien zur Entstehungsgeschichte der Metaphysik des Aristoteles* (Berlin: Weidmann, 1912); idem, *Aristoteles: Grundlegung einer Geschichte seiner Entwicklung* (Berlin: Weidmann, 1923); idem, *Aristotle: Fundamentals of the History of His Development*, trans. Richard Robinson (Oxford: OUP, 1948).
5 G.E.L. Owen, 'The Platonism of Aristotle', *Proceedings of the British Academy* 50.1 (1965), 125–50; idem, 'The Platonism of Aristotle', in *Logic, Science, and Dialectic: Collected Papers in Greek Philosophy*, ed. M.C. Nussbaum (London: Duckworth, 1986), 200–20; Daniel W. Graham, *Aristotle's Two Systems* (Oxford: Clarendon, 1987); John M. Rist, *The Mind of Aristotle: A Study of Philosophical Growth* (Toronto, ON: University of Toronto, 1989); Mary Louise Gill, 'Aristotle's *Metaphysics* Reconsidered', *Journal of the History of Philosophy* 43.3 (2005), 223–51.
6 Alyssa Ney, *Metaphysics: An Introduction* (London: Routledge, 2014), 30.
7 Peter van Inwagen, 'Being, Existence, and Ontological Commitment', in *Metametaphysics: New Essays on the Foundations of Ontology*, ed. David Chalmers, David Manley, and Ryan Wasserman (Oxford: Clarendon, 2009), 472–506 (472).
8 Most importantly, see the dissenting comments made by Jody Azzouni, 'On "On What There Is"', *PPQ* 79.1 (1998), 1–18; Stephen Yablo, 'Does Ontology Rest on a Mistake?', *Aristotelian Society Supplement* 72.1 (1998), 229–83; Matti Eklund, 'Neo-Fregean Ontology', *PP* 20.1 (2006), 95–121; idem, 'The Picture of Reality as an Amorphous Lump', in *Contemporary Debates in Metaphysics*, ed. Theodore Sider, John Hawthorne,

and Dean W. Zimmerman (Malden, MA: Blackwell, 2008), 382–96; idem, 'Carnap and Ontological Pluralism', in *Metametaphysics: New Essays on the Foundations of Ontology*, ed. David Chalmers, David Manley, and Ryan Wasserman (Oxford: Clarendon, 2009), 130–56; Amie L. Thomasson, *Ordinary Objects* (New York: OUP, 2007); 'Existence Questions', *Philosohical Studies* 141.1 (2008), 63–78; Theodore Sider, 'Ontological Realism', in *Metametaphysics: New Essays on the Foundations of Ontology*, ed. David Chalmers, David Manley, and Ryan Wasserman (Oxford: Clarendon, 2009); idem, *Writing the Book of the World* (Oxford: Clarendon, 2011).

9 Manley, 'Introduction', 4.

10 This term is borrowed from Karen Bennett, 'Composition, Colocation, and Metaontology', in *Metametaphysics: New Essays on the Foundations of Ontology*, ed. David Chalmers, David Manley, and Ryan Wasserman (Oxford: Clarendon, 2009), 38–76. See, most importantly, Rudolf Carnap, 'Empiricism, Semantics, and Ontology', in *Meaning and Necessity*, 2nd ed. (Chicago, IL: University of Chicago, 1956), 205–21. For more recent dismissals of ontology, see Hilary Putnam, 'Words and Life', ed. James Conant (Cambridge, MA: Harvard University, 1994); Alan Sidelle, 'Is There a True Metaphysics of Material Objects?', *Noûs* 36.1 (2002), 118–45; Eli Hirsch, 'Quantifier Variance and Realism', *Philosophical Issues* 12.1 (2002), 51–73; idem, 'Against Revisionary Ontology', *PT* 30.1 (2002), 103–28; idem, 'Physical-Object Ontology, Verbal Disputes, and Common Sense', *Philosophy and Phenomenological Research* 70.1 (2005), 67–98; Stephen Yablo, 'A Priority and Existence', in *New Essays on the* A Priori, ed. P. Boghossian and C. Peacocke (Oxford: OUP, 2000), 197–228; idem, 'Does Ontology Rest on a Mistake?'

11 Hilary Putnam, *Ethics without Ontology* (Cambridge, MA: Harvard University, 2004), 79.

12 Thomas Hofweber, 'A Puzzle about Ontology', *Noûs* 39.2 (2005), 256–83 (256).

13 Jonathan Schaffer, 'On What Grounds What', in *Metametaphysics: New Essays on the Foundations of Ontology*, ed. David Chalmers, David Manley, and Ryan Wasserman (Oxford: Clarendon, 2009), 347–83 (350).

14 W.V.O. Quine, 'On What There Is', *The Review of Metaphysics* 2.5 (1948), 21–38 (21). The essay was later reprinted as W.V.O. Quine, 'On What There Is', in *From a Logical Point of View* (Cambridge, MA: Harvard University, 1953), 1–19. The above quote may be found on p. 1 of this text. In what follows, all page numbers refer to the 1948 edition of the essay.

15 Quine, 'On What There Is', 21–22.

16 Quine, 'On What There Is', 23–25. This observation encroaches onto the territory of modality, the study of possibilities, discussed in §6 of this chapter.

17 The theses may be found in full in Inwagen, 'Being, Existence, and Ontological Commitment', 476–92.

18 Inwagen has been accused of misrepresenting or misreading Quine in his construction of these five theses. See Karl Egerton, 'Getting Off the Inwagen: A Critique of Quinean Metaontology', *Journal for the History of Analytical Philosophy* 4.6 (2016), 1–22.

19 This statement does not give assent to the univocity of being as posited by John Duns Scotus or, at least, as he was later understood. This holds that God and creature share the same kind of existence, over against the classical Thomistic view that asserts God is 'being itself' (*ipsum esse*) in whose being all creation participates analogously (Thomas Aquinas, *Summa Theologiae*, 1a.13.5.). For Scotus and his adherents (most importantly, note the significance of the univocity of being for understanding Deleuze's concept of 'difference' in Gilles Deleuze, *Difference and Repetition*, trans. Paul Patton (New York: Columbia University, 1994), 39. Deleuze's scotist influences are detailed in Nathan Widder, 'John Duns Scotus', in *Deleuze's Philosophical Lineage*, ed. Graham Jones and Jon Roffe (Edinburgh: Edinburgh University, 2009), 27–43. God and creation exist in the same manner, only God does so to an infinite degree. The debate regarding Scotus' univocity of being has gained prominence in recent years due to

the sharp criticism it has garnered from the Radical Orthodoxy movement. See, most importantly, Catherine Pickstock, 'Duns Scotus: His Historical and Contemporary Significance', *Modern Theology* 21.4 (2005), 543–74; Simon Oliver, 'Introducing Radical Orthodoxy: From Participation to Late Modernity', in *The Radical Orthodoxy Reader*, ed. John Milbank and Simon Oliver (London: Routledge, 2009), 3–27. For a critical push-back against RO (and the movement's reading of Scotus in particular) see David F. Ford, 'Radical Orthodoxy and the Future of British Theology', *SJT* 54.3 (2001), 385–404; Daniel P. Horan, *Postmodernity and Univocity: A Critical Account of Radical Orthodoxy and John Duns Scotus* (Minneapolis, MN: Fortress, 2014). Debate continues as to the proper reading of Scotus' view of univocity, with proponents of the RO sensibility taking his comments on univocity as ontological in nature, and dissenters of this view preferring to read them as comments on linguistics and the nature of God-talk. Equivocy, univocity, and the *analogia entis* will be discussed in more detail in the conclusion to this study.

20 Anthony C. Thiselton, *Hermeneutics of Doctrine* (Grand Rapids, MI: Eerdmans, 2007), 377.

21 Plutarch, 'Theseus', in *Lives, Volume I: Theseus and Romulus. Lycurgus and Numa. Solon and Publicola*, trans. by Bernadotte Perrin, Loeb Classical Library, 46 (Cambridge, MA: Harvard University, 1914), §23.1-2.

22 John Hawthorne, 'Identity', in *The Oxford Handbook of Metaphysics*, ed. Michael J. Loux and Dean W. Zimmerman (Oxford: OUP, 2003), 99–130 (99).

23 Fred Feldman, 'Leibniz and "Leibniz" Law', *The Philosophical Review* 79.4 (1970), 510–22 (522).

24 It is not necessary to outline the formal proof of Leibniz's Law in this study; one can understand its essence and importance for present purposes without such details. For those wishing for a more in-depth treatment of the Law, Ney, *Metaphysics*, 91–98 is especially helpful.

25 Ofra Magidor, 'Arguments by Leibniz' Law in Metaphysics', *Philosophy Compass* 6.3 (2011), 180–95 is a worthwhile read on this point.

26 Note the reservations expressed by: William G. Lycan, 'Materialism and Leibniz's Law', *The Monist* 56.2 (1972), 276–87; Benjamin Schnieder, '"By Leibniz's Law": Remarks on a Fallacy', *PQ* 56.222 (2006), 39–54; Stephen Wright, 'The Leibniz's Law Problem (For Stage Theory)', *Metaphysica* 11.2 (2010), 137–51. Also helpful are the discussions found in Frank Jackson, 'On the Metaphysical Implications of Some Epistemological Commonplaces', in *From Truth to Reality: New Essays in Logic and Metaphysics*, ed. Heather Dyke (London: Routledge, 2009), 99–111; idem, 'Leibniz's Law and the Philosophy of the Mind', *Proceedings of the Aristotelian Society* 112.3 (2012), 269–83.

27 For example, see my article: Jonathan Rowlands, 'Jesus and the Wings of YHWH: Bird Imagery in the Lament over Jerusalem (Matt. 23.37-39; Luke 13.34-35)', *NovT* 61.2 (2019), 115–36. See, also, my comments in the conclusion to this article (134–36) on recent research on synoptic Christology.

28 For a helpful entry to the adoptionist debate, compare Bart D. Ehrman, *How Jesus Became God: The Exaltation of a Jewish Preacher from Galilee* (New York: HarperOne, 2014) with Michael F. Bird, *Jesus the Eternal Son: Answering Adoptionist Christology* (Grand Rapids, MI: Eerdmans, 2017). To my knowledge, an adoptionist reading of the baptism has most recently been advanced by Helen Bond, *The First Biography of Jesus: Genre and Meaning in Mark's Gospel* (Grand Rapids, MI: Eerdmans, 2020).

29 Graham Nerlich, 'Space-Time Substantivalism', in *The Oxford Handbook of Metaphysics*, ed. Michael J. Loux and Dean W. Zimmerman (Oxford: Oxford University, 2003), 281–314.

30 The letters were originally published shortly after Leibniz's death in 1716 as Samuel Clarke, *A Collection of Papers, Which Passed between the Late Learned Mr. Leibniz, and Dr. Clarke, in the Years 1715 and 1716* (London: James Knapton, 1717). The full

text of the correspondence may now be found in Roger Ariew, ed., *G. W. Leibniz and Samuel Clarke: Correspondence* (Indianapolis, IN: Hackett, 2000).

31 This is advanced most clearly in Immanuel Kant, *Critik der reinen Vernunft* (Riga: Johann Friedrich Hartknock, 1781); ET: *Critique of Pure Reason*, trans. Norman Kemp Smith, rev. 2nd ed. (Basingstoke: Palgrave MacMillan, 2007).

32 Most famously, see the work of Arthur Prior, especially A.N. Prior, 'Thank Goodness That's Over', *Philosophy* 34.1 (1959), 12–17; idem, *Past, Present, and Future* (Oxford: Clarendon, 1967); idem, *Papers on Time and Tense* (London: OUP, 1968); idem, 'The Notion of the Present', *Studium Generale* 23.3 (1970), 245–48; 'Some Free Thinking about Time', in *Logic and Reality: Essays on the Legacy of Arthur Prior*, ed. B.J. Copeland (Oxford: OUP, 1996), 47–51. More recently, see Roderick M. Chisholm, 'Referring to Things that No Longer Exist', *PP* 4.1 (1990), 545–56; idem, 'Endurance and Indiscernibility', *JP* 91.4 (1994), 165–84; idem, 'On the Incompatibility of Enduring and Perduring Entities', *Mind* 104.415 (1995), 512–31; idem, 'Persistence, Parts, and Presentism', *Noûs* 33.3 (1996), 421–38; John Bigelow, 'Presentism and Properties', *PP* 10.1 (1996), 35–52; Mark Hinchliff, 'The Puzzle of Change', *PP* 10.1 (1996), 119–36; idem, 'A Defense of Presentism in a Relativistic Setting', *PhilSci* 67.3 (2000), 575–86; Dean W. Zimmerman, 'Persistence and Presentism', *Philosophical Papera* 25.2 (1996), 115–26; idem, 'Chisholm on the Essences of Events', in *The Philosophy of Roderick M. Chisholm*, ed. L.E. Hahn (Chicago, IL: Open Court, 1997), 73–100; idem, 'Temporary Intrinsics and Presentism', in *Metaphysics: The Big Questions*, ed. Dean W. Zimmerman and Peter van Inwagen (Cambridge, MA: Basil Blackwell, 1998), 206–20.

33 Bertrand Russell, 'On the Experience of Time', *The Monist* 25.2 (1915), 212–33; Donald C. Williams, 'The Myth of Passage', *JP* 48.15 (1951), 457–72; J.J.C. Smart, *Philosophy and Scientific Realism* (London: Routledge and Kegan Paul, 1963); Adolf Grünbaum, *Philosophical Problems of Space and Time* (New York: Alfred A. Knopf, 1963); D.H. Mellor, *Real Time* (Cambridge: CUP, 1981); *Real Time II* (London: Routledge, 1998); Robin LePoidevin, *Change, Cause, and Contradiction* (New York: St. Martin's, 1991); Theodore Sider, *Four-Dimensionalism* (Oxford: OUP, 2001).

34 The label 'four-dimensionalism' is occasionally used with a different referent. See Mark Heller, *The Ontology of Physical Objects* (Cambridge: CUP, 1990); idem, 'Varieties of Four Dimensionalism', *Australasian Journal of Philosophy* 71.1 (1993), 47–59; Theodore Sider, 'Four-Dimensionalism', *The Philosophical Review* 106.2 (1997), 197–231; idem, *Four-Dimensionalism*.

35 For a helpful introduction to this debate and its wider context, see Thomas M. Crisp, 'Presentism', in *The Oxford Handbook of Metaphysics*, ed. Michael J. Loux and Dean W. Zimmerman (Oxford: OUP, 2003), 211–45; Michael C. Rea, 'Four-Dimensionalism', in *The Oxford Handbook of Metaphysics*, ed. Michael J. Louw and Dean W. Zimmerman (Oxford: OUP, 2003), 246–80.

36 C.D. Broad, *Scientific Thought* (New York: Harcourt, 1927); R.M. Adams, 'Time and Thisness', in *Midwest Studies in Philosophy*, ed. P. French, T. Uehling, and H. Wettstein, vol. xi (Minneapolis, MN: University of Minnesota, 1986), 315–30; David Zeilicovici, 'Temporal Becoming Minus the Moving-Now', *Noûs* 23.4 (1989), 505–24; Michael Tooley, *Time, Tense, and Causation* (Oxford: Clarendon, 1997); Nataša Rakić, 'Past, Present, Future, and Special Relativity', *British Journal for the Philosophy of Science* 48.2 (1997), 257–80.

37 For example, see the recent overviews: Sarit Kattan Gribetz and Lynn Kaye, 'The Temporal Turn in Ancient Judaism and Jewish Studies', *CBR* 17.3 (2019), 332–95; Lynne Moss Bahr, 'The "Temporal Turn" in New Testament Studies', *CBR* 18.3 (2020), 268–79.

38 Simon Oliver, *Philosophy, God and Motion* (London: Routledge, 2005).

39 Ma'afu Palu, *Jesus and Time: An Interpretation of Mark 1:15*, LNTS 468 (London: T&T Clark, 2012), 126–41.

40 For an accomplished work that deals with the metaphysics of time in relation to Jesus, see Lynne Moss Bahr, *'The Time Is Fulfilled': Jesus's Apocalypticism in the Context of Continental Philosophy*, LNTS 596 (London: T&T Clark, 2019). Similarly, for a work on space, see Karen J. Wenell, *Jesus and Land: Sacred and Social Space in Second Temple Judaism*, LNTS 334 (London: T&T Clark, 2007).

41 David Hume, *Abstract of the Treatise* (1740) 35.622. The full text is available online for free at http://www.davidhume.org/texts/abs.html (accessed 16/08/2018). For a discussion of Hume's account of causation in particular see, most importantly, J.L. Mackie, *The Cement of the Universe: A Study of Causation* (Oxford: OUP, 1980). More recently, see chapter 4 ("Why Causation Cannot be the Cement of the Universe") of Mariam Thalos, *Without Hierarchies: The Scale Freedom of the Universe* (Oxford: OUP, 2013). The Humean account of causation will also be discussed shortly.

42 See the discussion in Michail Peramatzis, 'Metaphysics A.7, 988b16-21: Artistotle's Conclusion about His Predecessors on Causes', *Philosophical Inquiry* 41.2-3 (2017), 55–65.

43 Aristotle's four causes are outlined in *Physics*, Book II, Chapter 3, and *Metaphysics*, Book V, Chapter 2.

44 See, for example, the comments in Michael Tooley, 'Causation and Supervenience', in *The Oxford Handbook of Metaphysics*, ed. Michael J. Loux and Dean W. Zimmerman (Oxford: OUP, 2003), 386–434 (esp. 387). Tooley suggests modern metaphysical accounts of causation may be divided into four approaches—(1) direct realism, (2) Humean reductionism, (3) non-Humean reduction, and (4) indirect (or, theoretical) realism—each of which takes important cues from Hume's initial account of causation.

45 One may find these in David Hume, *A Treatise of Human Nature*, Part III, Section XV.

46 Peter Simons, 'Events', in *The Oxford Handbook of Metaphysics*, ed. Michael J. Loux and Dean W. Zimmerman (Oxford: OUP, 2003), 357–85 (357).

47 Alain Badiou, *L'Être et l'Événement*, L'Ordre philosophique (Paris: Seuil, 1988); ET: Alain Badiou, *Being and Event*, trans. Oliver Feltham (London: Continuum, 2005).

48 Slavoj Žižek, *Event, Philosophy in Transit* (London: Penguin, 2014).

49 See, most importantly, his trilogy of works on concept of 'begivenheden' (event): Ole Fogh Kirkeby, *Eventum Tantum: Begivenhedens ethos* (København: Samfundslitteratur, 2005); idem, *Skønheden sker: Begivenhedens æstetik* (København: Samfundslitteratur, 2007); idem, *Selvet sker. Bevidsthedens begivenhed* (København: Samfundslitteratur, 2008).

50 See, for example, the detailed overview in Craig S. Keener, *Miracles: The Credibility of the New Testament Accounts*, 2 vols (Grand Rapids, MI: Baker Academic, 2011), I.85–208.

51 Here, the *ressourcement* of the *Nouvelle théologie* within Catholic theology in the mid-20th century is particularly useful. I am thinking here of the likes of Maurice Blondel, Henri de Lubac, and Hans Urs von Balthasar, who all sought to undermine the modern fabrication of the Grace/Nature divide to great effect.

52 Keener, *Miracles*, I.13.

53 Theodore Sider, 'Reductive Theories of Modality', in *The Oxford Handbook of Metaphysics*, ed. Michael J. Loux and Dean W. Zimmerman (Oxford: OUP, 2003), 180–208 (180).

54 Especially Aristotle, *Prior Analytics*, Book I, Chapters 8–22.

55 Clarence Irving Lewis, 'The Place of Intuition in Knowledge' (unpublished Ph.D. diss., Harvard University, 1910).

56 Clarence Irving Lewis, *A Survey of Symbolic Logic* (Berkeley, CA: University of California, 1918).

57 Clarence Irving Lewis and Cooper Harold Langford, *Symbolic Logic* (New York: Dover Publications, 1932).

58 G.E. Hughes and M.J. Cresswell, *An Introduction to Modal Logic* (London: Methuen, 1968), 216.

59 Ruth C. Barcan, 'A Functional Calculus of First Order Based on Strict Implication', *JSL* 11.1 (1946), 1–16; idem, 'The Deduction Theorem in a Functional Calculus of First Order Based on Strict Implication', *JSL* 11.4 (1946), 115–18; idem, 'The Identity of Individuals in a Strict Functional Calculus of Second Order', *JSL* 12.1 (1947), 12–15.

60 A.N. Prior, *Time and Modality* (Oxford: Oxford University, 1957).

61 David Lewis, *On the Plurality of Worlds* (Oxford: Blackwell, 1986). One can also see intimations towards this argument in some of Lewis' earlier works. For examples, see David Lewis, 'Counterpart Theory and Quantified Modal Logic', *JP* 65.5 (1968), 113–26; idem, 'General Semantics', *Synthese* 22.1 (1970), 18–67; idem, 'Counterparts of Persons and Their Bodies', *JP* 68.7 (1971), 203–11.

62 Although Lewis prefers the term 'concreteness' and its cognates, he acknowledges some reluctance in using it. See the comments in David Lewis, *On the Plurality of Worlds*, 81–86.

63 Sider, 'Reductive Theories of Modality', 187.

64 Lewis, *Plurality of Worlds*, 3.

65 Ibid., 4.

66 The text is now available in English as Francis Bacon, *Novum Organum and Associated Texts*, ed. Graham Rees, The Instauratio Magna, II (Oxford: Clarendon, 2004).

67 David Hume, *Philosophical Essays Concerning Human Understanding* (London: A. Millar, 1748), §132. (Emphasis original).

68 See, especially, Immanuel Kant, *Critik der reinen Vernunft* (Riga: Johann Friedrich Hartknock, 1781) [*Kritik der reinen Vernuft* in modern German]. ET: *Critique of Pure Reason*, trans. Norman Kemp Smith, rev. 2nd ed. (Basingstoke: Palgrave MacMillan, 2007).

69 Ludwig Wittgenstein, *Tractatus Logico-Philosophicus* (London: Kegan Paul, 1922).

70 Marie McGinn, 'Between Metaphysics and Nonsense: Elucidation in Wittgenstein's *Tractatus*', *PQ* 49.197 (1999), 492.

71 Frank P. Ramsey, 'Critical Notice of L. Wittgenstein's *Tractatus Logico-Philosophicus*', *Mind* 32.128 (1923), 465–78; Max Black, *A Companion to Wittgensetin's Tractatus* (Ithaca, NY: Cornell University, 1964); G.E.M. Anscombe, *An Introduction to Wittgenstein's Tractatus* (London: Hutchinson, 1971); Bertrand Russell, *Preface to Wittgenstein's* Tractatus Logico-Philosophicus (London: Routledge and Kegan Paul, 1971); P.M.S. Hacker, *Insight and Illusion: Themes in the Philosophy of Wittgenstein* (Oxford: Clarendon, 1972); idem, *Wittgenstein's Place in Twentieth-Century Analytic Philosophy* (Oxford: Blackwell, 1996); Norman Malcolm, *Nothing Is Hidden: Wittgenstein's Criticism of His Early Thought* (Oxford: Blackwell, 1986).

72 Cora Diamond, 'Throwing Away the Ladder', *Philosophy* 63.243 (1988), 5–27; idem, 'Rules: Looking in the Right Place', in *Wittgenstein: Attention to Particulars*, ed. D.Z. Phillips and P. Winch (Basingstoke: Palgrave MacMillan, 1989), 12–34; idem, 'Ethics, Imagination and the Method of Wittgenstein's *Tractatus*', in *Bilder Der Philosophie*, ed. R. Heinrich and H. Vetter, Wiener Reihe, 5 (Vienna: Oldenbourg, 1991), 55–90; James Conant, 'Must We Show What We Cannot Say?', in *The Senses of Stanley Cavell*, ed. R. Flemming and M. Payne (Lewisburg, PA: Bucknell University, 1989), 242–83; idem, 'The Search for Logically Alien Thought: Descartes, Kant, Frege, and the *Tractatus*', *PT* 20.1 (1991), 115–80; 'Kierkegaard, Wittgenstein, and Nonsense', in *Pursuits of Reason*, ed. Ted Cohen, Paul Guyer, and Hilary Putnam (Lubbock, TX: Texas Tech University, 1993); idem, 'The Method of the *Tractatus*', in *From Frege to Wittgenstein: Perspectives on Early Analytical Philosophy*, ed. Erich H. Reck (Oxford: OUP, 2002); Thomas Ricketts, 'Pictures, Logic, and the Limits of Sense in Wittgenstein's *Tractatus*', in *The Cambridge Companion to Wittgenstein*, ed. Hans D. Sluga and David G. Stern (Cambridge: CUP, 1996), 59–99; Warren Goldfarb, 'Metaphysics and Nonsense: On Cora Diamond's *The Realistic Spirit*', *Journal of Philosophical Research* 22.1 (1997), 57–73.

73 Wittgenstein, *TLP*, §4.003.
74 Russell, *Preface*, xxi.
75 See, especially, A.J. Ayer, *Language, Truth, and Logic* (Oxford: Oxford University, 1936); Rudolf Carnap, *Scheinprobleme in der Philosophie: Das Fremdpsychische Und der Realismusstreit* (Berlin: Weltkreis, 1928); idem, *Logische Syntax der Sprache* (Berlin: Julius Springer, 1934); idem, *Philosophy and Logical Syntax*, Psyche Miniatures General Series 70 (London: Kegan Paul, 1935).
76 Michael J. Loux and Dean W. Zimmerman, 'Introduction', in *The Oxford Handbook of Metaphysics*, ed. Michael J. Loux and Dean W. Zimmerman (Oxford: Oxford University, 2003), 1–7 (1).
77 Bruce Lindley McCormack, *The Humility of the Eternal Son: Reformed Kenoticism and the Repair of Chalcedon* (Cambridge: CUP, 2021), 7.

3 The Concept of a Worldview

3.1 Introduction

In this chapter I introduce and define a key concept for my study—'Worldview'—understood in relation to metaphysics (discussed and defined in the previous chapter). Although the concept of worldview is common within western philosophical discourse,[1] advancements in this field have yet to exert significant influence upon biblical studies and historical Jesus research. This negative assertion is, admittedly, hard to substantiate. However, readers seeking my justification for this claim would do well to consult the second part of the present study, wherein I chart the development of the 'Quest' for the historical Jesus. Therein, I tease out the philosophical and theological presuppositions operative in various key publications in the discipline. In doing so, I highlight the fact that, although historians operate with a historiographical worldview, this worldview is not clearly disclosed to the reader and, thus, worldview does not become a methodological category employed by these historians. Whilst one occasionally encounters scholars talking about worldviews,[2] the term is frequently used without attention to the wider (western) philosophical tradition to which it appeals.

As one example, Wright understands the epistemological category of narrative as more fundamental than worldview, insofar as he conceives of worldviews as comprising narratives.[3] He appeals to various Christian thinkers who employ the category of narrative, rather than to the western philosophical tradition appealed to in what follows here, from which the concept of worldview actually emerges.[4] And yet, as we shall see, the western philosophical tradition within which the term was birthed does not connect worldview and narrative at any point. Rather, it conceives of worldview initially as a means of sensory perception, and then finally as a metaphysical framework for assessing and adjudging new information pertaining to the external world.

One reason for this lack of engagement with the western philosophical tradition may be that many possess an intuitive understanding of the term worldview, making recourse to lengthy philosophical developments ostensibly unnecessary. When one speaks of worldview, one's intentions are broadly understood. Another reason might simply be the practicalities of doing so. To engage fully with the western philosophical tradition in this manner would require Jesus historians to

DOI: 10.4324/b23077-4

increase the depth and breadth of their research exponentially; certainly, what I outline in this chapter is the mere tip of an inexhaustible iceberg.

However, since the term is so central to the present study, it must be defined and explained with precision, so as to avoid ambiguity later on when it is put into practice as I assess the metaphysics of the 'Quest' for the historical Jesus. As such, I here offer an account of the origin and development of the concept of a worldview. As we shall see, 'the notion of a worldview turns out to be substantially more complex than it at first appears.'[5] The English term is a calque of the German *Weltanschauung*, a term that has enjoyed considerable influence in the western philosophical tradition. It is, as will become apparent as my argument progresses, an important category for understanding the ways in which historiographical decisions about the nature of plausibility are made. To better understand the relationship between worldview and metaphysics, it is helpful to chart the development of the term *Weltanschauung*, from its invocation by Kant to refer to one's sensory perception of the external world, to obtaining a primarily metaphysical referent by the end of the 20th century.

3.2 Worldview in the 18th Century

Following his *Critique of Pure Reason* (*CPuR*) and *Critique of Practical Reason* (*CPrR*) in 1781 and 1788, respectively, Immanuel Kant (1724–1804) published his third critique in 1790: *Critique of Judgement* (*CJ*).[6] Therein, Kant sought to argue that it was possible to make aesthetic judgements (i.e., concerning beauty and art) from within the rational framework he had expounded in *CPuR* and *CPrR*.[7] In a passing comment in *CJ*, Kant writes:

> If the human mind is nonetheless able to think the given infinite [*Das gegebene Unendliche*[8]] without contradiction, it must have within itself a power that is supra-sensible, whose idea of the *noumenon* cannot be intuited but can yet be regarded as the substrate underlying what is mere appearance, namely, our world-view [*Weltanschauung*]. For only by this power and its idea do we, in a purely intellectual estimation of magnitude, comprehend the infinite in the world of sense entirely under a concept, even though in a mathematical estimation of magnitude by means of numerical concepts we can never think it in its entirety.[9]

Here *Weltanschauung* assumes a particular meaning, referring primarily to one's sense-perception of the world. A *Weltanschauung* is, in other words, that which 'is mere appearance.' For Kant, as Malan helpfully summarises, 'we perceive objects in the world not as they really are ("noumena"), but as they appear ("phenomena"), because our senses act as filters for our consciousness.'[10] Since one can only interact with the world through one's senses, 'things as they are in themselves—"noumena", Kant called them—lie beyond the pale of these subjective filters, forever inaccessible and unknowable.'[11] As Kant himself puts it (above), the mind's ability to comprehend *noumena* is 'regarded … [through] our worldview.' It is this process of apprehending the world through one's senses, and one's inability thereby to apprehend the world in and of itself, that Kant refers to when speaking of one's *Weltanschauung*.

As Naugle writes, 'various phrases … such as "mere appearance" and the "world of sense," suggest that for Kant the word *Weltanschauung* means simply the sense perception of the world.'[12] Martin Heidegger, too, understood Kant's use of *Weltanschauung* to refer to the 'world-intuition in the sense of contemplation of the world given to the senses.'[13] Given that Kant only uses the term once in his entire corpus, *Weltanschauung*, therefore, began life as an obscure and secondary phenomenological concept.[14] However, it did not stay as such for long.

Johann Gottlieb Fichte (1762–1814) was an avid disciple of Kant who—in his very first book, published two years after *Critique of Judgement*, entitled *Attempt at a Critique of All Revelation*—developed the concept of *Weltanschauung*. Although it is not clear why, the preface to the book (including Fichte's name) was not included in the first edition of his *Critique* and, since Fichte's work followed Kant's thought so closely, many assumed the work to be authored by Kant himself. When Fichte was revealed as the author, he instantly rose to prominence within the German philosophical community.[15]

Fichte appeals to a 'higher law' that mediates between moral freedom and natural causality. This 'higher law' also governs one's sense-perception of the world:

> If one were able to take its principle as a basis for a worldview [*einer Weltanschauung*], then, according to this principle, one and the same effect would be recognized as wholly necessary, as an effect which appears to us in relation to the sensory world as *free*, according to moral law, and when attributed to the causality of reason, appears in nature as *contingent*.[16]

For Fichte it is God who is the foundation of this 'higher law,' and thus becomes 'the hypostasis of the moral law within us,'[17] as Beiser summarises. In uniting the moral and the natural in this way, God's view of the world (His '*Weltanschauung*') is such that He perceives no differentiation between objects in the world. Fichte therefore continues as follows:

> In him, therefore, is the union of both laws, and that principle on which they mutually depend under-pins his worldview [*seiner Weltanschauung*]. For him, therefore, nothing is natural and nothing is supernatural, nothing is necessary and nothing is contingent, nothing is possible and nothing is actual.

Importantly, Fichte's use of *Weltanschauung* remains the same as Kant's, from whom he has inherited the term. Only, instead of using *Weltanschauung* to refer to our sensory perception of the external world, Fichte uses the term to refer primarily to God's perception of the world. In any case, the basic meaning is the same, regardless of the referent. As Naugle puts it, Fichte simply 'adopts Kant's basic meaning of the term as the perception of the sensible world.'[18] Fichte's contribution to the development of the concept is that he would be the one to introduce the term to Schelling.

In 1794, Fichte moved from Königsberg to take up a new position in Jena where one of his new colleagues would be Friedrich Wilhelm Joseph von Schelling (1775–1854). The significance of this is that, during his time in Jena, Fichte seems to have been the vehicle by which Schelling was introduced to the Kantian concept of *Weltanschauung*. This, in turn, is significant because of the new-found significance Schelling would imbue to the category of *Weltanschauung*.

Shortly after Fichte's move, in an unpublished note, Schelling would assert that 'intelligence is of two kinds, either blind and unconscious or free and with productive consciousness; productive unconsciousness is a worldview [*Weltanschauung*], with consciousness in the creation of an ideal world.'[19] For Schelling, one's *Weltanschauung* does not refer to the sensory apprehension of the external world, but rather it is a cognitive process of intelligence, albeit an unconscious one.

It is in the thought of Schelling, therefore, that the *Weltanschauung* undergoes its first re-conceptualisation. As Heidegger notes, Schelling conceived of *Weltanschauung* not to refer to the sense-perception of the world, but as 'a self-realized, productive as well as conscious way of apprehending and interpreting the universe of beings.'[20]

Mere years after Kant first referred to 'worldview' in *Critique of Judgement*, Schelling made the decisive shift in using *Weltanschauung* to refer, not to the sensory perception of the external world, but to the unconscious cognitive process by which it is apprehended. *Weltanschauung* as a cognitive, rather than sensory, function would remain its basic meaning from this point onwards.

3.3 Worldview in the 19th Century

By the end of the 18th century, Schelling had transformed the meaning of *Weltanschauung* from the sensory perception of the world, to a cognitive means of apprehending it. When charting the concept's development in the century that followed, one must begin with Schelling's great rival, Hegel.

Georg Wilhelm Friedrich Hegel (1770–1831) adopted Schelling's basic conception of *Weltanschauung*. For Hegel, the act of philosophy is 'its own time comprehended in thought,' the disciplined explication of the prevailing *Weltanschauung* of a certain cultural milieu. In 1801, Hegel published *The Difference between Fichte's and Schelling's System of Philosophy*, containing his first reference to the concept of *Weltanschauung*. Writing on the act of philosophising and the employment of philosophical systems, Hegel writes:

> Reason then unites this objective totality with the opposition subjective totality to form the infinite worldview [*unendlichen Weltanschauung*], whose expansion has at the same time contracted into the richest and simplest identity.[21]

Here *Weltanschauung* refers to an important idea or concept within a larger framework. *Weltanschauung* appears more prominently in Hegel's later publication of 1807, *Phenomenology of Spirit*.[22] In a characteristically opaque section, Hegel asserts:

> There is formed and established a moral worldview [*moralische Weltanschauung*] which consists in a process of relating the implicit aspect of morality and the explicit aspect. This relation presupposes both thorough reciprocal indifference and specific independence as between nature and moral purposes and activity; and also, on the other side, a conscious sense of duty as the sole essential fact, and of nature as entirely devoid of independence and essential significance of its own. The moral worldview [*Die moralische Weltanschauung*], the moral attitude, consists in the development of the moments which are found present in this relation of such entirely antithetic and conflicting presuppositions.[23]

Here the 'moral worldview' consists of a conscious and practical way of viewing the surrounding world, filtered through the lens of one's moral obligations. It is a way 'of living and of looking at the universe.'[24] As 'the Absolute Spirit instantiated itself in human thought and culture on its dialectical journey through history toward eschatological self-understanding,' alternative worldviews are created.[25]

Later, in *Lectures in the History of Philosophy*, Hegel suggests that one's *Weltanschauung* could refer to an individual's outlook on the world, or that of a defined group. 'As everyone may have his [or her] particular way of viewing things generally [*Weltanschauung*], so he may also have a religion peculiar to himself [or herself],' he writes.[26] Elsewhere, he speaks of the 'Indian worldview [*indischen Weltanschauung*]' to refer to what he perceived to be the collective outlook on the world shared by the people of India.[27]

Like all the thinkers hitherto discussed, *Weltanschauung* is only a tangential concept for Hegel, not the focus of his endeavours, but by assessing his work it is possible to construct a Hegelian concept of *Weltanschauung*. In this respect, one might say that for Hegel, worldviews are either individual or communal perceptions of the world, the result of the given instance of the Absolute Spirit at that moment in dialectic history. The popularity of Hegel's philosophical work also resulted in the popularity of the concept of *Weltanschauung*. 'Thus, Hegel played a significant role in the promotion of *Weltanschauung* as an incisive concept in the nineteenth-century European intellectual scene.'[28]

The influence of the concept of *Weltanschauung* in 19th-century German philosophy was of such magnitude and such immediacy that traces of its impact can also be seen in the work of contemporaneous Danish philosophical theologian Søren Kierkegaard (1813–55). 'Worldview' and 'lifeview' are key terms in Kierkegaardian thought. The calque for *Weltanschauung* that Kierkegaard employs is *verdensanskuelse*, whilst *livanskuelse* takes the place of the German *Lebensanschauung*. *Livanskuelse* is clearly the more important term for Kierkegaard: the Dane uses the former five times in his corpus, and the latter

143 times.[29] As Naugle notes, Kierkegaard speaks of *livanskuelse* twice as much as he does even of philosophy itself.[30]

For Kierkegaard, the purpose of life entails finding something for which one is content to live and die, a satisfying *livanskuelse*.[31] A lifeview is not merely the sum of one's experiences, but the result of the process by which these experiences become an individual's self-assurance. In the same passage, Kierkegaard intimates that one's lifeview may be either humanistic (and here he suggests Stoicism) or theistic and religious (here he suggests Christianity). Both are valid instances of a lifeview for Kierkegaard. However, he suggests that not everyone possesses (or will ever possess) a lifeview, instead it is the preserve of select individuals:

> The person who does not allow his life, to far too great an extent, to fizzle out [*futte ud*] but as far as possible seeks to turn its individual expressions inwards again, there must of necessity come a moment in which a strange illumination spreads over life … there must, I say, come a moment when, as Daub observes,[32] life is understood backwards through the idea.[33]

This lifeview is not a series of answers about reality *per se*, but a framework within which one may make sense of one's experiences. As we have seen, this framework is itself the result the 'transubstantiation' of one's experiences. A lifeview is experience giving understanding to itself. Here the famous Kierkegaardian dictum is key: life is lived forward but understood backwards.

Despite the frequency with which many of the aforementioned thinkers refer to worldviews, none of them devoted any time to explicating the meaning of the word itself. Rather, their concepts of worldview had to be gleaned from the context(s) in which they use the term. This changed, however, with the work of Wilhelm Dilthey (1833–1911). Dilthey was the first to offer 'a full scale treatment of the genesis, articulation, comparison, and development of world-views.'[34]

Dilthey's analysis of the concept of worldview can be found in *Dilthey's Philosophy of Existence*.[35] He recognised that there were multiple competing philosophical frameworks that each stake a claim to the truth of reality and suggested that no one framework was able to provide a complete understanding regarding the nature of reality. Every worldview has some claim to the truth about the nature of reality, but no single one can adequately explain the totality of existence. Accordingly, one must be aware that one's worldview—and the beliefs one holds thereby—is necessarily incomplete. Instead, different worldviews offer a glimpse into some aspect of reality and every worldview may be categorised into one of the three fundamental worldviews outlined below. He describes this as the 'anarchy of philosophical systems' (17).

This philosophical anarchy, Dilthey suggests, begat the realisation that humans were historically contingent, and the realisation that all philosophical claims are products of the historical situations in which they are made (19–20). The meaning of life, therefore, is not to be found in philosophical contemplation, but in the lived experience of the world. Dilthey termed this a *Lebenswelt*. This *Lebenswelt*, in turn, gives birth to one's *Weltanschauung*. Based upon this, Dilthey asserts that there are three fundamental types of worldview.

1. *The religious worldview.* This type of worldview is characterised by a belief in unseen powers or forces that possess the ability to interact in the realm of human affairs, and routinely do so. He writes

   > from such a relationship to the invisible, there emerges the interpretation of reality, the appraisal of life and the ideal of practical conduct … [comprising] a conflict of beneficent and evil beings, of an existence according to the understanding of our senses, and of a higher world transcending the senses (34).

   Although these worldviews are metaphysical in nature, they are to be distinguished on the grounds of their unique conception of spiritual influence upon human experience (35). This is somewhat analogous to what Charles Taylor would later describe as the pre-secular conception of the 'porous self.'[36] Dilthey ultimately concluded that the religious worldview imposed too many ethical restrictions upon humans and was undesirable.
2. *The poetic worldview.* Art, for Dilthey, began as a means of religious expression. However, following the Enlightenment, artistic expression 'obtained its full freedom' (36) from religion. Dilthey followed Hegel in suggesting that poetry enjoyed a unique status among the arts since the language itself is the very medium of communication. Furthermore, over against the religious worldview which construed invisible forces at work in the external world, poetry begins with the lived experience of humans: 'life makes poetry always represent new aspects' (38). Poetry, thus, is a means by which one may promote their individual interpretation of the external world.
3. *The metaphysical worldview.* This worldview is itself comprised of three variants. The first is naturalism, as exemplified by the Epicureans who assert that humans are defined and determined by nature. The second is the Idealism of Freedom (which he also calls Subjective Idealism), exemplified by Friedrich Schiller and Kant, who suggest that humans are separated by nature as a result of their free will. The third is Objective Idealism, exemplified by G.W.F. Hegel, Baruch Spinoza, and Giordano Bruno, who suggest that humans live in harmony with nature and the natural processes.

To conclude with Sire's helpful summary, for Dilthey a worldview is '*a set of mental categories arising from deeply lived experience which essentially determines how a person understands, feels and responds in action to what he or she perceives of the surrounding world and the riddles it presents.*'[37] Worldviews are subjective perspectives from which one attempts to adjudicate on matters pertaining to the nature of reality. This relativistic and sceptical element of Dilthey's work on worldviews, however, is found in a more radical form in Friedrich Nietzsche.

It is somewhat fitting that I end my survey of the 19th-century conception of worldview with Friedrich Nietzsche (1844–1900). In many ways, his thought is the culmination of what went before, whilst simultaneously setting the agenda for what would follow: 'Nietzsche was not only the *terminus ad quem* of the nineteenth century but also the *terminus a quo* of the twentieth.'[38] Presenting Nietzsche's thought is notoriously problematic, due largely to his complete refusal to present a programmatic system of thought. As Eric Blondel notes, 'Nietzsche's "contradictions", far from being a defect … or praiseworthy … are surely the product of the impossibility in structuring them?'[39] Regarding my present purpose, the concept of *Weltanschauung* in particular was vital to the development of Nietzsche's thought, especially in his early years.[40]

Indeed, Nietzsche seems comfortable using *Weltanschauung* to refer to a great multiplicity of outlooks during this period: the Dionysian *Weltanschauung*,[41] the Christian *Weltanschauung*,[42] the Hellenistic *Weltanschauung*,[43] the tragic *Weltanschauung*,[44] the musical *Weltanschauung*,[45] and the metaphysical *Weltanschauung*,[46] to name but a few. For Nietzsche the human mind was unavoidably creative regarding the external world; to speak about the external world as a thing that exists independent from our comprehension of it is a meaningless proposition. He described the Kantian ideal of the *Ding an sich* as something to be ridiculed: 'the thing-in-itself [*das Ding an sich*] is worthy of Homeric laughter, that it seemed to be so much, even everything, and yet is actually empty, namely meaningless.'[47] This claim was driven by Nietzsche's belief that *Weltanschauungen* were vital to human flourishing: 'every living thing can become healthy, strong, and fruitful, only within a horizon [*nur innerhalb eines Horizontes*].'[48]

Although these *Weltanschauungen* are an unavoidable part of lived experience, humans forget that these worldviews are fundamentally human *creations*, and so they arbitrarily ascribe authority to particular ways of apprehending the external world, based on which *Weltanschauung* has assumed convention in their given society or culture.

And yet Richard Schacht is right to note that Nietzsche does not in fact lower philosophy as he conceives and commends it to the level of the mere mongering of *Weltanschauungen*, thus reducing it to a kind of 'quasi-literary enterprise of little or no cognitive significance.'[49] Whilst interpretation frequently offers more insight into the *Weltanschauung* of the interpreter then the object of study, it does not follow that one should cease all philosophical inquiry, only that one should factor in a certain level of intellectual humility into one's conclusions.

Nietzsche thus offers an extreme perspectivism as the antidote to philosophy's ills. Only nature exists, and it is apprehended through subjective, human-made *Weltanschauungen*. Nietzsche's key insight, therefore, is not in defining what constitutes a worldview, but in the fact that all humans perceive reality *through* a worldview: they are an unavoidable facet of all philosophical reflection. This insight remains largely congruous with the following chapter of this study, wherein I examine the role of worldviews in historiographical decision-making.

3.4 Worldview in the 20th Century

By the end of the 19th century, the term *Weltanschauung* had become so ubiquitous that in 1891 James Orr bemoaned the fact that 'the history of this term has yet to be written'[50] since it had become, 'in a manner indispensable.'[51] David Naugle highlights an unpublished dissertation on the concept of *Weltanschauung*[52] whose bibliography contains around 2,000 German monographs from the early 20th century with the word *Weltanschauung* in the title. In the 20th century, discussion regarding the concept of *Weltanschauung* became more prevalent and more diverse. It is possible here only to survey the most important thinkers from this period.

I begin my analysis of the 20th century with Edmund Husserl (1859–1938). Husserl's primary contribution to the concept of worldview is in his writings that oppose the role of worldviews within contemporaneous philosophical discourse. In 1910, Husserl published a landmark article in *Logos* (for which he was also an editor), best translated into English as 'Philosophy as a Rigorous Science.'[53] Husserl begins his essay by stating one of his core theses:

> From the very beginning, philosophy has claimed to be a rigorous science [*strenge Wissenschaft*], namely, a science which meets the highest theoretical needs and enables a life governed by pure reason, in an ethical-religious sense. (289)

However, despite the lofty ambitions, Husserl is also aware that philosophy 'has not been able to meet the claim to be a rigorous science in any epoch of its development' (289) and, furthermore, 'the true meaning of philosophical problems has not even come to scientific clarification [*wissenschaftlicher Klärung*]' (290). For Husserl, not only has philosophical reasoning fallen short of its ideal, but even the very nature of framing philosophical questions has become problematic. He summarises the problem thus:

> Therefore philosophy, in its historical deposition, the highest and most rigorous of all sciences, it, which represents the inalienable claim of humanity to pure and absolute knowledge (and what is inseparable from this: on pure and absolute values and will), cannot be shaped into a real science [*wirklicher Wissenschaft*]. (290)

For Husserl, the cause of this malaise is two-fold. Rigorous philosophy has become enslaved to both a naturalism ('*Naturalismus*') and a form of 'worldview philosophy' ('*Weltanschauungsphilosophie*'), both of which are direct consequences of the rise of Hegelian modes of philosophising (292–3).

Husserl's treatment of naturalism (294–322) will not be assessed here, since it is of little consequence for the present study. However, when he turns to address this 'new worldview-philosophy' (*neue[n] Weltanschauungsphilosophie*) (323–41) at the centre of Husserl's programmatic critique was a withering attack on Dilthey's work on the concept of *Weltanschauung*.

Husserl states that *Weltanschauungsphilosophie* is the result of 'the transposition of Hegel's metaphysical philosophy of history into a sceptical historicism [*einen skeptischen Historizismus*]' (293), but it is Dilthey who typifies this turn towards historicism. Husserl writes, 'we grasp the motives that push towards it [i.e., historicism] most easily if we follow Dilthey's account' (324). However, one should note that Dilthey privately objected to Husserl that he had made far too much of Dilthey's treatment of *Weltanschauung*.[54]

Husserl proceeds by offering an analysis of the methods of *Weltanschauungsphilosophie*, claiming there is much to commend about this school of thought. He writes, that 'having given full justice to the high values of the worldview-philosophy, there seems to be nothing to stop us from necessarily recommending the pursuit of such philosophy' (332). However, what *does* hold Husserl back from unreserved praise of *Weltanschauungsphilosophie* is that the standards of 'philosophical science' are higher and therefore, rigorous scientific philosophy is of a higher order than subjective, wisdom-orientated *Weltanschauungsphilosophie*: 'With regards to the idea of philosophy, there is still another [type] of higher value, from a certain point of view, namely that of a philosophical science [*einer philosophischen Wissenschaft*]' (332).

As Naugle notes, 'in this assertion we see the modern "fact/value" dichotomy in bold relief.'[55] For Husserl, the two are fundamentally irreconcilable to each other: 'so there are sharp differences: worldview-philosophy and scientific philosophy are thus two ideas which are, in a certain way, related to each other but not to be blended [*aber nicht zu vermengende*]' (333).

What is significant for the present study—and seldom noted—is that Husserl would later change his stance regarding this *Wissenschaft-Weltanschauung* dichotomy. In his later work he developed an understanding of the role of the lived experience in the work of the philosopher, which instead led him to admit 'the essentially historical character of philosophic thought,'[56] although, as Philip Buckley has recently argued, many of Husserl's later thoughts are pre-empted in his earlier work.[57] In turn, towards the end of his life, he wrote *The Crisis of European Sciences and Transcendental Phenomenology*, in which he proclaimed that 'philosophy as science, as a serious, rigorous, even apodictically rigorous science—the dream is over.'[58]

For Husserl, the 'dream' was over because of what he perceived to be a widespread turn towards 'personal' philosophies, or *Weltanschauung* philosophies, rather than rigorous, 'objective,' philosophies. In his commentary on this text from Husserl, Paci states Husserl's concern thus: 'must we, therefore, surrender to personal philosophies, to philosophies as "world-views" or as "subjective" philosophies, not in the sense of phenomenological subjectivity, but in the relativistic sense?'[59]

It is in response to this tendency towards *Weltanschauung* philosophies that Husserl posited the lifeworld, or *Lebenswelt*, a notoriously complicated and ambiguous term.[60] Fundamentally, however, the *Lebenswelt* is the world, as it truly is, prior to any human conception of it (similar to the Kantian *Ding an sich*). In Husserl's own words:

> The Lifeworld is the world that is constantly pregiven, valid constantly and in advance as existing, but not valid because of some purpose of investigation, according to some universal end. Every end presupposes it; even the

> universal end of knowing it in scientific truth presupposes it, and in advance; and in the course of (scientific) work it presupposes it ever anew, as a world existing, in its own way (to be sure), but existing nevertheless.[61]

It is this *Lebenswelt*, the world as it really is, with which rigorous philosophy must concern itself, and it is also that about which *Weltanschauung* philosophies can say nothing, due to their inherent subjectivity. It is telling that, for all his assertions that phenomenological philosophy is the means to access the *Lebenswelt*, he has little to say about *how* this might be achieved. Indeed, Husserl's phenomenology is as historically conditioned and as subjective as the *Weltanschauung* philosophies with which he takes such umbrage. As David Carr notes:

> Attempting and claiming to have set aside historically acquired prejudices which stood in the way of a phenomenological grasp of a structure of the world and world-consciousness, Husserl seems, at a deeper level, to exhibit such prejudices in his description of the lifeworld … The very motivation to overcome prejudice, historically or otherwise acquired, is itself the expression of a historical prejudice, i.e., what Gadamer calls the 'prejudice against prejudices.' Husserl's philosophy seems to end up in the same position as any other philosophy, according to the view of those who describe philosophy as *Weltanschauung*, or the culminating expression of a historical period's view of the world.[62]

Crucially, for the present study, Husserl's struggles against *Weltanschauung* philosophies suggest that, not only are worldviews subjective frameworks for apprehending reality, but they are unavoidable. As Sarna concludes, 'Husserl's postulate of presuppositionlessness is impossible to realize,' and any theory 'free from any worldview's domain … is impossible to construct.'[63] This particular insight will gain increasing significance as the present study continues.

German-Swiss psychiatrist and philosopher Karl Jaspers (1883–1969) offered his own contribution to the concept of worldview with his 1919 monograph, *Phsychology of Worldviews*.[64] The monograph remains an influential one, its reach stretching far beyond the field of psychiatry. As Webb writes, 'his ideas on the subject still offer useful insights, many of which have found echoes among later thinkers, from developmental psychologists such as Jean Piaget and Robert Kegan to such figures as Ernst Becker and René Girard.'[65] As Jaspers himself would later note, the work unknowingly serves as a philosophical treatise under the auspices of a different discipline.[66]

He begins by acknowledging the rather esoteric nature of his work ('"Psychology of Worldviews" is not a common term,' he writes [p. 1]), and so spends some time defining *Weltanschauung* to clarify his intentions in what follows.

> What is a worldview? In any case something whole and something universal. If, for example, of knowing as a wholeness, as a cosmos. But worldview is

> not merely a knowledge [*nicht bloß ein Wissen*], but manifests itself in ratings [*Wertungen*], in the ranking of values [*der Rangordnung der Werte*]. Or, in a different way of expressing besides: when we speak of worldviews, we mean the forces or the everything, at least the end and the totality of humankind, *both subjectively* as experience and power and attitude, *and objectively* as a designed world (1, emphases mine).

Importantly, he understands *Weltanschauung* both subjectively *and* objectively, since Jaspers proceeds to approach the term on two fronts: regarding subjectivity, he is concerned with 'attitudes' (*Einstellungen*), and regarding objectivity, 'world-pictures' (*Weltbilder*).

Crucial to understanding these terms is what Jaspers calls 'the life of the spirit' [*Das Leben des Geistes*], in which both *Einstellungen* and *Weltbilder* find their ground. Within the life of the spirit, Jaspers suggests there are situations that all humans experience that profoundly shape their lives, events such as grief, conflict, and suffering. 'These situations, which are felt, experienced, thought about everywhere at the borders of our existence, are therefore called border-situations [*Grenzsituationen*]' (202). The way one responds to these *Grenzsituationen* reflects what Jaspers calls their 'spirit-types' [*Geistestypen*], discussed in Chapter III of his work (190ff). In his own words, 'if we ask about the spirit-type, we ask where man has his footing [*wo der Mensch seinen Halt habe*]' (202).

World-pictures [*Weltbilder*]—found in a variety of forms[67]—are the response of the various *Geistestypus* to the various *Grenzsituationen*, crystallised into seemingly 'objective' conceptions, or pictures [*Bilder*] of the world. By comparison, *Einstellungen*—again which come in various forms[68]—are essentially the mental patterns and structures by which one apprehends and experiences the world, informed by one's *Weltbild*. In this respect, *Weltanschauungen*, under the auspices of *Einstellungen*, resemble rather closely the conception of *Weltanschauung* as understood from Hegel to Husserl: subjective cognitive frameworks for understanding the external world.

For Jaspers, one's *Weltanschauung* is comprised of a *Weltbild* and an *Einstellung*. Throughout one's life one is faced with profound experiences—*Grenzsituationen*—that leave a lasting mark on the individual. In response to these situations one forms a conception of the external world (*Weltbilder*) dictated primarily by the *Geistestypus* one possesses. *Weltbilder* informs one's *Einstellung*, culminating in patterns of behaviour and ways of apprehending and understanding the external world. (This is a simplified, 'one-way' explanation of Jaspers' theory; one's *Geistestypus*, *Einstellung*, and *Weltbild* and irrevocably enmeshed and each informs one another.)

One might criticise Jaspers' work on a few levels. First, his definition of *Weltanschauung* is a confused one. When he speaks of *Weltbilder* as 'objective' conceptions of the world, informed by *Grenzsituationen*, he means that they *appear* objective to the individual. Jaspers does not claim that every individual conception of the world is objectively 'true,' rather that what every individual *takes* to be objectively true regarding the external world, is the result of one's

Geistestypus responding to *Grenzsituationen*. Therefore, these *Weltbilder* are in fact subjective in and of themselves.

Second, one might describe his conception of *Grenzsituationen* as overly pessimistic. He speaks of *Grenzsituationen* 'of struggle, of death, of chance, of guilt [*des Kampfes, des Todes, des Zufalls, der Schuld*]' (204), but at no point gives any credence to the possibility of *positive Grenzsituationen*. In other words, for Jaspers, one's defining moments in the 'life of the spirit' are overwhelmingly traumatic, there is no possibility that people's lives might be shaped profoundly by moments of positivity, of love, and importantly for present purposes, by positive interaction with the divine or the transcendent.

Regardless, one can take numerous insights from Jaspers. In addition to his reinforcing of the definition of *Weltanschauungen* hitherto, Jaspers helpfully highlights that the formation of *Weltanschauungen* is primarily *experiential*. This is to say, worldviews are subjective responses to key, life-changing events experienced by the individual.

Between Husserl's unwavering critique of *Weltanschauungsphilosophie*, and Jaspers' assertions that *Weltanschauungen* form the natural human response to important life events, lies Martin Heidegger (1889–1976). Heidegger 'undoubtedly belong[s] among the most important thinkers of the entire twentieth century.'[69] However, his work is irrevocably enmeshed with debates concerning his involvement with Nazism in the 1930s and 40s. To overlook completely these elements of Heidegger's own views—which remain highly disputed[70]—and to feign ignorance of them in the following discussion would be something of a failure of morality. Though Heidegger's connections with the Nazi Party were long noted it was not until the late 1980s, following a string of publications by Farías,[71] Derrida,[72] Lyotard,[73] Ott,[74] and Habermas[75] that the apparent extent of his relationship and sympathies with the party were laid bare.

Such inclinations have been made more apparent by the subsequent publication of Heidegger's infamous 'Black Notebooks.' In 2014, sections of the *Schwarze Hefte* covering the years 1931–41 were published in the Heidegger *Gesamtausgabe* (GA 94–6),[76] with the remaining notebooks (covering the years 1942–45) remaining in private ownership. Compounded by his 'erstwhile member[ship] of the Nazi party,'[77] many view the *Hefte* as betraying a blatant anti-Semitism, although some Heidegger scholars have offered more sympathetic readings of the texts.[78] Heidegger himself stressed in a letter to Hannah Arendt that he was not anti-Semitic but, as Richard King notes, Arendt remained 'deeply disappointed by the failure of German intellectuals and academics, especially Martin Heidegger, to resist the Nazis.'[79] Therefore, it is with the significant caveat that the most unconscionable form of fascism is 'solidly rooted in the heart of Heidegger's theory'[80] that I examine his conception of *Weltanschauung*.

In this respect, a helpful starting point is his review of Jaspers' *Psychologie der Weltanschauungen*.[81] Initially not intended for publication,[82] the text comprises a piece of private communication from Heidegger to Jaspers, Husserl, and Rickert and, despite some methodological concerns with Jaspers' work, is generally effusive in its praise of Jaspers' innovations regarding the concept of *Weltanschauung*, a concept which would drive much of his later philosophy. Following Husserl before him, Heidegger was keen to reject the pervasive worldview-philosophy of his day, which he perceived to be providing an insecure foundation for outlining a metaphysics of *Dasein*. He thus differentiates between worldview and philosophy (here labelled 'phenomenology') as follows:

> Phenomenology is the investigation of life in itself. Despite the appearance of a philosophy of life, it is really the opposite of a worldview. A worldview is an objectification and immobilizing of life at a certain point in the life of a culture. In contrast, phenomenology is never closed off, it is always provisional in its absolute immersion in life as such.[83]

Heidegger's insight here is an important one. He notes that one's worldview, or the worldviews of certain cultures, are closed systems: a series of propositions taken for granted, or a way of thinking about the external world that evades challenge by the one to whom it belongs, whereas philosophy is—or at least ought to be—constantly open to challenge, to moving forward. Worldviews do not allow themselves to be challenged, since they are the means by which we evaluate the external world; they are 'an objectification and immobilizing of life,' as Heidegger puts it. However, as Merleau-Ponty would later articulate,[84] Heidegger's approach to philosophy was in large part a worldview-driven one, wherein he sought primarily to reformulate Husserl's concept of the *Lebenswelt*, insofar as he viewed philosophy as the means of explaining the phenomenon of being in the world. As Heidegger himself would state the problem:

> What is the mode of being of the entity in which 'world' is constituted? That is *Being and Time*'s central problem—namely, a fundamental ontology of *Dasein*. It has to be shown that the mode of being of human *Dasein* is totally different from that of all other entities and that, as the mode of being that it is, it harbours right within itself the possibility of transcendental constitution.[85]

Elsewhere, Heidegger would claim that 'something like a worldview [*Weltanschauung*] belongs to the essential nature of the *Dasein*.'[86] Or, as Alvis puts it, 'it was indeed to the question of the phenomenality of the world that Heidegger claimed to be offering an answer in *Being and Time*.'[87] Indeed, this was inescapable for Heidegger, who conceded that 'all great philosophy culminates in a worldview.'[88] Despite Heidegger's desire to explain and understand the nature of *Dasein*, he cannot help but approach the question aside from the given-ness of his historical and existential circumstances.

Precisely how Heidegger sought to explain the nature of *Dasein* itself is unimportant here, and, at any rate, would require an entire monograph-length treatment to outline sufficiently. Instead, what is important for the present purposes is that Heidegger, whose 'new beginning still presents probably the most profound turning point in German philosophy since Hegel,'[89] viewed Philosophy as fundamentally a response to *Weltanschauungen*, that is to say, concerned with understanding the means of apprehending the external world. In other words, the problem of *Weltanschauungen* is the very problem of human existence and human experience.

Moreover, Heidegger goes further than Jaspers or Husserl had before him. Whereas, for these thinkers, worldviews were problematic largely because they were subjective frameworks for apprehending the external world, for Heidegger, they were a source of concern because they existed unchallenged in the mind of the individual. They establish epistemological boundaries and they prevented the individual from practising 'true' philosophy that was open and objective. Whilst Heidegger viewed this as problematic because it hinders our ability to comprehend *Dasein*, for my concerns in this study, this is an important insight because it also hinders our ability to make historiographical decisions in the same manner, as will be discussed in the next chapter. Heidegger's observation that our worldviews are philosophical frameworks that we allow to exist without challenge will also have significant implications for historiographical decision-making.

No less important a thinker than Heidegger, Ludwig Wittgenstein (1889–1951) only published one short book during his lifetime: *Tractatus Logico-Philosophicus* (*TLP*).[90] He would later reject much of what he wrote in *TLP* in a work published posthumously in 1953 as *Philosophical Investigations* (*PI*).[91] Either work might rightfully lay claim to be the most important philosophical treatise of the 20th century.

Wittgenstein was largely silent on the issue of *Weltanschauungen*, using the term only six times throughout his corpus[92] (albeit, taking into consideration the minimal nature of his output). As such, I will not devote too much time to his thought here. However, it is worth highlighting a famous passage in *TLP*, wherein he writes:

> The whole modern worldview [*Der ganzen modernen Weltanschauung*] is founded on the illusion that the so-called laws of nature are the explanations of natural phenomena. Thus, people today stop at the laws of nature, treating them as something inviolable, just as God and Fate were treated in past ages.
> (§6.371–2)

Significantly, Wittgenstein here diagnoses the naturalism of his day as a *Weltanschauung*. Naturalism, with its claims about the nature of reality, and its attempts to explain worldly phenomenon, is a *Weltanschauung*. In other words, Wittgenstein correctly notes that *Weltanschauungen* are *metaphysical*, an insight that will prove vital in much of the present study.

3.5 Conclusion

Worldview as a concept began within the work of Kant, only to rapidly gain enormous influence within the western philosophical tradition. A coming together of Fichte and Schelling in Jena resulted in the concept coming to refer primarily to a cognitive means of apprehending the world. This basic meaning was also applied by Hegel, whose stature ensured the term quickly rose to prominence. By the end of the 19th century, conceptual musings on the nature of worldviews by Kierkegaard, Dilthey, and Nietzsche solidified this state of affairs. Nietzsche has been an influential figure in the history of the term, insofar as he has demonstrated that worldviews are an unavoidable—if not entirely desirable—part of human cognition.

The 20th century saw the concept of *Weltanschauung* take root as the primary problem of all philosophical discourse, at least, according to Husserl, Jaspers, and Heidegger. Heidegger is particularly important here, since he highlights the fact that worldviews are an inescapable facet of rational inquiry: one cannot approach the external world except through one's worldview. Additionally, Wittgenstein, in his hugely influential *Tractatus*, reinforced the notion that all *Weltanschauungen* are metaphysical in content. Thus, I define a worldview as *a series of metaphysical presuppositions taken for granted when assessing new information about the external world.*

It is worth noting that the 21st century has yet to see many key advancements insofar as this philosophical locus is concerned. Rather, a few important works have emerged—some of which I have already interacted with—whose main concern is similar to mine here; simply to chart the development of the concept, rather than contribute to it.[93] One might conclude, therefore, that one's worldview is 'a prime foundation … [a commitment] to naming the final foundation of reality—that is, what holds everything in existence'[94] it comprises a set of metaphysical presuppositions taken for granted when assessing new information about the external world.

In this and the preceding chapter I have defined two terms, metaphysics and worldview. I defined metaphysics as *the study of the essential nature of reality, and all its constituent parts, including how they relate to one another*. Given the foregoing discussion of 'worldview' in this chapter, I have defined worldview as a set of metaphysical principles taken for granted when assessing new information regarding the external world. Having defined the concept of a worldview, I now turn to the role of worldviews in historiographical decision-making in the chapter that follows.

Notes

1 In the 21st century, a few important textbook-style treatments of the development of 'worldview' in the western philosophical tradition have been published. See David K. Naugle, *Worldview: The History of a Concept* (Grand Rapids, MI: Eerdmans, 2002); James W. Sire, *Naming the Elephant: Worldview as a Concept*, 2nd ed. (Downers Grove, IL: IVP, 2015); Richard DeWitt, *Worldviews: An Introduction to the History and Philosophy of Science*, 3rd ed. (Oxford: Wiley-Blackwell, 2018). These works are important conversation partners in the present chapter and set out, in much more detail, what I summarise here. Readers seeking a more detailed account of what I am attempting here are encouraged to consult these works.

2 Currently Wright is the most high-profile figure who appeals to worldview within historical Jesus research. See Wright, *NTPG*, 38–44. Wright's historical method will be discussed in detail in Chapter 9 of this study.

3 Wright, *NTPG*, 38.

4 He builds upon Hans W. Frei, *The Eclipse of Biblical Narrative: A Study in Eighteenth and Nineteenth Century Hermeneutics* (New Haven, CT: Yale University, 1974); Robert Alter, *The Art of Biblical Narrative* (New York: Basic Books, 1981); Paul Ricœur, *Time and Narrative*, trans. Robert Czerny, Kathleen McLaughlin, and David Pellauer, 3 vols (Chicago, IL: Chicago University, 1984–88); Alasdair MacIntyre, *After Virtue: A Study in Moral Theology*, 2nd ed. (Notre Dame, IL: Notre Dame University, 1985); Robert W. Funk, *The Poetics of Biblical Narrative* (Sonoma, CL: Polebridge, 1988); Stanley Hauerwas and L. Gregory Jones, eds., *Why Narrative? Readings in Narrative Theology* (Grand Rapids, MI: Eerdmans, 1989).

5 DeWitt, *Worldviews*, 7.

6 The original German title, *Kritik der Urteilskraft*, is occasionally translated as *Critique of the Power of Judgement*. See, for example, Allen W. Wood, *Kant*, Blackwell Great Minds (Oxford: Blackwell, 2005), 16; Paul Guyer, *Kant*, Routledge Philosophers (London: Routledge, 2006), 3–5.

7 The traditional reading of *CPuR* and *CPrR* holds that Kant's rationalist framework is congruous with his predecessors such as Leibniz, Hume, and Berkeley. See, for example, Ernst Cassirer, *Kant's Life and Thought*, trans. James Haden (New Haven, CT: Yale University, 1981), 139–217; Otfried Höffe, *Immanuel Kant*, trans. Marshall Farrier (Albany, NY: State of University of New York, 1994), 31–137; Karl Ameriks, *Kant and the Historical Turn: Philosophy as Critical Interpretation* (Oxford: Oxford University, 2006), 33–160; Graham Bird, *The Revolutionary Kant: A Commentary on the Critique of Pure Reason* (Chicago, IL: Open Court, 2006).

8 The first edition reads "Das Unendliche" rather than "Das gegebene Unendliche."

9 Immanuel Kant, *Kritik der Urteilskraft*, ed. Karl Vorländer, Fünfte Auflage, Die philosophischen Bibliothek 39 (Leipzig: Felix Meiner, 1922), 99.

10 Gert J. Malan, 'Mythology, Weltanschauung, Symbolic Universe and States of Consciousness', *HTS Teologiese Studies* 72.1 (2016), 1–8 (4). See also J. Baird Callicott, 'The Worldview Concept and Aldo Leopold's Project of "World View" Remediation', *Journal for the Study of Religion, Nature, and Culture* 5.4 (2011), 510–28 (512–13).

11 Callicott, 'The Worldview Concept,' 513.

12 Naugle, *Worldview*, 59.

13 Martin Heidegger, *The Basic Problems of Phenomenology*, trans. Albert Hofstadter, Studies in Phenomenology and Existential Philosophy (Bloomington, IN: Indiana University, 1982), 4. Heidegger's own contribution to the understanding of *Weltanschauung* will be discussed later in this chapter (§4).

14 Phenomenology was, of course, not yet a formal philosophical discipline at the time of Kant's writing. I only mean that in speaking of a *Weltanschauung* in terms of sense-perception, he is making a claim that we might today describe accurately as phenomenological.

15 See Günter Zöller, 'Introduction', in *The Cambridge Companion to Fichte*, ed. David James and Günter Zöller (Cambridge: Cambridge University, 2016), 1–6 (2).

16 Johann Gottlieb Fichte, *Versuch einer Critik aller Offenbarung*, Zweite Auflage (Königsberg: Hartungsche Buchhandlung, 1793), 150–51. (Emphases original).

17 Frederick Beiser, 'Fichte and the French Revolution', in *The Cambridge Companion to Fichte*, ed. David James and Günter Zöller (Cambridge: Cambridge University, 2016), 38–64 (54).

18 Naugle, *Worldview*, 60.

19 To my knowledge, these words (or similar) did not appear in any of Schelling's published works. The full quote can instead be found in Helmut G. Meier, '"Weltanschauung": Studien zu einer Geschichte und Theorie des Begriffs' (unpublished PhD diss., Westfälischen Wilhelms-Universität zu Münster, 1967), 327 n.147.

20 Heidegger, *The Basic Problems of Phenomenology*, 4.

21 G.F.W. Hegel, *The Difference between Fichte's and Schelling's System of Philosophy*, trans. H.S. Harris and Walter Cerf (Albany, NY: State of University of New York Press, 1977), 725.
22 In German *Phänomenologie des Geistes*. The German 'Geist' can convey the meaning of 'spirit' or 'mind'. Accordingly, *Phänomenologie des Geistes* is alternatively translated into English as either *Phenomenology of Spirit* or *Phenomenology of Mind*.
23 G.F.W. Hegel, *The Phenomenology of Mind*, trans. J.B. Baillie, 2nd ed. (London: George Allen and Unwin, 1961), 615–16.
24 Jean Hyppolite, *Genesis and Structure of Hegel's Phenomenology of Spirit*, trans. Samuel Cherniak and John Heckman, Northwestern University Studies in Phenomenology and Existential Philosophy (Evanston, IL: Northwestern University, 1974), 469–70.
25 Naugle, *Worldview*, 70.
26 G.W.F. Hegel, *The Philosophy of History*, trans. J. Sibree (Chicago, IL: Encyclopaedia Britannica, 1952), 193.
27 Ibid., 221.
28 Naugle, *Worldview*, 73.
29 See the relevant entries in *Fundamental Polyglot Konkordans til Kierkegaards Samlede Værker* (Leiden: Brill, 1971).
30 Naugle, *Worldview*, 74–75.
31 *The Journals of Kierkegaard*, trans. Alexander Dru (London: Oxford University Press, 1938), 15–16.
32 Kierkegaard mistakenly attributes this insight to Karl Daub. It actually comes from Franz von Baader, *Vorlesnungen über speculative Dogmatik* (Stuttgart: Cotta, 1828), 80.
33 Søren Kierkegaard, *Af en endnu Levendes Papirer. Om Begrebet Ironi.*, ed. Niels Jørgen Cappelørn, Joakim Garff, and Johnny Kondrup, Søren Kierkegaards Skrifter, 1 (København: Gad, 1997), 32–33. The translation is from Alastair Hannay, *Kierkegaard: A Biography* (Cambridge: CUP, 2001), 110–11.
34 Michael Ermarth, *William Dilthey: The Critique of Historical Reason* (Chicago, IL: University of Chicago, 1978), 324.
35 Wilhelm Dilthey, *Dilthey's Philosophy of Existence: Introduction to Weltanschauunglehre*, trans. William Kluback and Martin Weinbaum (New York: Bookman Associates, 1957), 17–74.
36 Taylor, *A Secular Age*, 35–43.
37 Sire, *Naming the Elephant*, 27. (emphasis original)
38 Naugle, *Worldview*, 98.
39 Eric Blondel, *Nietzsche: The Body and Culture: Philosophy as a Philological Genealogy*, trans. Seán Hand (London: Athlone, 1991), 76.
40 Peter Levine, *Nietzsche and the Modern Crisis of the Humanities* (Albany, NY: State of University of New York, 1995), xv.
41 Nietzsche, *KSA*, I:551, 598.
42 Ibid., VII:13.
43 Ibid., VII:75.
44 Ibid., *KSA*, VII:79, 118, 123, 288.
45 Ibid., VII:116.
46 Ibid., XV:102.
47 Idem, *Menschliches, Allzumenschliches. Ein Buch für freie Geister*, Neue Ausgabe mit einer einführenden Vorrede., 2 vols (Leipzig: E.W. Fritzsch, 1886), I:§1.16.
48 Idem, *KSA*, I:251.
49 Richard Schacht, 'Nietzsche and the Method of Philosophy', in *Nietzsche as Affirmative Thinker: Papers Presented at the Fifth Jerusalem Philosophical Encounter, April 1983*, ed. Yirmiyahu Yovel, Martinus Nijhoff Philosophical Library, 13 (Dordrecht: Springer,

1986), 1–19 (1). This paper is also available as 'Nietzsche on Philosophy, Interpretation and Truth', *Noûs* 18.1 (1984), 75–85.

50 James Orr, *The Christian View of God and the World as Centering in the Incarnation* (New York: Scribner, 1887), 365; now available as *The Christian View of God and the World* (Grand Rapids, MI: Kregel, 1989).

51 Orr, *The Christian View of God and the World*, 365.

52 Cf., Meier, 'Weltanschauug'.

53 Edmund Husserl, 'Philosophie als strenge Wissenschaft', *Logos. Internationale Zeitschrift für Philosophie der Kultur* 1 (1910), 289–341. ET: Edmund Husserl, 'Philosophy as Rigorous Science', in *The New Yearbook for Phenomenology and Phenomenological Philosophy*, ed. Burt Hopkins and Steven Crowell, trans. Marcus Brainard (London: Routledge, 2002), II.249–95. In what follows, all page numbers refer to the German original; translations given are my own.

54 In a letter from Dilthey to Husserl dated 29 June 1911, the former declares, "I am neither an institutionist, nor a historicist, nor a skeptic." See Edmund Husserl and Wilhelm Dilthey, 'The Dilthey-Husserl Correspondance', in *Husserl: Shorter Works*, ed. Peter McCormick and Frederick A. Elliston (Notre Dame, IL: University of Notre Dame, 1981), 204.

55 Naugle, *Worldview*, 113.

56 Arthur Holmes, 'Phenomenology and the Relativity of World-Views', *Personalist* 48.3 (1967), 328–44; David Carr, *Interpreting Husserl: Critical and Comparative Studies* (Boston, MA: Martinus Nijhoff, 1987), 217–28.

57 Philip Buckley, 'Phenomenology as Soteriology: Husserl and the Call for *"Erneuerung"* in the 1920s', *Modern Theology* 35.1 (2019), 5–22.

58 Edmund Husserl, *Die Krisis der europäischen Wissenschaften und die transzendentale Phänomenologie*, ed. Walter Biemel, Gesammelte Werke, VI (The Hague: Martinus Nijhoff, 1954), 508. An English translation of the text can be found in Edmund Husserl, *The Crisis of European Sciences and Transcendental Phenomenology: An Introduction to Phenomenological Philosophy*, ed. & trans. David Carr, Northwestern University Studies in Phenomenology and Existential Philosophy (Evanston, IL: Northwestern University, 1970). The relevant quote in the ET is found on p. 389. The phrase here translated as 'the dream is over' reads, in the original German, 'der Traum ist ausgeträumt.'

59 Enzo Paci, *The Function of the Sciences and the Meaning of Man*, trans. Paul Piccone and James E. Hansen, Northwestern University Studies in Phenomenology and Existential Philosophy (Evanston, IL: Northwestern University, 1972), 240–41.

60 See, for example, David Carr, 'Husserl's Problematic Concept of the Life-World', *American Philosophical Quarterly* 7.4 (1970), 331–39; John Scanlon, 'The Manifold Meanings of "Life World" in Husserl's Crisis', *American Catholic Philosophical Quarterly* 66.2 (1992), 229–39.

61 Husserl, *Crisis*, 382.

62 David Carr, *Phenomenology and the Problem of History: A Study of Husserl's Transcendental Philosophy* (Evanston, IL: Northwestern University, 1974), 246. This irony has been noted by others also. See B.C. Postow, 'Husserl's Failure to Establish a Presuppositionless Science', *The Southern Journal of Philosophy* 14.2 (1976), 179–88; Jan W. Sarna, 'On Some Presuppositions of Husserl's "Presuppositionless" Philosophy', *Analecta Husserliana* 27 (1989), 239–50; Teresa Reed-Downing, 'Husserl's Presuppositionless Philosophy', *RP* 20.1 (1990), 136–51; Adrian Mirvish, 'The Presuppositions of Husserl's Presuppositionless Philosophy', *Journal of the British Society for Phenomenology* 26.2 (1995), 147–70.

63 Sarna, 'Some Presuppositions,' 240.

64 Karl Jaspers, *Psychologie der Weltanschauungen* (Berlin: Springer, 1919). There have been six German editions of the text, the most recent of which was first published in 1971. The work has been translated into many different languages, many of the trans-

lations based on different editions of the original. At the time of writing, however, no English translation has yet been published.

65 Eugene Webb, *Worldview and Mind: Religious Thought and Psychological Development*, The Eric Voegelin Institute Series in Political Philosophy (Columbia, TN: University of Missouri, 2009), 15.

66 He writes, "In my *Psychologie der Weltanschauungen* I was, naively, engaged already in philosophizing without knowing clearly as yet what I was doing." See Karl Jaspers, 'Philosophical Autobiography', ed. Paul Arthur Schlipp, Library of Living Philosophers (La Salle, IL: Open Court, 1981), 5–94 (27).

67 For example, as with his analysis of Einstellungen, Jaspers discusses three primary types of Weltbilder: Das sinnlich-räumlich Weltbild, Das seelisch-kulturelle Weltbild, and Das metaphysische Weltbild.

68 Throughout chapter I, Jaspers discusses three primary Einstellungen: Gegenständliche Einstellungen, Selbstreflektierte Einstellungen, and Die enthusiastische Einstellung. Each of these three are themselves comprised of various Einstellungen. For example, within the category of Gegenständliche Einstellungen is discussed Aktive, Kontemplative, and Mystische Einstellungen. He notes: "jede Einstellung mit unendlich mannigfaltigem Inhalte erfüllt sein kann" (43). There is simply not enough space here to present and discuss each 'attitude' in turn. At any rate, it would be of no significance for the present study. Instead, what is important for understanding Jaspers' view of Weltanschauung is his view of its relation to Einstellungen (broadly construed).

69 Stefano Marino, *Aesthetics, Metaphysics, Language: Essays on Heidegger and Gadamer* (Newcastle upon Tyne: Cambridge Scholars, 2015), 1.

70 A helpful and balanced introduction to the issue and its importance may be found in Jayne Svenungsson, 'Introduction: Heidegger and Theology after the Black Notebooks', in *Heidegger's Black Notebooks and the Future of Theology*, ed. Mårtin Björk and Jayne Svenungsson (Cham: Springer Nature, 2017), 1–22.

71 Víctor Farías, *Heidegger et le nazisme* (Paris: Verdier, 1987); ET: *Heidegger and Nazism*, trans. Joseph Margolis and Tom Rockmore (Philadelphia, PA: Temple University, 1989). Farías' monograph was originally published in French due to his inability to find a German publisher willing to promote the book. See Tracey B. Strong, 'Review of Heidegger and Nazism. By Victor Farias', *American Political Science Review* 84.3 (1990), 962–64 (962).

72 Jacques Derrida, *De l'esprit: Heidegger et la question* (Paris: Editions Galilée, 1987).

73 Jean-François Lyotard, *Heidegger et 'les juifs'* (Paris: Débats, 1988).

74 Hugo Ott, *Martin Heidegger: Unterwegs zur seiner Biographie* (Frankfurt: Campus, 1988). Though there is no English translation of this work, English speaking readers may wish to consult the later Hugo Ott, *Martin Heidegger: A Political Life* (London: HarperCollins, 1993).

75 Jürgen Habermas, 'Work and Weltanschauung: The Heidegger Controversy from a German Perspective', trans. John McCumber, *Critical Inquiry* 15.2 (1989), 431–56.

76 It is worth pointing out that the scholarly rigour with which the Gesemtausgabe was assembled has itself been subject to a broadside critique by Theodore Kisiel, 'Heidegger's Gesamtausgabe: An International Scandal of Scholarship', *Philosophy Today* 39.1 (1995), 3–15.

77 Conor Cunningham, *Genealogy of Nihilism: Philosophy of Nothing and the Difference of Theology* (London and New York: Routledge, 2002), 131.

78 For example, see two recent articles from the last five years: Jesús Adrián Escudero, 'Heidegger's *Black Notebooks* and the Question of Anti-Semitism', *Gatherings: The Heidegger Circle Annual* 5.1 (2015), 21–49; Tobias Keiling, 'Heidegger's *Black Notebooks* and the Logic of a History of Being', *RP* 47.3 (2017), 406–28.

79 Richard H. King, *Arendt and America* (Chicago, IL: The University of Chicago Press, 2015), 122.

80 Tom Rockmore, 'Philosophy or Weltanschauung? Heidegger on Hönigswald', *History of Philosophy Quarterly* 16.1 (1999), 97–115 (112).
81 Martin Heidegger, 'Anmerkungen zu Karl Jaspers' *Psychologie der Weltanschauung*', in *Wegmarken*, ed. F.-W. von Herrmann, Gesamtausgabe, 9 (Frankfurt: Klostermann, 1976), 1–44. There is no English translation available at the time of writing.
82 See Theodore Kisiel, *The Genesis of Heidegger's 'Being and Time'* (Berkeley, CA: University of California, 1993), 137.
83 Martin Heidegger, quoted in Kisiel, *Genesis*, 17.
84 Note the comments in Maurice Merleau-Ponty, *Phenomenolgie de la perception* (Paris: PUF, 1945), 1.
85 Quoted from Jason W. Alvis, 'How to Overcome the World: Henry, Heidegger, and the Post-Secular', *IJPS* 24.5 (2016), 663–84 (666).
86 Heidegger, *The Basic Problems of Phenomenology*, 10.
87 Alvis, 'How to Overcome the World', 667.
88 Martin Heidegger, quoted in George Kovacs, 'Philosophy as Primordial Science in Heidegger's Courses of 1919', in *Reading Heidegger from the Start: Essays in His Earliest Thought*, ed. Theodore Kisiel and John van Buren, SUNY Series in Contemporary Continental Philosophy (Albany, NY: State of University of New York, 1994), 91–108 (94).
89 Habermas, 'Work and Weltanschauung', 434.
90 The text was originally published in 1921 as Ludwig Wittgenstein, 'Logisch-Philosophische Abhandlung', ed. Wilhelm Ostwald, *Annalen Der Naturphilosophie* 14 (1921). It was then translated into English and given the more famous Latin title in the following year as Ludwig Wittgenstein, *Tractatus Logico-Philosophicus* (London: Kegan Paul, 1922).
91 Upon Wittgenstein's death, the incomplete manuscript for *PI* was published as Ludwig Wittgenstein, *Philosophical Investigations*, trans. G.E.M. Anscombe (London: MacMillan, 1953). Amongst the myriad editions of the text that followed, the most important is Ludwig Wittgenstein, *Philosophical Investigations*, trans. G.E.M. Anscombe, 50th Anniversary Edition (London: Blackwell, 2001), which also contains the original German text. In what follows I refer to the 50th Anniversary Edition of the text.
92 Naugle, *Worldview*, 150.
93 For example, in addition to the works of Naugle and Sire, cited already see André Droogers and Anton van Harskamp (eds.), *Methods for the Study of Religious Change: From Religious Studies to Worldview Studies* (Sheffield: Equinox, 2014) and David N. Entwistle, *Integrative Approaches to Psychology and Christianity: An Introduction to Worldview Issues, Philosophical Foundations, and Models of Integration*, 3rd ed. (Eugene, OR: Cascade, 2015).
94 Sire, *Naming the Elephant*, 16.

4 Worldviews and Historiographical Decision-Making

4.1 Introduction

Over the course of the previous two chapters, I have defined a worldview as a set of metaphysical presuppositions taken for granted when evaluating information about the external world. In this fourth chapter, I examine the role of worldviews in historiography. I argue all historiography is inescapably filtered through one's worldview and, therefore, the metaphysical framework(s) that comprise one's worldview. Therefore, I also make a distinction between a historian's worldview *per se* (their 'personal' or 'private' worldview) and their historiographical worldview (the worldview they adopt in order to undertake historical enquiry).

During the preceding overview of worldview in the western philosophical tradition, I examined Heidegger's conception of *Weltanschauung*. For Heidegger, worldviews are unavoidable, if not altogether desirable. Even if they hinder us in our task—as Heidegger thought they hindered his pursuit of *Dasein*—one cannot help but employ one's worldview when assessing the external world. As Heidegger himself noted, 'all great philosophy culminates in a worldview.'[1]

I make a similar contention here regarding historiographical decision-making: all historical judgements are at least in part the result of the metaphysical presuppositions held by the historian. All historiography, therefore, is metaphysical, and there can be no historical method that avoids making metaphysical assumptions when assessing historical data. My aim here, therefore, is not to make judgements concerning which worldview(s) historians ought to adopt, but merely to demonstrate they are an unavoidable framework that makes possible any historical enquiry.

In this chapter I demonstrate that all historical research encroaches upon metaphysics, that it is impossible to make claims about the past without first making metaphysical assumptions. I claim that if historiography is conducted from within the worldview of the historian, and worldviews comprise a series of metaphysical presuppositions, then it logically follows that these metaphysical presuppositions in some sense interact with the ensuing research any historian may wish to undertake. It is the precise nature of this 'interaction' that I draw out in what follows. To expand upon this claim, it is necessary to probe the relationship between the

DOI: 10.4324/b23077-5

historian and historical evidence. In other words, this is to ask the question, what makes something 'historically plausible' in the most fundamental sense?

The notion of historical plausibility remains central to the quest for the historical Jesus, despite the fragmentary nature of the discipline at present, as it does in all historically based disciplines. Theissen and Winter, for example, assert that historical claims are only reasonable insofar as they are historically plausible.[2] Pitre's most recent contribution to the discipline—largely building upon the method of Sanders—is framed with the language of 'plausibility.'[3] Elsewhere, Le Donne writes, '*the "historical Jesus" is the figure that becomes plausible on the basis of the historical evidence; there is no other.*'[4]

However, these claims beg two questions about the category of 'plausibility.' What *is* plausibility? Moreover, how does one *measure* plausibility? Jesus historians have not adequately reflected upon these foundational questions that underpin the 'Quest' for the historical Jesus, and yet the answers to these questions offer important implications regarding the principal task of the discipline: to make historical claims about Jesus of Nazareth.

The aim of this chapter is to answer these questions, making two claims in the process. First, historical knowledge might be described as any historical claim that seems plausible to the historian. This is to say, plausibility is a subjective category. Second, historical plausibility is measured in direct correlation to the historian's historiographical worldview (i.e., the specific set of metaphysical presuppositions taken as a pre-given framework for historical enquiry). One may thus approach the following chapter as an exercise in the discipline known as 'the philosophy of history.' Since the dawn of postmodernism and the linguistic turn, instigated by the likes of Derrida,[5] White,[6] Lyotard,[7] Rorty,[8] historians have become increasingly self-aware and self-reflective of the presuppositions that dominate their work. Accordingly, debates have arisen regarding the very possibility of historical knowledge. Even deciding which knowledge might be described as 'historical' may be problematic.[9] However, as Rahikainen and Fellman note, these debates have changed historical praxis very little: 'it is one thing to pursue philosophical and theoretical discourse on history writing, and quite another to make it part of research work in practice.'[10]

Methodological debates can be dated back far beyond the postmodern turn. Indeed, the term 'philosophy of history' was itself coined in the mid-18th century. François-Marie Arouet (1694–1778)—best known by his *nom de plume*, Voltaire—is, in many ways, the archetypal enlightenment thinker, exemplified by his fierce criticism of religion (especially Christianity) and his ardent commitment to reason. Regarding historiography, his most important work is his 1756 treatise *Essai sur les mœrs et l'espirit des nations*.[11] He begins his essay with a section entitled 'La Philosophie de l'histoire,' which refers to two things: the examination of traditional historiographical approaches, and the appropriation of moral, aesthetic, and religious elements of past societies and cultures.[12]

It is the former domain to which I refer when I speak of a philosophy of history. The reader should not understand this as alluding to attempts to provide a philosophical metanarrative explaining the course of history as, say, Hegel and Marx have offered (thereby understanding 'history' to refer to the series of events that make up the past and will comprise the future). Rather, the philosophy of history is an attempt to delineate the content of historiography: what is involved in the act of writing history (i.e., writing *about* history). Thus, it is a branch of epistemology, whereas the former would properly fall under the auspices of metaphysics (although there is a clear metaphysical element to the philosophy of history as understood in this sense also).

4.2 Three Philosophies of History

This being the case, I highlight three philosophers of history and outline their understanding of historiography: (1) R.G. Collingwood, (2) Friedrich Nietzsche, and (3) Maurice Blondel. I choose these thinkers because they represent three different traditions: a classically trained historian, a nihilistic philosopher, and a Catholic theologian. And yet they all come to the same conclusion: historical knowledge is a subjective category that requires the active input of the historian and is predicated upon pre-conceived or given notions of 'plausibility.'

By examining their historiographical methodologies, it will become clear that historical knowledge is best understood as a series of claims that—rather than lying upon a binary system of correct and incorrect—lie upon a scale of plausible and implausible: when dealing with historical knowledge, one is tacitly dealing with historical *plausibility*. In other words, to claim that one 'knows' something about the past (and therefore to claim concurrently that that thing forms a piece of historical knowledge), one is claiming that *it is more probable than not* that that event took place (for example). As noted already, therefore, historical knowledge might accurately be described as something that appears *plausible* to the historian.

More recent concerns with historical knowledge are often traced back to R.G. Collingwood although, as has been made clear already (regarding Voltaire) and will be so again shortly (regarding Nietzsche), Collingwood is not the sole progenitor of the discipline. In this regard, philosophers of history highlight his influential posthumous book *The Idea of History*,[13] although many of the key thoughts of this work were pre-empted in Chapter X of his autobiography, published seven years prior.[14]

In an article first published in 1922,[15] Collingwood rejected the widespread notion that science and historiography represent two different kinds of knowledge, since science is concerned with what is *universally* true, whilst history is concerned with what is—or *was*—*particularly* true. This is to say, this is concerned with what happened on a particular occasion. This notion had become so widespread that it was 'in general accepted without question.'[16] However, in practice, both disciplines are concerned with the universal *and* the particular:

> A working historian is critical in all the same ways as a working scientist, and a scientist who has come to a conclusion states it, everybody knows, as dogmatically as a Pope: it would be a pedantic and insincere affections if he

> did not … To erect such a dualism is to falsify both science and history by mutilating each.[17]

Historical claims are neither completely 'dead' nor 'finished,' and scientific claims are neither completely 'living' nor 'universal.' Collingwood, therefore, conceives of history (in the sense of *writing about* history) as a present-oriented discipline, just as science is. For this reason, Collingwood also conceives of historical writing as a *psychological* endeavour. In his autobiography he stresses that 'historical knowledge is the re-enactment in the historian's mind of the thought whose history he is studying.'[18] It involves imagination and requires historians 'to "re-enact" thoughts which originally passed through the minds of the people they study.'[19] Historiography involves evidence and imagination.

It is this that leads him to assert the 'inside-outside' nature of historiography. From the 'outside,' that is, the external context to an event, one is better equipped to examine the 'inside,' that is, the internal thoughts and motivations of the agents involved. In *The Idea of History*, he writes:

> The historian, investigating any event in the past, makes a distinction between what may be called the outside and the inside of an event. By the outside of the event I mean everything belonging to it which may be described in terms of bodies and their movements: the passage of Caesar, accompanied by certain men, across a river called the Rubicon at one date, or the spilling of blood on the floor of the senate-house at another. By the inside of the event I mean that in it which can only be described in terms of thought: Caesar's defiance of Republican law, or the clash of constitutional policy between himself and his assassins.[20]

Though one might object to various aspects of Collingwood's historical method—for example, he places too much stress on individual actors, and ignores unconscious motives[21]—his work was an influence upon key thinkers such as Thomas Kuhn[22] and Quentin Skinner.[23]

Collingwood's primary contribution is the importance he bestows upon the role of imagination in historiographical work, and his contention that history could—and *should*—be as systematic and present-oriented an endeavour as science. The significance in the latter is most realised in opposition to the prevailing historiographical norms of Collingwood's day, which conceived of historiography as an exclusively narrative-driven discipline. In 1939, Charles Oman famously defined history as 'a series of happenings.'[24] It is the job of the historian to present events in their subject in chronological order, it was even the mark of rigorous historiography. In the same year, the great Marc Bloch seemed almost apologetic for not applying a chronological structure to his work.[25] Finnish historian Louis Halphen wrote in 1951 that 'to the historian, obeying the sequence of events according to their own chronology is the rational advice, which cannot be forgotten without punishment.'[26]

Now, of course, the picture is markedly different, so much so that 'narrating events in a strictly chronological order would not even qualify as serious historical research.'[27] Nowhere is this more clear than historical Jesus research, wherein monographs routinely contain sections on various themes within Jesus' life: Jesus' use of parables, Jesus and/within Judaism, Jesus and conflict, and so on. However, Collingwood's insight that historical knowledge is always a judgement of plausibility in which the historian is an active participant, applying their subjective imagination to the process, remains a vital insight.

I have already discussed Nietzsche in the previous chapter, wherein I examined his assertion that worldviews are an unavoidable part of human cognition. Regarding historical knowledge, Nietzsche's most important contribution is found in the second of his four 'Untimely Meditations,' entitled 'On the Use and Abuse of History for Life.'[28] Nietzsche's concerns here are twofold, the latter of which will be my concern here. First, Nietzsche takes aim at recent historical studies which, he suggests, following the Franco-Prussian war had had an unduly nationalising effect. Second, he wishes to inaugurate a shift in historiography more broadly. Nietzsche's aim here was to point out that 'the German obsession with the past was disabling action in the present,' as one recent commentator summarises.[29]

Nietzsche begins by comparing historical and un-historical modes of cognition. Cows, he suggests, have no awareness of the past and live their lives only in the present. Humans, however, are unwaveringly aware that they stand at the end of a long procession of past events, and at the beginning of an even longer chain of future events, knowledge of which serves to burden humanity. He likens this dichotomy to 'forgetting' and 'remembering': Humanity's obsession with 'remembering the past is crippling it in the present.' He described un-historical beings (e.g., cows) as living with 'the forgetting [*das Vergessen*]—or, in more scholarly sense, the ability to feel un-historical [*unhistorisch*] during its existence.'[30] Nietzsche thus seeks to examine the manner in which historiography enables humans to live in the present, rather than simply shackling them to what has already taken place.

Therefore, he calls for humans to be 'suprahistorical' beings, unbound by what has gone before, no longer bound by the past and no longer seeking historical knowledge for its own sake. This would, Nietzsche contends, be 'a kind of life-ending and reckoning for humanity.'[31] He therefore identifies three types of historiography, 'monumental history,' 'antiquarian history,' and 'critical history,' which must be balanced carefully if one is to serve the needs of the present.

Monumental history is employed by 'workers and aspirants [*Thätigen und Strebenden*],'[32] and seeks to understand the past in order to inspire greatness in the present. It is a category that Nietzsche borrows from ancient historians (and especially from Livy's *Ab Urbe Condita*[33]), in which one scours the past to find inspiration and encouragement, to remind those in the present of the great things achieved in the past and of the possibility that similar feats could be achieved again. However, Nietzsche warns against such a historiography and criticises what he perceives to be a fundamental misunderstanding of the nature of cause and effect:

> Monumental history deceives by analogies [*täuscht durch Analogien*]: it tempts the courageous with seductive resemblances to boldness, the

> enthusiastic to fanaticism, and if one thinks this history is in the hands and minds of gifted egoists and the swarming villains, then empires are destroyed, princes murdered, wars and revolutions are instigated, and the number of historical 'effects in themselves' ['*Effecte an sich*'], that is, of the effects without sufficient causes, is increased anew.[34]

Nietzsche hereby warns against too fine a dichotomy between cause and effect. It is dangerous, he suggests, to look for desirable 'effects' and seek to replicate them without fully understanding their causes. Thus, by removing the cause and focussing only on effect, these people are concerned only with the 'effects in themselves,' [*Effecte an sich*], devoid of any context and risk re-enacting any undesirable causes that may have preceded them. In other words, just because something good came about during the past, this does not mean one should strive to replicate it in the present, as it may be a happy by-product of an unpleasant 'cause.' This reified approach to the past is therefore ultimately harmful to it, insofar as it distorts the reality of past events for the sake of the present.

Antiquarian history is employed by those 'preserving and worshipping [*Bewahrenden und Verehrenden*]' the past,[35] and takes historical knowledge as the *telos* of itself; it prizes knowledge for knowledge's sake. Its aims are, broadly speaking, conservative and favoured by the so-called 'less-favoured families and populations [*die minder begünstigten Geschlechter und Bevölkerungen*],'[36] who oppose historical change and wish to see a return to 'the way things used to be,' where conditions were more favourable. This entails a reification of the past at the expense of advancements in the present:

> If the purpose of a people becomes so hardened, if history serves a past life so as to undermine the future life and, especially, the higher life [*und gerade das höhere Leben untergräbt*], if the historical meaning no longer conserves life but mummifies it [*sondern mumisiert*]: the tree dies gradually from the top to the root—and finally the root itself is commonly destroyed.[37]

Finally, critical history, as the name suggests, attempts to examine and critique the events of the past, to prevent them repeating in the present. Importantly, 'critical' [*kritische*] is here used in the negative sense of condemnation, rather than the modern academic sense of dispassionate judgement. Nietzsche writes:

> It demands the same life that needs oblivion, the temporary annihilation of this oblivion; then it should become clear how unfair the existence of any thing, a privilege, a caste, a dynasty is, for example, how much this thing deserves its downfall [*wie sehr dieses Ding den untergang verdient*].[38]

But when should one apply this methodology? After all, 'every past is worthy to be condemned [*jede Vergangenheit aber ist werth verurtheilt zu werden*].'[39] For Nietzsche, critical history should be the sole preserve of those who find themselves in need of freedom in the present:

> Only the one who is troubled by a present calamity, and who wants to throw off his burden at any cost [*der um jeden Preis die Last von sich abwerfen will*], has a need for a critical—that is to say, a judging—and condemning history.[40]

Those in need, he asserts, are those who are superior to their peers, who need freedom from sedentary, antiquarian approaches to the past. He claims: 'only the superior force [*die überlegene Kraft*] can judge, the weak must tolerate, if they do not feign strength, and make justice an actress on the judge's seat.'[41]

However, critical history too comes with its pitfalls, as far as Nietzsche is concerned. Specifically, he warns that it is impossible completely to disassociate one's self from the past in a dispassionate manner. Since we are at least in part the product of our history, one remains an inexorable part of the very thing one attempts to appropriate: 'For, as we are the results of earlier generations, we are also the results of their aberrations, passions and errors, even crimes: it is not possible [*nicht möglich*] to completely break away from this chain [*von dieser Kette*].'[42]

Each of the approaches, then, has its failings. Regardless, what is clear is Nietzsche's insistence that the past and the present are not so easily untangled. Both present-minded historiographical approaches are described in more favourable terms than antiquarian history, despite their concurrent difficulties. For Nietzsche, there was no question that study of the past was in some way to inform life in the present. This underlying assumption would drive much of his later work.[43] The only question was *how* this was best done since, as demonstrated in the previous chapter, all rational inquiry is subject to one's *Weltanschauung*. It is for precisely this reason that Nietzsche, responding to the positivist obsession with pure facts, writes in *The Will to Power* [*Der Wille zur Macht*]: 'No, facts alone do not exist, only interpretations.'[44]

This understanding of history would later have a profound impact upon Michel Foucault (whose historical work would, in turn, become enormously influential in its own right). In August 1953, Foucault was holidaying in Italy with then-lover Jean Barraqué, during which the former began reading Nietzsche's *Unzeitgemässe Betrachtungen*. The second essay, discussed above, entitled 'Vom Nutzen und Nachteil der Historie für das Leben' had a significant effect upon Foucault.[45] He subsequently came to view himself as a philosophical historian, and wholeheartedly adopted Nietzsche's position that historical knowledge was not an end in itself, but the means by which one may affect the present for the better. In order to do so, Foucault developed a new historiographical method he termed *archéologie*, which underpinned his historical work on mental illness,[46] medicine,[47] and the origins of science.[48] Although implicitly driving all these works, Foucault's notion of *archéologie* would only be explicated in 1969, with the publication of *L'archéologie du savoir*.[49]

Thus, for Nietzsche, one's apprehension of the past is driven by one's needs in the present, be they inspiration (monumental history), preservation (antiquarian history), or freedom (critical history). Although Collingwood and Nietzsche are markedly different thinkers, both in the form and content of their writings, they converge on this point: history is a subject-driven (and thus, subjective) discipline. It is impossible to approach the past on its own terms, one can only do so through the lens of a pre-given framework taken for granted present. Even the very questions we think to ask of our predecessors is governed by our concerns in the present.

Finally, I turn to the work of Maurice Blondel (1961–49). A French Catholic philosopher writing as part of *la nouvelle theologie*, a theological sensibility amongst certain Catholic theologians in the early-to-mid 20th century, whose endeavours towards a Catholic *ressourcement* significantly shaped the second Vatican council. However, his work was not without controversy, and he became embroiled in fierce discussion with Descoqs concerning the Catholic church's response to the rise of secularism.[50]

Blondel is perhaps most known for his masterpiece *L'Action* which seeks to connect philosophical reasoning and Christian belief,[51] something which would remain 'his original and permanent intention' throughout his life.[52] However, for the present purposes his most important work is *Histoire et dogme*,[53] a work which de Lubac credited with instigating a 'return to a more authentic tradition' within Catholic theology.[54]

Despite his importance, Blondel remains 'a figure more frequently invoked than understood.'[55] As Paul Hartog notes, 'much of the scholarly neglect is Blondel's own fault,' due to his tendency to isolate himself from the academic community, and his dense writing style.[56] Regarding the latter point, when Blondel submitted *L'Action* as his Sorbonne thesis, examiner Paul Janet lambasted Blondel's prose, writing:

> Your thought is obscure; your way of writing obscures it still more. It takes me an hour to read one of your pages and then I fail to understand it; I calculated that it would take me forty-five days to read your thesis … as long as I tried to follow you, I took great pains and achieved no result.[57]

Similarly, following the reprint of the English translation of *Histoire et dogme*, one reviewer bemoaned Blondel's impenetrable mode of writing and appeared to be incapable even of summarising the argument of the text.[58] It is perhaps understandable, then, that Blondel's thought has yet to impact significantly the field of historiography in general, and historical Jesus research in particular. This is rather unfortunate because, as we shall see, Blondel's work proves to be particularly generative.

He begins from the conviction that 'history and dogma still continue and will continue to verify and vivify one another.'[59] Blondel thus seeks to elucidate the connection between the two, rejecting 'the thesis of the water-tight compartment between history and dogma … and still more, of course, the thesis of an opposition between them which results in double-thinking.'[60] In so doing, he rejects two of the most common approaches to history amongst Christian theologians: (1) the collection of historical desiderata for apologetic purposes, and (2) the construction of a historical foundation for Christian beliefs. These approaches he uneasily titles 'extrinsicism' and 'historicism,' respectively, terms he later describes as 'barbarous neologisms.'[61]

Christian theology neither comprises historical facts nor is built upon them, and yet dogma and history remain irremovably enmeshed. As Paul warns the church in Corinth, 'if Christ has not been raised, then our proclamation has been in vain and your faith has been in vain,' (1 Cor. 15.14). Whilst this assertion clearly invokes (on some level) the historicity of Jesus' resurrection, it is also clearly something *more* than a mere statement of fact. As Michel Henry notes:

> The truth of Christianity … is not a matter of a truth of the type: 'The French took the Bastille on July 14, 1789.' Nor of another kind of truth, formally similar to the preceding one: 'Christ came into the world in order to save humankind.' In these two examples, our attention is drawn to a certain content, specifically a historical fact or—since a fact of this type is never present in isolation—to a certain state of things that is itself historical.[62]

In response to the problem, Blondel proposes a model of history that resides between history for history's sake and history for faith's sake, where history is no longer viewed as a wholly independent, disinterested, or self-sufficient discipline, fuelled by arbitrary divisions within the academy. He writes:

> The moment a science concludes from its independence within its own field of research to a sort of self-sufficiency, it becomes guilty of fraudulently converting a simple method of work into a negative and tyrannical doctrine. Willy-nilly it is led into the subtly crude illusion that because it is legitimate and necessary to divide the work of the mind, the divisions subsist in the reality.[63]

This being the case, Blondel proposes a distinction between 'real history' and 'reconstructed history,' which recognises the fact that certain facets of history, even though they in some sense 'true' or 'real,' lie beyond the realms of empirical apprehension. In his own words, 'real history' includes 'what the historian does not see … [i.e.,] the spiritual reality, the activity of which is not wholly represented or exhausted by the historical phenomena,' whereas 'reconstructed history' comprises those elements of the past that can be reconstructed using empirical methods. Where reconstructed history may be cognisant of the external events and actions that have taken place in the past, access to internal motivations of the actors, or to the actions of unseen spiritual elements of reality remain elusive. Thus, it will always be an incomplete account of the past that has replaced 'the fact for the actor, the testimony for the witness, the portrait for the person.' In other words, Blondel insists upon the distinction—now commonly recognised by Jesus historians—between 'what actually happened,' and 'what historians can say about what happened.'

This distinction between real and reconstructed history forms the basis for Blondel's criticism of historicism (the view that faith ought to be based upon historical reconstruction), since it draws solely upon the findings of reconstructed history which is, itself, merely the sum of flawed and incomplete methodologies. Thus, any faith built upon a foundation of reconstructed history will ultimately be the result of these same methodologies: 'an ontology, purely phenomenological in character, will be extracted from a methodology and a phenomenology.'[64] Instead, Christian theology can only be built upon real history:

> One realizes through the practice of Christianity that its dogmas are rooted in reality. One has no right to set the facts on one side and the theological data on the other without going back to the sources of life and of action, finding the indivisible synthesis … the link between facts and beliefs can never be rationally justified by scholarship or dialectics, as though each human reason separately performed its dogmatic task.[65]

To provide this link between history and dogma, what is needed is not a historical Christianity, but a Christian historiography that eschews all pretences of dispassionate inquiry and objective neutrality:

> While it is true that Christian knowledge does not disdain the support of history (for the facts in this instance are both the redemptive reality and the revelatory message), history cannot, without leading to the shipwreck of faith, disregard Christian knowledge, by which I mean the results methodologically acquired by the collective experience of Christ verified and realized in us.[66]

I will not consider in any greater detail here the way in which Blondel proposes to navigate a *via media* between history and dogma, since that is not directly relevant to my purposes in the present chapter. Rather, by way of concluding this section, it is worth highlighting the insight that Blondel's dichotomy between real and reconstructed history offers, not least regarding how one understands the nature of historical knowledge and its production.

To use Blondel's terminology, when one participates in modern historical Jesus research (or any number of other historically based academic enterprises) one tacitly participates in the outlining of reconstructed history (as opposed to real history). This is to say, one concerns oneself, not with 'what really happened' and all the attendant questions that accompany it (for example, the motives of those involved, the possible role played by unseen transempirical agents[67]), but instead concerns oneself with reconstructing those elements of the past to which one has access. However, as Blondel makes clear, this neglects a great unknown number of elements about the past that remain inaccessible to the historian.

The fact that modern historiography of this type remains detached from real history means any claims produced under the auspices of reconstructed history are themselves necessarily incomplete, imperfect, and uncertain. In other words, they are *probabilities*; claims tacitly proceeded by the words 'notwithstanding any factors I am unable to assess ….' To employ the metaphysical categories established in the previous chapter, they are *modal claims*, claims that deal first and foremost, in plausibility, doing so with reference to a pre-given 'reconstructed history' that stands in conflict with the 'real history' Blondel speaks of.

4.3 Measuring Historical Plausibility

When attempting to draw parallels between Collingwood, Nietzsche, and Blondel, one point strikes the reader: each of the three stresses the subjectivity of historical knowledge and the inevitability of a pre-given framework underpinning any historiographical enquiry used to assess historical plausibility. For Collingwood, historiography is an act of imagination on the part of the historian; for Nietzsche, it is a means of scouring the past and appropriating for benefit in the present; for Blondel it is an incomplete reconstruction that involves a tacit confession of its own limitations. In each instance—and there are more thinkers one might highlight who stand in congruity with this point—the three make it plain to see that there is simply no unfettered access to the past in all its totality. Historians actively engage in reconstruction of the past, doing so with incomplete sets of data and their own subjectivities and prejudices ascribed to them by their social and cultural setting in the present. Ultimately, then, one might best understand historical judgements as statements of *plausibility*. In other words, it is not possible to view such judgements as mere binaries (i.e., either X event 'happened,' or it didn't), but rather as situated upon a degree of probability that comprises a potentially infinite amount of nuance. If a historian claims, for example, that a saying of Jesus recorded in the gospels is accurate, the implication is not that it was definitely uttered by Jesus, but that it is more likely to have come from the historical Jesus than not: it is *plausible*.

This is true even of historical data that are seemingly taken for granted. Let us return to the example cited by Michel Henry, above: 'the French took the Bastille on July 14, 1789.' No historian would wish to argue against the claim that the storming of the Bastille in Paris took place at this point in time. However, even an event surrounded by such ubiquity and consensus regarding its historicity is not—and indeed cannot—be a certainty, logically and metaphysically speaking. It may be, for example, that the Cartesian problem of the evil demon is accurate and that the external world (including events thought to have occurred in the past) is simply an illusion. Historians, presumably, proceed from the assumption that the external world is *not* an illusion, as would be reasonable to do, but the Cartesian doubt regarding the external world (elsewhere famously encapsulated by Descartes' *cogito ergo sum*[68]) makes it clear that such an assumption cannot be proven logically, it must simply be assumed as a first principle. Indeed, the very existence of the body is, for Descartes, 'only probable,'[69] and the Cartesian doubt regarding the external world is one to which the western philosophical tradition has yet to offer a solution. In other words, to proceed as though the possibility of historiography is a given is to make a metaphysical judgement that has no logical backing. This is not to say that this is an unreasonable means of proceeding, or even that there is any alternative, but it must be borne in mind nonetheless.

Alternatively, one might state the problem in terms of personhood. As Blondel's conception of real history demonstrates, events in the past are moved forward (at least in part) by the internal motives of varying agents. For example, a Jesus historian might legitimately wish to ask the question, 'Why did Jewish and Roman authorities seek to kill Jesus?' But implicit within the question one finds numerous metaphysical assumptions being made. The question assumes the existence of personhood; that the Jewish authorities at the time of Jesus comprised a group of autonomous, free-willed agents capable of making moral judgements based upon rational motives.

However, some would reject this metaphysical claim altogether, not least those operating under the auspices of the so-called 'new atheist' movement. For example, Francis Crick asserts that:

> You, your joys and your sorrows, your memories and your ambitions, your sense of personal identity and free will, are in fact no more than the behaviour of a vast assembly of nerve cells and their associated molecules … you're nothing but a pack of neurons.[70]

Properly understood, this is a metaphysical claim about the nature of humanity, one that rejects the notion of personhood altogether, and renders the possibility of historiography impossible altogether, insofar as it asserts that both the historian and their object of study are simply inert bundles of atoms. To engage in the act of historiography at all, then, is to tacitly reject some metaphysical frameworks from the outset.

To some readers, these claims about historical plausibility and the inherent metaphysical dimension of all historical claims might seem merely trivial. This may seem like unnecessarily extreme scepticism, but it highlights one of the central points made in this chapter: the very notion of 'the past' is something that cannot be proven logically, only taken as a given within a metaphysical framework that operates cognitively prior to the historiographical act. Accordingly, any judgements made about what may or may not have been must always be accompanied by at least some acknowledgement that it is a *plausibility*, rather than a certainty.

To say that historical claims rest upon subjective plausibility judgements may hardly seem innovative. And yet it is important to explicate, since it raises a secondary—more important—question. When one describes an event as 'plausible,' what does one mean? Oliver Laas suggests that plausibility is best understood as a measure of 'truthlikeness' in historical terms.[71] This does little to help, however, and merely begs the question, since the phrase 'truthlikeness' appears to be even more impenetrable than does 'plausible.' Indeed, in the current (at the time of writing) 'post-truth' climate of fake news and wilful subjectivity, to refer casually to 'truth' in this manner might strike the reader as somewhat naïve. Laas, perhaps cognisant of this, argues that 'a hypothesis or claim is plausible if it appears true under normal circumstances and familiar types of situations, in light of the credentials represented by the basis of its credibility.'[72] But this begs further questions:

what comprises 'normal circumstances and familiar types of situations'? What passes for 'credible'? Who is well positioned to judge these most intangible of phenomena? How does one *measure* plausibility? Laas' definition only pushes the problem further back out of sight.

A more accurate and helpful way in which one might understand historical plausibility is in relation to *Weltanschauung*. The degree to which pieces of data appear historically plausible to the historian is in direct correlation to the degree to which those data cohere with the historian's *Weltanschauung*. In other words, something is plausible if it stands in agreement with a pre-established worldview. Stated differently still, if historical judgements are (at least implicitly) made in accordance with one's *Weltanschauung*, and these *Weltanschauungen* are comprised of metaphysical truth claims, then we might say that *metaphysics is prior to historiography*; that one must subscribe (even if only tacitly) to a metaphysical stance before one can make any historical judgement.

For example, let us return to the Cartesian problem of the external world. One logically cannot prove that the external world (including the past) forms part of the 'real,'[73] it must instead be taken as given. If one wishes to engage in historiography, the first (almost always implicit) step is to assert that the external world is 'real,' as is the past. Two points should be noted about this. First, as mentioned already, this step cannot be supported by appeal to reason. Second, that the external world (including the past) exists is a metaphysical claim.

Significantly, it was demonstrated in the previous chapter that *Weltanschauungen* are defined by (1) a lack of a logical foundation, and (2) a metaphysical content. This is to say, worldviews might be described as a series of metaphysical presuppositions taken for granted about the external world. One might accurately say, then, that moving beyond the Cartesian doubt about the external world to engage in historiography involves (in some sense) the positing of something that resembles a worldview. The perceived plausibility of historical data directly correlates with the degree to which it coheres with the historiographical worldview.

An important distinction to make here is between a historian's worldview *per se*, and their historiographical worldview. By the former I mean the worldview that frames the day-to-day life of an individual and is used for assessing new information about the external world. By the latter I mean the worldview that a historian *adopts* to conduct historiographical research. It is the latter with which I am concerned in this study, even if we might reasonably think of the latter as residing 'within' and being shaped by the former. For example, in Chapter 9 of this study I am not concerned with identifying the metaphysical presuppositions that comprise N.T. Wright's worldview *per se*, but identify the metaphysical presuppositions present in his *historiographical worldview*, the metaphysical presuppositions that comprise the framework within which he conducts historical research.

To substantiate this claim, I examine the role of plausibility in Bayes' theorem (or Bayesian inference, as it is also known). Bayes' theorem has endured a tumultuous history within academia.[74] It was widely taught in the 18th and 19th centuries until, in the early 20th century, a new paradigm was born amidst the so-called 'frequentist' approaches of the likes of Pearson, Fisher,[75] and Heyman, prompting something of a schism amongst statisticians.[76] Spurred on by the work of Frank Ramsey[77] and Bruno de Finetti[78] in particular, a neo-Bayesian approach to statistics emerged in the 1950s and 60s, spearheaded by the likes of Lindley,[79] Savage,[80] and Raiffa and Schlaifer,[81] who all published important works during this period that ensured that Bayesian inference would enjoy significant influence within statistical analysis until the present day.[82]

I choose Bayes' theorem as the subject of this test case for three reasons. First, it is a well-established theorem within the field of decision-making and probability theory, and has begun to impact fields as disparate as management studies[83] and child development,[84] so much so that Zyphur and Oswald might speak of a 'Bayesian revolution.'[85] Indeed, 'the past 20 years has seen a veritable explosion of Bayesian applications across the social and physical sciences.'[86] Second, Bayesian reasoning has become the subject of debate within certain corners of New Testament scholarship too, following the publication of Christoph Heilig's *Hidden Criticism?*[87] In it, Heilig uses Bayes' theorem to assess the various criteria occasionally employed to identify anti-imperial overtones in the Pauline corpus. Although Bayesian reasoning is hardly ubiquitous in New Testament scholarship, it has been employed elsewhere in discussions regarding historical method[88] and, by assessing Bayesian reasoning as a test case, I demonstrate the place of plausibility in decision-making, and the role of one's *Weltanschauung* in ascribing plausibility to an event. Third, and most significantly, it allows me to demonstrate with precision the central claim made in this chapter, that all historiography inevitably and inescapably proceeds from, and operates within, a pre-given metaphysical framework, a framework I have already described as a historian's historiographical worldview. As such, it is a helpful test case for stating the same point in different terms.

My point in what follows is not to advocate for or against the use of Bayesian inference within historical research *per se*. Rather, I demonstrate that judgements of plausibility—specifically *historical* plausibility judgements—rest upon other implicit judgements of metaphysical plausibility made at the uncritical level of one's historiographical worldview. One is predisposed to make certain historical judgements before engaging with the evidence, and this pre-disposition is governed by the metaphysical framework that constitutes one's worldview. My interaction with Bayes' theorem in what follows is one example of how one might quantify and explicate this claim. It is not presented as, in any sense, paradigmatic of the way Jesus historians should assess and evaluate evidence or hypotheses.

I would also like to make it clear that my own historical judgements are subject to the same methodological problem. I do not claim to have a 'solution' to this 'problem.' Rather, I suggest a more appropriate course of action is to acknowledge the impossibilities entailed in making neutral historical judgements, and instead to allow a plurality of metaphysical historiographies that are explicit about their starting point(s).

I begin by offering an overview of Bayesian reasoning and how it is employed. In his review of Heilig's monograph, Given criticises Heilig's decision not to offer an extensive outline of Bayes' theorem,[89] a criticism Heilig graciously acknowledged in a later response.[90] Accordingly, it is appropriate to offer a brief outline of the theorem here. The theorem is named after Thomas Bayes (1702–61), who first posited the theorem in a 1763 work entitled 'An Essay towards solving a Problem in the Doctrine of Chances,'[91] although Bayes' theorem was later popularised by Pierre-Simon Laplace (1749–1827).[92] It proceeds from the presupposition that—as Harney puts it—'probability can be interpreted as the value of available knowledge.'[93] This being the case, Bayes' theorem seeks to ascertain the probability of an event by assigning value to the available evidence. Therefore, Heilig is right to describe it as '*not* another new method,' but rather a meta-method which 'simply means to *make the logical substructure more explicit that underlies all solid historical conclusions.*'[94] The theorem is expressed as a formula, which reads as follows:[95]

$$p(H|E) = \frac{p(E|H) \times p(H)}{P(E)}$$

The formula is used to ascertain the probability ('p') of a hypothesis ('H') being true, in the light of (here symbolised by '|') any given evidence ('E'). Hence, 'p(H|E)' is the desired outcome of the theorem.

To ascertain this value, one first needs to identify the 'predictive power' of hypothesis H. The 'predictive power' of a hypothesis is the accuracy of the E, if one presupposes hypothesis H to be correct. In other words, it is the probability ('p') of the evidence ('E'), in the light of ('|') a given hypothesis ('H'). This can therefore be written mathematically as 'p(E|H),' as seen in the larger formula of Bayes' theorem, above.

The other two values in the formula—'p(H)' and 'p(E)'—are known as 'priors.' This is because they are ascertained before one considers the evidence ('E') itself. Accordingly, the value 'p(H|E)' is known as the 'posterior,' since it is calculated after one has taken the evidence ('E') into account and it is, thus, dependent upon the evidence. 'p(H)' and 'p(E)' are the probability of the hypothesis and the evidence, independent of one another. In other words, this is the 'background knowledge on the parameters of the model being tested,'[96] or, as Heilig helpfully writes, the '*background plausibility* of a hypothesis.'[97]

In other words, 'p(H)' is an attempt to answer the question: 'is there any reason—independent of the evidence in question—why this hypothesis might be accurate?' Similarly, 'p(E)' seeks to ascertain the probability of evidence 'E' being reliable, independent of the hypothesis. As Heilig puts it, 'for every inference one has to consider both the predictive power *and* the background plausibility of a hypothesis together.'[98]

In many ways, this is not a new insight: Jesus historians have long been aware of the need to evaluate evidence and hypotheses on their own terms—'p(E)' and 'p(H),' respectively—before applying them to questions of the historical Jesus. Brant Pitre asserts that 'a scholar must first *interpret* the evidence in the Gospels *before* drawing any conclusions about the historical plausibility of a saying or deed of Jesus.'[99] However, one of the most helpful characteristics of Bayes' theorem for biblical research is that it quantifies many of the methods scholars use already, such as evaluating the strength of one's sources. Bayes' theorem seeks simply to make these methods more consistent. However, Bayes' theorem does have limits to its usefulness, not least when it comes to historiographical decision-making.

It may be helpful, at this point, to include a simple example of Bayes' theorem applied in practice. Let us assume that there is a 30% chance of rain on day 1 and, subsequently, there is a 70% chance of rain on day 2 *if it rained on day 1.* Let's assume that we also know that if there was no rain on day 1, there will be a 45% chance of rain on day 2. Suppose, then, we wished to ascertain the probability that it rained on day 1, given that we know it rained on day 2. One can employ Bayes' theorem to answer this question:

$$p(H|E) = \frac{p(E|H) \times p(H)}{p(E)}$$

We are attempting to ascertain the probability of the hypothesis 'H', *that it rained on day 1*, given the evidence 'E' *that it rained on day 2*. Hence, we wish to find the value of $p(H \mid E)$. In order to do so, we must fill in the values for the right-hand side of the equation.

$p(E \mid H)$ is the probability of rainfall on day 2 given that there was rainfall on day 1. We know from above that there is a 70% chance of rain on day 2 if there was rain the previous day.

$p(H)$ is the probability of rainfall on day 1, regardless of the evidence 'E' concerning rainfall on day 2. We know this to be 30%.

$p(E)$ is the probability of rainfall on day 2, regardless of whether or not it has rained on day 1. We can work out this value to give what we know already, since this value is simply the sum of the probabilities of it raining on both days, and not raining on day 1 but still raining on day 2. The probability of rain on both days is the result of multiplying the probability of rain on day 1 by the probability of it raining on day 2, given it rained on day 1. In other words:

$$p(\mathit{Rain\,on\,both\,days}) = 0.30 \times 0.70$$

The probability of rainfall on day 2, but not on day 1 is ascertained by multiplying the probability of no rain on day 1 (expressed as 1 – 0.30=0.60), by the probability of rain on day 2, given there was no rain on day 1 (0.45, see above). This may be expressed as:

$$p(\mathit{Rain\,on\,day\,2\,only}) = 0.60 \times 0.45$$

To ascertain $p(E)$, the probability of rainfall on day 2, regardless of rainfall on day 1, we need to add together these two probabilities. Expressed mathematically, this reads:

$$p(E) = (0.30 \times 0.70) + (0.60 \times 0.45) = 0.48$$

In other words, there is a 48% chance of rain on day 2, regardless of the weather on day 1. We now know the values of $p(E \mid H)$, $p(H)$ *and* $p(E)$, and so we can ascertain the value of $p(H \mid E)$, or, the probability of rainfall on day 1, given that it rained on day two. Given that Bayes' theorem is as follows:

$$p(H|E) = \frac{p(E|H) \times p(H)}{p(E)}$$

The probability of rain on day 1, given rain on day 2 is expressed thus:

$$p(H|E) = \frac{0.70 \times 0.30}{0.48}$$

$$p(H|E) = 0.4375$$

Expressed as a percentage, this means that there is a 43.75% chance that it rained on day 1, if there was rainfall on day 2.

However, while Bayesian reasoning can be of clear value in instances such as this, it is less helpful when making judgements of historical plausibility since it works most effectively when one can accurately ascertain the values for 'p(H)' and 'p(E).' In other words, when one can be sure of the 'background plausibility' of a hypothesis and of the evidence—to use Heilig's terminology—the theorem works with little hindrance. In the example outlined above, for instance, one can be sure that the answer is accurate, given the values for 'p(H)' and 'p(E)' are also accurate. However, in the disciplines of the humanities, and not least within historiographically informed disciplines, ascertaining these values is far more difficult. Historians frequently deal with hypotheses and evidence that are impossible to quantify.

Say, for example, one wishes to employ Bayesian reasoning to test the hypothesis that 'Jesus was risen from the dead.' Assuming, then, that this is our hypothesis, we must then ascertain $p(H \mid E)$; we are seeking to find the probability (p) of the hypothesis that Jesus was risen from the dead (H) in the light of ($\mid$) the available evidence (E). To do so, however, one must first outline the 'background plausibility.' But this poses a problem: how does one seek to ascertain the inherent or background likeliness of the claim that Jesus was risen from the dead? One might suggest it is very unlikely indeed, since there are no verified accounts of anyone having returned from the dead, suggesting a value of 0 for H. However, one might retort that Jesus was not simply 'another person' and, indeed, God would only have risen from the dead if he *was* different from any other human (i.e., if he was the Son of God), such that appealing to the lives of other humans is an inappropriate connection to make. This may seem like a glib or extreme example, but it is helpful for two reasons. First, historical approaches to the resurrection will take centre stage in the following chapter on the methodology of N.T. Wright. Second, the extreme and controversial nature of the hypothesis ensures that it makes my point as clear as possible, a point which I suggest is true of all claims about the historical Jesus (or any historical figure).

My point here is not to determine what set of metaphysical presuppositions are most helpful or most reasonable for studying the historical Jesus. Rather, my aim instead is to demonstrate that it is impossible to study the historical Jesus *without* operating first from a given set of presuppositions about what is and is and is not 'historically plausible'; a set of given presuppositions that, properly understood, are metaphysical (since they refer to the ultimate nature of reality and all its constituent parts), and theological (since they refer to God and all things in relation to God).

Berg and Rollins claim that 'historical Muḥammed scholars can help their historical Jesus counterparts by pointing out that many of them treat Jesus as an utterly unique person, and as such they evince a cryptotheological perspective.'[100] However, it must also be recognised that the inverse is also a 'cryptotheological' perspective. To study the historical Jesus precisely as though he were a person like any other is not to take a metaphysically or theologically neutral methodological stance. Rather, it is to take a methodological stance that is *differently* metaphysical, and *differently* theological; not *less* so. It is to proceed from a methodological framework, the theological content of which differs in the *quality* of theological potency, not the *quantity*.

If the aim of any 'Next Quest'[101] for the historical Jesus involves an attempt to remove altogether metaphysical and theological presuppositions from the discipline, it can only fail, for such a task is an impossibility for historiography. Rather than asking 'how might we be *less* metaphysical, or *less* theological?' the discipline of historical Jesus research must begin to ask 'in *what ways* will we permit participants to be metaphysically and theologically grounded?'

Ultimately, one might decide that the only way to ascertain the 'background probability' of a hypothesis is to evaluate the evidence for its 'background probability.' This is certainly not an unreasonable move, but it only relocates the problem, rather than solves it. Mathematically, we could write this manoeuvring thus:

$$p(H|E)=\frac{p(E|H)\times\left(p(H|E)=\dfrac{p(E|H)\times p(H)}{p(E)}\right)}{p(E)}$$

This 'theorem within a theorem' can theoretically go on endlessly. My point is that Bayesian inference can (and logically does) lead to infinite regress once one really begins to scrutinise the reasons for ascribing a certain 'background plausibility' to a historiographical hypothesis.

Let us return to the example from earlier in the chapter—borrowed from Michel Henry—of the hypothesis that 'the French took the Bastille on July 14, 1789.' How might one assess the 'background plausibility' of this hypothesis? One might say it is very likely: the French Revolution began in 1789; one can observe that the Bastille is no longer in operation; an act like this might be expected to occur during a revolution. However, as noted previously in this chapter, all these claims implicitly build upon fundamental metaphysical claims about the nature of reality, not least a belief in the reality of the external world and the agency of human beings. This is to say, the 'background plausibility' of any hypothesis will necessarily be dependent upon the metaphysical framework within which the historian operates. In other words, the 'background plausibility' of any historically based hypothesis will necessarily be directly correlated to the historian's worldview, in some sense. There can be no historical hypothesis that does not—however implicitly or inchoately—impinge upon metaphysics.

4.4 Conclusion

In this chapter, I have made two points about the nature and production of historical knowledge. First, by engaging with Collingwood, Nietzsche, and Blondel on historiography, I examined the nature of historical knowledge, what it means to 'know' something about the past. I asserted all claims about the past are based on probabilities and that issues such as the Cartesian doubt about the external world and our inability to access what Blondel described as 'real history' preclude any attempts to ascertain information about the past with certainty. Thus, all historical judgements are made based on what seems *plausible* to the historian.

Second, having ascertained this, I addressed the question, 'how does one measure plausibility?' If the historicity of an event rests upon its plausibility, how does one arbitrate between what is plausible and implausible? In response, I asserted the most effective way to apprehend the category of historical plausibility is through the lens of worldview. More specifically, an event becomes more plausible to the historian to the degree to which it coheres with his or her historiographical worldview.

Therefore, one might claim that historiography is always a metaphysical act. To make a historical judgement is tacitly to make secondary and tertiary claims regarding the very nature of reality itself: claims about the nature of ontology, time and space, identity agency, cause and effect, and the nature of plausibility. This is never more the case than within historical Jesus research, the subject of which is a man about whom it has been claimed that he is God incarnate: ultimate reality in the form of a human man.

But all of this begs the question: which *Weltanschauungen* are at play within modern historical Jesus research? It is my contention that it is possible to identify a shared characteristic common to the metaphysical frameworks operative amongst Jesus historians. More specifically, all modern historical Jesus research has operated from within a series of historiographical worldviews one might reasonably describe as 'secular.' Before I substantiate this claim, however, I will outline in detail what I mean when I refer to 'secular' scholarship.

Notes

1 Martin Heidegger, quoted in George Kovacs, 'Philosophy as Primordial Science in Heidegger's Courses of 1919', in *Reading Heidegger from the Start: Essays in His Earliest Thought*, ed. Theodore Kisiel and John van Buren (Albany, NY: State of University of New York, 1994), 91–108 (94).
2 Gerd Theissen and Dagmar Winter, *The Quest for the Plausible Jesus: The Question of Criteria*, trans. M. Eugene Boring (Louisville, KY: Westminster John Knox, 2002), 37.
3 Brant Pitre, *Jesus and the Last Supper* (Grand Rapids, MI: Eerdmans, 2015), esp. 31–52. Pitre explicitly acknowledges, at numerous points, his debt to E. P. Sanders, *Jesus and Judaism* (London: SCM, 1985).
4 Anthony Le Donne, *The Historiographical Jesus: Memory, Typology, and the Son of David* (Waco, TX: Baylor University, 2005), 7. (emphasis original)
5 Here, see Derrida's famous 1967 trilogy of works: Jacques Derrida, *La Voix et le Phénomène* (Paris: PUF, 1967); idem, *De la grammatologie* (Paris: Minuit, 1967); idem, *L'écriture et la différence* (Paris: Seuil, 1967).
6 Hayden White, *Metahistory: The Historical Imagination in Nineteenth-Century Europe* (Baltimore, MD: John Hopkins University, 1973); *Tropics of Discourse: Essays in Cultural Criticism* (Baltimore, MD: John Hopkins, 1978).
7 Lyotard, *La condition postmoderne*.
8 Most importantly, see Richard Rorty, *Philosophy and the Mirror of Nature* (Princeton, NJ: Princeton University, 1979).
9 For example, see Ernest Wamba-dia-Wamba, 'How Is Historical Knowledge Recognized?', *History in Africa* 13 (1986), 331–44.
10 Marjatta Rahikainen and Susanna Fellman, 'Introduction', in *Historical Knowledge: In Quest of Theory, Method and Evidence*, ed. Susanna Fellman and Marjatta Rahikainen (Newcastle upon Tyne: Cambridge Scholars, 2012), 1–3 (1).
11 As of 2019, the complete text of this essay is available as a critical edition. See Voltaire, *Essai sur les mœurs et l'esprit des nations et sur les principaux faits de l'histoire depuis Charlemagne jusqu'à Louis XIII*, ed. Bruno Bernard et al., Œuvres complètes de Voltaire vols. XXI–XXVII (Oxford: The Voltaire Foundation, 2009–19). Voltaire constantly revised the essay during his life, and the text presented in the *Œuvres complètes* is based on the last version of the text authorized by Voltaire, published in 1775.
12 See the helpful summary in Jerome Roesenthal, 'Voltaire's Philosophy of History', *Journal of the History of Ideas* 16.2 (1955), 151–78 (esp. 151).
13 R.G. Collingwood, *The Idea of History* (Oxford: Clarendon, 1946).
14 Idem, *An Autobiography* (Oxford: Oxford University, 1939).
15 Idem, 'Are History and Science Different Kinds of Knowledge?', *Mind* 31.124 (1922), 443–51. A Reprint of the essay can be found in R.G. Collingwood, *Essays in the Philosophy of History*, ed. W. Debbins (Austin, TX: University of Texas, 1965).
16 Collingwood, 'Different Kinds of Knowledge?', 443.
17 Ibid., 450–51.
18 Idem, *Autobiography*, 112.
19 R.B. Smith, 'R.G. Collingwood's Definition of Historical Knowledge', *History of European Ideas* 33.3 (2007), 350–71 (351).
20 Collingwood, *The Idea of History*, 213.
21 So William Twining, 'R.G. Collingwood's Autobiography: One Reader's Response', *Journal of Law and Society* 25.4 (1998), 603–20 (611).
22 Cf., Kuhn, *The Structure of Scientific Revolutions*.
23 Quentin Skinner, *The Foundations of Modern Political Thought*, 2 vols (Cambridge: Cambridge University, 1978). See the comment about Collingwood in I.xi.
24 Charles Oman, *On the Writing of History* (London: Methuen, 1939), 7.

25 Marc Bloch, *La société féodale*, L'Évolution de l'humanité (Paris: Albin Michel, 1939), I:xxi.
26 Louis Halphen, *Johdatus historiantutkimukseen. Alkuteos Introduction à l'histoire*, Suom. Eino E. Suolahti. Historiallinen kirjasto, XIV (Helsinki: WSOY, 1951), 66. The translation is taken from Matti Peltonen, 'The Method of Clues and History Theory', in *Historical Knowledge: In Quest of Theory, Method and Evidence*, ed. Susanna Fellman and Marjatta Rahikainen (Newcastle upon Tyne: Cambridge Scholars, 2012), 45–76 (52).
27 Marjatta Rahikainen and Susanna Fellman, 'On Historical Writing and Evidence', in *Historical Knowledge: In Quest of Theory, Method and Evidence*, ed. Susanna Fellman and Marjatta Rahikainen (Newcastle upon Tyne: Cambridge Scholars, 2012), 5–44 (10).
28 In German: "Vom Nutzen und Nachteil der Historie für das Leben." This is alternatively translated into English as 'On the Use and *Disadvantage* of History for Life.' While this is technically more accurate, 'Use and Abuse' conveys a better sense of Nietzsche's intentions in the title, insofar as he wishes to target an academic approach to history that actively perverts the telos of historiography. This is perhaps also evidenced by Nietzsche's use of 'Historie' (i.e., the academic discipline) rather than 'Geschichte' (i.e., the past itself).
29 Sue Prideaux, *I Am Dynamite! A Life of Friedrich Nietzsche* (London: Faber & Faber, 2018), 121.
30 *UM*, II.§250.
31 Ibid., II.§257.
32 Ibid., II.§258.
33 See Scott Jenkins, 'Nietzsche's Use of Monumental History', *Journal of Nietzsche Studies* 45.2 (2014), 169–81 (170–72).
34 *UM*, II:§263.
35 Ibid., II:§258.
36 Ibid., II:§266.
37 Ibid., II:§268.
38 Ibid., II:§270.
39 Ibid., II:§269.
40 Ibid., II:§264.
41 Ibid., II:§289.
42 Ibid., II:§270.
43 Here Jenkins, 'Monumental History', is especially insightful.
44 *WP*, §481. In German: "Nein, gerade Tatsachen gibt es nicht, nur Interpretationen."
45 Didier Eribon, *Michel Foucault*, trans. Betsy Wing (Cambridge, MA: Harvard University, 1991), 52; James Miller, *The Passion of Michel Foucault* (New York: Simon & Schuster, 1993), 64–67; David Macey, *The Lives of Michel Foucault* (London: Hutchinson, 1993), 50.
46 Foucault, *Folie et déraison*.
47 Foucault, *Naissance*.
48 Michel Foucault, *Les mots et les choses: Une archéologie des sciences humaines* (Paris: Gallimard, 1966).
49 Foucault, *L'archéologie*.
50 A comprehensive treatment of the controversy can be found in Peter J. Bernardi, *Maurice Blondel, Social Catholicism, and Action Française: The Clash over the Church's Role in Society during the Modernist Era* (Washington, DC: The Catholic University of America, 2009).
51 Maurice Blondel, *L'Action: Essai d'une critique de la vie et d'une science de la pratique* (Paris: Alcan, 1893).
52 John Simons, 'Maurice Blondel: Philosophy and Christianity', *Canadian Journal of Theology* 13.4 (1967), 241–53 (241).

53 Maurice Blondel, *Histoire et dogme: les lacunes philosophiques de l'exégèse moderne* (Impr.: Libraire de Montligeon, 1904); ET: Maurice Blondel, *The Letter on Apologetics & History and Dogma*, trans. Alexander Dru and Illtyd Trethowan, Ressourcement: Retrieval and Renewal in Catholic Thought (Edinburgh: T&T Clark, 1994). The text originally appeared as three separate articles in *La Quinzaine*.
54 Henri de Lubac, *A Brief Catechesis on Nature and Grace*, trans. Richard Arnandez (San Francisco, CA: Ignatius, 1984), 37.
55 David Grumett, 'Review: *Maurice Blondel: A Philosophical Life* by Olivia Blanchette', *The Thomist: A Speculative Quarterly Review* 27.4 (2011), 708–12 (708).
56 Paul Hartog, 'Blondel Remembered: His Philosophical Analysis of the "Quest for the Historical Jesus"', *Themelios* 33.1 (2008), 5–15 (7).
57 Quoted in Alexander Dru's introduction to Maurice Blondel, *History and Dogma*, 40.
58 Bernard M.G. Reardon, 'Review of Maurice Blondel, *The Letter on Apologetics and History and Dogma*', *ExpTim* 107.1 (1995), 29.
59 Blondel, *History and Dogma*, 224.
60 Ibid., 258–59 n. 1.
61 Ibid., 225.
62 Michel Henry, *I Am the Truth: Toward a Philosophy of Christianity* (Stanford, CA: Stanford University, 2003), 21.
63 Blondel, *History and Dogma*, 238.
64 Ibid., 240.
65 Ibid., 286.
66 Ibid., 287.
67 The term 'transempirical' is here borrowed from Thiselton, *Hermeneutics of Doctrine*, 377.
68 The phrase—asserting one's own existence is all one can logically be certain of—originally appeared in French ('je pense, donc je suis') in Descartes' *Discours de la Méthode*, easily accessible online. See René Descartes, *Discours de la Méthode Pour bien conduire sa raison, et chercher la vérité dans les sciences* (Leiden: Ian Maire, 1637), 33.
69 Shai Frogel, 'Descartes: Truth and Self-Deception', *Philosophy* 91.1 (2016), 93–108 (108).
70 Francis Crick, *The Astonishing Hypothesis: The Scientific Search for the Soul* (London: Simon & Schuster, 1994), 3.
71 Oliver Laas, 'Toward Truthlikeness in Historiography', *European Journal of Pragmatism and American Philosophy* 8.2 (2016), 1–29.
72 Laas, 'Toward Truthlikeness', 21.
73 Here meaning it forms a constituent part of reality. 'The real' is not used here in the Lacanian/Žižekian psychoanalytical sense of referring to that which is beyond the imaginary and the symbolic, but is not to be equated with reality, *per se*. See Jacques Lacan, 'Le symbolique, l'imaginaire et le réel', *Bulletin de l'Association Freudienne* 1.1 (1982), 4–13; Slavoj Žižek, *The Ticklish Subject: The Absent Centre of Political Ontology* (London and New York: Verso, 1999), 222.
74 For a more complete overview of the use of Bayes' theorem (or lack thereof), see Laure Cabantous and Jean-Pascal Gond, 'The Resistible Rise of Bayesian Thinking in Management: Historical Lessons from Decision Analysis', *JM* 41.2 (2015), 441–70 (esp. 443–50).
75 R.A. Fisher, 'Frequency Distribution of the Values of the Correlation Coefficient in Samples from an Indefinitely Large Population', *Biometrika* 10.4 (1915), 507–21; R.A. Fisher, *Statistical Methods for Research Workers* (Edinburgh: Oliver and Boyd, 1925).

76 The history of this 'split' is helpfully laid out in Ian Hacking, *The Emergence of Probability: A Philosophical Study of Early Ideas about Probability, Induction and Statistical Inference* (Cambridge: Cambridge University, 1975); Sharon Bertsch McGrayne, *The Theory that Would Not Die: How Bayes' Rule Cracked the Enigma Code, Hunted Down Russian Submarines, and Emerged Triumphant from Two Centuries of Controversy* (New Haven, CT: Yale University, 2012), 61–86.

77 Frank P. Ramsey, *The Foundations of Mathematics and Other Logical Essays* (London: Kegan Paul, 1931).

78 Most important here is de Finetti's 1931 essay 'Probabilism,' now available as Bruno de Finetti, 'Probabilism: A Critical Essay on the Theory of Probability and on the Value of Science', *Erkenntnis* 31.2/3 (1989), 169–223.

79 Dennis V. Lindley, 'Statistical Inference', *Journal of the Royal Statistical Society. Series B (Methodological)* 15.1 (1953), 30–76; idem, 'A Statistical Paradox', *Biometrika* 44.1/2 (1957), 187–92.

80 Leonard J. Savage, *The Foundations of Statistics* (Oxford: John Wiley & Sons, 1954). This is now available as idem, *The Foundations of Statistics*, 2nd rev. ed. (New York: Dover Publications, 1972).

81 Raiffa and Schlaifer published important works during this period, both independently and collaboratively. See (in chronological order), Robert O. Schlaifer, *Probability and Statistics for Business Decisions* (New York: McGraw-Hill, 1959); Howard Raiffa and Robert O. Schlaifer, *Applied Statistical Decision Theory* (Cambridge, MA: Harvard University, 1961); Howard Raiffa, *Decision Analysis* (Reading, MA: Addison Wesley, 1968).

82 The birth of the neo-Bayesian movement is helpfully outlined by Stephen E. Fienberg, 'When Did Bayesian Inference Become "Bayesian"?', *Baysian Analysis* 1.1 (2006), 1–40; Stephen E. Fienberg, 'The Early Statistical Years: 1947–1967. A Conversation with Howard Raiffa', *Statistical Science* 23.1 (2008), 136–49.

83 So, for example, Michael J. Zyphur, Frederick L. Oswald, and Deborah E. Rupp, 'Rendezvous Overdue: Bayes Analysis Meets Organizational Research', *JM* 41.2 (2014), 387–89; Cabantous and Gond; Rob Austin McKee and C. Chet Miller, 'Institutionalizing Bayesianism within the Organizational Sciences: A Practical Guide Featuring Comments from Eminent Scholars', *JM* 41.2 (2015), 471–90; Michael J. Zyphur and Frederick L. Oswald, 'Bayesian Estimation and Inference: A User's Guide', *JM* 41.2 (2015), 390–420.

84 Rens van de Schoot et al., 'A Gentle Introduction to Bayesian Analysis: Applications to Developmental Research', *Child Development* 85.3 (2014), 842–60.

85 Zyphur and Oswald, 'Bayesian Estimation and Inference,' 472.

86 Zyphur, Oswald, and Rupp, 'Rendezvous Overdue,' 387.

87 Originally published as Christoph Heilig, *Hidden Criticism? The Methodology and Plausibility of the Search for a Counter-Imperial Subtext in Paul*, WUNT II, 392 (Tübingen: Mohr Siebeck, 2015), this monograph is now available as Christoph Heilig, *Hidden Criticism? The Methodology and Plausibility of the Search for a Counter-Imperial Subtext in Paul* (Minneapolis, MN: Fortress, 2017). In what follows, all page numbers refer to the 2017 edition of the text.

88 Aviezer Tucker, *Our Knowledge of the Past: A Philosophy of Historiography* (Cambridge: CUP, 2008), 92–140; Mark Day, *The Philosophy of History: An Introduction* (London: Continuum, 2008), 31–49; Mark Day and Gregory Radick, 'Historiographic Evidence and Confirmation', in *A Companion to the Philosophy of History and Historiography*, ed. Aviezer Tucker, BCP (Oxford: Blackwell, 2009), 87–97.

89 Mark D. Given, '2019.03.23. Heilig, Hidden Criticism?', *RBL*, 2019, available online: http://rblnewsletter.blogspot.com/2019/03/20190323-heilig-hidden-criticism.html [accessed 9 April 2019].

90 See Christoph Heilig, 'What Bayesian Reasoning Can and Can't Do for Biblical Research', *Zürich New Testament Blog*, 2019, available online: https://www.uzh.ch/blog/theologie-nt/2019/03/27/what-bayesian-reasoning-can-and-cant-do-for-biblical-research/?fbclid=IwAR1yI8Xy2Y15OnGcPKkTuKomR1I69E5KZPS8d3whGEEm4tpYyzQqGDBPCR4 [accessed 9 April 2019].

91 For the text of the original essay in which Bayes' theorem was first posited, see Richard Swinburne, ed., *Bayes's Theorem*, PBA 113 (Oxford: Oxford University, 2002), 117–49.

92 See, most importantly, Pierre-Simon Laplace, 'Mémoire sur la probabilité des causes par les événements', in *Œuvres complète de Laplace Tome VIII* (Paris: Gauthier-Villars, 1878), 27–65. For a helpful overview of the origins of Bayes' theorem, see A.I. Dale, 'Bayes or Laplace? An Examination of the Origin and Early Applications of Bayes' Theorem', *Archive for History of Exact Science* 27.1 (1982), 23–47.

93 Hanns Ludwig Harney, *Bayesian Inference: Data Evaluation and Decisions*, 2nd ed. (Basel: Springer, 2016), 4.

94 Heilig, *Hidden Criticism?*, 28.

95 The complete technical derivation of the theorem can be found in Harney, *Bayesian Inference*, 11–25.

96 van de Schoot, et al., 'Gentle Introduction', 844.

97 Heilig, *Hidden Criticism?*, 29. (emphasis original)

98 Ibid. (emphasis original)

99 Pitre, *Jesus and the Last Supper*, 50. (emphases original)

100 Berg and Rollins, 'Historical Muḥammad', 280.

101 As in the introduction to this study, here this phrase is borrowed from Crossley, 'Next Quest.'

5 Characterising Secular Scholarship

5.1 Introduction

In this chapter, I examine three theories of secularisation to suggest we may describe something as 'secular' if it evidences a metaphysical tendency to refuse to allow religious perspectives the authority to contribute to public discourse. Therefore, the historiographical worldviews operative in modern academic historical Jesus research may be described as secular if they evidence a tendency not to allow religious metaphysics to contribute to their historical method.

In Chapters 2–4, I argued that historiographical research must operate—logically speaking—within a bespoke historiographical worldview. In Chapters 6–9, I argue that modern academic historical Jesus research operates within a metaphysical framework one might accurately label as 'secular.' However, before I come to those chapters, it is important to discuss secularism and the nature of secular scholarship. As with metaphysics and worldview before it, 'secular' is a term whose meaning is at once assumed and obfuscated. In the first instance it seems reasonable to imagine that something is 'secular' if, as Taylor writes, it has been 'allegedly emptied of God, or of any reference to ultimate reality.'[1] However, when dealing with a historical figure such as Jesus, about whom many claims have been made that refer to 'God' and 'ultimate reality,' this definition can become a confusing one since the entire field of historical Jesus research concerns itself with a historical figure later understood by some to be God.

To describe any discipline as 'secular' based only upon such a brief definition is therefore unhelpful; it lacks detail, and engagement with contemporary debates concerning the nature and essence of secularism. It is important, then, to engage in some discussion about what I mean when I speak of modern academic historical Jesus research as secular: to what does secular refer?

Etymologically, the term secular was coined in 1851 by G.J. Holyoake, who employed the term when arguing in favour of society's independence from religion.[2] However, arguments in favour of a division between church and state had been made earlier by thinkers as diverse as Hugo Grotius[3] and Martin Luther,[4] to name but two. This is to say, debates concerning secularism have a long and multivalent tradition.

DOI: 10.4324/b23077-6

In the current chapter, I outline three accounts of secularisation: (1) accounts focussed on religious belief, (2) accounts focussed on religious institutions and their authority, and (3) accounts that focus upon religio-economic factors. Later, in Chapters 6–9 of this study, I substantiate the claim that historical Jesus research is a secular discipline based upon the extent to which they cohere with the conception of secularism I outline here in this chapter. Thus, in this chapter, I discuss what characteristics scholarship must portray before we may describe it as 'secular.' The ultimate claim I make in this chapter is that secular historical Jesus scholarship is best characterised by a refusal to allow theistic perspectives the opportunity to inform historiographical scholarship if it is to be academically permissible. I use the term theistic rather than religious here due to the debated nature of the latter term. As we shall see, precisely what constitutes a religion is unclear. By using the term 'theistic' and its cognates, I make clear that a secular worldview refuses to confer credence to any beliefs that involve the existence of a deity, or any divine activity, rather than engagement with religion *per se*.

Before I begin it is important to offer some clarity regarding the scope and focus of what follows. First, one should note the distinction between 'the secular' and 'secularism.' The distinction is an important one, to the extent that Asad's work on secularism is predicated upon identifying the connection between the two.[5] In what follows, I understand 'the secular' to be synonymous with the public sphere, and 'secularism' as the series of beliefs that are prevalent in forming and upholding the secular. In other words, 'the secular' is a *place* (for want of a better word) while 'secularism' is a philosophical framework: 'the secular' is where 'secularism' is put into action. Therefore, when I describe something as secular (in the adjectival sense), this is not to be confused with *the* secular. Rather, I mean it stands in coherence with the ideals of *secularism*. Thus, I contend modern historical Jesus research is a secularised discipline located within 'the secular' (i.e., the public sphere or, more accurately in the case of modern academic historical Jesus research, publicly funded, government regulated universities). This is important because I am not concerned here with saying anything about 'the secular' but instead discuss the nature of the philosophical framework of secularism itself.

Second, a word on geography and the scope of my discussion. The secularism debate is a global issue, insofar as every nation and continent has some relationship with religion, whether if it is an overwhelmingly positive or negative one. Despite the fact that 'secularism as a political doctrine arose in modern Euro-America,'[6] its relationship with modernity means the secularism debate is relevant for every society that identifies as 'modern,' as Taylor argues.[7] To outline the development of secularism across the globe is an almost impossible task. However, in what follows, I will try to ensure the discussion is not confined to my immediate context in the United Kingdom, even if the total picture of religion in the current geopolitical landscape will inevitably escape the following discussion.

In 1967, Larry Shiner claimed 'in both empirical research and interpretation today there is a total lack of agreement as to what secularization is and how to measure it.'[8] Over half a century later these words still largely ring true; there remains considerable debate about how best to define secularism. Among sociologists of religion, three primary frameworks for understanding the phenomenon of secularisation have been offered, each of which is of varying degrees of usefulness when applied to modern academic historical Jesus research. The first of these suggests secularism involves declining levels of *participation* in religious belief, the second suggests secularism involves the waning of the *authority* of religious institutions, and the third seeks to understand the phenomenon primarily in *economic* terms, as a supply-demand transaction that will always (and inevitably) inhibit its own progress. In what follows I characterise secular scholarship in discussion with these three dominant paradigms.

These three paradigms seek to understand *what* secularism is, rather than *how* or *why* it came to be. In other words, in what follows I am concerned with *quantifying* and *qualifying* rather than *explaining* the secular phenomenon. Offering a definition before an explanation is difficult, not least because definitions of secularism occasionally invoke such explanations in the process. However, for the structure and flow of my argument, it is helpful to distinguish the two tasks and treat them separately. In offering such a definition, I will suggest declining religious *authority* is the best category for understanding secularism. This provides a warrant for describing modern historical Jesus research as secular, insofar as it refuses to allow religious metaphysics to contribute to the historical task.

5.2 Secularism as Declining Religious Belief

We might be tempted to say that a work of scholarship is secular if it has been authored by a scholar who does not subscribe to any religious tradition. Accordingly, the first secularisation theory I examine conceives of the process in terms of declining religious belief. Stated simply, this theory describes the phenomenon in terms of a decreasing number of people either identifying with certain religious traditions or participating in the ongoing life of religious institutions. Thus, the extent to which one may describe a society (or, in our case, a discipline) as secular is enmeshed with figures of religious participation.[9] Certainly, there are figures to support the notion that we may describe much of the global population as secular in this respect. In 2015, the Pew Research Center for Religion and Public Life estimated the following demographic of religious communities across the world (see Table 5.1).[10]

Where once it was almost unthinkable to reject religion altogether, now nearly one-sixth of the world's population (or roughly 1.2 billion people) actively do not identify with any religious tradition, making it the third largest demographic group pertaining to religious affiliation (or lack thereof).

This being the case, to what extent is it possible to describe modern academic historical Jesus research as a secular discipline, regarding the religious faith(s) of its participants? Clearly, if secularism is the decline of religious belief in public life, then historical Jesus research can hardly be called a 'secular' discipline. Although it is difficult to quantify with precision the amount of Jesus historians who have a religious faith (of whatever stripe), we may highlight a few key figures about whom we have some insight into their worldview. In the third quest alone

Table 5.1 Religious affiliation, 2015 ©Pew Research Center 2017.

Religious Group	*Followers*	*% of Global Population*
Christians	2,276,250,000	31.2
Muslim	1,752,620,000	24.1
Unaffiliated	1,165,020,000	16
Hindus	1,099,110,000	15.1
Buddhists	499,380,000	6.9
Folk Religionists[a]	418,280,000	5.7
Other Religions[b]	59,710,000	0.8
Jews	14,270,000	0.2

[a]This comprises those who identify with various African religions, Chinese folk religions, Native American Religions and Australian aboriginal religions.
[b]This includes Bahai's Jains, Sikhs, Shintoists, Taoists, Wiccans, and Zoroastrians, among others.

there are many such figures: N.T. Wright formerly served as Bishop of Durham in the Church of England; Crossan still understands himself to be a Roman Catholic, despite his grievances with those in power in the church;[11] Allison describes himself as a 'lifelong churchgoer.'[12] One could highlight many more men and women who engage with the quest having come from a place of religious faith, even if they attempt to put their faith aside when doing so. This perhaps comes with the territory: the person of Jesus attracts people with theological interests, and those with theological interests are drawn to Jesus. It seems, then, that 'most of us writing about Jesus have theological interests.'[13] If to describe something as 'secular' is to suggest it is largely devoid of religious participants, then it seems problematic to couch modern historical Jesus research in these terms.

However, one might object to this paradigm of secularisation for numerous reasons and, therefore, one may also object to conceiving of the secularity of scholarship in relation to the beliefs of a discipline's participants. Most importantly, it is wholly unclear whether religious belief is, in fact declining. Despite claims that 'never before have we seen secularity so widespread,'[14] this picture is not uniformly true across the globe. As just one example of this, at the turn of the 20th century, one important survey demonstrating the decline in religious belief in Britain[15] was shortly followed by another demonstrating its growth in other parts of Europe.[16]

Furthermore, as Talal Asad notes, 'the contemporary salience of religious movements around the globe, and the torrent of commentary on them by scholars and journalists, have made it plain that religion is by no means disappearing in the modern world.'[17] The Pew Research Center has also projected the following relating to religiously unaffiliated people for 2060.

While these projected figures show an increase in the *number* of religiously unaffiliated persons by 2060, the Pew Research Center notes that 'as a share of all people in the world, religious "nones" are projected to decline from 16% of the

Table 5.2 Number of religiously unaffiliated, 2060 ©Pew Research Center 2017.

Religious Group	*Followers*	*% of Global Population*	*Population Growth*
Christians	3,065,460,000	31.8	+778,210,000
Muslim	2,987,390,000	31.1	+1,234,770,000
Unaffiliated	1,202,300,000	12.5	+37,280,000
Hindus	1,392,900,000	14.5	+293,790,000
Buddhists	461,980,000	4.8	−37,400,000
Folk Religionists[a]	440,950,000	4.6	+22,670,000
Other Religions[b]	59,410,000	0.6	−290,000
Jews	16,370,000	0.2	+2,100,000

[a]This comprises those who identify with various African religions, Chinese folk religions, Native American religions, and Australian aboriginal religions.

[b]This includes Bahai's Jains, Sikhs, Shintoists, Taoists, Wiccans, and Zoroastrians, among others.

Table 5.3 Number of religiously unaffiliated, 2060 (by region) ©Pew Research Center 2017.

Region	*% Global Unaffiliated Population 2015*	*% Global Unaffiliated Population 2060*	*Natural Change 2055–60*
Asia-Pacific	75%	66%	−25,870,000
Europe	12%	14%	−1,790,000
N. America	6%	10%	+2,640,000
Latin America/Caribbean	4%	5%	−30,000
Sub-Saharan Africa	2%	5%	+3,240,000
Middle East/North Africa	0.2%	0.3%	+50,000
Global	**100**	**100**	**−21,780,000**

total population in 2015 to 13% in 2060 (see Table 5.2).'[18] These figures may also be broken down further by region (see Table 5.3).

While some regions are projected to see an increase in religiously unaffiliated persons by 2060 (North America, sub-Saharan Africa, and Middle East/North Africa regions), the overall global change in the number of religiously affiliated persons is projected as a decrease of nearly 22 million. While North America and Europe—the two regions who have contributed most to what might be called, rightly or wrongly, 'mainstream' modern academic historical Jesus research as understood in this study[19]—are both expected to comprise a larger proportion of the total global number of religiously unaffiliated persons by 2060 (regardless of growth change within these regions), the overall global picture is one of increased religious participation by this point (by virtue of decreased religious unaffiliation). In this respect, it is telling that Europe is projected to see both a *decrease* in the number of religiously unaffiliated persons and an *increase* in this number *as a proportion* of the total global number of religiously unaffiliated persons.

To describe secularisation as the decline in religious belief, then, overlooks other factors that might account for how so-called secular societies can be the place of religious growth. Furthermore, it is somewhat problematic to refer to secularisation in terms of *religious* belief since the term 'religion' is itself devoid of fixed meaning. Must something refer to god(s) to be truly a religion? Even if one answers affirmatively,[20] the Pew Research Center notes that many of those who identified as 'unaffiliated' in 2015, still believe in phenomena one might describe as 'spiritual,' 'deistic,' or 'theistic.' For example, of those unaffiliated individuals in the U.S., 68% also 'hold some religious or spiritual beliefs … [including] belief in God or a higher power.'[21] At the very least, if historical Jesus research is indeed undertaken within a secular context, then secularity must be more than simply the lack of 'religious belief,' however construed.

Additionally, some commentators have identified the fact that certain societal phenomena have all the appearance of religious belief without reference to god(s), most notably Christmas[22] and football (or any major sport).[23] Certainly these two phenomena represent two industries whose social significance and participation have grown exponentially. Additionally, it is possible to observe a growth in the belief of low-level superstitions which, although distinct from participation in the major religious institutions, indicate that at least on some level something approaching religious belief may be on the rise.[24] All this is to say that the claim 'religious belief is in decline' approaches meaninglessness, since the phrase 'religious belief' is itself somewhat nebulous. It is precisely these issues (and apparent rises in religious belief) that led sociologists to reformulate this theory of secularisation in the early 1990s, into a paradigm that understands the phenomenon in terms of religious authority.

In addition to this, construing secularism in these terms is not a helpful one for the present purposes. Certainly, one would not wish to suggest that modern historical Jesus research is a secular discipline in the sense that most of its participants reject the notion of divinity. In this sense, historical Jesus research (and indeed Theology and Religious Studies broadly construed) would be one of the least secularised disciplines within the academy. In claiming modern historical Jesus research operates from within a secular metaphysical framework, it should be clear that this is not a reference to the personal metaphysical beliefs of those who partake in the quest.

5.3 Secularism as Declining Religious Authority

The second account of secularisation I highlight conceives of the phenomenon primarily in terms of authority and seeks to stress the perceived decline in authority that religious beliefs and institutions possess in secularised societies. This authority-focussed account was first inaugurated by Mark Chaves' 1994 article in *Social Forces*.[25] By the early 1990s, radical changes were taking place regarding how sociologists understood secularisation. It had largely been understood as the decline of participation in religious belief, rituals, and institutions, so much so that in 1985 Bryan Wilson could describe this as 'the inherited model' of secularisation for his generation of sociologists.[26] However, in the early 1990s it had become apparent that such a decline in participation had not only ceased but, in some instances, had begun to reverse (as noted above). In 1991, therefore, Frank J. Lechner noted that:

> Secularization used to be part of the conventional sociological wisdom … Recently, however, the conventional wisdom has come under attack, and secularization theory in particular has become suspect in the eyes of the sociologists. … [There is now] a new conventional wisdom: religion is not a spent force, the critics would argue … in many ways, people today are more 'religious' than they were in the past.[27]

In the same year Bryan Turner characterised the problem as an 'analytical cul-de-sac.'[28] In the late 1980s and early 1990s, therefore, a string of publications emerged pronouncing the death of secularisation theory,[29] with others seeking to reformulate the theory in a manner that better fitted the recent growth in religious participation.[30] In the same manner that Bruno Latour had famously noted that society had never, in fact, been modern (at least in terms of how 'modernity' is frequently conceived),[31] sociologists began to wonder whether, in fact, society had ever been secular. Was secularism a myth? Or had our understanding of secularism been misconstrued? Faced with this 'dead-end' caused by 'religion's stubborn refusal to disappear,'[32] Chaves seeks to reformulate secularisation theory in a manner that considers the issues raised by its critics. In so doing, he advances a relatively simple thesis: 'Secularization is best understood not as the decline of religion, but as the declining scope of religious authority.'[33]

He begins by distinguishing carefully between religious belief *per se* and the religious institutions that mediate this belief (in a manner dependent upon Tschannen's important work on the issue[34]). Following a Parsonian model of social theory which identifies 'differentiation' as 'a paradigm of evolutionary change,'[35] Chaves advances a view of society as 'an interinstitutional system,' whereby institutions constitute the fabric of society, rather than ethical or religious belief systems themselves.[36] In such a society, religion—as mediated by religious *institutions*—is understood primarily:

> as another mundane institutional sphere or organizational sector; it can no longer claim any necessary function as primary … It is one relativized sphere among other relativized spheres, whose elites jockey to increase or at least maintain their control over human actions, organizational resources, and other societal spheres.[37]

This view is therefore consonant with Charles Taylor's insight that in secularised societies religion is understood as simply one option among many: 'belief in God is no longer axiomatic. There are alternatives.'[38] This distinction is also a helpful one insofar as historical Jesus research is concerned (or, indeed, any academic historiography). It is of no concern what the individual historian believes if those beliefs do not contribute to the construction of a non-secular framework by which one makes claims about the person of Jesus. As Bryan Wilson states, it is not *people* who are secular; rather, 'it is the *system* that becomes secularized.'[39] As an example—and, as will be substantiated in the Chapter 9 of this study—it is of no (real) concern to the wider academy that N.T. Wright was formerly Bishop of Durham (and therefore Christian) as long as he continues to operate within a secular metaphysics (or historiographical worldview) when he approaches the historical person of Jesus.

Chaves is not the first to make such a claim—Wilson,[40] Dobbelaere,[41] and Lechner[42] are important precursors to Chaves' work—but his argument was advanced at such a crucial time for sociological analysis of secularism that it has come to be seen as one of the discipline's landmark studies. Where Chaves seeks to go beyond previous attempts to identify religious authority as the key loci of secularisation is where he seeks to ensure that a focus on religious institutions does not completely overshadow analysis of individual religious belief. As he states:

> The approach I am developing here moves beyond this [prior] work by explicitly and relentlessly maintaining the focus on religious authority, and hence on religion's social significance, at all analytical levels, including the individual level.[43]

This balance is achieved by the abandonment of one category and the adoption of another; replacing 'religion' for 'religious authority' when referring to secularism. In support of this, Chaves highlights the fact that, while Weber famously refused to define religion, he did define what constituted a religious institution, and did so in terms of religious authority:

> A *hierocratic organisation* is an organisation which guarantees order through psychic coercion [*psychische Zwang*] by distributing or denying religious benefits … a compulsory hierocratic organization will be called a *church* insofar as its administrative staff claims a *monopoly* on the legitimate use of hierocratic coercion [*hierokratischen Zwanges*].[44]

This *hierokratische Zwang* constitutes the methods and means by which religious institutions enforce their authority upon communities. In the case of religious institutions, this comes in the form of *psychische Zwang* (as opposed to political authorities, for example, who might resort to physical or violent coercion). However, as Chaves notes, the category of 'psychic coercion,' is not necessarily a helpful one since it is neither easy to define nor to observe. Instead, he proposes to define religious institutions as those structures which seek to enforce their will 'by controlling the access of individuals to some desired goods, where the legitimation of that control includes some supernatural component, however weak.'[45]

Religious institutions, therefore, are societal structures which offer the means to possessing various 'goods' (health, wealth, salvation, etc.) but control access to these 'goods' by referring to them in terms of the 'supernatural' which they alone have special insight into. Stated in these terms, secularisation is understood as 'the declining influence of social structures whose legitimization rests on reference to the supernatural.'[46] In other words, in a secularised society, religious institutions possess less authority because the means by which they enforce this authority (with reference to the 'supernatural') have become less compelling in the imaginative interior life of the individual.

This approach to secularism is helpful for numerous reasons. Practically, it offers an approach that is perhaps easier to quantify than approaches based on individualistic belief. Regarding the present study, as noted above, the focus of systemic secularisation helps to identify and explain the presence of secular frameworks within which non-secular individuals might operate. One might suggest that historical Jesus research is not a secular endeavour by surveying several participants in the quest and finding that the majority profess to be Christian. However, it is quite another thing to state that Christian individuals must operate within a secular *framework* in order to participate in the discipline and its discussions.

Moreover, one can also identify a number of difficulties with Chaves' approach. Whereas Chaves objected to Weber's category of *psychische Zwang* for being unhelpful and nebulous, one might similarly object to his introduction of the term 'supernatural' into discussion about religion and religious institutions. Not only is the term 'supernatural' unclear, it is equally unclear whether a belief system must make reference to the 'supernatural' for it to be properly *religious*.[47] Similarly, a more charitable critic of religion may read Chaves' definition of religious institutions and wonder *why* they might seek to control access to certain 'goods' by means of referring to the supernatural. The motives behind the enforcing of authority (if this is the correct means of comprehending secularisation) are left to the imagination.

Despite its attendant problems, 'maintaining such a distinction between religion's influence and the mere existence of religious beliefs and sentiments among individuals represents an enduring contribution and will be fundamental to any valid notion of secularization.'[48] While the particularities of Chaves' framework may be accused of lacking specificity, practically it offers a conception of secularism that is of help when understanding the state of modern historical Jesus research. Thus, we may carry forward this understanding of secularism that 'does not even suggest that most individuals have relinquished all their interest in religion, even though that may be the case.'[49]

5.4 Religio-economic Rejections of Secularisation

The third and final conception of secularisation I assess is the religio-economic approach made famous by the likes of Rodney Stark, William Sims Bainbridge, Roger Finke, and Laurence Iannaccone: that of secularisation as a self-limiting process, an approach which has now become one of the most discussed theories of secularisation among sociologists.[50] Broadly speaking, this theory suggests that when we apply economic categories of analysis to the religious elements of society, it becomes clear that theories of secularisation have been problematic in proclaiming the decline of religion. These scholars and their counterparts have offered a serious challenge to the secularisation theories and religio-economic (or supply-side) approaches to secularisation have become so prevalent that any discussion of secularisation would be incomplete without some assessment of them. Moreover, these religio-economic approaches are to be carefully distinguished from the work of (among others) Goodchild[51] and Tanner[52] who highlight the religious element of modern economics (rather than the economic element of modern religion, discussed here). In the second chapter of this study, when defining metaphysics, I examined several rejections of metaphysics, and why they did not impact upon the argument I am making. Likewise, before offering some final thoughts on the characteristics of secular scholarship, it is important to address the challenge this religio-economic approach poses to my argument.

In assessing these economics-driven attempts to describe secularisation, it is helpful to note that they take their cue from Nobel prize-winning economist Gary Becker. His work is so crucial in serving as a logical forerunner to these religio-economic approaches to secularisation that it is worth saying a few brief words about his work here. Becker, himself influenced by the work of Milton Friedman and Theodore Schultz, viewed economics as a method of analysis, rather than a field in its own right.[53] Accordingly, Becker was among the first economists to apply traditional economic categories to areas previously thought to be beyond the realms of economic analysis, including issues of racial discrimination,[54] politics,[55] crime,[56] human capital,[57] family organisation,[58] and education,[59] among many other issues. Becker outlined his project in his own words, during his acceptance speech for the reception of the Nobel Prize: 'My research,' he begins, 'uses the economic approach to analyse social issues that range beyond those usually considered by economists … it is a *method* of analysis, not an assumption about particular motivations.'[60] Rather than seeking to describe why individuals behave in certain ways, Becker 'uses theory at the micro level as a powerful tool to derive implications at the group or macro level.'[61] Following Becker's basic conviction that economics may be used to analyse any given facet of society, the aforementioned group of thinkers (Stark et al.) have attempted to apply economic principles to the study of religion and secularisation. In reality, Stark, Bainbridge, Fink, Iannaccone, and others have each advanced their own variations upon the religio-economic theory of secularisation, so that we should, more accurately, speak of religio-economic *theories* of secularisation. However, rather than outline each version of this theory individually, I will synthesise what is most common to the work of these scholars and treat them together.

These religio-economic approaches proceed from two basic convictions that underpin their analysis of the religious sectors of life. The first of these is the notion of rewards and compensators, initially outlined in Stark and Bainbridge's 1987 work *A Theory of Religion*. While Becker, resisting the Marxist claim that individuals are driven primarily by greed, preferred to speak of 'individuals maximiz[ing] welfare *as they conceive it*,'[62] Stark and Bainbridge in turn conceive of individuals as motivated by 'reward,' defined broadly as 'anything humans will incur costs to obtain.'[63] However, in cases where desired rewards are not available, they instead seek compensators, or 'postulations of rewards according to explanations that are not readily susceptible to unambiguous evaluations.'[64] Religious institutions may well offer rewards but are ultimately concerned with compensators for rewards unavailable at present, including previously inaccessible webs of relationships, a promise of an 'afterlife' in some sense, and material help when in need.

Those in positions of power will seek to gain a monopoly on the available rewards, leaving little for the rest who must instead turn to compensators to satiate their desire for reward.[65] Religious institutions, therefore, become one of the main means by which compensators are obtained by those without the ability to obtain rewards, and these same religious institutions are, in turn, rewarded by the powerless for their distribution of compensators. For example, one may give money to a church (a reward for the church) in order to strengthen one's participation in the faith and conviction of reward after death (a compensator for the individual). Thus, church and congregant enact a mutually beneficial relationship.

What, then, of secular societies? How do we explain secularisation in terms of religious institutions and their societal role as distributors of compensators? Stark and Bainbridge define the secular as referring to 'any parts of society and culture that are substantially free of supernatural assumptions.'[66] Thus, we may expect that the socio-economically powerful will be among the most secular parts of society, given they have most access to rewards and least need for compensators such as belief in the afterlife. However, they note two developments that have led to 'the progressive loss of power by religious organizations,' and these are external competition, by which societal elites make more rewards available to others in order to maximise their utility (e.g., they incentivise working in areas the elites deem a priority) and internal democracy, whereby individuals gradually become more cognisant of the prevalence of rewards and lose interest in compensators.[67]

The second basic premise underpinning the supply-side theory of secularisation claims that free-market principles apply also to religious institutions: the more competition there is among religious groups in any given society, the more likely they are to flourish as a whole.[68] As with business, competition promotes quality: where there is a great multiplicity of religious options, these institutions must raise standards in order to entice prospective congregants, and where there is hegemony of religion, it can become stagnant and unappealing. Moreover, the more religious choice available in a society, the more likely it is that an individual can find an institution that offers compensators in the form that best suits them. Again, hegemony of religion appeals to fewer people-groups. Stark even goes as far as to suggest that privately-funded religious figures will work harder to attract new members to their institutions than will publicly funded religious officials whose livelihood does not depend upon such things (although in response to this we might wish to suggest that at least some religious officials work hard because they conceive their religion's message to be important, and not necessarily to earn a salary).[69]

These two fundamental guiding principles of supply-side analyses of religion explain why religio-economists are broadly sceptical of secularisation theories. Stark, writing in 1990, notes that 'after nearly three centuries of utterly failed prophesies and misrepresentations of both present and past, it seems time to carry the secularization doctrine to the graveyard of failed theories, and there to whisper, "*requiescat in pace*."'[70] First, the human desire for reward means that secularisation will always be a self-limited process. Rewards, however construed, are a finite resource that the socio-economically powerful will always seek to control and monopolise at the expense of the less powerful. This will result in a constant demand for compensators like the ones provided by religion.

It is to the benefit of those in power that religious institutions continue to exist and (to a degree) flourish, insofar as they provide individuals with a satisfactory alternative to the pursuit of the rewards which those in power seek to monopolise. Likewise, it is in the interests of religious institutions that the powerful remain powerful and rewards lie beyond the reach of most individuals, so that they can provide compensators and, in turn, obtain rewards from their congregants. It is therefore in the interests of both parties that the effects of secularism are limited, that religious institutions continue to exist and attract new individuals.

Second, the free-market principles that exist concurrently with the capitalist economics ubiquitous in modern societies turn out to be conducive to the flourishing of religion. They encourage religions to be competitive and ensure their survival. If a given religious institution fails to provide a more attractive service than their competitors, their intake of rewards will slow to a trickle and their existence will become compromised over time. The relegation of religion to the private sphere thus allows competition to be introduced and results in the most effective compensator-distributors to thrive at the expense of the less effective ones who go out of 'business,' as it were. This ensures that the mutually beneficial relationship between the powerful and religious institutions is at its most effective and, again, serves to limit the effects of secularisation.

What has been called secularism, then, or the retreat of religion from public life, is better understood as part of the natural, ongoing process of religious metamorphosis. What has hitherto been conceived of as decline is instead the less competitive elements of religion dying away and the more competitive gaining prominence among those unable to obtain the rewards they desire. Stark therefore views it as problematic that theories of secularisation can only account for religious decline, and not for the more fundamental category of religious *change*: 'the secularization theory is as useless as a hotel elevator that only goes down,' he writes.[71] We should, therefore, disregard notions of secularism: not only are they inaccurate, they are unhelpful and only hinder sociological analyses.

What bearing do these ideas have for my argument, then? Is it possible to speak of secular metaphysics if the very notion of secularism is fundamentally misguided to begin with? I argue, despite the analyses of religio-economic sociologists, we have good reason to hold on to the notion of secularisation. First, we might wonder which theories of secularisation lie in the sights of these religio-economic approaches. It appears that they have little to say about the decline of religious authority and instead choose to focus upon the decline of religious participation, a notion already found to be problematic earlier in the present chapter. Stark, for example, resists theories of secularisation on the basis that individuals do not seem to be turning away from religion as predicted. However, he acknowledges the loss of power and influence on the part of religious institutions, noting 'if this were all that secularization means, there would be nothing to argue.'[72] Although he is not alone in doing so,[73] it appears that he has defined secularism as the apparent decline in religious participation in order to reject it (and the notion of secularisation writ large). This is to say that this approach to secularisation is only compelling if one defines secularism in a manner which is problematic to begin with.

Elsewhere, Steve Bruce notes that 'when Rodney Stark and William S. Bainbridge wanted to represent the secularization paradigm (in order to show it false), they ignored the sociologists who had developed those ideas and instead cited a 1960s undergraduate textbook written by an anthropologist.'[74] We might criticise supply-side approaches to secularisation, then, for erecting a straw-man version of the secularisation paradigm to make their refutation of it more compelling. Few would agree with the notion of secularisation as they present it. By failing to engage with the strongest form of the secularisation paradigm, all they have accomplished is to undermine a theory in which few were invested in the first place.

Moreover, when it comes to the two fundamental premises behind religio-economic approaches to secularisation—the first of these being the human desire for reward and/or compensators—we might note some objections. To begin with, the claim that humans universally desire reward is not only reductive, but unsubstantiated. Human behaviour is complicated and multifaceted, and it is not apparent that every individual (or enough individuals to call it a trend) are motivated primarily by reward.

To take a specific case more familiar to modern historical Jesus research, we might briefly consider the role of 'gift' in antiquity. The sociological category of 'gift' was introduced first via Marcel Mauss,[75] discussed at length by Derrida[76] and later popularised among theologians by the work of John Milbank, who has considered the nature of gift at length.[77] Central to this category of gift is that of reciprocity, the notion that individuals give to receive. Gift, conceived in correlation to reciprocity, has subsequently become an important point of discussion in many disciplines, not least in biblical studies and ancient history. Accordingly, a recent study by Seth Schwartz has argued that 1st-century Mediterranean Jews had 'profound reservations about [the notion of] the gift'[78] and that their social ordering was centred upon a 'rejection of reciprocity,'[79] which we might re-conceive as a rejection of reward, to use the nomenclature of supply-side economics. Although John Barclay has recently disputed this conclusion—he suggests Jews in this context expected a delayed reward from God, similar to the notion of a compensator[80]—it is important to note that even if we concede that reward plays an important and universal part in human motivation, this is not to say that it is the sole motivator behind human behaviour. Such a claim reduces human agency to the mere pursuit of profit, a move for which there does not appear to be sufficient warrant.

We might also note a reservation about the other fundamental premise of supply-side theories of secularisation: that religious expansion is positively linked with religious pluralism and free-market principles. While Finke and Stark have presented figures to support the notion that religious multiplicity leads to religious expansion,[81] others have conducted similar studies and come to the conclusion that 'religious *monopoly*—not religious diversity—fuels religious expansion.'[82] Chaves and Gorski, having undertaken an analysis of the data collected in numerous works of scholarship on the issue, found that 'empirical evidence does not support the claim that religious pluralism is positively associated with religious participation in any sense.'[83] Elsewhere, Daniel Olson has highlighted serious methodological reservations about the manner in which supply-side theorists have collected data to support their case.[84] In short, it does not seem to be the case that diversity of religion leads to an increase in religiosity. Not directly, at least. Despite Rodney Stark appearing to have declared dead the very notion of secularisation, it is here to stay.

5.5 Conclusion

In this chapter, I examined three theories of secularisation to determine what traits a work of historical Jesus scholarship must evidence for it to be properly described as 'secular.' The first of these theories conceived of secularisation merely as the decline in religious participation. In other words, it suggested that the extent to which societies were secular stood in direct correlation to the proportion of its population that actively engages with a religious faith. Despite this theory seemingly initially plausible and substantiated by various statistics, it was ultimately found to be unsatisfactory for several reasons. First, I offered reasons to doubt the trustworthiness of the statistics available, due to the vague nature of what constitutes a 'religion' and (subsequently) what constitutes 'participation' in a religion. In this respect, the example of non-institutionalised spirituality was highlighted as an outlier to this paradigm. Furthermore, I raised questions regarding the trustworthiness of self-identification, also. For the available figures to be deemed useful involves an uncritical acceptance of people's religious self-identification as accurate, a claim for which I found limited support. Moreover, even if the figures *are* deemed to be trustworthy, another problem arises. Namely, that the number of religiously unaffiliated individuals is projected to fall over the course of the 21st century. If we are to say that secularism is a category that accurately describes a genuine facet of the reality of the world around us, it cannot merely refer to the number of religious participants. Thus, if we are to refer to an academic discipline as secular, this cannot simply refer to the individual, private faiths of those who engage in the discipline.

The second theory with which I engaged conceived of secularisation as the decline in religious authority. In other words, religious traditions lost their monopolistic influence over the public sphere and came to be viewed as simply one option among many. In reality the two theories are not only irrevocably enmeshed—as they are with other factors also—and, as Steve Bruce has noted, 'causally related,' with a decline in one area followed by a decline in the others also (and *vice versa*).[85] By the 1990s sociologists had come to realise that the secularisation paradigm centred on religious participation did not adequately explain or express what could be observed taking place within various societies. It soon became apparent that secularism did not necessarily refer to the number of religious observants or participants, but to the authority that religious institutions and beliefs enjoyed within public discourse. While the language of 'religion' and 'religiosity' again proved problematic for the religious authority paradigm, I found it to be far more compelling than the religious participation paradigm and suggested it more accurately described the phenomenon described as secularism.

Finally, I examined the various religio-economic approaches to secularism. These approaches—taking Becker's totalising system of economic analysis as their cue—apply economic categories and criteria to the study of religion and proceed from two fundamental principles: (1) that humans are primarily motivated by reward, and (2) free-market principles also apply to religious institutions. This being the case, religio-economists argue that the secularism paradigm is destined to fail, due to secularism itself being a self-limiting process. Religious institutions are required to dispense and distribute compensators to those less powerful members of society who cannot access the rewards they desire. Moreover, free-market principles, inseparable from the widespread modern capitalist system of economics encourage religious institutions to be competitive with one another and ensures that the most effective and enticing forms of religious institutions are the most successful.

However, I identified numerous problems with religio-economic approaches to theories of secularism. First, the two bulwarks of these approaches—humans as reward-driven, and religious institutions as competitive—was naïve, insofar as it propagated a reductive view of human behaviour and motivation. Perhaps more troubling was the work of various scholars who not only questioned the statistical analysis advanced by religio-economists, but also raised the possibility of statistical manipulation in order to obtain a more desirable conclusion. I therefore claimed religio-economic challenges to theories of secularisation had not been successful.

Thus, when I speak of modern academic historical Jesus research I will not speak of secularism (and its cognates) as though this refers to the private beliefs of any individuals, but instead will employ a conception of secularism as the systematic refutation of the authority of religious beliefs. Although not without its problems, this conception of secularism will be the one that I carry over into my discussion regarding the metaphysical framework(s) present within modern academic historical Jesus research. In other words, we may describe scholarship—be it an individual contribution to scholarship or an entire discipline such as the 'Quest' for the historical Jesus—as secular, insofar as it refuses to allow religious perspectives to contribute to the discipline's historical method.

Notes

1 Taylor, *A Secular Age*, 2.
2 The text is accessible online as G.J. Holyoake, *English Secularism: A Confession of Belief* (Chicago, IL: Open Court, 1896). Among those who identify Holyoake as the first to use the term 'secularism' are Taha Parla, Andrew Davison, and Janet R. Jakobsen, 'Secularism and Laicism in Turkey', in *Secularisms*, Social Text Books (Durham, NC: Duke University, 2008), 58–75 (60); András Sajó, 'Preliminaries to a Concept of Constitutional Secularism', *International Journal of Constitutional Law* 6.3–4 (2008), 605–29 (607); T. Randolph Beard et al., 'Secularism, Religion, and Political Choice in the United States', *Politics and Religion* 6.4 (2013): 753–77 (756); Michael Rectenwald, *Nineteenth-Century British Secularism*, Histories of the Sacred and the Secular, 1700–2000 (Basingstoke: Palgrave MacMillan, 2016), 71–106.
3 Hugo Grotius, *The Law of War and Peace*, trans. Francis W. Kelsey et al. (Indianapolis, IN: Bobbs-Merrill, 1925). On the one hand, some credit Grotius with the secularization of many modern legal systems (so Hilaire McCoubrey, 'Natural Law, Religion and the Development of International Law', in *Religion and International Law*, ed. Mark W. Janis and Carolyn Evans (The Hague: Martinus Nijhoff, 1999), 177–90; John D. Haskell, 'Hugo Grotius in the Contemporary Memory of International Law: Secularism, Liberalism, and the Politics of Restatement and Denial', *Emory International Law Review* 25.1 (2011), 269–98) while others highlight his importance in the secularising of the political sphere (for example, see Benedict Kingsbury and Adam Roberts, 'Introduction: Grotian Thought in International Relations', in *Hugo Grotius and International Relations*, ed. Hedley Bulls, Benedict Kingsbury, and Adam Roberts (Oxford: Oxford University, 1990), 1–64; Edward Keene, *Beyond the Anarchical Society: Grotius, Colonialism and Order in World Politics* (Cambridge: Cambridge University, 2002), esp. 143–44).
4 Luther posits a distinction between church and state most explicitly in Martin Luther, 'Temporal Authority: To What Extent It Should Be Obeyed', in *Luther's Works*, ed. Walther I. Brandt and Helmut T. Lehmann, vol. 45: The Christian in Society II (Philadelphia, PA: Fortress, 1962), 77–133. The concept of the two governments borrows heavily from that of the two cities found in Augustine of Hippo, *De Civitate Dei*, ed. and trans. P.G. Walsh (Oxford: Oxbow Books, 2005). For an introductory discussion regarding Luther's view of the two governments and the intellectual influences upon this doctrine, see John R. Stephenson, 'The Two Governments and the Two Kingdoms in Luther's Thought', *Scottish Journal of Theology* 34.4 (1981), 321–37; Richard Marius, *Martin Luther: The Christian between God and Death* (Cambridge, MA: Belknap Press, 1999), 366–67; Bernhard Lohse, *Martin Luther's Theology: Its Historical and Systematic Development*, trans. Roy A. Harrisville (Edinburgh: T&T Clark, 1999), 314–24.
5 See the comments in Talal Asad, *Formations of the Secular: Christianity, Islam, Modernity*, Cultural Memory in the Present (Stanford, CA: Stanford University, 2003), esp. 1.
6 Asad, *Formation of the Secular*, 1.
7 The case is made most explicitly (and most compellingly) in Charles Taylor, 'Modes of Secularism', in *Secularism and Its Critics*, ed. Rajeev Bhargava (Delhi: Oxford University, 1998). However, as we will see in due course, the likes of Rodney Stark and the religio-economic theorists might suggest the very things that characterise modernity also allow religious institutions to flourish (or perhaps even demand it). Although modernity is a term used at various points in this study, it is one not without contention. Most importantly Latour argues modernity is a state that is still yet to be manifest in society, since those phenomena we associate with so-called modern societies are yet to actually manifest themselves. Thus, to borrow from the title of his work, 'we have never been modern.' See Bruno Latour, *Nous n'avons Jamais Été Modernes: Essai*

d'anthropologie Symétrique (Paris: La Découverte, 1991), ET: *We Have Never Been Modern*, trans. Catherine Porter (Cambridge, MA: Harvard University, 1993). Despite this, the term 'modernity' and its cognates will be used here and in what follows, to refer to the period following the enlightenment until the present day or, in other words, the period roughly contemporaneous with the quest for the historical Jesus, as outlined in Chapter 6 of the present study.

8 Larry Shiner, 'The Concept of Secularization in Empirical Research', *JSSR* 6.2 (1967), 207–20 (207).

9 So Shiner 'The Concept of Secularization in Empirical Research'.

10 Here, and in what follows, all statistics are taken from the Pew Research Centre website: https://www.pewforum.org/wp-content/uploads/sites/7/2017/04/FULL-REPORT-WITH-APPENDIXES-A-AND-B-APRIL-3.pdf (accessed: 7 March 2020). At the time of writing, these figures from 2015 (but published in 2017) remain the most recent. All figures are rounded to the nearest 10,000.

11 John Dominic Crossan, *A Long Way from Tipperary: A Memoir* (New York: HarperCollins, 2000), 198–204.

12 Dale C. Allison, Jr., *The Historical Christ and the Theological Jesus* (Grand Rapids, MI: William B. Eerdmans, 2009), ix.

13 Allison, Jr., *Historical Christ*, 19.

14 Phil Zuckerman, *The Nonreligious: Understanding Secular People and Societies* (Oxford: Oxford University Press, 2016), 76.

15 Robin Gill, C. Kirk Hadaway, and Penny Long Marler, 'Is Religious Belief Declining in Britain?', *JSSR* 37.3 (1998), 507–16.

16 Paul Froese and Steven Pfaff, 'Replete and Desolate Markets: Poland, East Germany, and the New Religious Paradigm', *Social Forces* 80.2 (2001), 481–507.

17 Asad, *Formation of the Secular*, 1.

18 See p. 10 of the report cited in note 10, above.

19 In other words, the 'Quest' for the historical Jesus, traditionally understood as comprising works of scholarship from Reimarus to the present day (see the chapters in the second part of this study for further detail).

20 So Steve Bruce, 'Defining Religion: A Practical Response', *Revue Internationale de Sociologie* 21.1 (2011), 107–20.

21 These and additional figures are available at in Appendix E of the aforementioned report on the 2015 statistics, available here: https://assets.pewresearch.org/wp-content/uploads/sites/11/2017/04/04104610/Appendix-E-DefiningReligiousGroups.pdf (accessed: 7 March 2022). This particular statistic, the report notes, is taken from 2012 data but remains the most recent statistic available from the Pew Research Centre for this particular phenomenon.

22 Christopher Deacy, *Christmas as Religion: Rethinking Santa, the Secular, and the Sacred* (New York: Oxford University, 2016).

23 Frieder Ludwig, 'Football, Culture and Religion: Varieties of Interaction', *Studies in World Christianity* 21.3 (2015), 201–22.

24 David Voas, 'The Rise and Fall of Fuzzy Fidelity in Europe', *European Sociological Review* 25.2 (2009), 155–68 (esp. 161).

25 Mark Chaves, 'Secularization as Declining Religious Authority', *Social Forces* 72.3 (1994), 749–74.

26 Bryan Wilson, 'Secularization: The Inherited Model', in *The Sacred in a Secular Age*, ed. Phillip E. Hammond (Berkeley, CA: University of California, 1985), 9–20.

27 Frank J. Lechner, 'The Case against Secularization: A Rebuttal', *Social Forces* 69.4 (1991), 1103–19 (1103–4).

28 Bryan S. Turner, *Religion and Social Theory*, 2nd ed. (New York: City University of New York, 1991), 3.

29 Most importantly, see Michael Hout and Andrew M. Greeley, 'The Center Doesn't Hold: Church Attendance in the United States, 1940–1984', *ASR* 52.3 (1987), 325–45;

Jeffrey K. Hadden, 'Toward Desacralizing Secularization Theory', *Social Forces* 65.3 (1987), 587–611; Rodney Stark and Laurence R. Iannaccone, 'Sociology of Religion', in *The Encyclopedia of Sociology*, ed. Edgar F. Borgatta and Marie L. Borgatta (New York: MacMillan, 1992), 2029–37.

30 In addition to Chaves' article, see Lechner, 'Case against Secularization'.

31 Latour, *Nous n'avons Jamais Été Modernes*.

32 Chaves, 'Secularization', 749.

33 Ibid., 750.

34 Oliver Tschannen, 'The Secularization Paradigm: A Systematization', *JSSR* 30.4 (1991), 395–415.

35 Talcott Parsons, *Societies: Evolutionary and Comparative Perspectives* (Englewood Cliffs, NJ: Prentice-Hall, 1966), 21.

36 On this point, see also Roger Friedland and Robert R. Alford, 'Bringing Society Back In: Symbols, Practices, and Institutional Contradictions', in *The New Institutionalism in Organizational Analysis*, ed. Walter W. Powell and Paul J. DiMaggio (Chicago, IL: University of Chicago, 1991), 232–63.

37 Chaves, 'Secularization', 751–52.

38 Taylor, *Secular Age*, 3.

39 Wilson, 'Secularization', 19.

40 Bryan Wilson, *Contemporary Transformations of Religion* (Oxford: OUP, 1976); idem, 'The Return of the Sacred', *JSSR* 18.3 (1979), 268–80; idem, *Religion in Sociological Perspective* (Oxford: OUP, 1982); idem, 'Secularization'.

41 This distinction is implicit or explicit in many of Dobbelaere's key publications, including (but not limited to) Karel Dobbelaere, 'Secularization: A Multi-Dimensional Concept', *Current Sociology* 29.2 (1981), 1–216; 'Secularization Theories and Sociological Paradigms: A Reformulation of the Private-Public Dichotomy and the Problem of Societal Integration', *SR* 46.4 (1985), 377–87; 'Some Trends in European Sociology of Religion: The Secularization Debate', *SR* 48.2 (1987), 107–37; 'Secularization, Pillarization, Religious Involvement, and Religious Change in the Low Countries', in *World Catholicism in Transition*, ed. Thomas M. Gannon (New York: MacMillan, 1988), 80–115; 'The Secularization of Society? Some Methodological Suggestions', in *Secularization and Fundamentalism Reconsidered*, ed. Jeffrey K. Hadden and Anson Shupe (New York: Paragon House, 1989), 27–43.

42 Lechner, 'Case against Secularization'.

43 Chaves, 'Secularization', 754.

44 Max Weber, *Wirtschaft and Gesellschaft* (Tübingen: J. C. B. Mohr (Paul Siebeck), 1922), 29. (emphases original)

45 Chaves, 'Secularization', 755–56.

46 Ibid., 756.

47 A helpful introduction to the problem of the category of 'religion' may be found in Bruce, 'Defining Religion'.

48 Chaves, 'Secularization', 752.

49 Wilson, *Religion in Sociological Perspective*, 150.

50 For a sympathetic introduction to the theory, see *Rational Choice Theory and Religion*, ed. Lawrence A. Young (London: Routledge, 1997); Ted G. Jelen, *Sacred Markets, Sacred Canopies: Essays on Religious Markets and Religious Pluralism* (Lanham, MD: Rowman & Littlefield, 2002). Among the more critical introductions to the topic are Steve Bruce, *Choice and Religion: A Critique of Rational Choice* (Oxford: OUP, 1999); Joseph M. Bryant, 'Cost-Benefit Accounting and the Piety Business: Is *Homo Religiosus*, at Bottom, a *Homo Economicus*?', *Method and Theory in the Study of Religion* 12.1/4 (2000), 520–48.

51 Most importantly, see Philip Goodchild, *Capitalism and Religion: The Price of Piety* (London: Routledge, 2002); *Theology and Money* (London: SCM, 2007). Goodchild's

argument is that one may conceive of economics as a pseudo-religious framework, insofar as it is dependent upon a faith-based system of absent credit.

52 See the recent monograph, Kathryn Tanner, *Christianity and the New Spirit of Capitalism* (New Haven, CT: Yale University, 2019). Here Tanner turns Weber's 'protestant ethic' on its head and posits Christianity and Capitalism as competing systems of belief, in order to posit the former as a much needed genuine alternative to the latter.

53 Becker has an extensive bibliography. In what follows I will only refer to a few key publications on a given topic, rather than offer an exhaustive list of his work.

54 Gary S. Becker, *The Economics of Discrimination* (Chicago, IL: University of Chicago, 1957).

55 Idem, 'Public Policies, Pressure Groups, and Dead Weight Costs', *Journal of Public Economics* 28.3 (1985), 329–47; idem, 'Pressure Groups and Political Behaviour', in *Capitalism and Democracy: Schumpeter Revisited*, ed. R.D. Coe (Notre Dame, IL: University of Notre Dame, 1985), 120–46.

56 Idem, *The Economics of Crime* (Richmond, VA: Federal Reserve Bank of Richmond, 1995).

57 Idem, *Human Capital: A Theoretical and Empirical Analysis, with Special Reference to Education* (New York: National Bureau of Economic Research, 1964).

58 Idem, 'A Theory of Marriage: Part I', *JPE* 81.4 (1973), 813–46; idem, 'A Theory of Marriage: Part II', *JPE* 82.2 (1974), 11–26; idem, *A Treatise on the Family* (Cambridge, MA: Harvard University, 1981).

59 Idem, William H.J. Hubbard, and Kevin M. Murphy, 'The Market for College Graduates and the Worldwide Boom in Higher Education of Women', *American Economic Review* 100.3 (2010), 229–33; idem, 'Explaining the Worldwide Boom in Higher Education of Women', *Journal of Human Capital* 4.3 (2010), 201–41.

60 Gary S. Becker, 'Nobel Lecture: The Economic Way of Looking at Behaviour', *JPE* 101.3 (1993), 385–409 (385).

61 Ibid., 402.

62 Becker, 'Nobel Lecture', 386 (emphasis original). The full quote better outlines the borders of what Becker means here: "[economic] analysis assumes that individuals maximize welfare *as they conceive it*, whether they be selfish, altruistic, loyal, spiteful, or masochistic. Their behaviour is forward-looking, and it is also assumed to be consistent over time. In particular, they try as best they can to anticipate the uncertain consequences of their actions. Forward-looking behaviour, however, may still be rooted in the past, for the past can exert a long shadow on attitudes and values."

63 Rodney Stark and William Sims Bainbridge, *A Theory of Religion* (New York: Peter Lang, 1987), 27.

64 Ibid., 30.

65 Ibid., 33.

66 Ibid., 289.

67 Ibid., 293.

68 Laurence A. Iannaccone, 'The Consequences of Religious Market Structure: Adam Smith and the Economics of Religion', *Rationality and Society* 3.2 (1991), 156–77; Roger Finke, 'An Unsecular America', in *Religion and Modernization: Sociologists and Historians Debate the Secularization Thesis*, ed. Steve Bruce (Oxford: Oxford University, 1992), 145–69; Roger Finke and Rodney Stark, *The Churching of America, 1776–1990: Winners and Losers in Our Religious Economy* (New Brunswick, NJ: Rutgers University, 1992); Roger Finke and Iannaccone, 'Supply-Side Explanations for Religious Change', *Annals of the American Academy of Political and Social Science* 527.1 (1993), 27–39.

69 He makes this argument specifically in relation to the German Lutheran church in Rodney Stark, 'German and German-American Religiousness', *JSSR* 36.2 (1997), 182–93.

70 Rodney Stark, 'Secularization, R.I.P.', *SR* 60.3 (1990), 249–73 (270).
71 Stark, 'Secularization, R.I.P.', 269.
72 Ibid., 252.
73 The same straw-man conception of the secularization theory is also present in, for example, Hout and Greeley; Hadden; Stark and Iannaccone.
74 Steve Bruce, *God Is Dead: Secularization in the West*, Religion and Spirituality in the Modern World (Oxford: Blackwell, 2002), 1.
75 The text was originally published as "Essai sure le don. Forme et raison de l'échange dans les sociétés archaïques" in *L'Année Sociologique* in 1923-24 and first published as a single-volume monograph as Marcel Mauss, *Essai sur le don in sociologie et anthropologie* (Paris: Universitairs de France, 1950), ET: Marcel Mauss, *The Gift: The Form and Reason for Exchange in Archaic Societies* (London: Routledge, 2002).
76 Most importantly, see Jacques Derrida, *Given Time, Vol. 1: Counterfeit Money*, trans. P. Kamuf (Chicago, IL: University of Chicago, 1992).
77 John Milbank, 'Can a Gift Be Given? Prolegomena to a Future Trinitarian Metaphysic', *Modern Theology* 11.1 (1995), 119–61; idem, *Being Reconciled: Ontology and Pardon*, Radical Orthodoxy (London: Routledge, 2003); idem, *The Gift Exchanged: The Gift in Religion* (Oxford: Blackwell, 2017).
78 Seth Schwartz, *Were the Jews a Mediterranean Society?* (Princeton, NJ: Princeton University, 2010), 75.
79 Schwartz, *Were the Jews a Mediterranean Society?* 5.
80 See the argument outlined in John M.G. Barclay, *Paul & the Gift* (Grand Rapids, MI: Eerdmans, 2015), 39–45. Barclay claims Jews gave to those who could not give in return (such as beggars) "not because they did not care about a return, but because they had stronger ideological grounds for expecting one—not, of course from the beggar, but from God" (45).
81 In addition to the works cited above, see Roger Finke and Rodney Stark, 'Religious Economies and Sacred Canopies: Religious Mobilization in American Cities, 1906', *ASR* 53.1 (1988), 41–49.
82 Judith R. Blau, Kenneth C. Land, and Kent Redding, 'The Expansion of Religious Affiliation: An Explanation of the Growth of Church Participation in the United States, 1850–1930', *Social Science Research* 21.4 (1992), 329–52 (329, emphasis mine). See also the similar arguments made in, for example, Kenneth C. Land, Glenn Deane, and Judith R. Blau, 'Religious Pluralism and Church Membership: A Spatial Diffusion Model', *ASR* 56.2 (1991), 237–49; Pippa Norris and Ronald Ingelhart, *Secular and Sacred: Religion and Politics Worldwide* (Cambridge: Cambridge University, 2004).
83 Mark Chaves and Philip S. Gorski, 'Religious Pluralism and Religious Participation', *Annual Review of Sociology* 27.1 (2001), 261–81 (261). This article, in particular, is an incredible scholarly feat and deals with the issue at hand in minute detail. Chaves and Gorski assess 26 works of scholarship that considers the link between religious pluralism and religious expansion. Ten found a positive correlation between the two, while eleven found a negative correlation. The remaining five found no correlation at all.
84 Most importantly, see Daniel V. A. Olson, 'Religious Pluralism in Contemporary U.S. Counties', *ASR* 63.5 (1998), 759–61; idem, 'Religious Pluralism and US Church Membership: A Reassessment', *SR* 60.2 (1999), 149–73.
85 Steve Bruce, *Secularization: In Defense of an Unfashionable Theory* (Oxford: Oxford University, 2011), 2.

Part II

Worldviews and Historical Jesus Research

6 Metaphysics and the First 'Quest'

6.1 Introduction

In this chapter, I begin to build upon the technical foundation laid down in Chapters 2–5 to examine the metaphysical presuppositions that have influenced modern academic historical Jesus research. To do so, I offer a critical overview of the Quest for the historical Jesus, and the method(s) used by several of its participants. I highlight the extent to which these participants refuse to allow religious metaphysical commitments to contribute to their historiographical worldview. This refusal coheres with the definition of secularism constructed in Chapter 5, and I therefore claim it is reasonable to describe the historiographical worldviews employed by these scholars as secular. In this chapter, I undertake this task with reference to the first 'Quest' for the historical Jesus, with a similar approach in the next two chapters with reference to the second and third 'Quest' respectively. Finally, in Chapter 9, the overview of these three chapters is complemented with a detailed analysis of N.T. Wright's work in particular. This combination of macro- and micro-analyses of the discipline, when *taken together*, gives warrant to claim mainstream historical Jesus research operates within a secular metaphysical historiographical worldview.

To be clear, in what follows I will not outline the entire historiographical worldview operative in the work of every figure mentioned. Rather, I identify whether one constituent part of their historical worldview(s) might be a totalising secular metaphysical presupposition that it is proper not to allow religious metaphysical presuppositions to influence one's historical method. As such, I am not suggesting that everybody discussed in these chapters shares the same historiographical worldview operating within the same metaphysical framework. Rather, it is possible to observe this single, shared metaphysical presupposition among participants in the 'Quest(s)' for the historical Jesus, and that commitment to this presupposition warrants the description of concomitant historiographical methodologies as 'secular.' Based on my discussion on the characteristics of secular scholarship in the previous chapter, one might describe any historiographical worldview that displays this metaphysical presupposition as secular.

Offering a history of the quest is a complicated task, not least because the proper starting point is unclear. Issues of history have been present throughout

DOI: 10.4324/b23077-8

church history, from the earliest Church Fathers; indeed, one might view the gospels themselves in this vein. As James Carleton Paget summarises:

> Any attempt at introducing a narrative of the 'Quest' has to contend with the basic problem of origins: where to begin one's story ... Much of the problem, as implied above, lies in how one understands the subject. If, contra Schweitzer, one perceives the Quest in terms simply of an interest or a concern with the figure of Jesus as he lived and died, it is difficult to deny that it was with the Christian church from a very early stage.[1]

Similarly, Birch suggests that 'depending on how loosely one defines the project, [the quest] could be considered as old as the earliest attempts to keep alive the memory of the Galilean.'[2] To discuss the metaphysical presuppositions of the 'Quest(s)' for the historical Jesus, one must outline the scope of this task. In this study I am concerned with modern historical Jesus research undertaken within an academic setting; by this I mean attempts to reconstruct the life and teaching of Jesus from the Enlightenment onwards. It is therefore reasonable to begin with those figures who first sought to understand Jesus as a historical figure by employing modernist historiographical presuppositions and techniques.

This chapter (and the two that follow) will adhere to the traditional three-quest structure of the history of the discipline. Although some have rightly criticised this division of the quest,[3] it remains the *communis opinio* among Jesus historians in practice, even if not in theory. One reason for this is that it introduces an element of clarity into an otherwise kaleidoscopic field of study. As Bond writes, 'these division are still broadly useful and will enable us to see some of the major trends over the last two hundred years.'[4] Despite critiques of the three-quest structure I nevertheless use it as my starting point for the overview that follows.

In engaging with the key figures presented in the second part of this study, I wish also to uphold and reiterate the distinction (introduced in Chapter 4) between a historian's worldview *per se*, and their historiographical worldview. It is the latter I will be concerned with presently. For example, it would certainly not be accurate to say that figures such as Kähler, Schillebeeckx, and Dunn are 'naturalists' or 'secular,' *in and of themselves*. However, in what follows, I hope to demonstrate the same is perhaps not true of the historiographical worldview that is manifest in their attempt(s) to apprehend the historical Jesus.

This is also not to say that the figures discussed herein are to be understood as being subject to criticism for having approached the historical Jesus from within a secular historiographical worldview. Let me reiterate here what was said in the introduction to this study, that I wish to *add* to historical Jesus research by discussing the metaphysical foundations of the discipline, not to subtract from it. My aim is to describe and demonstrate the dominance of secular metaphysical presuppositions within historical Jesus research while subsequently encouraging the discipline to permit alternative frameworks *alongside* what has gone before. This being the case, I begin my overview with the first quest (alternatively known as the old quest), from Reimarus to Schweitzer. By examining the metaphysical presuppositions operative in the work of key figures in the first quest of the historical Jesus, from Reimarus to Schweitzer, I observe within the first quest a shared metaphysical presupposition that religious perspectives cannot (or should not) positively contribute to reconstructions of the historical Jesus. Therefore, one may describe this first quest as significantly influenced by secular metaphysical presuppositions.

6.2 Hermann Samuel Reimarus

Reimarus (1694–1768) is the starting point for my overview of the metaphysics of the first quest. Reimarus did not publish any work on the historical Jesus during his lifetime. In 1777, G.E. Lessing posthumously published one of Reimarus' works,[5] entitled *An Apologie, or Short Defense of, Rational Worshippers of God*, in Lessing's own *Zur Geschichte und Literatur aus den Schätzen der Wolfenbüttelschen Bibliothek* in 1774–78.[6] The *Apologie*—described recently as a 'masterpiece of early biblical criticism'[7]—was presented as *Wolfenbüttelsche Fragmente eines Unbekannten*.[8] The *Fragmente* were translated into English in 1879,[9] at which point Reimarus remained relatively unknown in the Anglophone world,[10] and the full text of the *Apologie* was published in 1972.[11]

Therein Reimarus claimed Jesus was a politically motivated figure who desired to be a king, only to be crucified instead. The disciples, either unwilling or unable to accept that Jesus had failed in his mission, stole his body and fabricated the resurrection: out of the aftermath of a failed messianic ministry, the early church was born. In Reimarus' own words, 'the new system of a suffering spiritual Saviour, which no one had ever known or thought of before, was invented *after* the death of Jesus.'[12] Or, as Birch writes, Reimarus construes 'the birth of Christianity as the deliberate miscarrying of Jesus' aims.'[13] Reimarus suggests the earliest Christians 'deliberately miscarried' Jesus' message so as to 'tread in the paths leading to influence and aggrandisement' within society.[14] Bermejo-Rubio writes that 'Reimarus' work had an impact on the scholarly world—particularly in German quarters—which was unparalleled by any previous writer tackling the historical figure of Jesus,'[15] and his influence is such that, in 2015, Per Bilde could assert that 'Reimarus's work should still be regarded as the most important contribution to modern Jesus research.'[16]

However, while Reimarus' work enjoyed considerable influence, his ideas were 'not intensely ground-breaking,'[17] and, in fact, many of his ideas—insofar as their *content* is concerned—were not well received: 'most of the details of Reimarus's thesis were quickly repudiated.'[18] Nonetheless, the methodological approach of his work had an impact of such magnitude that 'from this modest rivulet, a mighty stream has grown by stages.'[19] However, as Nathan MacDonald has noted, 'whilst Hermann Samuel Reimarus has justly received a chapter in the history of biblical criticism, he has lacked a dedicated treatment of his work and methods until recently.'[20] When one undertakes such a critical appraisal, Reimarus' claims no longer strike the reader as surprising, given the historiographical worldview within which he operates. Indeed, James Carleton Paget asserts that his work 'should not be viewed as the bolt from the blue that Schweitzer claimed it to be.'[21] Scepticism regarding the miraculous claims concerning Jesus' ministry was commonplace in post-Enlightenment Europe. The example *par excellence* can be found in section X of David Hume's 1748 treatise *An Enquiry Concerning Human Understanding*.[22] Equally, Reimarus owes evident debt to the work of the so-called 'English Deists' and the philosophical work of Christian Wolff (1679–1754).[23] Colin Brown's claim that Reimarus' approach is simply 'evocative'[24] of sources such as English Deism understates their influence upon Reimarus. Rather, there is little methodological forethought evident in Reimarus' work, he simply proceeds in a manner typical of his day.[25]

In particular, one element of his historiographical worldview deserves further attention: his treatment of the miracles of Jesus' ministry, concerning which Reimarus writes that 'it is always a sign that a doctrine or history possesses no depth of authenticity when one is obliged to resort to miracles in order to prove its truth.'[26] He here suggests that the gospel writers fabricated the miracle stories in order to add weight to their claim(s) that Jesus was the Messiah. But, Reimarus contends, since miracles are by definition infringements against natural law, they not only cannot have occurred but also subsequently cannot be used as historical evidence for assessing Jesus' life and teaching: 'contradiction is a devil and father of lies, who refuses to be driven out by fasting and prayer, or by miracles.'[27] He also applies this approach to prophetic sayings, too: 'in short, I may affirm that one cannot refer to a single quoted prophecy that is not false.'[28] This approach, as intimated above, borrows heavily from multiple sources, including the English Deists. Orr correctly summarised the Deists' position as follows:

> The antisupernaturalism of the deists led them not only to reject the miracles of the Bible but also to reject the church doctrine of the inspiration of the Bible. Having rejected these, the deists felt the necessity for supplying some plausible theory of the origin of the Books and its contents. This led to a study of the origin of the Books of the Bible, to investigations of questions of canon and authorship.[29]

This is significant because it evidences a metaphysical tendency, shared by Reimarus, not to permit religious perspectives to influence critical study of the biblical texts and the historical Jesus. As we have seen, Reimarus adopts this framework too. Baird notes, 'in all of this, Reimarus sounds like a noisy echo of the English deists.'[30] This approach (in both Reimarus' and the Deists' thought) to miracles and prophecy are important, insofar as it evidences a metaphysical tendency in Reimarus' work to refuse religious perspectives the opportunity to contribute to his reconstruction of the historical Jesus. These phenomena are dismissed without critical engagement because they are offhandedly assumed to be impossible, his metaphysical framework not allowing for these phenomena to take place.

All this is to say that Reimarus operates from within a secular metaphysical framework that rejected divine agency as a methodological problem for his historical enquiry, and equally denied that a faith-informed perspective might serve as a starting point for his work. Reimarus was among the first to synthesise these thoughts and place them into the wider holistic context of Jesus' life and teaching and, in doing so, he offered a (literally and deliberately) un-orthodox narrative regarding Jesus' ministry. Reimarus employs a historiographical worldview that displays evidence of the secular metaphysical presupposition that refuses religious metaphysics the possibility of contributing to historiography; he is an 'enlightenment radical in disguise,' as one biographer puts it.[31]

6.3 David Friedrich Strauss

One of the most important figures to emerge in the period following Reimarus was David Friedrich Strauss (1808–74). His 1835 monograph *The Life of Jesus Critically Examined* is a landmark publication in historical Jesus research,[32] which had a profound effect among protestant and catholic thinkers alike[33] with Strauss himself declaring it an 'inspired book.'[34] Elsewhere Kümmel calls it a work of 'epoch-making significance,'[35] while Baird describes its publication as 'a theological bombshell.'[36] Although Strauss stood in the same rationalist tradition as Reimarus, he believed such approaches had stripped the gospels of their religious potency. Strauss' contribution to the quest was twofold. First, he wrote one of the first exhaustive treatments of Reimarus' *Apologie* in 1862.[37] Second, he claimed the gospels were mythical re-tellings of the origins of the Jesus movement, a claim that Backhaus argues was 'an important step forward in historical insight.'[38] History and myth had become so intertwined as to be inseparable: one could not distinguish between the historical Jesus and the later mythologies applied to him.[39]

Yet for Strauss the significance of the gospels was to be located precisely in this mythological dimension of their accounts. As Kümmel notes, 'Strauss at every point ... plays off rationalist over against conservative interpretation ... only to show that both interpretations are untenable and to put the "mythical" in their stead.'[40] A side effect of Strauss' mythical reading of the gospels was its impact upon the use of John's gospel among scholars.[41] Strauss labelled the Fourth Gospel as mythic in content, even more so than the synoptics, 'mark[ing] the beginning of the devaluation of the historical value of John's gospel.'[42] Coupled with advancements that would soon be made regarding the synoptic problem,[43] this led to John falling out of use as a viable source for knowing about the historical Jesus. Indeed, one of Schweitzer's main criticisms of psychiatric analyses of the historical Jesus was their historical reliance upon John's gospel.[44]

Upon the publication of *The Life of Jesus*, Carl August von Eschenmayer, professor of philosophy at Tübingen, described it as 'the Iscariotism of our days,' and 'the offspring of the legitimate marriage between theological ignorance and religious tolerance, blessed by a sleep-walking philosophy.'[45] The Earl of Shaftesbury described it as 'the most pestilential book ever vomited out of jaws of hell.'[46] The controversy marked the end of Strauss' academic career: Eschenmayer ensured that his view of Strauss' work became 'accepted officially by the president of the regional Evangelische Verein (Lutheran Synod) as the official church view of the book.'[47] He was dismissed from Tübingen in 1835 and, although appointed to chair of Theology at the University of Zürich in 1839, the furore meant the institution pensioned him off before he began his post.[48]

One may glimpse the worldview within which Strauss operates in his critique of Schleiermacher's[49] work *The Life of Jesus* in his own study *The Christ of Faith and the Jesus of History*.[50] For Strauss, 'whoever undertakes to write the life of a person finds, as a rule, a widespread conception of this person which he himself also more or less shares.'[51] This is described by Strauss as a 'prejudice,' and he suggests it is the role of the historian to correct prejudices about the past through their work. Regarding Jesus, Strauss claimed 'in the common conception of Christendom, Jesus is taken to be the God-man, a being—in spite of his human appearance—different from all other men.'[52] This is the prejudiced starting position regarding Jesus and, therefore, it is the claim which historians must seek to correct by close analysis of the sources.

However, even if an accurate reading of the sources results in the same conception of Jesus, then 'the sources would show themselves as transmitting not the pure facts but only a later conception.'[53] This is a key point in understanding Strauss' historiographical worldview because he contends that it is not possible to historically reconstruct the life of Jesus in a manner concurrent with Christian orthodoxy; even if proper historical criticism results in such a reconstruction, the sources themselves are prejudiced.[54] Strauss contends from the beginning that historical rigour will always stand opposed to Christian orthodoxy. This is because, for Strauss, history is a closed system of cause and effect, with which no external divinity—*even if* there is such a thing—may interfere. Strauss writes that, from this point of view 'at which nature and history appear as a compact tissue of finite causes and effects, it was impossible to regard the narratives of the Bible, in which this tissue is broken by innumerable instances of divine interference, as historical.'[55] As Kaye notes, here Strauss articulates 'a fundamentally deist world-view stated with the utmost clarity.'[56]

This rejection of religious metaphysical presuppositions is apparent elsewhere in Strauss' writings. In *The Life of Jesus Critically Examined*, Strauss describes Christian faith as a 'prejudice,' whereas properly conducted historiography ought to be presuppositionless: 'if theologians regard this absence of presupposition from his [i.e., Strauss'] work as un-Christian, he regards the believing presuppositions of theirs as unscientific.'[57] Not only is scientific (i.e., non-faith-based) historiography assumed to be value-neutral as far as metaphysical presuppositions are concerned, Strauss also explicitly refutes the possibility that religious perspectives might contribute to historiography. As such, scientific historiography is to assume primacy over faith-perspectives within the academy, such that even a diluted or compromised faith is still not to be afforded an opportunity to contribute:

> Now if, in the renunciation of a personal divine element in Christ, faith allows itself to be 'tuned' to science, the latter still cannot somehow avoid making

> a concession to faith. In this case, science should be on its guard lest it is cheated, the way secular authorities commonly are cheated in compacts with religious authorities.[58]

This final sentence is especially illuminating concerning Strauss' historiographical worldview. He explicitly seeks to compare faith-less, scientific historiography with secular authorities, in direct opposition to religious authorities and perspectives. That academic historiography should resist religious perspectives, in Strauss' view, is made equally apparent in his damning indictment of Schleiermacher's reconstruction of the historical Jesus:

> If previous theologians were like the companions of Ulysses who stopped their ears against the Sirens of criticism, then Schleiermacher indeed kept his ears open, but had himself tied with cables to the mast of the Christian faith in order to sail past the dangerous island unharmed. His conduct is only half-free, therefore also only half-scientific. The truly scientific conduct is to engage in criticism unfettered and with open ears.[59]

Like Reimarus before him, in this respect Strauss clearly repeats the secular presuppositions of his Deist forebears. Following Reimarus and Strauss, however, were two thinkers whose work have enjoyed lasting influence upon historical Jesus research as a result of their critique of the discipline itself: Kähler and Troeltsch.

6.4 Martin Kähler

Martin Kähler (1835–1912) was a German theologian most famous for his work *The So-Called Historical Jesus and the Historical, Biblical Christ* (at least, among biblical scholars),[60] a work which had a profound effect upon Tillich, among others.[61] The gospels, Kähler suggests, are of limited use for reconstructing the life of the historical Jesus. Although Kähler did not disregard the 'Quest' altogether,[62] he was sceptical of the results it could achieve. Jesus, being truly man and truly God, was unlike anyone else who has ever lived. Historians, therefore, are without analogy for Jesus' life, and so cannot comprehend him in a purely historical mode.[63] Instead, one finds the value of Jesus' life 'in the church that has been going throughout the centuries, in the confessing word and life of the brothers, in one's own powerful faith, which he has gained from Him.'[64]

What is important for Kähler is not historical facts about Jesus' life or even his teaching, but actual experience of Christ himself. In this manner, one might view Kähler as a precursor to the Bultmannian and Barthian focus on the *kerygmatic* readings of the New Testament, paving the way for the historical Jesus to be left at the wayside. Kähler's assertion that it is impossible to get 'behind' the texts to Jesus himself has still not been answered, with modern historical Jesus research finding itself 'in a sort of stalemate' ever since.[65] When he inaugurated the 'new quest' in 1953, Käsemann claimed Kähler's argument 'after sixty years, is hardly dated and, in spite of many attacks and many possible reservations, has never really been refuted.'[66]

But this influential distancing of the historical Jesus and the Christ of faith only entrenches secular metaphysical presuppositions about the nature of historiography. Kähler's observation that the historical Jesus and the 'real' Jesus are incompatible stems from a recognition of the incompatibility of the methods that lie behind the apprehension of each of these figures. The two are not the same because, while the historical Jesus is constructed from a pursuit of Enlightenment rationality, pursuit of the real Jesus takes place in the community of the church (as noted in the above quotation). It is not necessarily accurate to describe Kähler's scholarship *per se* as 'secular,' insofar as he is concerned with making claims about a Jesus who is fully human and fully divine, in whom the second person of the trinity dwells bodily. However, his conception of *historical Jesus research* conceives of it as a secular discipline that cannot speak to these concerns. In this manner, one may suggest Kähler perpetuates the secular framework for historical Jesus research, in contrasting the Jesus of history and the Christ of faith.

6.5 Ernst Troeltsch

Alongside Kähler, the very possibility of historical Jesus research was also questioned by Ernst Troeltsch (1865–1923). Deines notes, 'although not a biblical scholar himself, the influence of the historian, philosopher, and theologian Ernst Troeltsch on New Testament scholarship can hardly be overstated.'[67] Troeltsch's most famous contribution to the field is his 1898 essay 'On Historical and Dogmatic method in Theology,'[68] written in response to Friedrich Niebergall, who assigned Troeltsch the label of historical relativist.[69] Troeltsch himself, however, was equally wary of such relativism: later, Troeltsch came to view historicism as 'the chief factor in precipitating the great cultural crisis of the time by relativizing all values and denying all shape to history.'[70] In addition, both men were adamant that Christianity was the highest form of religion.[71] Where they disagreed, however, was in Troeltsch's assertion that one could not appeal to history to support Christianity's superiority. Echoing Kähler's dichotomy between the Jesus of history and the Christ of faith, Troeltsch thought theologians must choose between historical and dogmatic approaches to theological reflection.

There can be no middle ground between the two approaches, and no way to integrate them either. If one begins from a historical starting point, one must explain everything in historical terms; if one begins from a dogmatic starting point, one must explain everything in dogmatic terms. As with the claims of Kähler, Troeltsch's work builds upon a secular metaphysical conception of historiography, such that religious metaphysics cannot contribute to historical reconstruction. The divide between historical and dogmatic scholarship in Kähler is thus realised in its most thoroughgoing form in Troeltsch who posits historiography and faith as two totalising epistemological categories who cannot engage with one another.

Martin Kähler and Ernst Troeltsch introduced a dichotomy that questioned the very possibility of historical Jesus research and stifled the optimistic and positivist historical studies that had preceded them: a dichotomy between the Jesus of history and the Christ of faith; between historicism and dogmatism. This dichotomy serves as the context to Albert Schweitzer, the man who brought the first quest to an end.

6.6 Albert Schweitzer

Albert Schweitzer (1875–1965) is known for many things outside of theology and biblical studies: his campaigns against nuclear weapons, his musical scholarship, and his complicated relationship with Africa,[72] to name but a few. Within historical Jesus research, however, he commands 'fabulous authority'[73] and is known for his 1906 work, *Von Reimarus zu Wrede: eine Geschichte der Leben-Jesu-Forschung*.[74] As Thate writes, 'Schweitzer's writings on Jesus rank among the most influential and well-known texts within biblical scholarship,' although he is also right to warn that 'their familiarity has bred a peculiar ignorance.'[75]

Regarding Schweitzer's historiographical worldview, one may again observe a metaphysical framework that denies religious perspectives the opportunity to inform his historical programme. His approach to historiography is taken largely from Strauss' *Life of Jesus*, about which he writes:

> Strauss' first Life of Jesus is one of the most perfect things in the whole range of learned literature. In over fourteen hundred pages he has not a superfluous phrase; his analysis descends to the minutest details but he does not lose his way among them; the style is simple and picturesque, sometimes ironical, but always dignified and distinguished.[76]

Strauss was right, he argues, to pursue myth as central to questions of the historical Jesus, if one is to avoid repeating unhistorical elements of Jesus' life fabricated by the early church: 'no sooner is a great man dead than legend is busy with his life.'[77] Rather than preserving the truth about the historical Jesus, 'what was operative [within the early church] was a creative reminiscence.'[78] Thus, like Strauss, Schweitzer suggests those elements of the gospel narratives that cohere with the orthodox Christian view of Jesus are unhistorical, a product of the church itself.[79]

Like Weiss before him,[80] Schweitzer emphasised the eschatological dimension of Jesus' teaching, only more so. Jesus expected that God would bring about the end of history through a figure known as the Son of Man and realised that he himself must become this Son of Man by suffering a violent death, in accordance with the image of the suffering servant of Isaiah 53. Jesus therefore willingly went to the cross, hoping it would force God to bring about the eschaton. Of course, his predictions did not come to pass. Schweitzer asserted that when the eschatological dimension of Jesus' ministry was reconstructed in this way, the historical Jesus became elusive. Instead, building upon the mythological element of

Strauss' work, Schweitzer stressed 'the absolute indifference of early Christianity towards the life of the historical Jesus.'[81] Indeed, the Christian faith in its present form equally has no need for the historical Jesus: Baird notes that 'according to Schweitzer, faith does not rest on the result of historical research.'[82]

He instead located the religious significance in the timeless, 'spiritual' Jesus (over against his historical counterpart). His famous concluding remarks are indicative of this 'spiritual' conception of Jesus:

> He comes to us as One unknown, without a name, as of old, by the lake-side, He came to those men who knew Him not. He speaks to us the same word: 'Follow thou me!' and sets us to the tasks which He has to fulfil for our time. He commands. And to those who obey Him, whether they be wise or simple, He will reveal Himself in the toils, the conflicts, the sufferings which they shall pass through in His fellowship, and, as an ineffable mystery, they shall learn in their own experience Who He is.[83]

Comments such as these are ever more present in Schweitzer's second edition, which contained 'tentative moves towards a demythologized eschatology and [a] call for a kind of existential engagement with Jesus' will.'[84] To continue the dichotomy first established by Kähler, it is the Christ of faith who holds religious significance. Schweitzer is thus the culmination of what preceded him, and his faith is thus 'a Christian faith owing so much to the Enlightenment and Kant.'[85]

Regarding his historiographical worldview, one may again observe the influence of secular metaphysics in his method. He begins *The Quest of the Historical Jesus* by claiming that 'the greatest achievement of German theology is the critical investigation of the life of Jesus,' because it is 'of higher intrinsic value than the history of the study of ancient dogma or of the attempts to create a new one.'[86] Indeed, for Schweitzer, the quest was inaugurated to counteract unfettered religious speculation about the person of Jesus in the first place, noting:

> The historical investigation of the life of Jesus did not take its rise from a purely historical interest; it turned to the Jesus of history as an ally in the struggle against the tyranny of dogma. Afterwards when it was freed from this πάθος it sought to present the historic Jesus in a form intelligible to its own time.[87]

Over against the thoroughgoing scepticism of Wrede, Schweitzer instead offered a thoroughgoing eschatology and notes that 'in the critical basis of these two schools … there has entered into the domain of the theology of the day a force with which it cannot possible ally itself. Its whole territory is threatened.'[88] This 'critical basis'—the scientific approach to history—makes notions of the historical Jesus problematic for Christians today.

Thus, the pursuit of the historical Jesus in these terms can be of no use for Christian theology, since the metaphysical framework within which one must operate when conducting history, itself stands apart from Christian theology.

Faith cannot speak to matters of history, and history cannot speak to matters of faith. For example, he notes, 'that the historic Jesus is something different from the Jesus Christ of the doctrine of the Two Natures seems to us now self-evident.'[89] This is why, for Schweitzer, the historical Jesus can possess no religious significance for us in the present:

> Primitive Christianity was therefore right to live wholly in the future with the Christ who was to come, and to preserve of the historic Jesus only detached sayings, a few miracles, His death and resurrection. By abolishing both the world and the historical Jesus it escaped the inner division described above [between scientific study and faith] and remained consistent in its point of view.[90]

In terms of his method, at least, Schweitzer stands in congruity with the like of Reimarus and Strauss before him in refusing to allow religious metaphysical commitments to contribute to his reconstruction of the life of the historical Jesus. Furthermore, like Kähler and Troeltsch, Schweitzer's criticism of the quest for the historical Jesus is enmeshed with his sharp distinction between the Jesus of history and the Christ of faith. Like these scholars, Schweitzer conceives of the quest as a scientific discipline with which religious perspectives may not engage, while simultaneously conceiving of theological reflection about the person of Jesus as an enterprise within which the theologian may not borrow from the quest, due to its competing metaphysical presuppositions.

6.7 Conclusion

In this chapter, I have argued that key indicative figures in the first 'Quest' for the historical Jesus evidence the same tendency of refusing to allow religious metaphysical presuppositions to contribute to their historical task. This is reinforced by the work of Kähler and Troeltsch who propose a sharp distinction between the Jesus of history and the Christ of faith (so Kähler), and between historical and dogmatic scholarship (so Troeltsch). In both instances there is an (explicit) acceptance that proper historical reconstruction of the life of Jesus will result in one markedly different from that found in orthodox Christian theology, due to their (implicit) conception of history (i.e., history the academic discipline rather than history as the past itself) as something with which religious metaphysical presuppositions may not engage. This divide between the Jesus of history and Christ of faith is only so stark because the historical enterprise is perceived to rest upon a secular metaphysics estranged from orthodox Christian metaphysics.[91] From the very outset of the 'Quest's' inauguration, notions of historiography were enmeshed with secular metaphysical claims about history and divine agency. Throughout this first instantiation of the Quest, we may observe a tendency for historians to suppress the religious elements in their historiographical worldview(s) so their reconstruction might cohere with post-Enlightenment secular metaphysical conceptions concerning historiography.

Notes

1 James Carleton Paget, 'Quests for the Historical Jesus', in *The Cambridge Companion to Jesus*, ed. Markus Bockmuehl (Cambridge: CUP, 2001), 138–55 (139).
2 Jonathan C.P. Birch, 'Revolutionary Contexts for the Quest: Jesus in the Rhetoric and Methods of Early Modern Intellectual History', *JSHJ* 17.1–2 (2019), 35–80 (36).
3 Walter P. Weaver, *The Historical Jesus in the Twentieth Century 1900–1950* (Harrisburg, PA: Trinity International, 1999); Stanley E. Porter, *The Criteria for Authenticity in Historical-Jesus Research* (Sheffield: Sheffield Academic, 2000), 28–62; Graham N. Stanton, *The Gospels and Jesus*, 2nd ed. (Oxford: Oxford University, 2002), 165; Fernando Bermejo-Rubio, 'Historiografía, exégesis e ideología. La ficción contemporánea de las "tres búsquedas" del Jesús histórico (I)', *Revista Catalana de Teología* 30.2 (2005), 349–406; idem, 'Historiografía, exégesis e ideología. La ficción contemporánea de las "tres búsquedas" del Jesús histórico (II)', *Revista Catalana de Teología* 31.1 (2006), 53–114; idem, 'The Fiction of the "Three Quests": An Argument for Dismantling a Dubious Historiographical Paradigm', *JSHJ* 7.3 (2009), 211–53; idem, 'Theses on the Nature of the *Leben-Jesu-Forschung*: A Proposal for a Paradigm Shift in Understanding the Quest', *JSHJ* 17.1–2 (2019), 1–34 (esp. 9–11).
4 Helen Bond, *The Historical Jesus: A Guide for the Perplexed* (London: Bloomsbury, 2012), 7.
5 As Baird notes, this posthumous publication by Lessing does not mean that Lessing wholeheartedly agreed with Reimarus' work: there were significant departures in thought between the two. See the discussion in Baird, *HNTR*, I:172–3.
6 The *Fragmente* is available in volumes 8 and 9 of *Gotthold Ephraim Lessing Werke und Briefe*, ed. Wilfred Barner and others, Bibliothek Deutscher Klassiker, 12 vols (Frankfurt am Main: Deutscher Klassiker, 1989).
7 Robert Morgan, 'Reimarus, Schweitzer, and Modern Theology', *ExpTim* 129.6 (2018), 254–64 (254).
8 The original title (*Wolfenbüttelsche Fragmente eines Unbekannten*) is occasionally translated so as to refer to an 'unknown' writer, but the sense of the German 'unbekannten' here means 'anonymous' (i.e., 'known', but not wilfully communicated).
9 G.E. Lessing, *Fragments from Reimarus Consisting of Brief Critical Remarks on the Object of Jesus and His Disciples as Seen in the New Testament*, ed. & trans. Charles Voysey (London: Williams and Nogate, 1879).
10 In the preface, editor and translator Charles Voysey notes that "the name of Reimarus is scarcely known in this country beyond a very select circle of English students, while his writings, so far as I know, have never been popularly known, nor frequently quoted by English commentators." See, Lessing, *Fragments*, iii.
11 *Apologie oder Schutzschrift für die vernünftigen Verehrer Gottes / Hermann Samuel Reimarus*, ed. Gerhard Alexander, 2 Bänden (Hamburg: Insel, 1972).
12 Reimarus, *Fragments*, 28.
13 Birch, 'Revolutionary Contexts', 36.
14 Reimarus, *Fragments*, 92.
15 Bermejo-Rubio, 'Theses', 23.
16 Per Bilde, 'Can It Be Justified to Talk about Scholarly Progress in the History of Modern Jesus Research since Reimarus?', in *The Mission of Jesus: Second Nordic Symposium on the Historical Jesus, Lund, 7–10 October 2012*, ed. Samuel Byrskog and Tobias Hägerland, WUNT II.391 (Tübingen: Mohr Siebeck, 2015), 5–24 (23).
17 Ernst Baasland, 'Forth Quest? What Did Jesus Really Want?', in *HSHJ,* I:31–56 (32).
18 John S. Kloppenborg, 'Sources, Methods and Discursive Locations in the Quest of the Historical Jesus', in *HSHJ,* I:241–90 (242).
19 Jürgen Becker, 'The Search for Jesus' Special Profile', in *HSHJ,* I:57–89 (57).
20 Nathan MacDonald, 'Review: *Hermann Samuel Reimarus (1694–1768): Classicist, Hebraist, Enlightenment Radical in Disguise*. By Ulrich Groetsch', *JTS* 68.1 (2017),

412–13. In addition to Groetsch's work (reviewed by MacDonald) we might also note the work of Dietrich Klein, *Hermann Samuel Reimarus (1694–1768): Das theologische Werk*, Beiträge zur historischen Theologie 145 (Tübingen: Mohr Siebeck, 2009).

21 Carleton Paget, 'Quests', 141.

22 David Hume, *Of Miracles* (La Salle, IL: Open Court, 1985).

23 Bermejo-Rubio, '*Leben-Jesu-Forschung*', goes as far as to suggest the quest, when properly contextualised, begins with the English Deists, not Reimarus himself (12–13). He does, however, later note that Reimarus' work signifies an important "turning point in the history of research" (22). Similarly, Charlesworth writes that "Schweitzer attributed the origin of the 'Old Quest' to Reimarus (1694–1768) but surely the English Deists are the real precursors of critical Jesus study." James H. Charlesworth, 'The Historical Jesus: How to Ask Questions and Remain Inquisitive', in *HSHJ*, I:91–128. Likewise, in the same publication Hagner notes that Reimarus' approach to miracles and prophecy was "anticipated by the English Deists." See Donald A. Hagner, 'The Jesus Quest and Jewish-Christian Relations', in *HSHJ,* II:1055–77 (1056). The impact of the English Deists on New Testament studies broadly construed (including historical Jesus research and the work of Reimarus) is recounted in Baird, *HNTR*, I:31–57; Kümmel, *NTHIP*, 51–61.

24 Colin Brown, 'The Quest of the Unhistorical Jesus and the Quest of the Historical Jesus', in *HSHJ,* II.855–86 (862).

25 A very helpful overview of Reimarus' influence and the intellectual milieu in which he writes can be found in Jonathan Israel, 'The Philosophical Context of Hermann Samuel Reimarus' Radical Bible Criticism', in *Between Philology and Radical Enlightenment: Herman Samuel Reimarus (1694–1768)*, ed. Martin Mulsow, Brill's Studies in Intellectual History, 203 (Leiden: Brill, 2011), 183–200; Jonathan C.P. Birch, 'Reimarus and the Religious Enlightenment: His Apologetic Project', *ExpTim* 129.6 (2018), 245–53. Another helpful treatment of the issue can be found in the first three chapters of Colin Brown, *Jesus in European Protestant Thought, 1778–1860* (Grand Rapids, MI: Baker Academic, 1988).

26 Reimarus, *Fragments*, 74–5.

27 Ibid., 76.

28 Ibid., 78.

29 James Orr, *English Deism: Its Roots and Its Fruits* (Grand Rapids, MI: Eerdmans, 1934), 246.

30 Baird, *HNTR*, I:172.

31 Note the subtitle of Ulrich Groetsch, *Hermann Samuel Reimarus (1694–1768): Classicist, Hebraist, Enlightenment Radical in Disguise*, Brill's Studies in Intellectual History 237 (Leiden: Brill, 2015). Morgan ('Reimarus, Schweitzer, and Modern Theology', 254) similarly describes him as "an outstanding Enlightenment scholar."

32 D.F. Strauss, *Das Leben Jesu, kritisch bearbeitet*, 2 vols (Tübingen: C. F. Osiander, 1835–36); ET: idem, *The Life of Jesus: Critically Examined*, 2 vols (London: Chapman, 1846).

33 The Catholic reception of Strauss (still under-evaluated in some corners of scholarship) has been most helpfully charted by Madges. See William Madges, *The Core of Christian Faith: D. F. Strauss and His Catholic Critics*, Theology and Religion 38 (Paris: Peter Lang, 1987); idem, 'D. F. Strauss in Retrospect: His Reception among Roman Catholics', *HeyJ* 30.3 (1989), 273–92. Contrary to notions that Strauss' *Life of Jesus* had little impact amongst Catholic scholarship, Madges notes that "it evoked considerable attention among Strauss's Catholic contemporaries," and "the Catholic response to Strauss's book included four book-length critiques and eight article in the decade immediately following its publication" (Madges, 'D. F. Strauss in Retrospect', 274).

34 Cited in Edwina G. Lawler, *David Friedrich Strauss and His Critics: The Life of Jesus Debate in Early Nineteenth-Century German Journals* (New York: Peter Lang, 1986), 18.

35 Kümmel, *NTHIP*, 121.
36 Baird, *HNTR*, I:246.
37 D.F. Strauss, *Herman Samuel Reimarus und seine Schutzschrift für die vernünftigen Verehrer Gottes* (Leipzig: Brodhauß, 1862).
38 Knut Backhaus, 'Echoes from the Wilderness: The Historical John the Baptist', in *HSHJ,* II, 1747–85 (1748).
39 See the discussions in Raymond E. Brown, *An Introduction to the New Testament* (New York: Doubleday, 1996), 818; James D.G. Dunn, *Jesus Remembered*, Christianity in the Making, 1 (Grand Rapids, MI: Eerdmans, 2003), 29–34; Edwin K. Broadhead, 'Implicit Christology and the Historical Jesus', in *HSHJ,* II:1169–82 (1169–71).
40 Kümmel, *NTHIP*, 121.
41 See James H. Charlesworth, 'The Historical Jesus in the Fourth Gospel: A Paradigm Shift', *JSHJ* 8.1 (2010), 3–46; Matti Kankaanniemi, 'Mission as Reaction: Exhausted Jesus at the Well of Sychar', in *The Mission of Jesus: Second Nordic Symposium on the Historical Jesus, Lund, 7–10 October 2012*, ed. Samuel Byrskog and Tobias Hägerland, WUNT II 391 (Tübingen: Mohr Siebeck, 2015), 164–67. Kümmel writes "Strauss' judgement on the Fourth Gospel had possibly a still more revolutionary effect than his radical criticism" (*NTHIP*, 124).
42 James D.G. Dunn, 'Remembering Jesus: How the Quest of the Historical Jesus Lost Its Way', in *HSHJ*, I:183–205 (184).
43 I do not deal in depth with these advancements here, since they did not alter the metaphysical presuppositions of the quest. Suffice it to say, the dominant paradigm was that advanced in Johann Jakob Griesbach, *Commentatio qua Marci Evangelium Totum e Matthaei et Lucae Commentariis Decerptum Esse Monstratur* (Jena: Officina Stranckmannio-Fickelscherria, 1790), but pre-empted by Henry Owen, *Observations on the Four Gospels; Tending Chiefly to Ascertain the Time of Their Publication, and to Illustrate the Form and Manner of Their Composition* (London: Payne, 1764) and the anonymous author of 'Von Interpolationen im Evangelium Matthaei', in *Repertorium für biblische und morgenlandische Literature 9*, ed. J.G. Eichhorn (Leipzig: Weidmann, 1781) (Stroth is identified as the author of this document in J.G. Eichhorn, *Einleitung in das Neue Testament*, 2nd ed. (Leipzig: Weidmann, 1820), 1.465 n.1). Between the time of Strauss and Kähler the two-source hypothesis has been proposed (by Weisse) and popularised (by Holtzmann). See, Christian Hermann Weisse, *Die evangelische Geschichte, kritisch und philosophisch bearbeitet* (Leipzig: Breitkopf und Hartel, 1838); Heinrich Julius Holtzmann, *Die synoptischen Evangelien: ihr Ursprung und geschichtlicher Charakter* (Leipzig: Wilhelm Engelmann, 1863).
44 See Schweitzer's MD thesis: Albert Schweitzer, *Die psychiatrische Beurteilung Jesu. Darstellung und Kritik* (Tübingen: J. C. B. Mohr, 1913); ET: *The Psychiatric Study of Jesus: Exposition and Criticism*, trans. Charles R. Joy (Boston, MA: Beacon, 1948).
45 Carl A. Eschenmayer, *Der Ischariotismus unserer Tage: Eine Zugabe zu dem Werke: Das Leben Jesu von Strauß* (Tübingen: Fues, 1835).
46 See Gregory W. Dawes, *The Historical Jesus Question: The Challenge of History to Religious Authority* (Louisville, KY: Westminster John Knox Press, 2001), 77–9.
47 Bruce N. Kaye, 'D. F. Strauss and the European Theological Tradition: "Der Ischariotismus Unsere Tag"?', *The Journal of Religious History* 17.2 (1992), 172–93 (172).
48 Information on this period of Strauss' life is scarce. See, however, Douglas R. McGaughey, 'On D.F. Strauß and the 1839 Revolution in Zurich', http://www.chora-strangers.org/files/chora/mcgaughey_1994.pdf (blog), accessed 30 June 2018.
49 Baird details the difficult relationship between Strauss and Schleiermacher that provides the context for this work: Strauss moved to Berlin in 1831 to study under his idol, Hegel, which upset Schleiermacher, Hegel's colleague. See the overview in Baird, *HNTR*, I:247. Although Strauss stayed in Berlin after Hegel's death and attended

Schleiermacher's lectures on Jesus, he later admitted "the truth is I found myself repelled by almost every aspect of these lectures" (D.F. Strauss, *In Defense of My Life of Jesus against the Hegelians*, trans. Marilyn Chapin Massey (Hamden, CT: Archon, 1983), 6).

50 D.F. Strauss, *The Christ of Faith and the Jesus of History: A Critique of Schleiermacher's* Life of Jesus, trans. Leander E. Keck, Lives of Jesus Series (Philadelphia, PA: Fortress, 1977). Cf., Friedrich Schleiermacher, *The Life of Jesus*, trans. S. MacLean Gilmour, Lives of Jesus Series (Philadelphia, PA: Fortress, 1975).

51 Strauss, *The Christ of Faith*, 19.

52 Ibid., 19

53 Ibid., 20.

54 On this point in particular, see also the discussion in Kaye, 'D. F. Strauss', 180–4.

55 Strauss, *Life of Jesus*, 78.

56 Kaye, 'D. F. Strauss', 184. See also the discussion in Madges, 'D. F. Strauss in Retrospect,' 276–8.

57 These comments are found in the preface to the first German edition of the text. See idem, *Das Leben Jesu*, lii.

58 Strauss, *The Christ of Faith*, 25.

59 Ibid., 36–7.

60 The German text is available as Martin Kähler, *Der sogenannte historische Jesus und der geschichtliche biblische Christus* (Munich: Kaiser, 1892); ET: idem, *The So-Called Historical Jesus and the Historical Biblical Christ*, ed. & trans. Carl E. Braaten (Philadelphia, PA: Fortress, 1964). In what follows I translate from the most recent German reprint: Martin Kähler, *Der sogenannte historische Jesus und der geschichtliche biblische Christus* (Berlin: Berlin University, 2013).

61 See the comments in *The Cambridge Companion to Paul Tillich*, ed. Russell Re Manning (Cambridge: CUP, 2009), xix. See also the helpful comments on Kähler's work and legacy in Deines, *Acts of God*, 105–12. Also helpful here is Dunn, 'Remembering Jesus', I:189–90.

62 See the article on his later apologetic work, Karl-Wilhelm Niebuhr, 'Welchen Jesus predigen wir? Überlegungen im Anschluss an Martin Kähler', *Sacra Scripta* 10.2 (2011), 123–42.

63 Kähler, *Der sogenannte historische Jesus*, 25–6.

64 Ibid., 56.

65 Bilde, 'Scholarly Progress?', 5.

66 Ernst Käsemann, *Essays on New Testament Themes* (London: SCM, 1964), 16.

67 Deines, *Acts of God*, 10.

68 The essay first appeared as 'Über historische und dogmatische Methode in der Theologie,' in response to Friedrich Niebergall, 'Über Die Absolutheit Des Christentums', *Studien Der Rheinischen Predigervereins*, 4 (1898). The text of the original can be found in *Ernst Troeltsch Lesebuch: Ausgewählte Texte*, ed. Friedemann Voigt, UTB, 2452 (Tübingen: Mohr Siebeck, 2003), 2–25; Ernst Troeltsch, 'Historical and Dogmatic Method in Theology', in *Religion in History*, ed. J.L. Adams and W.F. Bense (Minneapolis, MN: Fortress Press, 1991), 11–32; Dawes, 29–53; Ernst Troeltsch, *Zur Religiösen Lage, Religionsphilosophie Und Ethik*, Gesammelte Schriften, II, 2nd ed. (Tübingen: Mohr Siebeck, 1922), 729–53.

69 This is to simplify Troeltsch's motivations somewhat. See Hans-Georg Drescher, *Ernst Troeltsch: Leben und Werk* (Göttingen: Vandenhoeck & Ruprecht, 1991), 160–6.

70 Judith Wolfe, 'The Eschatological Turn in German Philosophy', *Modern Theology* 35.1 (2019), 55–70 (60). Cf., Ernst Troeltsch, 'Die Krisis des Historismus', *Die neue Rundschau* 33.1 (1922), 572–90; idem, *Der Historismus und seine Probleme* (Tübingen: Mohr Siebeck, 1922).

71 C.f., Ernst Troeltsch, *Die Absolutheit des Christentums und die Religionsgeschichte: Vortrag gehalten auf der Versammlund der Freunde der Christlichen Welt zu Mühlacker*

am 3. Oktober 1901 (Tübingen: J. C. B. Mohr (Paul Siebeck), 1902). The English translation of this text is based upon the later 3rd edition from 1929. See Ernst Troeltsch, *The Absoluteness of Christianity and the History of Religions*, trans. David Reid (London: SCM, 1971).

72 The scholarly understanding of Schweitzer's relationship with Africa is currently undergoing revision following the publication of James Carleton Paget, 'Albert Schweitzer and Africa', *Journal of Religion in Africa* 42.3 (2012), 277–316, and Ruth Harris, 'Schweitzer and Africa', *The Historical Journal* 59.4 (2016), 1107–32. The former has published extensively on all aspects of Schweitzer's life. See James Carleton Paget, 'Theologians in Context: Albert Schweitzer', *Journal of Ecclesiastical History* 62.1 (2011), 116–31; idem, 'Albert Schweitzer and Adolf von Harnack: An Unlikely Alliance', *Zeitschrift für Kirchengeschichte* 122.2–3 (2011), 257–87; idem, 'Schweitzer and Paul', *JSNT* 33.3 (2011), 223–56; idem, 'Albert Schweitzer and the Jews', *HTR* 107.3 (2014), 363–98.

73 Anthony Giambrone, 'Schweitzer, Lagrange, and the German Roots of Historical Jesus Research', *JSHJ* 17.1–2 (2019), 121–44 (123).

74 Albert Schweitzer, *Von Reimarus zu Wrede: eine Geschichte der Leben-Jesu-Forschung* (Tübingen: J. C. B. Mohr, 1906). ET: *The Quest of the Historical Jesus*, trans. W. Montgomery (Mineola, NY: Dover, 2005).

75 Michael J. Thate, *Remembrance of Things Past? Albert Schweitzer, the Anxiety of Influence, and the Untidy Jesus of Markan Memory*, WUNT II, 351 (Tübingen: Mohr Siebeck, 2013), 6.

76 Schweitzer, *The Quest*, 78. Elsewhere notes that "the critical study of the life of Jesus … falls, immediately, into two periods: that before Strauss and that after Strauss" (ibid., 10).

77 Ibid., 79.

78 Ibid., 80.

79 See, as just one example of this sensibility of Sweitzer's approach, his reconstruction of the relationship between Jesus and John the Baptist: ibid., 81–2.

80 Johannes Weiss, *Die Predigt Jesu vom Reiche Gottes* (Göttingen: Vandenhoeck & Ruprecht, 1892).

81 Ibid., 2.

82 Baird, *HNTR*, II:234. See, further, David Dungan, 'Albert Schweitzer's Disillusionment with the Historical Reconstruction of the Life of Jesus', *Perkins (School of Theology) Journal* 29.1 (1976), 27–48.

83 Ibid., 401.

84 James Carleton Paget, 'Albert Schweitzer's Second Edition of *The Quest of the Historical Jesus*', *Bulletin of the John Rylands Library* 88.1 (2006), 3–39 (39).

85 Robert Morgan, 'Reimarus, Schweitzer, and Modern Theology', *ExpTim* 129.6 (2018), 254–64 (264).

86 Schweitzer, *The Quest*, 1, 2.

87 Ibid., 4.

88 Ibid., 329.

89 Ibid., 3–4.

90 Ibid., 3.

91 I distinguish here between secular metaphysics and *orthodox* Christian metaphysics because, as we shall see in Chapter 10, the likes of John Milbank and Charles Taylor have convincingly argued that secular metaphysics might accurately be reconceived of a *heterodox* Christian metaphysics.

7 Metaphysics and the Second 'Quest'

7.1 Introduction

Following Schweitzer's critique of the Victorian 'lives' of Jesus, received wisdom notes that there followed what many call the 'no Quest period.' Wright, for example, claims the influence of Barth and Bultmann led scholars to believe historical Jesus research could not contribute to theological reflection, resulting in a dearth of publications on historical questions regarding Christ.[1] However, as we shall see, to claim Jesus historians were entirely silent during this period would be inaccurate.

As one commentator notes:

> for decades, it has been contended that in the first half of the 20th century there was no historical quest regarding Jesus, although it suffices only to take a look at the shelves of a good library to see the opposite.[2]

Weaver has meticulously detailed the output of participants of the 'Quest' in this period;[3] elsewhere Allison has argued that we may reasonably view the 'Quest' as one continuous endeavour, without any meaningful breaks to speak of.[4] Landmark publications in this period include the historical reconstructions by Headlam[5] and Guignebert.[6] Accordingly, Scott could still speak of 'the endless procession of Lives of Jesus' in 1934.[7]

Rather than attempting to synthesise a wholistic picture of the entire life of Jesus, it became more common in this period to study *individual aspects* of Jesus' ministry, typified by the work of C.H. Dodd on the parables,[8] Joachim Jeremias on (among other topics) the parables and the eucharist,[9] and T.W. Manson on Jesus' teaching.[10] Moreover, the priority of Mark and 'Q' was solidified as the *communis opinio* following Streeter's 1924 monograph *The Four Gospels*, which argued fervently for the priority of Mark.[11] Stevenson summarises the state of affairs thus: 'despite being an obvious misnomer, the term "no quest" highlights the temporary attenuation of German interest and the fact that the enduring relevance of the work of this period is not widely endorsed.'[12]

Thus, although few of the works mentioned hitherto in this section left much by means of lasting impact upon the 'Quest,' to speak of a 'no Quest' period is

DOI: 10.4324/b23077-9

misleading, to say the least. Moreover, besides the works already highlighted, it is worth discussing the form the 'Quest' took in the Nazi-sympathetic factions of the German Church in the 1930s and 1940s.

7.2 The 'Aryan Quest'

Once an overlooked aspect of the 'Quest' for the historical Jesus, it is now widely noted that historical Jesus research played a role in the Nazi-sympathetic quarters of the German Church in the build-up to the Second World War, the standard treatment of which is Heschel's *The Aryan Jesus*.[13] Head is right to note that 'the standard histories of New Testament research have not adequately dealt with this aspect of the Quest'[14] and, as Marsh notes, 'labelling this period that of "No Quest" is at best misleading, and at worse a sinister abdication of moral responsibility.'[15] Furthermore, Bormann has demonstrated how certain founding members of the *Studiorum Novi Testamenti Societas* itself were also supporters of the Nazi regime (Kittle, Kuhn, and Grundmann), and that the admittance of these members into the society at its inception was made possible due to Kittel's considerable political power and influence.[16] At this time in the history's discipline, Nazi ideology and academic study of the person of Jesus of Nazareth became inescapably enmeshed in certain quarters of the field.[17] As such, it remains important to also examine the metaphysical presuppositions underlying this period in the 'Quest.'

In 1899 H.S. Chamberlain published 'perhaps the single most influential book [of the 19th century]'[18] entitled *The Foundations of the Nineteenth Century*.[19] A native Englishman, Chamberlain settled in Germany and—like other contemporaries of his—thought western civilisation was built upon race struggle and that the Aryan race was superior to all others. The notion that Jesus was a Jew was unconscionable for Chamberlain, who viewed Christianity as the highest form of religious life. As Arnal notes, for Chamberlain 'the greatness of the Christian message owes nothing to Judaism, or, indeed, to individuals tainted by Jewish ethnicity.'[20] Chamberlain wrote that 'the fact that Christ was not a Jew, that he did not have a drop of genuine Jewish blood in his veins, is so great that it is almost a certainty.'[21] While there were some scholars who resisted this conception of Jesus—notably Bonhoeffer and Lohmeyer,[22] among others—Chamberlain's claims exerted considerable influence within historical reconstructions of Jesus' life in this period. It is impossible to survey this development comprehensively, and here I follow Casey who notes two scholars that serve as good examples of this phenomenon: Paul Fiebig and Walter Grundmann.[23]

By the early 1930s, Fiebig published on a variety of issues connected to historical Jesus research, including the 'Son of Man' problem, and Jesus' teaching in the Sermon on the Mount and in the Lord's Prayer.[24] Most pertinently, however, he gave three lectures in 1935, entitled *New Testament and National Socialism*.[25] He suggested Jesus was fundamentally opposed to the Judaism of his time: while the gospels record many accounts of Jesus as coming into conflict with various facets of Jewish leadership (which he cited to support his case), Fiebig also cited Jesus' mother Mary as a figure who had colluded with his opponents.

Grundmann joined the Nazi Party in 1930 and the Party's influence upon his work is well-documented.[26] He was an active member of the *Deutsche Christen* movement, which attempted to synthesise a Christianity in line with Nazi ideals, a movement opposed by the 'Confessing Church' (of which Barth, Bonhoeffer, and Bultmann were all members). Grundmann also assisted Gerhard Kittel (well-known for his anti-Semitic views[27]) in preparing his *Theologisches Wöterbuch zum Neuen Testament* and was appointed a Professor at Jena in 1936 despite not having written a *Habilitationsschrift* as the rector of the university sought to make the university the intellectual centre of National Socialism.[28]

Grundmann gave the address at the opening of the *Institut zur Erforschung und Beseitigung des jüdischen Einflusses auf das deutsche kirchliche Leben*, entitled 'The De-Judaization of the Religious Life as the Task of German Theology and Church.'[29] Therein he outlined his belief that it was vital the German church rid itself of its Jewish heritage, an endeavour Grundmann himself contributed to with his 1940 monograph entitled *Jesus der Galiläer und das Judentum*.[30] In a similar manner to Chamberlain, Grundmann sought to put distance between Jesus and the Judaism of his time, instead pitting the two as conflicting opposites by analysing the history of Galilee and placing great emphasis on the Gentile occupation of Galilee, suggesting the Galileans of Jesus' time were Gentile, not Jewish (and thus so was Jesus himself). There is much more one would ideally like to say about this period, given its importance. Suffice it to say, while these ideas have not permeated into the consciousness of 'mainstream' historical Jesus research, far from being a period of 'no Quest' the 1930s and 1940s saw a great deal of publications under the auspices of historical Jesus research.

Insofar as the metaphysical framework of the 'Aryan Quest' is concerned, it is significant that, as with the first 'Quest' before it, the possibility of divine agency and/or activity is once again absent. In other words, it is possible to identify the same methodological tendency to suppress religious metaphysical presuppositions in the 'Aryan Quest' as observed in the first 'Quest.' It is striking that even in a period of the 'Quest' so explicitly driven by ideological concerns—concerns frequently enmeshed with theological commitments—one may still observe a secular metaphysical refusal to permit religious metaphysical commitments to influence historical-critical methodology, ostensibly for the sake of academic credence. There is much more one might say about this period: it remains an overlooked shadow in the history of the 'Quest.' And yet suffice it to say here that the participants of this period of the 'Quest,' in refusing to incorporate religious metaphysics into historiographical methodology, continue to operate within a historiographical worldview we may describe as fundamentally secular. Indeed, this was precisely one of the purposes of the 'Aryan Quest' for the historical Jesus. By attempting to suppress avowedly religious metaphysical presuppositions, participants in the 'Aryan Quest' sought to give academic credence to their ideologically driven reconstructions of the life and teaching of the historical Jesus.

Here the language of 'religion' begins to reach the limit of its utility in this conversation. Many will reasonably wonder whether the Nazi party (and the pseudo-scholarship produced in support of its aims and ideologies) was not a 'religious' group or, at least possessed some characteristics of a religious group in their organisation and ideology. This is certainly the case and the Nazi party quite clearly built upon religious imagery, concepts, and figures in pursuit of its aims (hence its usurpation of Jesus of Nazareth, as discussed here). When I speak here of the 'Aryan Quest' operating with a (set of) historiographical worldview(s) that refuse 'religious' metaphysical presuppositions to be operative in its historical methodology, I merely mean that its participants *at least* wish to *appear* to be operating with the same standards of academic acceptability, even if that wish is enacted in pursuit and service of clear ideological and religious motivations.

7.3 Rudolf Bultmann

Outside of the alleged 'no Quest' period, it again becomes possible to observe a metaphysical continuity between the first and second 'Quests,' insofar as it is again possible to notice a tendency to refuse to allow religious metaphysical presuppositions to contribute to one's historical method and (therefore) one's historical reconstruction of the life and teaching of Jesus. Thus, it is reasonable to also describe this stage of the 'Quest' as secular in the manner outlined in Chapter 5 of this study.

Before discussing the second 'Quest' in earnest, one must mention the work of Rudolf Bultmann (1884–1976). Although not primarily known for his work on the historical Jesus, in 1926 he did offer some thoughts on the topic in his monograph *Jesus*. He begins his work with a now famous quote about the futility of such endeavours, writing:

> For I believe, of course, that we can know next to nothing about the life and the personality of Jesus, since the Christian sources are not interested in it and, moreover, are very fragmentary and overgrown with legend, and since other sources about Jesus do not exist.[31]

Like Schweitzer before him (who pre-empted Bultmann's demythologising endeavours[32]), he rejected the work of the liberal 'lives' of Jesus but was more sceptical about the success with which one might reconstruct the life of the historical Jesus. For Bultmann, much that was written about Jesus in the gospels were re-interpretations of his life in light of the Easter event; hindsight-fuelled faith-statements masquerading as history. These are of little use to the historian since they tell us more about the early church than Jesus himself, thus rendering the 'Quest' almost untenable.

Instead, Bultmann advocated a process of demythologising. This stemmed from the assertion that Jesus was as much a product of the primitive worldview of his day as was the early church. By stripping away this mythologised worldview it was possible to replace these categories with the existentialist ones of his colleague, Martin Heidegger. By re-discovering the demythologised truth that forms the core of Jesus' message, it was possible to see Jesus as an existential figure with meaning for present-day believers, not just a Jesus whose importance was tethered to his historical situation. Thus, in this respect 'Bultmann is one with Kähler in emphasizing the central Christian proclamation (kerygma) of Jesus' death and resurrection and in rejecting the historical Jesus as the basis or the content of Christian faith.'[33] It is one of the great ironies of 20th-century historical Jesus research that Bultmann, whose demythologising programme emerged in response to his lack of confidence in historical-critical attempts to reconstruct the life of the historical Jesus, ultimately paved the way for the explosion of work that would follow, not only in the second 'Quest,' but the third, dominated by North American scholarship.[34]

7.4 Ernst Käsemann

Bultmann exerted considerable influence over much 20th-century scholarship and the new 'Quest' about to begin. Indeed, it was one of his doctoral students, Ernst Käsemann (1906–98), who would provide the catalyst for this new 'Quest' in a 1953 lecture, 'The Problem of the Historical Jesus.'[35] Käsemann suggested Bultmannian demythologising only further reinforced the problems highlighted by Martin Kähler during the first 'Quest': 'in essence, Bultmann has merely, in his own way, underpinned and rendered more precise the thesis of this [i.e., Kähler's] book.'[36] Thus, Käsemann sought to restate the necessity of reconstructing the historical Jesus: without knowing something of the historical Jesus, he claimed, there was nothing to arbitrate between true and false representations of the gospel:

> Neither am I prepared to concede that … defeatism and scepticism must have the last word and lead us on a complete disengagement of interest from the earthly Jesus. If this were to happen, we should either be failing to grasp the nature of the primitive Christian concern with the identity between the exalted and the humiliated Lord; or else we should be emptying that concern of any real content, as did the docetists.[37]

While Käsemann remained broadly sceptical of the historical value of the gospels, he believed it was possible to identify several facts about the historical Jesus that provided a historical groundwork to anchor theological reflection about Jesus: his existence, his Jewishness, his baptism, and his death. For Käsemann, historical Jesus research had to play its part if Christological reflection was to retain a critical reference point. With one short but provocative lecture showing the importance of a historical grounding for Christological theology, Käsemann marked the start of a new phase in the field of historical Jesus research.

Methodologically, Käsemann sought not to advance a new metaphysical basis for a historical method for reconstructing the life of the historical Jesus: 'the issue today is not whether criticism is right, but where it is to stop,' he claims.[38] Thus, Käsemann, like the participants of the first 'Quest,' refuses to allow religious metaphysical presuppositions to influence methods within the discipline. Indeed, he describes 'supernaturalist' approaches—i.e., theologically motivated approaches that incorporate religious metaphysical presuppositions into their method—as 'succeeding only in depicting the miraculous aura of the θεῖος ἀνήρ, who can be accepted only by means of the *sacrificium intellectus*.'[39] While Käsemann's lecture reinforced the need for a historical reconstruction of the life of Jesus, and instigated a new 'Quest' for the historical Jesus, methodologically, Käsemann's approach to the discipline concurrently reinforced the secular metaphysical presupposition that religious metaphysics are not to influence one's historical reconstruction.

7.5 Günther Bornkamm

This new beginning saw a series of monographs on the topic, the most important by Günther Bornkamm (1905–90). His *Jesus von Nazareth* appeared in 1956, and quickly became one of the most important historical reconstructions of the life on Jesus and remained such for some time.[40] In 1969 Keck described it as 'clearly the dominant book about Jesus since World War II' and 'the only comprehensive book on Jesus which the new questers and the new hermeneuts have produced.'[41] Bornkamm approached the historical Jesus in a similar manner to Käsemann, asserting that only a few facts about the historical Jesus could be established. Beyond essential facts (that Jesus was a Jew, born in Nazareth, who spoke Aramaic, and was baptised by John), Bornkamm instead focussed on Jesus' *teaching*. In this respect, Bornkamm viewed Jesus as proclaiming the imminence of the Kingdom of God alongside a radical reinterpretation of many aspects of the Torah, which ultimately led to his death.

Regarding Bornkamm's historical method and historiographical worldview, he adopts a positive stance towards historical-critical methodology and proceeds in a manner that is largely Bultmannian and, as such, adheres to the same divide (instigated by Kähler and Troeltsch in the first 'Quest'), perpetuated by Bultmann and reinforced by Käsemann, between the Jesus of history (the study of which is informed by secular metaphysical presuppositions) and the Christ of faith (with which religious metaphysics may engage).

Bornkamm notes that 'without the process of criticism and counter-criticism there is no knowledge of historical truth in this field or any other.'[42] And yet his opening remarks suggest he will proceed in a manner that incorporates religious metaphysical presuppositions. He suggests, for example, that a belief in the resurrection of Jesus is central to a complete reconstruction of his life: 'this understanding of history is therefore an understanding from the end backward and to the end forward.'[43] However, it soon becomes clear that by this Bornkamm means to appeal to his *Doktorvater*'s demythologising approach to allow the historical Jesus to speak today. He notes, as did Bultmann, the impossibility of historical reconstruction: 'no one is any longer in the position to write a life of Jesus,' and instead suggests that what is truly important for believers is 'the tradition [which] is not really the repetition and transmission of the word he spoke once upon a time, but rather *is* his word today.'[44]

Moreover, Bornkamm suggests that it is the proper application of already established critical techniques that allow us to demythologise the texts of the New

Testament and recapture the living Christ who is able to speak to the Church today. In this respect, he writes that 'it is precisely historical criticism which, rightly understood, opened up our way anew to this history, by disposing of attempts along biographical, psychological lines.'[45] For Bornkamm, then, if religious metaphysical presuppositions are to influence Christological reflection, it may not be in terms of the historical Jesus, but only in reflecting upon the demythologised Jesus, who lives and speaks to believers today.

7.6 Edward Schillebeeckx

Alongside Bornkamm's work, one of the most enduring publications from this period—and one of the most detailed—is that written by the Dutch Dominican theologian Edward Schillebeeckx (1914–2009) in 1974.[46] Echoes of Bultmannian demythologising are present throughout Schillebeeckx's work. He writes:

> We are confronted in the gospels not just with Jesus of Nazareth but with a portion of ancient religious culture. Jesus is indeed hidden beneath religious ideas belonging to that time, ideas which, if it comes to that, were themselves not altogether alien to him—rather the opposite. Moreover, the original experience of salvation in Jesus gets filled out in the gospels with doctrinal and practical problems of the later Christian congregations.[47]

This Bultmannian tone would hardly have been surprising to Schillebeeckx's primary audience: the subtitle to the first Dutch edition (*het verhaal van een levende*) may be translated into English as *The Story of a Living Person*. Most famously, he suggests that belief in Jesus' bodily resurrection was not the result of an empty tomb, or resurrection appearances, rather 'the resurrection was believed in before there was any question of appearance.'[48] Moreover, as Simut notes, 'Schillebeeckx is not ready to say that a bodily resurrection implies a real body, because we are historically bound to live in the same body we were born with.'[49] This brought him into conflict with the Catholic *Congregation for the Doctrine of the Faith* who, on 20 October 1976, wrote to Schillebeeckx with numerous objections they had regarding his historical reconstruction of Easter.[50] Alongside this, Schillebeeckx's portrayal of Jesus popularised a Bultmannian approach that sought to release Jesus from the shackles of history to emphasise experience with him in the present.

Regarding Schillebeeckx's historical method, it is clear from the outset that he employs a method that is akin to a historical equivalent of Gadamerian *Wirkungsgeschichte*,[51] whereby the starting point for apprehending the historical Jesus is the *effect* his life and teaching had upon his followers. (This is similar to the method employed by Dunn, discussed in §6 of the next chapter.) Schillebeeckx writes:

> The starting-point for any Christology or Christian interpretation of Jesus is not simply Jesus of Nazareth, still less the Church's *kerygma* or creed. Rather

> it is the movement which Jesus himself started in the first century of our era … The only knowledge we possess of the Christ event reaches us via the concrete experience of the first local communities of Christians.[52]

Significantly, Schillebeeckx here conceives of his historical reconstruction of the life of Jesus as a 'Christology or Christian interpretation of Jesus.' However, this does not mean that Schillebeeckx's historiography is informed, on a practical level, by religious metaphysical presuppositions. Instead, Schillebeeckx's historical method shows clear evidence of the secular metaphysical tendency highlighted throughout this chapter. The starting point for understanding Schillebeeckx's historical method is the attention he draws to the impact of the historical Jesus' life and teaching. Schillebeeckx notes that:

> 'Historically', that is, in the occurrent reality of his earthly existence, something is present which is in principle inaccessible by way of purely historico-critical methods … In Jesus' case this 'something', experienced in the encounter with him, was expressed by Christians in images such as son of man, messianic son of David, and so forth.[53]

Here Schillebeeckx hints at the limits of historical-critical methods influenced by secular metaphysical presuppositions, in referring to 'something' in the life of Jesus inaccessible by these minds (akin to Blondel's notion of 'real history,' discussed in Chapter 4 of this study). However, rather than engaging fully with this line of thought and positing a means to access this 'something' in Jesus' life, he instead enquires as to the effect that Jesus' ministry had upon the early church. Therefore, Schillebeeckx claims it is incumbent upon the historian, if they are to produce the fullest reconstruction of Jesus' life possible from within this secular metaphysical historiographical worldview, to ask whether the representations of Jesus' ineffability found in the writings of the New Testament do indeed reflect the historical reality of the person of Jesus himself. As Schillebeeckx himself writes, 'we are really enquiring after the historical basis and source of what we have called the "Christian movement,"' rather than enquiring after Jesus himself.[54] This is what Schillebeeckx means when he speaks of the historical importance of Jesus' impact upon the earliest Christians, and its role in historical Jesus research: the study of early Christianity speaks to the life of the historical Jesus.

Schillebeeckx suggests traditional historical-critical methods are not adequate: these methods are concerned 'to recover the past, as we say, on a value-free basis,' but have failed in this endeavour since 'this so-called value-free stance itself serves to conceal another set of positive evaluations that are equally real.'[55] In response to these methods, Schillebeeckx speaks of 'negative' and 'positive' criteria, the former employed to identify inauthentic traditions, and the latter authentic ones. He chooses to disregard negative criteria in his historical method, writing that

> those negative criteria—a sure pointer, we are told, to the absence of authenticity—are completely unsafe and moreover operate with all kinds

> of presuppositions which *a priori* isolate Jesus from the Old Testament and Judaic tradition as also from any continuity with the later thinking prompted by the faith of the Church, whereas what we want to trace is the continuity as well as the discontinuity.[56]

As such, he therefore posits five 'positive criteria' that one may employ to 'legitimately (and with fluctuating certainty) regard a logion or New Testament story as going back to the earthly Jesus.'[57] It is these criteria that form Schillebeeckx's historical method and, thus, it is within these criteria that one may find traces of the historiographical worldview operative within his scholarship. Specifically, in outlining these criteria Schillebeeckx demonstrates a reluctance to allow religious metaphysical presuppositions to influence his historiographical worldview.

First, he suggests we might contrast traditions with the editorial interests of the evangelists in whose gospels the tradition appears and 'whenever they hand on material not markedly in accord with their own theological view of things, we may take this to be a sign of deference in face of some revered tradition.'[58] Second, Schillebeeckx seeks to employ *Formgeschichte*, conceived of as the act of distinguishing authentic material insofar as it is historically distinct from the content of both contemporaneous Jewish thought and the proclamation(s) of the early church, this method being 'primarily a legacy of Bultmann.'[59] He is clear that this is not to deny that in many respects Jesus may stand in congruity with both Jewish and early Christian thought, but that 'in such cases of continuity this criterion affords us no historical or critical certainty as to whether the source is Jesus himself or the Jewish-Christian church.'[60] Third, Schillebeeckx introduces the criterion of tradition. By this he means the more independent attestations one may observe for a tradition, the more likely it is this tradition is authentic. In his own words:

> this criterion carries more weight where the same sort of content is to be found in diverse forms (whatever the relationship between them, *qua* tradition, may be); such concordance gives obvious weight to the genuineness of a logion.[61]

Fourth, one's historical reconstruction must be consistent, insofar as every part of this reconstruction must cohere with the overall, broader view of Jesus it advances. Thus, 'both the total view of what emerges on strictly historical grounds as a picture of Jesus on the one hand, and detailed exegesis on the other, are involved in a mutual process of verification.'[62] Fifth, Schillebeeckx calls his final criterion the 'execution' criteria, 'for it is based on the view that the fact of Jesus' trial and execution has a hermeneutical bearing on precisely what it was that he taught and did.'[63] Thus, any reconstruction of the historical Jesus must necessarily convincingly explain why Jesus' life and teaching were such that they lead to his execution by contemporaneous Jewish and Roman leaders.[64]

What might this criteria-based method of Schillebeeckx's suggest about his historiographical worldview? I contend that, like many of the figures highlighted in this chapter, he does not allow any religious metaphysical presuppositions to influence his method, despite suggesting his historical reconstruction is a 'Christology' or 'Christian interpretation of Jesus' (noted above). Central to Schillebeeckx's work (beyond his contribution to historical Jesus research) is 'a strong sense of the importance of linking orthodoxy with orthopraxis,'[65] insofar as orthodox belief should manifest itself practically in one's scholarship. He notes that such 'praxis is decisive' in Christian scholarship.[66] This is born from his conviction that 'the indefectibility and infallibility of the church from God's promise to preserve the church in truth.'[67] Importantly, Schillebeeckx explicitly notes that this is true 'of the Church as a whole, before any distinction is made between the community and its office-bearers,' such that 'the whole "body of the faithful, anointed as they are by the Holy One, cannot err in matters of belief," [as] the Second Vatican Council declared.'[68]

Thus, one might expect Schillebeeckx's conception of the *sensus fidelium* to feature in his historical method. And yet Schillebeeckx advances a set of criteria that cohere largely with what has gone before him in the 'Quest' for the historical Jesus. Although he does not make this explicit at any point, for Schillebeeckx, faith (and therefore religious metaphysical presuppositions) cannot contribute to the historical task in the same way it is an integral part of his *theological* reflection. Thus, one might suggest that for Schillebeeckx, 'God is not a *Deus ex machina*, meaning that he left history to mankind.'[69] In practice, this conception of God results in a secular historical-critical method. The historiographical worldview of Schillebeeckx coheres with those employed by many figures discussed in this chapter, insofar as one may observe a secular metaphysical tendency within his method, to not allowing religious metaphysical presuppositions to contribute to his historiographical worldview and, thus, his reconstruction of the life and teaching of the historical Jesus.

7.7 Conclusion

As was the case with the first 'Quest,' the 'no Quest' and second 'Quest' stages of the discipline saw a continuation of the tendency not to permit religious metaphysical presuppositions to influence historical methods. This tendency is present in the indicative figures I have examined in this stage of the 'Quest' and provides evidence that this stage of the 'Quest' operated with historiographical worldviews I may reasonably describe as secular. Strikingly, this remains the case in the so-called 'Aryan Quest.' Even in an example such as this, with scholarship so clearly and explicitly driven by ideological aims and agendas, there remains a commitment not to allow explicitly 'religious' presuppositions, notwithstanding complications surrounding the use of the word 'religious' in this context.

Notes

1 N.T. Wright, 'Jesus, Quest for the Historical', in *ABD*, 1992, III, 796–802; idem, *JVG*, 21–23.

2 Bermejo-Rubio, '*Leben-Jesu-Forschung*', 4.
3 Walter P. Weaver, *The Historical Jesus in the Twentieth Century: 1900–1950* (Harrisburg, PA: Trinity International, 1999).
4 Dale C. Allison, Jr., 'The Secularizing of the Historical Jesus', *PRS* 27.2 (2000), 135–51.
5 A.C. Headlam, *The Life and Teaching of Jesus the Christ* (London: Murray, 1923).
6 C. Guignebert, *Jésus* (Paris: Renaissance du Livre, 1933); ET: idem, *Jesus*, trans. S. H. Hooke (London: Kegan Paul, 1935).
7 E.F. Scott, 'Recent Lives of Jesus', *HTR* 27.1 (1934), 1–31.
8 C.H. Dodd, *The Parables of the Kingdom* (London: Nisbet & Co., 1935).
9 Joachim Jeremias, *Die Gleichnisse Jesu* (Zürich: Zwingli Verlag, 1947); *Die Abendmahlsworte Jesu* (Göttingen: Vandenhoeck & Ruprecht, 1949).
10 T.W. Manson, *The Teaching of Jesus: Studies of Its Form and Content* (Cambridge: Cambridge University, 1931).
11 B.H. Streeter, *The Four Gospels: A Study of Origins* (London: MacMillan, 1924).
12 Austin Stevenson, 'The Self-Understanding of Jesus: A Metaphysical Reading of Historical Jesus Studies', *SJT* 72.3 (2019), 291–307 (293).
13 Susannah Heschel, *The Aryan Jesus: Christian Theologians and the Bible in Nazi Germany* (Princeton, NJ: Princeton University, 2008).
14 Peter M. Head, 'The Nazi Quest for an Aryan Jesus', *JSHJ* 2.1 (2004), 55–89 (57).
15 Clive Marsh, 'Quests of the Historical Jesus in New Historicist Perspective', *BibInt* 5.4 (1997), 403–37 (414).
16 Lukas Bormann. '"Auch unter politischen Gesichtspunkten sehr sorgfältig ausgewählt": Die ersten deutschen Mitglieder der Studiorum Novi Testamenti Societas (SNTS) 1937–1946', *NTS* 58.3 (2012), 416–52.
17 For insight into the continuing post-war significance of Nazi-sympathetic biblical scholarship, see the incredibly moving chapter: Hermann Lichtenberger, 'Karl Georg Kuhn (1906–1976)—Two Academic Careers in Germany', in *Protestant Bible Scholarship: Antisemitism, Philosemitism and Anti-Judaism*, ed. Arjen F. Bakker, René Bloch, Yael Fisch, Paula Fredriksen, and Hindy Najman (JSJS 200; Leiden: Brill, 2022), 1–23. Lichtenberger reflects in the chapter on the work of his *Doktorvater* Karl-Georg Kuhn (himself a student of Kittel), Kuhn's connections to Nazi Party, and the extent of his "denazification" after the war, speaking of Kuhn's "(fictitious) rehabilitation" from 1949 to 1976 (13). On the influence of the likes of Kittel, Lichtenberger notes "in 1988 I became the successor (after an interlude of Ernst Bammel) of Karl Heinrich Rengstorf in Münster, who had been habilitated by Gerhard Kittel in Tübingen (1930). In 1993, I became the successor of Martin Hengel in Tübingen. He was the successor Otto Michael, who followed Gerhard Kittel (1946). That is the small world of academics" (2).
18 Maurice Casey, *Jesus of Nazareth: An Independent Historian's Account of His Life and Teaching* (T&T Clark, 2000), 5. See, also, his earlier article on the *TWNT/TDNT*: Maurice Casey, 'Some Anti-Semitic Assumptions in the "Theological Dictionary of the New Testament"', *NovT* 41.3 (1999), 280–91.
19 H.S. Chamberlain, *Die Grundlagen des neunzehnten Jahrhunderts*, 2 vols (München: Bruckmann, 1899). ET: idem, *The Foundations of the Nineteenth Century*, trans. J. Lees, 2 vols (London and New York: Lane; Bodley Head, 1910).
20 William E. Arnal, *The Symbolic Jesus: Historical Scholarship, Judaism and the Construction of Contemporary Identity*, Religion in Culture (London: Equinox, 2005), 9.
21 Chamberlain, *Die Grundlagen*, I:218–19.
22 Regarding the latter, see James R. Edwards, *Between the Swastika and the Sickle: The Life, Disappearance, and Execution of Ernst Lohmeyer* (Grand Rapids, MI: Eerdmans, 2019).
23 Casey, *Jesus*, 5–9.
24 P. Fiebig, *Der Menschensohn: Jesu Selbstbezeichnung* (Tübingen: J. C. B. Mohr, 1901); *Altjüdische Gleichnisse und die Gleichnisse Jesu* (Tübingen: J. C. B. Mohr, 1904);

Die Gleichnisreden Jesu im Lichte der rabbinischen Gleichnisse des neutestamentlichen Zeitalters (Tübingen: J. C. B. Mohr, 1912); *Jesu Bergpredigt. Rabbinische Texte zum Verständnis der Bergpredigt, ins Deutsche übersetzt, in ihren Ursprachen dargeboten und mit Erläuterungen und Lesarten versehen*, FRLANT NF 20 (Göttingen: Vandenhoeck & Ruprecht, 1924); *Das Vaterunser. Ursprung, Sinn und Bedeutung des christlichen Hauptgebetes*, BFChT 30 (Gütersloh: Bertelsmann, 1927).

25 P. Fiebig, *Neues Testament und Nationalsozialismus. Drei Üniversitätsvorlesungen über Führerprinzip - Rassenfrage - Kampf*, Schriften der Deutschen Christen (Dresden: Deutsch-christliche Verlag, 1935). At the time of writing no English translation of this text exists.

26 A. Gerdmar, *Roots of Theological Anti-Semitism: German Biblical Interpretation and the Jews, from Herder and Semler to Kittel and Bultmann*, SJHC, 20 (Leiden: Brill, 2009), 531–76; *Walter Grundmann: Ein Neutestamentler im Dritten Reich*, ed. Roland Deines, Volker Leppin, and Karl-Wilhelm Niebuhr, Arbeiten zur Kirchen- und Theologiegeschichte, Band 21 (Leipzig: Evangelische Verlagsanstalt, 2007); Heschel, *Aryan Jesus*.

27 Gerdmar, *Roots*, 417–530.

28 The role of the Faculty of Theology at the University of Jena in facilitating the aims of the Nazi party in the 1930s and 1940s, and Grundmann's role therein, is summarised in Heschel, *Aryan Jesus*, 201–41.

29 Walter Grundmann, *Die Entjudung des religiösen Lebens als Aufgabe deutsche Theologie und Kirche* (Weimar: Verlag Deutsche Christen, 1939). As above, there is currently no English translation of the text.

30 Walter Grundmann, *Jesus der Galiläer und das Judentum* (Leipzig: Wigand, 1940). Again there is no English translation at present.

31 Rudolf Bultmann, *Jesus* (Berlin: Deutsche Bibliothek, 1926), 8.

32 See, especially, the comments in Carleton Paget, 'Schweitzer's Second Edition', 39.

33 John P. Meier, 'Basic Methodology in the Quest for the Historical Jesus', in *HSHJ*, I:291–331 (300).

34 See, on this point, Stephen J. Patterson 'Bultmann's Jesus in America', in *"To Recover What Has Been Lost": Essays on Eschatology, Intertextuality, and Reception History in Honor of Dale C. Allison Jr.*, ed. Tucker S. Ferda, Daniel Frayer-Griggs, and Nathan C. Johnson, NovTSup 183 (Leiden: Brill, 2021), 405–28.

35 Ernst Käsemann, 'Das Problem des historischen Jesus', *ZTK* 51.2 (1954), 125–53. ET: idem, 'The Problem of the Historical Jesus', in *Essays on New Testament Themes*, trans. W. J. Montague (London: SCM, 1964), 15–47.

36 Käsemann, 'The Problem', 16.

37 Ibid., 46.

38 Ibid., 34.

39 Ibid., 19.

40 Günther Bornkamm, *Jesus von Nazareth*, Kohlhammer Urban-Taschenbücher 19 (Stuttgart: Kohlhammer, 1956). ET: Günther Bornkamm, *Jesus of Nazareth*, trans. Irene McLuskey, Fraser McLuskey, and James M. Robinson (London: Hodder & Stoughton, 1960), translated from the third German edition published in 1959. In what follows, all quotes are taken from the 1960 English translation.

41 Leander E. Keck, 'Bornkamm's *Jesus of Nazareth* Revisited', *JR* 49.1 (1969), 1–17 (1).

42 Bornkamm, *Jesus*, 15.

43 Ibid., 16.

44 Ibid., 1, 17 (emphasis original).

45 Ibid., 24.

46 Edward Schillebeeckx, *Jezus, het verhaal van een levende* (Bloemendaal: Uitgeverij H. Nelissen B.V., 1974). ET: idem, *Jesus: An Experiment in Christology* (London: Collins, 1979).

47 Schillebeeckx, *Jesus*, 21.

48 Ibid., 354.
49 Ramona Simut, 'Edward Schillebeeckx's Position on the Resurrection and the Time Test: What Is Resurrection Today?', *Journal for the Study of Religions and Ideologies* 16.48 (2017), 16–30 (17).
50 Full details of the controversy between Schillebeeckx and the CDF can be found in *The Schillebeeckx Case*, ed. Ted Schoof (New Haven, CT: Paulist, 1984).
51 Advanced most famously in Hans-Georg Gadamer, *Wahrheit und Methode* (Tübingen: J. C. B. Mohr (Paul Siebeck), 1960). ET: Hans-Georg Gadamer, *Truth and Method*, trans. Joel Weinsheimer and Donald Marshall, 2nd rev. ed. (London: Continuum, 2004).
52 Schillebeeckx, *Jesus*, 44-45.
53 Ibid., 69.
54 Ibid., 69.
55 Ibid., 79. I will make a similar point in chapter ten, that secular metaphysics (and therefore historical-critical methods that proceed from secular metaphysical presuppositions) are not value-neutral, or value-free, to use Schillebeeckx's language. I will also suggest that this should encourage the field of historical Jesus research to operate with a wider variety of metaphysical presuppositions allowed to influence historical methods.
56 Ibid., 90.
57 Ibid., 91.
58 Ibid., 91.
59 Ibid., 92.
60 Ibid., 93.
61 Ibid., 95.
62 Ibid., 96.
63 Ibid., 97.
64 A similar criterion has also been advanced recently by Ernst Baasland, 'Forth Quest? What Did Jesus Really Want?', in *HSHJ*, I:31–56 (49).
65 Martin G. Poulsom, 'Schillebeeckx and the *Sensus Fidelium*', *New Blackfriars* 98.1074 (2017), 203–17. See, also, the discussion of theory and praxis in idem, *The Dialectics of Creation: Creation and the Creator in Edward Schillebeeckx and David Burrell* (London: T&T Clark, 2014), 112–21.
66 Edward Schillebeeckx, *Jesus in Our Western Culture: Mysticism, Ethic and Politics*, trans. John Bowden (London: SCM, 1987), 75.
67 Daniel Speed Thompson, *The Language of Dissent: Edward Schillebeeckx on the Crisis of Authority in the Catholic Church* (Notre Dame, IL: University of Notre Dame, 2003), 129.
68 Edward Schillebeeckx, 'The Problem of the Infallibility of the Church's Office', in *The Language of Faith: Essays on Jesus, Theology and the Church*, trans. Smith (London: SCM, 1995), 55–69 (57, 64).
69 Simut, *Schillebeeckx's Position on the Resurrection*, 24.

8 Metaphysics and the Third 'Quest'

8.1 Introduction

In this chapter, I seek to demonstrate that it is again possible to observe a tendency not to allow religious metaphysical presuppositions to contribute to the task of historically reconstructing the life of Jesus and, again, this observation invites us to describe the third 'Quest' as adhering to secular metaphysical presuppositions regarding the nature of historiography. Following the decline of the second 'Quest' there began a new 'Quest.' Though hard to discern a singular event or publication from which this new 'Quest' began, it is occasionally suggested that N.T. Wright inaugurated the new 'Quest' in 1992. Mark Powell, for example, identifies Wright's *The New Testament and the People of God* as containing the first reference to a new 'Quest.'[1] In reality, the term was used as early as 1988.[2] Looking back even further, Deines suggests that

> the 'New Schürer' (1973-87) under the editorship of Geza Vermes, Fergus Millar, and Matthew Black, can be seen as the starting line of the new wave in second temple studies which has not yet subsided and which runs parallel to the third 'Quest', the starting date of which is often connected with the publication of Geza Vermes' *Jesus the Jew* and E. P. Sanders's *Jesus and Judaism*.[3]

By the end of the 1980's, it was clear that a new development in the 'Quest' was underway.

Whereas in 1971 Leander Keck described historical Jesus research as 'a dead-end street,'[4] in 1988 Marcus Borg was outlining what he viewed as a renaissance in the discipline.[5] The reappraisal of Judaism at the time of Jesus by Vermes and Sanders led to a reappraisal of Jesus himself. Accordingly, one of the most distinctive features of this 'Quest' is the givenness of Jesus' Jewishness: 'this generation reached a consensus that Jesus' Jewishness was central to his identity, aims, and impact.'[6] Jesus' Jewishness is no longer seen as a question for debate, but a starting point, with scholars instead seeking to ask *what kind of Jew was Jesus*?

The amount of publications of the historical Jesus increased exponentially since the start of this third 'Quest.' In what follows, there will inevitably be

DOI: 10.4324/b23077-10

scholars whose work has also contributed to the third 'Quest' but is not included here. These figures include Gerd Theissen,[7] Gerd Lüdemann,[8] Maurice Casey,[9] James H. Charlesworth,[10] Richard Horsley,[11] and David Flusser,[12] among many others. Similarly, I do not discuss Wright in what follows, since his scholarship is the focus of Chapter 9.

8.2 Géza Vermes

One finds intimations of the third 'Quest' in the work of Géza Vermes (1924–2013). Vermes' highly influential *Jesus the Jew* remains an important contribution to the 'Quest,'[13] as do his two later works on the subject, *Jesus and the World of Judaism,*[14] and *The Religion of Jesus the Jew*.[15] Vermes attempted to study Jesus alongside Galilean *Hasidim*, or, charismatic holy-men. These *Hasidim*, he argued, were considered to stand in the tradition of Israel's ancient prophets and it was understood that their close relationship with God manifested itself in miraculous events, with contemporaneous examples of such figures including Honi the Circle Drawer and Hanina ben Dosa.[16] Vermes thus concludes that 'the logical inference must be that the person of Jesus is to be seen as part of a first-century charismatic Judaism and as a paramount example of the early Hasidim or Devout.'[17] While the particularities of Vermes' argument have long since passed from influence, his methodological decision to study Jesus as a man congruent with the Judaism of his day in part set the agenda for years to come. Despite the disparate nature of the third 'Quest,' one of the only points of congruence between the vast majority of contemporary Jesus historians is Jesus' Jewishness, and the great variety of forms in which second temple Judaism manifested itself.[18] It is Vermes who first introduces these loci of discussion into the 'Quest' for the historical Jesus.

Examining Vermes' metaphysical presuppositions is difficult because he does not outline his historical method in any of his works on the historical Jesus. However, he does make it clear that he believes religious metaphysical presuppositions should not influence one's historiographical decision-making. For example, regarding historiography, he writes:

> When a committed Christian embarks on such a task with a mind already persuaded by the dogmatic suppositions of his church … he is bound to read the gospels in a particular manner and to attribute the maximum possible Christian traditional significance even to the most neutral sentence, one that in any other context he would not even be tempted to interpret that way.[19]

Over against this approach, Vermes stresses that 'I seek to re-assert in my whole approach to this problem [of the historical Jesus] the inalienable right of the historian to pursue a course *independent of beliefs*.'[20] Therefore, although Vermes does not expound a historical method *per se* there is clear evidence that he presupposes the same secular metaphysical tendency highlighted throughout the previous two chapters, namely the conviction that religious metaphysical presuppositions may not inform ones historical decision-making. This is made more explicit in Vermes' review of Joseph Ratzinger's work on Jesus, wherein he criticises Ratzinger for attempting to foist religious metaphysical presuppositions into his historical reconstruction of the life of Jesus.[21] As Witherington notes, Vermes 'attempts to place Jesus in a category that says something less about Jesus than Christians have traditionally wanted to assert.'[22] Vermes' historical method thus remains influenced by secular metaphysical presuppositions regarding historiography. As Deines note, 'if anything, it is the *Jewish* heritage of the Christian faith that rejects the deistic assumption of a distant God removed from the world,' and yet Vermes remains silent as to how this might (or should) impact his historical reconstruction.[23]

8.3 E.P. Sanders

Vermes' Jewish framework for Jesus research was later taken up by E.P. Sanders (1937–). Sanders' most important contribution to the 'Quest' was his 1985 monograph *Jesus and Judaism*.[24] He situated Jesus within an apocalyptic strand of ancient Judaism and argued that the core of Jesus' ministry was the imminent end of the temple cult, to be replaced by the Kingdom of God. Not merely an apocalyptic prophet, Sanders' Jesus is thoroughly Jewish in every way. The conflict stories are seen as later Christian interpolations arising from disputes between the early Christians and the Jewish authorities; Jesus himself was a strict observant of the Torah. Instead, what brought about his death was Jesus throwing out the money changers in the temple, which prompted anger from the Sadducees and set in motion the events that would lead to Jesus' crucifixion.[25]

The metaphysical presuppositions that influence Sanders' historiographical worldview are again most effectively apprehended via analysis of his historical method. He begins by suggesting historians should 'begin with what is relatively secure and work out to more uncertain points.'[26] Thus, he posits 'several facts about Jesus' career *and its aftermath* which can be known beyond doubt.'[27] These 'facts' are (1) that Jesus was baptised by John, (2) that Jesus was a Galilean, a preacher, and a healer, (3) Jesus had disciples and a discreet group of followers called 'the twelve,' (4) Jesus' ministry was confined to Israel, (5) Jesus engages in controversy with the temple, (6) Jesus was crucified by the Romans, (7) an identifiable group of 'Jesus followers' continued to exist after his death, and (8) some Jews persecuted this new movement in some sense. Taking these 'facts' as a preliminary framework for approaching the historical Jesus' ministry, Sanders then posits a set of criteria by which he will assess various sayings attributed to Jesus: 'each saying must be tested by appropriate criteria and assigned (tentatively) to an author—either to Jesus or to an anonymous representative of some stratum in the early church.'[28]

To be clear, Sanders does not posit a set of criteria *per se* (as, say, Norman Perrin did), but rather a method born of form criticism. He writes that one of the principle arguments of the form critics—namely, that we have the material as it was handed down by the church, and that it has been adapted for use by the church—is to be maintained.'[29] However, in Sander's view, 'tests which were used to establish the earlier form of tradition ... are unreliable,'[30] and so while the overarching principle behind form criticism is adopted, the means of applying it is not, which is problematic due to our lack of knowledge regarding the early texts outside of the New Testament to which Sanders seeks to apply form criticism in the first place. Thus, 'we must conclude that the material [concerning Jesus] was subject to change and may have changed, but that we do not know just how it changed.'[31]

In addition to this, Sanders highlights the test of double dissimilarity, that material not born of the early church, nor identifiable with Jesus' Jewish contemporaries, are most likely to have originated with Jesus himself. However, while the *theory* behind this test is again commendable, Sanders once more takes issue with its results: it rules out too much material for it to be meaningfully useful. He claims it leaves 'too little material to allow a satisfactory reconstruction of the life and teaching of Jesus'[32] and what little is identified by these means must still be interpreted by the historian and a judgement decision must still be made regarding where in Jesus' life these sayings fit. As Witherington notes, 'Sanders does not have the same confidence Crossan and others do that we can readily get back to the earliest layer of the sayings tradition by using criteria.'[33] Thus, given the problems inherent in these criteria, historians 'need to move beyond the saying themselves to a broader context than a summary of their contents if they are to address historical questions about Jesus.'[34] Thus, Sanders' method is significantly influenced by a sceptical view of the sources available for reconstructing the life and teaching of the historical Jesus. He contends that little beyond a broad sketch of Jesus in his Jewish context is possible, given the extant evidence. Where he does talk more explicitly about historical method, however, he neglects to mention the impact that religious metaphysical presuppositions might positively exert upon the discipline. Therefore, I claim (albeit tentatively due to his lack of explicit discussion on the issue) Sanders operates with a historiographical worldview that evidences the secular metaphysical presupposition at the centre of the present chapter, namely that religious metaphysical presuppositions cannot influence historical decision-making.

8.4 John Dominic Crossan

After the third 'Quest' was inaugurated by the studies of the Jewish Jesus by Vermes and Sanders, came the 'Jesus Seminar' from the mid-1980s onwards. Based in North America (and primarily comprising North American scholars), the seminar was founded by Robert W. Funk (1926–2005) in 1985. The seminar displayed some noticeable differences from what had preceded it. First was the conscious employment of a greater variety of sources. Rather than restricting themselves to the canonical gospels in their historical reconstruction, they made use of non-canonical texts such as the Gospel of Thomas. Second, they were keen to publicise their results as widely as possible, resulting in the seminar becoming the sensibility within the 'Quest' that the general public has had perhaps the greatest awareness of (or, at least, did at the time). At one point there were even plans to make a film documenting the seminar's work.[35] Third is the manner in which they categorise the sayings of Jesus by colour, according to their plausibility.[36] If David Bentley Hart is right to bemoan the results of committee-based biblical translations,[37] then one might equally wonder what might be gained when committees attempt historiography. The picture of Jesus drawn by the seminar is certainly an unusual one. For those in the seminar, Jesus was an illiterate peasant who began his ministry as a disciple of John, ultimately breaking away from the Baptist and initiating his own ministry. This ministry was said to be characterised by an awareness of (and call to) social justice; the Seminar's Jesus seems to take great pleasure in mocking the religious institutions of the Judaism surrounding him. However, when it comes to the historiographical works of individual members of the seminar, these works are often of much greater value that the work published under the auspices of the seminar itself.

One such member is the Irish American former Catholic Priest, John Dominic Crossan (1934–). His work on the historical Jesus has enjoyed considerable influence within the academy and without, thanks to his rigorous scholarly work[38] and his more accessible output on the subject,[39] although the latter was also partly conceived to be a response to what Crossan considered to be 'incomplete readings' of the former.[40] As the Seminar itself had concluded, Crossan also conceives of Jesus as an illiterate peasant. Furthermore, Crossan agrees that Jesus was initially a disciple of John the Baptist, later splitting from him to begin his own ministry. The reasons for this split was that Jesus wished to stress the *present* nature of the Kingdom of God (over against its *coming* nature in John's proclamation), and he rejected John's asceticism, instead choosing to dine controversially with those whom society had cast out.

Crossan is also significant in that he breaks from the trend amongst scholars of the third 'Quest' to view Judaism as the primary context for Jesus' life. Instead, Crossan conceives of a strong connection between Jesus and the Hellenistic group known as the Cynics, a view which has had limited influence upon other Jesus historians.[41] Amongst the criticism Crossan has faced is his use of the gospels of Thomas and Peter, both of which he assigns an early date (and therefore considers them to be more historically useful than many would). Elsewhere, writing in review of Crossan's later work, Robert Lyon ponders if it is 'not another "Life of Jesus" that reflects again the culture of the times.'[42] Despite this, Crossan remains an important voice within the 'Quest.' His choice of sources has prompted discussions about methodology, and his work is one that scholars following in his footsteps are duty-bound to consult.

Crossan's historiographical worldview is, like other scholars whose work is discussed in this chapter, most evident in his method. This is significant because one of the most evident characteristics of his work is his discussion of methodology at the start of his work. Therein he suggests:

> Methodology in Jesus research at the end of this [20th] century is about where methodology in archaeological research was at the end of the last [19th] …

> [Therefore] this book had to raise most seriously the problem of methodology and then follow most stringently whatever theoretical method was chosen.[43]

His chosen method involves a 'triple triad process: the campaign, the strategy, and the tactics, as it were.'[44] To be clear, Crossan means here three levels of his method, each of these themselves comprising three distinct layers. Crossan's prose regarding his method is, at times, not as clear as it could be.

The first of these triads involves a three-pronged approach which seeks to invoke (1) social anthropology, (2) history, and (3) literature to reconstruct the life of the historical Jesus: 'I presume an equal and interactive cooperation in which weakness in any element imperils the integrity and validity of the others ... my method, then, demands an equal sophistication on all three levels at the same time.'[45] The second triad is concerned with the literary and textual elements of historical Jesus research. Here Crossan seeks to (1) compile an inventory of texts relevant to the study of the historical Jesus, (2) to order the texts chronologically (which Crossan describes as *stratification*), and (3) identify independent attestations of traditions regarding the historical Jesus. Finally, the third triad 'focuses on the methodological manipulation of that inventory already established according to chronological hierarchy of stratification and numbered hierarchy of attestation.'[46] In other words, here Crossan seeks to make sense of the texts *as ordered and categorised* under the second methodological triad. This final triad involves (1) investigating the various textual traditions *in chronological order*, (2) constructing a hierarchy of attestation in accordance with the number of independent attestations a tradition has, and (3) disregarding any traditions only attested once, regardless of when they are attested.

Crossan is careful to avoid labelling this triadic process as objective or metaphysically neutral. He writes:

> My methodology does not claim a spurious objectivity, because almost every step demands a scholarly judgement and an informed decision. I am concerned, not with an unattainable objectivity, but with an attainable honesty. My challenge to colleagues is to accept these formal moves or, if they reject them, to replace them with better ones.[47]

He does, however, suggest that the wider discipline might adopt this approach, noting that 'historical Jesus research would at least have some common methodology instead of a rush to conclusion that could then only be accepted or denied.'[48] To be clear, at no point does Crossan explicitly claim that religious perspectives cannot inform historical Jesus research. However, it is equally true that Crossan does not actively employ anything that might resemble a religious perspective within his methodological discourse. Instead, he seems to reimagine the criteria already advanced by previous participants of the 'Quest'; we might suggest that he develops previous methods rather than expounding new ones.

This is significant because, when he invites scholars to 'accept these formal moves or ... replace them with better ones,' at no point does he acknowledge the possibility of constructing a formal historical method from within another metaphysical framework. Although Crossan himself does not explicitly operate from within a secular worldview, he also does not explicitly allow religious perspectives the opportunity to contribute to the discipline, or to his historiographical worldview. As such, I tentatively suggest it is reasonable to infer that Crossan operates within a historiographical worldview that might be described as 'secular,' in accordance with the definition of 'secular' derived at in Chatper 5 of the present study.

8.5 John P. Meier

In contrast to Crossan's single-volume contribution to the 'Quest,' the work of John P. Meier (1942–) on the historical Jesus—entitled *A Marginal Jew*—is the largest work by a single author on the historical Jesus.[49] At the outset of his work, Meier describes an imaginary 'unpapal conclave' of historians and seeks to ascertain a consensus on which all might agree. He writes:

> Suppose that a Catholic, a Protestant, a Jew, and an agnostic—all honest historians cognizant of 1st-century religious movements—were locked up in the bowels of the Harvard Divinity School library, put on a spartan diet, and not allowed to emerge until they had hammered out a consensus document on who Jesus of Nazareth was and what he intended in his own time and place … such a limited consensus statement, which does not claim to act as a substitute for the Christ of faith, is the modest goal of the present work.[50]

The sheer amount of Meier's output suggests that this goal is anything but 'modest.' In response Meier posits a Jesus who in many ways is not dissimilar from Sanders'. Meier depicts a Jewish prophet from Galilee who, initially his disciple, rejected John the Baptist's stern call for repentance and stressed God's mercy and love which would be manifest in the coming Kingdom of God. Unlike Sanders' Jesus, however, Meier's Jesus conceived of himself as possessing the authority to alter the Torah, and did so freely and it was this, coupled with his activity in Jerusalem, which ultimately lead to his death. Most critiques of Meier's work focus on his methodology, especially his use of criteria,[51] many of which were inaugurated by Norman Perrin in the late 1960's and have since been significantly problematised.[52]

As with Crossan, Meier himself notes the impossibility of objective historiography, writing: 'whether we call it a bias, a *Tendenz*, a worldview, or a faith stance, everyone who writes on the historical Jesus writes from some ideological vantage point; no critic is exempt.'[53] This begs the question, from which 'ideological vantage point'—or historiographical worldview—does Meier conduct his historiography? To Meier's credit, he is quite clear about his own personal faith perspective: 'I must candidly confess that I work out of a Catholic context,' he writes.[54] However, he is equally clear that he conceives of his faith as an inappropriate framework for speaking about the historical Jesus: 'I hope non-Catholic scholars in particular will point out where I may fail to observe my own rules by reading Catholic theology into the quest.'[55]

As is intimated by his imagined 'unpapal conclave' Meier seeks to reconstruct the figure of Jesus in a conciliatory manner that seeks not to exclude anyone from any tradition or worldview. We might describe this, in an entirely underogatory manner, as the 'lowest common denominator' approach to the historical Jesus, whereby Meier seeks to employ only those methodological criteria to which the majority will consent. In practice, this means that Meier seeks actively to resist allowing his faith perspective to inform his reconstruction of the life of Jesus. Elsewhere he writes:

> By the 'historical Jesus' I mean the Jesus whom we can recover, recapture, or reconstruct by using scientific tools of modern historical research. Granted the fragmentary state of our sources and the often indirect nature of the arguments we must use, this 'historical Jesus' will always remain a scientific construct, a theoretical abstraction that does not and cannot coincide with the full reality of Jesus of Nazareth as he actually lived and worked in Palestine during the 1st century of our era.[56]

Thus, within the scope of Meier's project, the pursuit of the historical Jesus is irrevocably distinct from knowledge of the 'real' Jesus: 'the historical Jesus is not the real Jesus, and vice versa.'[57] This is of particular importance here because it demonstrates that Meier operates with a conception of historiography that seeks not to 'read theology into' the sources, while simultaneously pointing towards the theological limitations of historical Jesus research. For example, he acknowledges the importance of faith-informed enquiry regarding the person of Jesus, *as well as* historical considerations.

However, these are, for Meier, distinct questions: 'it is simply a matter of asking one question at a time. I would be delighted if systematic theologians would pick up where this book leaves off and pursue the line of thought further.'[58] Importantly, however, Meier is quite clear that theology is for theologians, and history for historians; one's faith cannot lay claim to insight regarding the historical Jesus. Meier thus stands as an interesting case regarding his worldview and the way this interacts with his historiographical decision-making. He freely admits his own personal faith perspective, and simultaneously acknowledges that all historiography takes place within what I have described as a worldview. And yet Meier chooses to adopt a different—and markedly *secular*—historiographical worldview in order to reconstruct the life of Jesus in a manner he believes will appeal to individuals of all perspectives. It is clear that his own 'personal' worldview and the historiographical worldview he adopts in his scholarly output stand in contradiction to each other. And yet Meier is unequivocal in stressing that the religious metaphysical presuppositions that influence his 'personal' worldview should not be afforded the same influence over his historiographical worldview.

8.6 James D.G. Dunn

Like Meier, James Dunn (1939–2020) is known (amongst Jesus historians at least), for a multi-volume work on the historical Jesus,[59] although he is also a seminal figure in the field of NT Christology[60] and the so-called 'New Perspective' on Paul,[61] and his doctoral thesis on baptism in the spirit remains one of the standard treatments of the topic.[62] Dunn's most significant contribution to historical Jesus studies lies in his methodology, or more specifically, in his use of oral traditions, about which he has also written elsewhere.[63] Dunn views the texts of the NT (and the gospels in particular) as the crystalised form of pre-existing oral tradition, tradition which remained in flux even after having been written down in this manner. Dunn thus seeks to move beyond the texts themselves to the oral tradition behind them, and beyond these traditions even further, to the impact of the historical Jesus himself which brought about these traditions. In other words, by tracing Jesus' impact, one might say something about Jesus himself. This approach might be described as a historical counterpart to Gadamer's *Wirkungsgeschichte* hermeneutics.[64] Thus, in Dunn's own words:

> The first impact (sequence of impacts) made by Jesus resulted in the formation of tradition, which was itself formative and constitutive of community/church through Easter, beyond Galilee and into Greek, and was preserved and celebrated through regular performance (whether in communal or specifically liturgical gatherings) or reviewed for apologetic or catechetical purposes. In other words, what we today are confronted with in the Gospels is not the top layer (last edition) of a series of increasingly impenetrable layers, but the living tradition of Christian celebration which takes us with surprising immediacy to the heart of the first memories of Jesus.[65]

Dunn's use of these traditions results in a familiar portrayal of Jesus' life. Originally a disciple of John the Baptist, Jesus began to preach the imminence of the Kingdom of God and the coming renewal of the nation of Israel, urging his disciples to repent and ignore the unnecessarily legalistic purity codes advocated for by religious groups such as the Pharisees, leading to his death. Although Dunn's portrayal of Jesus is ultimately a conventional one, his introduction of orality into debates regarding the historical Jesus remains his most important—and most controversial—contribution to the 'Quest.'

Insofar as Dunn's historical method is concerned, again it is possible to identify a secular metaphysical worldview in operation within his scholarship that informs the way he makes historical judgements. As noted already, Dunn's method borrows from Gadamerian hermeneutics. This is because, in Dunn's words, 'that will no doubt be part of the reason for the failure of history and faith to be well together: hermeneutics is the too little acknowledged third partner—a somewhat uncomfortable *ménage à trois*.'[66] But Dunn also makes clear that by this he does not envision an integration of history and faith on an epistemological level where both are operative upon the other, but that hermeneutics is the key for allowing history to influence faith. He writes that hermeneutics is key to 'any attempt to reassert the importance of history for faith.'[67] The direction of influence is apparent. Dunn envisions history impacting upon faith *through* proper hermeneutical sensitivity; at no point does he envision faith having a similar impact upon history through any means. He writes that 'faith could and does have a theologically legitimate interest in the history of Jesus. Honest historical inquiry may be granted insights regarding Jesus which are crucially (in)formative of honest (self-critical) faith.'[68] Moreover, he speaks of historical Jesus research 'correct[ing] faith (when faith makes statements of fact beyond its competence).'[69]

This direction of influence of history *upon* faith is the result of Dunn's distinction between the *quality* of knowledge produced by history and faith, whereby the former offers a greater degree of certainty than does faith, allowing it to correct beliefs held by faith. Dunn explicitly writes that historical knowledge is based upon probabilities, not certainties. However, he suggests historical knowledge offers a greater degree of *probability* than knowledge produced by faith and that, therefore, historical knowledge introduces *a greater degree of certainty* to faith-based knowledge. This is not the same, however, as saying historical knowledge introduces certainty *per se* to knowledge produced by faith. When discussing the possibility of miracles, for example, Dunn suggests Reimarus (and the English Deists that influenced him) were right to reject notions of the historicity of Jesus' miracles: 'as David Hume had earlier pointed out, it is more probable that the account of a miracle is an untrue account than that the miracles recounted actually took place.'[70] History can, thus, inform faith, while faith is of no use for historiography; faith is uncritical trust, history is constant self-criticism. In Dunn's words, 'faith deals in trust, not in mathematical calculations, nor in a "science" which methodologically doubts everything can be doubted … faith is commitment, not just conviction.'[71]

When discussing the resurrection, Dunn is clear that even here he holds fast to his methodology: 'I do not for a moment retract my methodological principle, that our only viable subject matter for historical investigation is the impact made by Jesus as it has impressed itself into the tradition.'[72] Interestingly, immediately after reaffirming his commitment to studying the impact of the Jesus tradition, he writes:

> It is the impact summarized in the word 'resurrection' which requires us to conclude that there was a something which happened 'on the third day' which could only be apprehended/conceptualized as 'resurrection' … Despite the inconsistencies and tensions which the diversity of traditions evidences only too clearly, it is in the end of the day the tradition itself which pushes us to the conclusion that it was something perceived as having happening to *Jesus* (resurrection evidenced in empty tomb and resurrection appearances) and not just something which happened to the *disciples* (Easter faith) which provides the more plausible explanation for the origin and core content of the tradition itself.[73]

Here, in affirming the historicity of the resurrection, Dunn clearly goes beyond the boundaries of what might be affirmed within a purely naturalistic framework.

However, Dunn has not sufficiently laid the metaphysical groundwork necessary to claim that the resurrection is the most *plausible* explanation.

The historical plausibility of a claim—discussed in detail in Chapter 4 of this study—is measured in coherence to one's historiographical worldview. But Dunn's historiographical *Wirkungsgeschichte*, in the form he presents it (detailed above), does not incorporate or leave space for the agency of trans-empirical realities or agents. It is not clear how such 'a something' as that which Dunn speaks of as happening to Jesus might be said to be *possible* (let alone *probable* or *most plausible*) within this framework. Dunn does not, for example, suggest that the evidence before us, once assessed by means of his historiographical *Wirkungsgeschichte*, might lead us to think afresh about our metaphysical commitments, that the impact of the Easter event suggestively exposes the very limits of Dunn's methodology, pointing to something beyond itself.

Rather, Dunn helpfully (and correctly) states that the resurrection 'is not so much a historical fact as a foundational fact or meta-fact, the interpretative insight into reality which enables discernment of the relative importance and unimportance of all other facts.'[74] But this does not change the fact that, in Dunn's work, the resurrection is something argued *for*, not something argued *from*. In other words, Dunn (rightly) notes that the tradition's claims about the resurrection of Jesus have immediate and significant implications for the way in which history functions (history here meaning both the past itself and the study of the past), but does not address what implications this might have for his own historiographical worldview and, indeed, whether it is even possible to make such a claim from within his own historiographical worldview.

Dunn, as has been the case throughout my methodological overview of the 'Quest,' proposes a historical-critical method that does not allow for religious metaphysical presuppositions of any kind to be incorporated into his historical reconstruction of the life of Jesus. Hermeneutics, Dunn suggests, is the vital emulsifying agent that allows historical Jesus research to speak into the content of faith. Consequently, when Dunn later claims that Jesus' actual resurrection is the most plausible explanation for the phenomena described in the Easter narratives, the result is a conclusion without a sufficient prior metaphysical framework into which this conclusion might fit. In this manner, Dunn's scholarship shows evidence of the secular metaphysical tendency highlighted throughout this chapter.

8.7 Dale C. Allison Jr.

Finally, I come to Dale C. Allison Jr. (1955–), whose first monograph-length contribution to the 'Quest' came in 1998.[75] Allison's scholarship on the historical Jesus has resulted in a variety of contributions and any attempt to engage and describe his oeuvre in an overview such as the one undertaken in this chapter will necessarily have to conflate and elide the multivalency of his work into one narratable historiographical worldview. What follows is not intended as a comprehensive summary of Allison's methodology (or, indeed, methodologies), but rather a means of discussing the role of non-secular metaphysical presuppositions present in his historiographical worldview(s).[76]

For Allison, Jesus understood himself to be the Coming One that John the Baptist proclaimed and expected to reign over the Kingdom of God in God's place. Allison also intimates that Jesus and his disciples viewed themselves as societal outcasts, practising a mild form of asceticism. He has since noted that this portrayal of Jesus was largely influenced by the circumstances in which he found himself at the time of writing.[77] Following this, in 2010 Allison released *Constructing Jesus*, one of the first monographs to examine the life of Jesus through the lens of memory theory.[78] In so doing, Allison highlights the many pitfalls of human memory, including its unreliability and malleability. He therefore goes one step further than even Dunn, suggesting that, even if one might gain access to the memories of the earliest witnesses of Jesus, this alone would not be an entirely unproblematic source of historical knowledge. He begins *Constructing Jesus* with the claim that 'the frailty of human memory should distress all who quest for the so-called historical Jesus.'[79] The best one can hope for is to sketch a general overview of Jesus' life and teaching; the specificities remain unfortunately beyond our reach.

Regarding Allison's methodology, however, one may observe a tendency to refuse to allow religious metaphysical presuppositions to operate within Allison's historical-critical method. Like Sanders before him, Allison questions the usefulness of criteria in historical Jesus research, suggesting that 'we just do not know enough about first-century Judaism or early Christianity to make the criterion very reliable.'[80] And yet (again in a manner similar to Sanders) he notes that 'this state of affairs does not, however, mean that we should lay them aside. For in truth we have nothing better in the toolshed.'[81] Thus he ultimately paints a somewhat pessimistic picture of the possibility of reconstructing the life and teaching of the historical Jesus:

> Until we become literal time travellers, all attempts to find the historical Jesus will be steered by instinct and intuition. Appeals to shared criteria may, we can pray, assist us in being self-critical, but when all is said and done we look for the historical Jesus with our imaginations—and there too is where we find him, if we find him at all.[82]

Despite this, Allison does not claim 'the ax[e] of scepticism must be laid unto the roots of the trees in the Jesus tradition,'[83] although this sense of scepticism towards the task only becomes more apparent in his later work applying memory theory to the discipline, wherein he notes that 'the fallibility of memory should profoundly unsettle us would-be historians of Jesus.'[84]

Instead, he suggests progress might be made if one views historiography as a form of storytelling, whereby the historian 'aspire[s] to fashion a narrative that is more persuasive than competing narratives.'[85] This is done by a process of hypothesis verification, advancing a general framework of Jesus' life and assessing the extent to which it coheres with the available data. Allison appears not to recognise the problem in this method, namely that what one takes to be the 'available data' is ascertained by applying the criteria he seeks to move beyond: Allison wishes to eschew a detailed historical reconstruction in favour of a broad historical sketch, but advances an approach that allows him only to outline in this broad sketch one of these very details that have been identified and isolated in the manner of which he is sceptical.

Allison then suggests a set of criteria that might be used to ascertain the authenticity of broad themes in the life of the historical Jesus (rather than specific details or sayings),[86] in relation to his hypothesis of Jesus as an eschatological prophet.[87] First, a theme's plausibility is increased 'if it illumines or is illumined by the paradigm of Jesus as an eschatological prophet or known biographical information about him.'[88] Second, its plausibility is increased if the early church appears to have struggled to understand, or seems to have been embarrassed by, this aspect of Jesus' life. Third, plausibility is increased if one cannot conceive of a compelling reason for its fabrication by the early Church after the Easter event. Fourth, a theme's probability is increased if it is expressed in a manner that evidences similarity with the formal linguistic and technical aspects of Jesus' teaching.[89] Fifth, a theme's plausibility is increased if one may demonstrate 'inconspicuous or unexpected connections' with a theme already deemed to be authentic, which Allison calls 'the index of intertextual linkage.'[90] Thus, regardless of whether one refers to Allison's criteria for assessing small details concerning the historical Jesus or broader themes, he does not indicate that he is allowing religious metaphysical presuppositions to influence his historical decision-making. This remains the case in his recent magnificent work on the resurrection, wherein he cautions that 'those looking for religious bread will find here only a historical-critical stone.'[91] While Allison does not explicitly reject the possibility that such presuppositions might meaningfully contribute to the historical task, one struggles to find the impact of any non-secular metaphysical presuppositions in his historiographical worldview(s).

However, Allison has not been averse to addressing the 'extra-secular' phenomena described in the gospel accounts. For example, in his 2005 work, he is clear that the disciples' belief in the resurrection cannot be explained by the common phenomenon of post-mortem visions alone. A certain 'something else' must also be present, Allison suggests.[92] Interestingly, in his most recent work, Allison tackles the issue of the resurrection head-on. But even here he explicitly describes this most recent monograph as 'an exercise in the limits of historical criticism,' in which he seeks 'only' to 'collect data, make observations, pose questions, develop arguments, and offer suggestions and speculations about this and that.'[93] He seeks to navigate a path between 'the anemic arguments of apologists' and 'the low-wattage arguments of polemicists.'[94] He notes himself to be both religiously sympathetic and a church goer, stating that he is 'not … equidistant from the two entrenched camps.'[95] But—and this is crucial for present purposes—Allison is explicit in refusing to allow his 'personal beliefs and predilections' a say in his historiographical worldview, writing 'I have, however, sought to do my best, hoping that my conclusions derive not from reflexive prejudices and rigged starting points, but from the data, limited as they are.'[96] For Allison, historical-critical enquiry is clearly authorised to inform his faith, but it is certainly not clear that the opposite is also true; if anything, theological presuppositions appear to have conformed to what is permitted within a historical-critical (i.e., secular) metaphysics, if they are to speak into the discussion at all.

Noting the direction of travel here is key. Allison is content to allow historical-critical methodology to inform theological reflection upon the resurrection of Jesus and, in my opinion, rightly so. Certainly, I do not wish to suggest theology be detached from historical enquiry. However, the inverse is absent from Allison's methodology, even as he interrogates that most theological of historical events, the resurrection of Jesus. He does not appear to interrogate the theological content of his historiographical methodology, resulting in a historical method that is implicitly and uncritically theological and metaphysical. The lack of genuine integration of theology and history in Allison's methodology—where each is permitted to inform the other, where the direction of influence is not one way, where one does not enjoy pre-eminence over the other—results in a historical discussion of the resurrection that remains, in theological terms, precisely secular, even as it is utilised to make theological claims about the resurrection of Jesus.

There is, of course, much more one can and would like to say about Allison, were space permitting. He is, in my opinion, the foremost Jesus historian of our day and, any discussion of his oeuvre in an overview such as this will necessarily result in some oversimplification and reductionism in presenting his work. Suffice it to say here that, despite Allison's undeniable sophistication as a Jesus historian, he too is unsuccessful in genuinely integrating theological and metaphysical considerations into his historiographical method. The direction of travel remains 'one-way,' with a secular historiographical worldview permitted to shape his theological conclusions, but not *vice versa*.

8.8 Conclusion

Again, regarding the metaphysics of the third 'Quest,' it seems reasonable to suggest there was a broad trend towards a secular worldview for conducting historical Jesus research. In some cases—such as Meier's notion of an 'unpapal conclave'—religious perspectives are treated in a secular manner, insofar as they are explicitly denied the authority to engage in or influence the 'Quest.' However, while the emphasis to restate the Jewishness of Jesus is a commendable characteristic of the third 'Quest,' ultimately the third 'Quest' again proceeds from the presupposition that historiography is in its most pure form when religious interests are suppressed.

As just one example, it is rather telling that, when discussing Hengel and Dunn, Fernando Bermejo-Rubio speaks of 'respected scholars boasting of doing historical research [who also] explicitly state that it is impossible to understand Jesus' and then suggests that 'any secular-minded historian making this kind of obscurantist statements about any other figure of the past would become the laughing stock of the guild.'[97] Here we may observe two related metaphysical presuppositions behind this statement. The first is that Hengel and Dunn must be 'secular-minded' because they are respected historians. In other words, there is an implicit assumption to engage in historiography in a manner that conforms to scholarly standards and is acceptable to the academy. The second metaphysical presupposition is that to study Jesus from within this secular worldview means to treat him as though he were like any other figure from the past, to use Bermejo-Rubio's language. But this stands in direct contradiction to Christian theology which takes, as its starting point, the self-revelation of God in the person of Jesus.

At the present time there seems to be some agreement that the 'Quest' is encountering a period of change. As Bock and Webb noted in 2009, 'historical Jesus research is not only alive and well, it is also fascinatingly fruitful.'[98] Elsewhere, Ernst Baasland writes, 'the history of Jesus research shows that every new wave levels out and the scholarly effort reaches certain impasses. The "Third Quest" is definitely at this stage, and needs to be replaced by a "Fourth Quest."'[99] In addition to Hooker's withering responses to Norman Perrin in the early 1970's,[100] the 21st century has seen a number of challenges to the criteria of authenticity so that they now seem fundamentally problematic.[101] In response to this, various paths forward have been offered. Some suggest memory holds the key.[102] Elsewhere, the critical realist movement rumbles ever forward.[103]

Another shape the future of the discipline may take is intimated in Brant Pitre's *Jesus and the Last Supper*. Pitre notes that 'if there is any aspect of the historical quest for Jesus that is currently in a remarkable state of flux, it is the question of method'[104] and so seeks to frame his methodology in terms of 'plausibility' rather than 'authenticity.' However, in so doing, he explicitly builds upon the methodology of E.P. Sanders' *Jesus and Judaism*, a work deeply steeped in the language and criteria of authenticity.[105] Pitre states this most explicitly when he writes:

> I have chosen to model my approach herein on the method laid out by E.P. Sanders in his rightly famous work, *Jesus and Judaism*. Although Sanders's study is not without its own problems and methodological inconsistencies, it remains to my mind (and in the opinion of many others) one of the most brilliant and enduring contributions to the historical study of Jesus.[106]

As such, Pitre posits numerous criteria of plausibility which closely resemble the now defunct criteria of authenticity. Jordan Ryan is therefore correct to note that Pitre's *Jesus and the Last Supper* is a transitional work, with 'one foot in the previous generation of scholarship and one foot in the future of the discipline.'[107] Moreover, as I have already argued (Chapter 4), 'plausibility' lies at the centre of the 'Quest' for the historical Jesus, as it does in any historical discipline. Pitre has simply made this more explicit than others.

While there seems to be a collective acknowledgement that something 'new' is needed (or indeed inevitable), nothing has yet galvanised the discipline in a way that might provide the impetus needed to propel the 'Quest' forward. This new

'Quest,' it seems, is yet to begin in earnest. What we can say, however, is that the methods and aims evident in these first inklings of a new 'Quest' resemble those of the third 'Quest.' While critical realism will be discussed in more detail in the following chapter, memory theorists, for example, employ social memory theory to move from the gospels to that which is behind the gospels. However, to my mind this is simply to move the same problems further back; it is to ask the same questions and apply the same methods to the authors of the sources (rather than the sources themselves). If genuine change is to happen within the 'Quest,' what is needed is not new methods at answering the same questions, but rather new metaphysical frameworks altogether.

At the beginning of Chapter 6, I set out to answer the question 'to what extent may we describe modern academic historical Jesus research as secular?' This was to be done with reference to the definition of secular as outlined in Chapter 5 of the present study, whereby scholarship may be described as 'secular' if it refuses (implicitly or explicitly) to bestow any authority upon any given religious perspective. In the previous two chapters, I surveyed this one aspect of the implicit metaphysical foundations of the first and second 'Quests,' and in this chapter I have added to this by undertaking the same task with reference to the third 'Quest.' These three chapters, therefore, comprise a macro-evaluation of the secular dimension of the metaphysical frameworks upon which many of the most significant contributions to the 'Quest' for the historical Jesus have been undertaken, starting with Reimarus and ending with the 'Quest' in its current state. There is, of course, much more one would ideally like to say in such an overview, both of the figures already mentioned and discussed, and of these figures whom I have neglected entirely. What I have sought to do in these three chapters is merely to provide and begin to analyse a number of indicative figureheads for each of the three 'Quests' and their historiographical worldviews to identify whether religious metaphysical presuppositions might be observed as operative within those historiographical worldviews. In so doing, I offered the first half of my answer to the question that provoked this survey. One may suggest modern academic historical Jesus research is a secular discipline insofar as it is possible to identify a trend in the various stages of the 'Quest,' common amongst its various participants, towards a series of methods that preclude (either explicitly or implicitly) the possibility of divine agency.

In other words, despite the various forms and shapes the 'Quest' has taken, a refusal to engage with divine agency as a methodological problem for historical exegesis has remained a characteristic of the 'Quest' for the historical Jesus. In this broad sense, then, the 'Quest' has been a secular one, even when considering the so-called 'Aryan Quest' for the historical Jesus, a moment in the 'Quest' so clearly dominated by ideological impetus and yet still operating within a historiographical worldview we might term as 'secular.' So far, I have only been able to offer a broad reading of the 'Quest' and have occasionally been unable to engage in more detailed readings of individual participants in the 'Quest.' In the next chapter, however, I rectify this by interacting in detail with the contribution of N.T. Wright.

Notes

1 Mark A. Powell, *Jesus as a Figure in History* (Louisville, KY: Westminster John Knox, 1998), 22.

2 S. Neill and N.T. Wright, *The Interpretation of the New Testament 1961–1986*, 2nd ed. (Oxford: Oxford University, 1988), 363, 379.

3 Deines, *Acts of God*, 99–100. Regarding the 'new Schürer', see also Martin Hengel, 'Der alte und der neue "Schürer"', *JSS* 35.1 (1990), 19–72.

4 Leander E. Keck, *A Future for the Historical Jesus* (Nashville, TN: Abingdon, 1971), 9.

5 Marcus J. Borg, 'A Renaissance in Jesus Studies', *ThTo* 45.3 (1988), 280–92.

6 Anthony Le Donne, 'The Third Quest in Retrospect', *JSHJ* 14.1 (2016), 1–5 (1).

7 Gerd Theissen, *The Shadow of the Galilean: The Quest of the Historical Jesus in Narrative Form* (Minneapolis, MN: Fortress, 1986); idem and Annette Merz, *The Historical Jesus: A Comprehensive Guide* (Minneapolis, MN: Fortress Press, 1998); idem and Winter, *Plausible Jesus*.

8 Gerd Lüdemann, *Jesus nach 2000 Jahren. Was er wirklich sagte und tat.* (Lüneburg: zu Klampen, 2000). ET: Gerd Lüdemann, *Jesus after 2000 Years: What He Really Said and Did* (London: SCM, 2000).

9 Casey, *Jesus of Nazareth*; idem, *Jesus: Evidence and Argument or Mythicist Myths?* (London: T&T Clark, 2014).

10 James H. Charlesworth, *Jesus within Judaism: New Light from Exciting Archaeological Evidence* (London: SPCK, 1989).

11 Richard A. Horsley, *Jesus and the Spiral of Violence: Popular Jewish Resistance in Roman Palestine* (San Francisco, CA: Harper & Row, 1987); idem, *Jesus and Empire: The Kingdom of God and the New World Disorder* (Minneapolis, MN: Fortress, 2003); idem, *Jesus in Context: Power, People, and Performance* (Minneapolis, MN: Fortress, 2008); idem, *Jesus and the Politics of Roman Palestine* (Columbia, TN: University of South Carolina, 2013); idem, *Jesus and Magic: Freeing the Gospel Stories from Modern Misconceptions* (Eugene, OR: Cascade, 2014).

12 David Flusser, *Jesus: The Sage from Galilee*, 2nd augmented ed. (Jerusalem: Magnes; The Hebrew University, 1998).

13 Géza Vermes, *Jesus the Jew: A Historian's Reading of the Gospels* (Minneapolis, MN: Fortress Press, 1973). See, for example, the important recent study on Vermes' legacy: Hilde Brekke Moller, *The Vermes Quest: The Significance of Géza Vermes for Jesus Research*, LNTS, 576 (London: T&T Clark, 2017).

14 Géza Vermes, *Jesus and the World of Judaism* (London: SCM, 1983).

15 Idem, *The Religion of Jesus the Jew* (London: SCM, 1993).

16 Idem, *Jesus the Jew*, 69–78.

17 Ibid., 79.

18 However, Barnett would rightfully remind us that there is "a minority of scholars … [who] emphasize Jesus' Hellenistic environment above the Judaic. See Paul W. Barnett, *Jesus and the Logic of History*, New Studies in Biblical Theology 3 (Downers Grove, IL: IVP, 1997), 16.

19 Idem, *Jesus and the World of Judaism*, 1.

20 Ibid., 2. (emphasis mine)

21 Vermes' critique of Ratzinger's work is also addressed in Deines, *Acts of God*, 353–57. Vermes' review of the first volume of Ratzinger's *Jesus of Nazareth* was published in *The Times*, May 19th, 2007. In my own engagement with Ratzinger's work in the introduction to this study I claimed Ratzinger is actually unsuccessful in his attempt to present a genuinely Christian historiographical approach and that his historiographical method remains under the influence of secular metaphysical presuppositions.

22 Ben Witherington III, *The Jesus Quest: The Third Search for the Jew of Nazareth* (Carlisle: Paternoster, 1995), 108.

23 Deines, *Acts of God*, 356–57.
24 Sanders.
25 See, for example, the comments of this and the Sander's under-representation of Jesus' conflict with the pharisees in Ben Witherington III, *The Jesus Quest: The Third Search for the Jew of Nazareth* (Downers Grove, IL: IVP, 1995), 116–32.
26 Sanders, *Jesus and Judaism*, 3.
27 Ibid., 11. (emphasis original)
28 Ibid., 13.
29 Ibid., 14.
30 Ibid., 15.
31 Ibid., 15.
32 Ibid., 16.
33 Witherington, *Jesus Quest*, 119.
34 Sanders, *Jesus and Judaism*, 17.
35 Wright, *JVG*, 30.
36 See, for example, *The Parables of the Jesus: Red Letter Edition*, ed. Robert W. Funk, Bernard B. Scott, and James R. Butts (Sonoma, CL: Polebridge, 1988), 21.
37 See the comments in David Bentley Hart, *The New Testament: A Translation* (New Haven, CT: Yale University, 2017), xiv.
38 John Dominic Crossan, *The Historical Jesus: The Life of a Mediterranean Jewish Peasant* (New York: HarperCollins, 1991).
39 Idem, *Jesus: A Revolutionary Biography* (San Francisco, CA: HarperCollins, 1994).
40 Idem, *A Long Way from Tipperary: A Memoir* (New York: HarperCollins, 2000), 175.
41 Burton L. Mack, *A Myth of Innocence: Mark and Christian Origins* (Philadelphia, PA: Fortress, 1988); F. Gerald Downing, *Cynics and Christian Origins* (Edinburgh: T&T Clark, 1992).
42 Robert W. Lyon, '*Jesus: A Revolutionary Biography*. By John Dominic Crossan', *Journal of Church and State* 37.3 (1995), 660.
43 Crossan, *Historical Jesus*, xxviii.
44 Ibid., xxviii.
45 Ibid., xxix.
46 Ibid., xxxii.
47 Ibid., xxxiv.
48 Ibid., xxxiv.
49 John P. Meier, *A Marginal Jew: Rethinking the Historical Jesus*, 5 vols (New York: Doubleday, 1991–2016).
50 Ibid., I.1–2.
51 Ibid., I.167–95.
52 See, for example, two reviews of Meier's third volume which both share similar methodological concerns: Clive Marsh, 'Review: John P. Meier, *A Marginal Jew Volume III: Companions and Competitors*', *JSNT* 26.3 (2004), 374–76; John S. Kloppenborg, 'Review: Meier, John P., *A Marginal Jew: Rethinking the Historical Jesus* Volume III: *Companions and Competitors*', *BibInt* 12.2 (2004), 211–15.
53 Meier, *A Marginal Jew*, I.5.
54 Ibid., I.6.
55 Ibid.
56 Ibid., I.1.
57 Ibid., I.25.
58 Ibid., I.6.
59 James D.G. Dunn, *Christianity in the Making*, 3 vols (Grand Rapids, MI: Eerdmans, 2003–15).
60 Idem, *Christology in the Making: An Inquiry into the Origins of the Doctrine of the Incarnation*, 2nd ed. (London: SCM, 1989).
61 Most importantly, see idem, *New Perspective*.

62 Idem, *Baptism in the Holy Spirit: A Re-Examination of the New Testament Teaching on the Gift of the Spirit in Relation to Pentecostalism Today*, Studies in Biblical Theology *Second Series* 15 (London: SCM, 1970).
63 Idem, *The Oral Gospel Tradition* (Grand Rapids, MI: Eerdmans, 2013).
64 As first outlined in Gadamer, *Wahrheit und Methode*. Note, also, the similarity to Edward Schillebeeckx's (discussed in §6 of the previous chapter) who takes the *impact* of the historical Jesus as key to reconstructing the historical Jesus himself.
65 Dunn, *Christianity in the Making*, I.254.
66 Ibid., I.99. The Gadamerian influence is clear here and, on the same page, Dunn quotes the Gadamerian dictum: "the foundation for the study of history is hermeneutics" (Gadamer, *Truth and Method*, 198–99).
67 Dunn, *Christianity in the Making*, I.100.
68 Ibid., I.101.
69 Ibid.
70 Ibid., I.103–4.
71 Ibid., I.104.
72 Ibid., I.876.
73 Ibid. (emphases original)
74 Ibid., I.878. There are clear and significant parallels (as well as important points of contrast) with N.T. Wright's arguments concerning the resurrection here. Wright's argument is assessed more fully in the following chapter to this study.
75 Dale C. Allison, Jr., *Jesus of Nazareth: Millenarian Prophet* (Philadelphia, PA: Fortress, 1998).
76 Readers seeking an overview of Allison's career to present should consult Tucker S. Ferda, Daniel Frayer-Griggs, and Nathan C. Johnson, 'Introduction', in idem. (eds), *"To Recover What Has Been Lost": Essays on Eschatology, Intertextuality, and Reception History in Honor of Dale C. Allison Jr.*, NovTSup 183 (Leiden: Brill, 2021), 1–11.
77 See, Allison, Jr., *Historical Christ*, 17. He writes: "I wrote *Jesus of Nazareth* during an exceedingly miserable period in my life … in retrospect, an alienated Jesus with a transcendent hope was probably the Jesus I needed at the time."
78 Dale C. Allison, Jr., *Constructing Jesus: Memory, Imagination, and History* (Grand Rapids, MI: Baker Academic, 2010).
79 Allison, Jr., *Constructing Jesus*, 1.
80 Allison, Jr., *Millenarian Prophet*, 5.
81 Ibid., 6.
82 Ibid., 7.
83 Ibid., 35.
84 Allison, Jr., *Constructing Jesus*, 1, 8.
85 Allison, Jr., *Millenarian Prophet*, 36.
86 These criteria are outlined in ibid., 52–54.
87 His reasons for choosing this hypothesis are outlined in ibid., 39–44.
88 Ibid., 52.
89 These formal aspects are set out in *ibid.*, 49–50 and include: parables, antithetical parallelism, rhetorical questions, prefatory 'amens', divine passives, exaggeration or hyperbole, aphorisms, and anything apparently unexpected or paradoxical.
90 Ibid., 52, 53.
91 Dale C. Allison, Jr., *The Resurrection of Jesus: Apologetics, Polemics, History* (London: T&T Clark, 2021), 6.
92 Idem., *Resurrecting Jesus: The Earliest Christian Tradition and its Interpreters* (New York: T&T Clark, 2005), 321–26.
93 Allison, *The Resurrection*, 3.
94 Ibid., 323.
95 Ibid., 3.

96 Ibid., 7.
97 Bermejo-Rubio, 'Theses', 5.
98 Darrell L. Bock and Robert L. Webb, 'Introduction to Key Events and Actions in the Life of the Historical Jesus', in *Key Events in the Life of the Historical Jesus: A Collaborative Exploration of Context and Coherence*, ed. Darrell L. Bock and Robert L. Webb, WUNT 247 (Tübingen: Mohr Siebeck, 2009), 1–8 (1).
99 Ernst Baasland, 'Forth Quest? What Did Jesus Really Want?', in *HSHJ,* I.31–56 (56). Another helpful essay on the notion of a new quest is Roland Deines, 'Jesus and the Jewish Traditions of His Time', *Early Christianity*, 1.3 (2010), 344–71, now available in idem, *Acts of God*, 95–120.
100 Cf., Norman Perrin, *Rediscovering the Teaching of Jesus* (London: SCM, 1967); M.D. Hooker, 'Christology and Methodology', *NTS* 17.4 (1971), 480–87; idem, 'On Using the Wrong Tool', *Theology* 75.629 (1972), 570–81.
101 Keith and Le Donne, *Criteria*; Tobias Hägerland, 'The Future of Criteria in Historical Jesus Research', *JSHJ* 13.1 (2013), 43–65; Jordan J. Ryan, 'Jesus at the Crossroads of Inference and Imagination: The Relevance of R.G. Collingwood's Philosophy of History for Current Methodological Discussions in Historical Jesus Research', *JSHJ* 13.1 (2015), 66–89; Anthony Le Donne, 'The Third Quest in Retrospect', *JSHJ* 14.1 (2016), 1–5.
102 Le Donne, *Historiographical Jesus*; Rafael Rodríquez, *Structuring Early Christian Memory: Jesus in Tradition, Performance, and Text*, LNTS 407 (London: T&T Clark, 2010); Chris Keith, *Jesus' Literacy: Scribal Culture and the Teacher from Galilee*, LNTS 413 (London: T&T Clark, 2011); Chris Keith, *Jesus against the Scribal Elite: The Origins of the Conflict* (Grand Rapids, MI: Baker Academic, 2014); Zeba A. Crook, 'Collective Memory Distortion and the Quest for the Historical Jesus', *JSHJ* 11.1 (2013), 53–76; Richard Bauckham, *Jesus and the Eyewitnesses: The Gospels as Eyewitness Testimony*, 2nd ed. (Grand Rapids, MI: Eerdmans, 2017); Alan Kirk, *Memory and the Jesus Tradition*, The Reception of Jesus in the First Three Centuries 2 (London: Bloomsbury, 2018); Craig S. Keener, *Christobiography: Memory, History, and the Reliability of the Gospels* (Grand Rapids, MI: Eerdmans, 2019).
103 Here Wright remains the figure head. His work will be analysed in detail in chapter ten. Other important Critical realist works include Donald L. Denton, 'Being Interpreted by the Parables: Critical Realism as Hermeneutical Epistemology', *JSHJ* 13.2–3 (2015), 232–54; Jonathan Bernier, *The Quest for the Historical Jesus after the Demise of Authenticity: Toward a Critical Realist Philosophy of History in Jesus Studies*, LNTS 540 (London: Bloomsbury, 2016). See also the exchange between Porter and Pitts on the one hand and Bernier on the other: Stanley E. Porter and Andrew W. Pitts, 'Critical Realism in Context: N. T. Wright's Historical Method and Analytic Epistemology', *JSHJ* 13.2–3 (2015), 276–306; Jonathan Bernier, 'A Response to Porter and Pitts' "Wright's Critical Realism in Context"', *JSHJ* 14.2 (2016), 186–93; Stanley E. Porter and Andrew W. Pitts, 'Has Jonathan Bernier Rescued Critical Realism?', *JSHJ* 14.3 (2016), 241–47.
104 Pitre, *Jesus*, 28.
105 Ibid., 31–52.
106 Ibid., 31–32.
107 Jordan J. Ryan, 'The Historian's Craft and the Future of Historical Jesus Research: Engaging Brant Pitre's *Jesus and the Last Supper* as a Work of History', *JSHJ* 15.1 (2017), 60–87 (82).

9 Metaphysics and N.T. Wright

9.1 Introduction

In this chapter, I examine the use and misuse of the critical realist method adopted by N.T. Wright in his *Christian Origins and the Question of God* project and beyond, and the extent to which one may describe his method as secular.[1] In the previous chapters, I examined the metaphysical presuppositions operative in key, indicative figureheads throughout historical Jesus studies (broadly construed) and observed a shared tendency throughout the 'Quest' to resist methodological influence from religious metaphysics. I supplement this broad claim here by examining the metaphysical presuppositions operative in the work of one particular scholar. I examine Wright's critical realist method, or 'the way he chooses to move from the evidence to his particular reconstruction of the past,'[2] as described elsewhere. Wright attempts to move beyond the logical limits of his critical realist method and this attempted manoeuvre shows the secular character of his method, where Wright, like many figures highlighted already in the previous chapters, refuses to allow religious metaphysics to contribute to his historical task.

My reasons for choosing Wright as a test case for detailed analysis (over against any other historian) are as follows. In declaring its inauguration in 1988,[3] Wright is a figurehead of the third 'Quest,' and—as we shall see—his work is extremely methodologically aware, making his scholarship conducive to the methodological analysis undertaken here. Wright devotes a great deal of time to discussing the resurrection of Jesus which allows the implicit metaphysical aspects of his worldview to be more easily teased out than might be the case with other scholars. This is because, as will be discussed in detail shortly, the resurrection is *a worldview-defining event*: one's opinions regarding the historicity of the resurrection says something about one's worldview (and, thus, metaphysical framework).

I have resisted choosing a conversation partner whose historiographical worldview would be obviously supportive of my argument. It would not be a noteworthy contribution to argue that, say, Funk operates within a secular metaphysics; to apply this conclusion to suggest the discipline is secular would not be a convincing argument. Wright was formerly the Bishop of Durham within

DOI: 10.4324/b23077-11

the Church of England and, as already noted, has argued in some detail in favour of the historicity of the bodily resurrection of Jesus; one may describe Wright as an orthodox Christian. While Wright is routinely criticised for allowing his religious presuppositions to influence his historical reconstruction, my argument in what follows is actually the opposite: he has not yet thoroughly or consistently acknowledged the influence his religious metaphysical presuppositions should have upon his methodology.

If I can show how Wright's methodology bears the characteristics of secular scholarship, outlined earlier in Chapter 5, this will be a more noteworthy point than if this is true of Funk (to repeat the example from above). If my argument is accurate *even* in the case of N.T. Wright, it will be more reasonable to apply this conclusion to other participants in the 'Quest.' Though many historians could have staked an equal claim to be an ideal conversation partner representing the 'Quest' for the historical Jesus, Wright's scholarship is the most suitable for my aims in this chapter.

9.2 Critical Realism, from Lonergan to Wright

In this section, I outline Wright's critical realist historical method by first tracing its use by Lonergan and Meyer (from whom Wright receives the method) and then by assessing the method as Wright understands its function. Wright's *Christian Origins and the Question of God* series has become known for its use of a critical realist method.[4] Wright was not the first to formulate such a method: he borrowed the term from Meyer who borrowed it from Lonergan. If one is to assess Wright's historical method—and the historiographical worldview within which he conducts his scholarship—one must engage with the critical realist tradition in which he stands.

Before I begin in earnest, however, two points are worth making briefly. First, my tracing of Wright's method back to Lonergan does not preclude the possibility of other influences upon his method. Certainly, as Losch argues, the influence of Ian Barbour upon Wright's critical realist method is apparent.[5] However, in what follows I am concerned with what Wright perceives himself to be doing; if he has uncritically conflated the approaches of Barbour and Lonergan (so Losch), this does not negate the point I make in this chapter, that Wright has also uncritically adopted the theological presuppositions that accompany Lonergan's critical realism. Second, and related to this, is that there are competing readings of Lonergan. Scholars of Lonergan may take issue with my reading of Lonergan (although, as I hope will become apparent, there are also many who would agree with it). Again, it is Wright's work that is determinative here: I hope that those who read Lonergan differently to the presentation below can agree that this is how Wright (through Meyer) reads Lonergan, and that this reading (accurate or otherwise) proceeds from a set of theological and metaphysical presuppositions that Wright uncritically adopts, and which subsequently become problematic for his argument.

In this section, I examine the critical realist method for theological reflection advanced by Lonergan, which is eventually inherited by Wright as the basis of his historical-critical method. Lonergan's efforts to divorce form from content in theology are unsuccessful in that, far from presenting a theologically neutral method (as is his intention), Lonergan instead bestows secular metaphysical presuppositions with ultimate authority in his method. This is significant for the aims of the present chapter because I will later claim that Wright's work evidences a similar implicit secular metaphysics.

Bernard Lonergan (1904–84) was a Jesuit priest and philosophical theologian. He understood himself as standing in the Thomistic tradition and authored two monographs on Thomas himself.[6] Where Thomas attempted to apply Aristotelian philosophy to a Christian worldview, Lonergan sought to conceive of modern modes of thinking (be they scientific, historical, or hermeneutical) in a similar manner.[7] This leads him construct his critical realist approach. In the broadest sense of the term, critical realism refers to Lonergan's attempt to create a hermeneutical approach that upholds the independent existence of the external world without undue trust in our sensory perception of it. 'Realism,' as Porter and Pitts write, 'is the view that the world and its properties exist independently of being experienced.'[8] That is to say, there is an objective reality that remains unchanged in the face of one's opinions about the nature of that reality. For example, one's belief in the universe as created by a god does nothing to *determine* whether this is the case. Accordingly, *critical* realism—broadly construed—is the acknowledgement that there is an objective reality and the attempt to make claims about that reality while being critically aware that our perceptions of reality may be inaccurate. Or, as Porter and Pitts write 'by critical realist, Lonergan means a combination of a Thomistic understanding of having the ability to make real, accurate value judgements (thus realism) and the Kantian notion of a critique of the mind (thus critical).'[9] One need not stand within any given religious tradition to be a critical realist. In its most basic form, it merely comprises the concurrent affirmation of an objective external reality and a subjective means of apprehending that reality.

Although critical realism may refer to a plethora of traditions and methods,[10] when Wright speaks of critical realism, he means the critical realist approach proposed by Lonergan and advanced by Meyer. As Bernier notes, '[his] critical realism is that of Meyer, and Meyer's that of Lonergan.'[11] Accordingly, one must trace this development if one is to properly evaluate Wright's historical-critical method and, thus, his historiographical worldview. For this reason, Porter and Pitts claim that 'in an[y] attempt to situate Wright's critical realism it will be essential to understand Lonergan.'[12] Building upon his earlier work *Insight*, Lonergan's critical realist approach is outlined in *Method in Theology*.[13] Herein he posits a fundamental method for theological reflection in a higher education context; he thus seeks to achieve something comparable to what Wittgenstein had done for philosophy earlier in the 20th century.[14] Lonergan defines his critical realist approach in relation to what he calls empiricism and idealism. Critical realism, by contrast, is a kind of epistemological *via media*. He writes:

> The empiricist restricts objective knowledge to sense experience; for him, understanding and conceiving, judging and believing are merely subjective activities. The idealist insists that human knowing always includes understanding as well as sense; but he retains the empiricist's notion of reality, and so he thinks of the world mediated by meaning as not real but ideal. Only the critical realist can acknowledge the facts of human knowing and pronounce the world mediated by meaning to be the real world.[15]

Lonergan differentiates between four levels of consciousness and intentionality:[16]

1. *The empirical level.* This is the level at which sense-data are received. Lonergan describes this as the level 'on which we sense, perceive, imagine, feel, speak, move.'[17] Here the recipient stands in relation to reality by means of their sensory organs as pieces of data concerning the external world are apprehended by the senses.
2. *The intellectual level.* In this level the knower interrogates the data gathered by the sensory organs, analysing each piece of information to form a basic, cognitive picture of the external world. This picture is presented as a series of hypotheses or propositions about the external world. It is '[the] level on which we inquire, come to understand, express what we have understood, work out the presuppositions and implications.'[18]
3. *The rational level.* At this level the knower attempts to verify hypotheses formulated based on the cognitive picture established in the *intellectual level.* This requires the knower to 'reflect, marshal the evidence, pass judgement on the truth or falsity, certainty or probability, of a statement.'[19] Here the knower attempts to transform this cognitive picture into knowledge by assessing the truth or falsity of propositions arising from the cognitive picture established in the previous level of consciousness.
4. *The responsible level.* At this level the knower attempts to respond to the sense-data about the external world and the truth or falsity of the hypotheses that they prompt. This may involve the formation of beliefs or deciding upon a course of action to take in response to this new information, and is 'concerned with ourselves, our own operations, our goals, and so [allows us to] deliberate about possible courses of action, evaluate them, decide, and carry out our actions.'[20] The process is thus:

   Data → Hypothesis → Verification → Reflection

It is important to recognise that this does not itself constitute a method; rather, it is a theory by which one might construct a method. Bernier writes:

> Theory is to method as carpentry is to hammering. To hammer is to practice a method; to know carpentry is to think about what one does when hammering. Theories of knowledge are not methods but rather aid us in generating methods suitable for achieving a particular aim.[21]

Thus, Lonergan is not advocating critical realism as a method that theologians may or may not employ but rather a series of propositions about the production of knowledge that, when spelled out as he has done, allow for theological methods to be constructed with greater clarity, precision, and accuracy. In this way, he seeks not to establish a method or set of methods by which theologians might make claims about God but a framework within which theological studies may be undertaken.

For Lonergan's supporters, his critical realist approach allows for theology (and its constituent parts) to be studied within the context of secular universities without sacrificing their content to secular metaphysics.[22] But this is not the case. Lonergan makes explicit in the opening of *Method in Theology* that he is 'writing not theology but method in theology.'[23] However, Lonergan does not address the appropriateness of such a division between form and content in Christian theology. Thus, Lash rightly raises the question in response to Lonergan's *Method*: 'is the Christian response to truth such that so sharp a distinction between method and content in Christian theology is legitimate?'[24] Lonergan is unsuccessful in neatly divorcing form from content in the manner he envisions. Discussions pertaining to the proper methodological approach for theological reflection presume, for example, that one has made judgement on the sources of theology and the correct starting point for theology. To say something about the shape theology should take is concurrently to imply something about the content of that theology also; it is to imply theological presuppositions.

However, Lonergan does not make these theological presuppositions clear to the reader. As Meynell writes, Lonergan 'does not argue here for or from any (first-order as opposed to methodological) doctrine at all—for example, that of the existence of God or the special authority of the Catholic church.'[25] Meynell is sympathetic to Lonergan's work and means this statement in support of Lonergan against his critics. What Meynell overlooks, however, is that it is precisely Lonergan's refusal to appeal to a first-order doctrine with which his critics take issue, since it allows for a secular metaphysics instead to operate as first principle in his methodological system. For this reason, Dulles writes, 'method in theology cannot be adequately treated without some attention to these questions. In theology as in other sciences, method and content are dialectically interdependent.'[26] Similarly, Sullivan notes of Lonergan's method:

> The authentically converted Christian theologian is uniquely suited to be an instrument of the Holy Spirit's work in transmitting the faith precisely because the tradition he or she investigates and guides is Christian reflection upon the revelation of Jesus Christ; united are the person and that to which he or she is explicitly 'witnessing'.[27]

Thus, in attempting to construct a method for theology that does not take a religious metaphysical foundation, Lonergan instead produces a method one cannot describe as 'Christian'; one that refuses the influence of religious metaphysics. Or, as Rahner puts it, 'Lonergan's theological method abstracts …from the very particular, unique reference to the concrete person of Jesus.'[28] In positing a theological method without also engaging in the content of Christian theology, Lonergan has inadvertently secularised Christian theology. I do not suggest he has done this wilfully, but that Lonergan's attempt to divorce theological form from theological content is the result of an adoption of certain secular metaphysical presuppositions that ultimately reinforces these same presuppositions.

In divorcing form from content, Lonergan implicitly posits that something other than God's self-revelation in Christ is the ultimate and authoritative source of Christian theological reflection. As Kelly argues, this 'suggests presuppositions about what is absolute and original in Christian experience, and more basically, an implicit approach to theological knowing.'[29] However, Lonergan does not outline what these presuppositions might be. The result of this is not a neutral method, as Lonergan would hope, but instead a method that implicitly rejects anything distinctively Christian from being the ultimate authority for theological reflection.

As Reynolds writes, 'if one makes no theological assumptions concerning revelation and authority, what is to prevent a neutral method from rejecting the dogmas of the Church which it is meant to serve?'[30] Similarly, Aidan Nichols writes that 'the distinctiveness of the Christian faith on [Lonergan's] view is not a very interesting distinctiveness.'[31] Thus, Lonergan's critical realist approach posits method as prior to theology. But in doing so, he implicitly adopts secular theological presuppositions into this method. This is significant in my assessment of Wright's historical method (which is the ultimate concern of this chapter) because Wright inherits this method via Ben Meyer, including the implicit secular metaphysical presuppositions embedded within.

Meyer (1927–95) builds upon the work of Lonergan, explicitly acknowledging the debt he owes to his work. Meyer writes that his 'philosophical stance is entirely that of Lonergan. He is often cited; intended originality vis-à-vis his work is negligible … no attempt is made to improve on the master.'[32] Denton is therefore right to suggest, 'it would not be an exaggeration to say that Meyer everywhere assumes Lonergan's cognitional theory as the epistemological world within which he conducts his enquiries.'[33]As such, I will not devote as much time to Meyer as I will to Lonergan and Wright. For the present purposes, Meyer is merely a vehicle by which the thought of the former is transferred to the latter.

In *The Aims of Jesus*, Meyer begins by highlighting the importance of method in historical Jesus research. He asks, 'is it possible that progress in the development of historical techniques … might resolve the dilemmas of historical-Jesus research?'[34] Though many might answer affirmatively here, Meyer does not. Instead, he suggests that the problem of the historical Jesus is one step removed even from this. He claims that historical method is not the problem, but rather the underlying philosophical assumptions that guide the construction of these methods.[35] Thus, he suggests, Lonerganian hermeneutics might serve as one such way beyond the impasse.[36]

For Meyer, if methods are constructed upon improper philosophical grounds, then they will always be doomed to inadequacy. What is required of Jesus historians is a more robust philosophical framework that might lead to better historical methods that, in turn, might lead to more accurate historical reconstructions of Jesus' life and teaching. As Bernier puts it, for Meyer the discipline's 'methodological impasse is typically a symptom of a deeper malaise and … the quest for methodological solutions will be incomplete, inadequate, and not improbably unsuccessful until we engage with the deeper concerns.'[37] But Meyer seeks to move beyond even the philosophy of history and seeks to identify the problem as, first and foremost, a *cultural* one. He describes historiographical problems as a 'basic and baffling dilemma, not a technical but a cultural one.'[38] The dilemma in question concerns what Meyer views as the mutually exclusive claims about the historical Jesus made by centuries of Christian tradition on the one hand and the limits of modern historical enquiry on the other. In his own words, 'the heritage of Christian belief affirms as indispensable what the heritage of modern culture excludes as impossible.'[39]

Meyer then suggests that philosophy alone can mediate between this cultural framework and the production of knowledge, based on Lonergan's claim that 'theology mediates between a cultural matrix and the significance and role of a religion in that matrix.'[40] As to *which* philosophical approach might best mediate between culture and historiography, Meyer posits Lonergan's critical realism, without modification, as the most expedient solution. In so doing, Meyer provides the mediatorial platform through which Wright repurposes Lonergan's critical realism framework.

In his *Christian Origins and the Question of God* series, Wright builds upon this epistemological framework advanced by Lonergan and introduced to New Testament studies by Meyer, debts which Wright openly acknowledges. In *PFG*, Wright describes critical realism, in the broadest sense, as follows:

> What I mean by this is the application of history to the same overall procedure as is used in the hard sciences: not simply the mere assemblage of 'facts', but the attempt to make sense of them through forming hypotheses and then testing them against the evidence.[41]

This approach is one he labels as 'abduction'[42] and he posits critical realism as the key to the successful abduction of historical evidence, a historical method first set out in *NTPG*. Therein Wright describes critical realism as:

> A way of describing the process of 'knowing' that acknowledges the *reality of the thing known, as something other than the knower* (hence 'realism'), while also fully acknowledging that the only access we have to this reality lies along the spiralling path of *appropriate dialogue or conversation between the knower and the thing known* (hence 'critical'). This path leads to critical reflection on the products of our enquiry into 'reality', so that our assertions about 'reality' acknowledge their provisionality.[43]

In a similar manner to Lonergan's fourfold depiction of consciousness, Wright offers a threefold parallel (and in so doing conflates the second and third level of Lonergan's schema).

1. *Initial observation.* Wright does not explicate what he means by this, but it is clear that he is referring to subjective sense-perception. He writes:

   > the observer is looking from one point of view, and one only; and there is no such thing as a god's-eye view (by which would be meant a *Deist* god's-eye view) available to human beings, a point of view which is no human's point of view.
   >
   > (36)

   Here he builds upon the notion of a worldview, that all human knowledge and experience of the external world is conditioned by and filtered through one's set of presuppositions. Later he appeals to the concept of worldview explicitly. Although his definition of worldview lacks any explicit grounding in, or engagement with, the western philosophical tradition from whence it emerged, he notes that:

   > worldviews are thus the basic stuff of human existence, the lens through which the world is seen, the blueprint for how one should live in it, and above all the sense of identity and place which enables human beings to be what they are.
   >
   > (124)

   Although there are intimations that Wright appeals to the purely Kantian notion of worldview as sense-perception ('worldviews are … the lens through which the world is seen'), in practice, the cognitive understanding of worldview drive Wright's method. Elsewhere he makes clear that this lens is metaphorical and refers to how one conceives of the external world (36).
2. *Critical reflection.* This is essentially a conflation of what Lonergan called *the intellectual level* and *the rational level.* Here, upon gathering one's initial observations about the external world, one reconfigures this data into a series of hypotheses about the external world (Lonergan's *intellectual level*) and attempts to verify the truth or falsity of these hypotheses (Lonergan's *rational level*). 'We make a hypothesis about what is true, and we go about verifying or falsifying it by further experimentation,' he notes (37). Furthermore, Wright suggests that the *means* by which one verifies or falsifies these hypotheses is one's worldview: 'one needs a larger framework on which to draw, a larger set of *stories* about things that are likely to happen in the world … [one asks] in what way do the large stories and the specific data arrive at a "fit"?' (37). Later, he clarifies that it is 'worldview [which] provides the *stories* through which human beings view reality' (123). In other words, here the individual attempts to understand the sense-data ascertained in the *initial observation* by ordering this data into hypotheses to find the hypothesis that most compellingly explains the sense-data initially received.
3. *Ability to speak about reality.* Any hypothesis which one verifies by means of one's worldview, therefore, is then taken as a 'true' statement about the external world. This level of Wright's critical realist approach thus aligns

with Lonergan's *responsible level*; here (according to both Wright and Lonergan) the individual reflects upon the implication of the truth/falsity of these hypotheses and decides upon a course of action in light of this.

Wright's critical realism is essentially Meyer's, then, which is essentially Lonergan's. There are two main differences between Wright and Lonergan: (1) Wright conflates Lonergan's *intellectual* and *rational* levels into one that comprises hypothesis construction and verification, and (2) Wright explicitly construes worldview as the means by which one verifies these hypotheses.

9.3 The Implied Metaphysics in Wright's Methodology

As intimated above, this critical realist methodology has enjoyed considerable influence within the field of historical Jesus research. Those who have adopted this model following *NTPG* include Dunn,[44] Denton,[45] McKnight,[46] and Bernier.[47] However, its use has not acquired universal assent amongst historians. Porter and Pitts have raised concerns about critical realism's epistemological foundation[48] and, while such an objection is valid, it fails to identify the underlying metaphysical presuppositions embedded in this methodology (and to be fair, this is not Porter and Pitts' intention). It is this that I wish to identify. If Wright suggests that all epistemology is filtered through one's worldview and, thus, all historical judgements are filtered through one's worldview, then he and I stand in congruity regarding worldview's place as prior to historiography (logically speaking). Or, to use my concluding language from Chapters 2 to 4 of the present study, *metaphysics is prior to historiography*. This begs the question, then, what metaphysical framework stands prior to Wright's historical reconstruction?

While my analysis of Wright hitherto has focussed on his *NTPG*, to understand the metaphysical framework within which Wright is operating, one must instead turn to his later work *RSG*. It is there that his metaphysical framework becomes clearest. He begins with the surprising admission that 'all the arrows of history cannot reach God … the transcendence of the god(s) of Judaism, Christianity and Islam provides the theological equivalent of the force of gravity. The arrows of history are doomed to fall short.'[49] And yet Wright asserts that in Jesus—God incarnate—the transcendent God 'appeared within the gravitational field of history' so that 'the transcendence of this god [has] come within bowshot' (11). I do not wish to query Wright on this point. Regardless of one's views on Christ's relationship to history, Wright's claim that Christ is the historically bound manifestation of the historically sovereign God is not a secular claim. Any historical method that takes this as its starting point may be said to be a genuinely Christian historiography.

My criticism of Wright is that this observation fails to impact his methodology in any meaningful way, meaning that his historical method is *de facto* secular. Regardless of what he *says*, the way Wright *does* history is devoid of any concept of divine agency or extra-secular metaphysical presupposition. He proceeds without reference to God or divine activity, so that his methodology may reasonably be labelled 'secular' in practice, regardless of how it is framed in theory. This subsequently becomes problematic due to Wright's willingness to move beyond the limits of this secular metaphysical framework in his discussion of the Easter event. As I discuss in more detail below, Wright fails to apply this secular, critical realist historiographical method consistently at the very moment divine agency is introduced into this discussion on the historicity of Jesus' resurrection.[50]

Following Wright's opening remarks on the transcendence of God being made manifest in history through Christ, he helpfully and carefully defines what it means to speak of the resurrection as a historical event. In so doing, he distinguishes between five different senses of the word 'history' and its cognates (12–13):

1. *History as event.* This refers to things that have happened, regardless of whether such events are known or if they can be proved to have taken place. As such, this use of 'historical' refers simply to things that have existed.
2. *History as significant event.* This refers not only to things that have happened or people that have existed, but to those events and people that have left a lasting impact upon the world. To say, 'the fall of the Berlin wall was a historic event,' is not merely to say that it happened, but that it had profound consequences too.
3. *History as provable event.* To describe something as 'historical' in this sense means that it can, in some way, demonstrably be shown to have happened.
4. *History as writing about the past.* This sense of history refers to the act of speaking about the past, whatever form that may take. *Saving Private Ryan* may be described as a historical film in two different ways. It is historical in the sense that it enjoyed enormous success and had an impact upon the films that followed it. But it is also a historical film in the sense that it attempts to say something about the past.
5. *History as that which modern historians can say about history.* This is something of a combination of senses 3 and 4 of history and its cognates. Wright notes that 'in this sense, "historical" means not only that which can be demonstrated and written, but that which can be demonstrated and written *within the post-Enlightenment worldview*' (13, emphasis original).

In what sense does Wright imagine himself to be speaking about the historicity of the resurrection? It is a combination of sense 1 and sense 5: he speaks of 'the question at stake throughout much of this book: was the resurrection something that actually happened?' (sense 1) but he also notes that 'it is sense 5 that has caused the real headache' for Jesus historians (14). In what follows Wright continues to lay the foundation for his study by assessing the work of those scholars who object to the very notion of studying the resurrection as a historical event. Following Crossan,[51] he divides these scholars into those who say the resurrection *cannot* be studied as a historical event (15–20), and those who suggest it *should not* (20–28). It is Wright's treatment of the theological objections to such an endeavour—those who say the resurrection *shouldn't* be studied historically to use his terminology—that are pertinent for present purposes.

Here Wright deals with the notion that the resurrection is the starting point of Christian epistemology, an argument he traces back primarily to Hans Frei.[52] The resurrection forms the basis of knowledge within a Christian worldview. Stated otherwise, the resurrection is the foundation of Christian metaphysics. From the confines of a Christian worldview, the resurrection is the starting point of rational enquiry, and so to treat it as one object of study amongst others would require conformity to a different epistemological foundation, at which point any observations made about the resurrection would be the product of a non-Christian worldview. Wright's response to this is the point at which his methodology begins to collapse. For him, this argument 'simply begs the question.' He asserts that 'even if some Christians might wish to rule it off limits, they have (presumably) no *a priori* right to tell other historians, whether Muslims, Jews, Hindus, Buddhists, New Agers, gnostics, agnostics, or anyone else, what they may and may not study' (21). But it is unclear that this is Frei's intention. Frei wishes to demonstrate that, from within the confines of a Christian worldview, it is a logical fallacy to suggest that one may approach the resurrection historically since that event itself forms the basis of the Christian worldview and, thus, marks the starting point of Christian epistemology and, therefore, Christian scholarship. Frei does not demand that non-Christians conform to this worldview, nor does he suggest that the resurrection is in any sense 'off limits' to non-Christians.

If anyone is in danger of prescribing conformity in this situation, it is Wright himself. In his five senses of 'history' and its cognates, the fifth possible sense refers not only to 'that which can be demonstrated and written, but that which can be demonstrated and written *within the post-Enlightenment worldview*' (13, emphasis original). And yet at no point does Wright contemplate the possibility of anything *other than* a post-Enlightenment metaphysics. In this respect, it is telling that Wright asserts:

> even if it were true that a fully Christian epistemology would want to begin all its knowing with Jesus, confessed as the crucified and risen Messiah, that does not mean that there is no access to Jesus and his death and resurrection in the public world.
>
> (22)

Wright does not take issue with the notion that the resurrection is the starting point of Christian epistemology. Rather, he takes issue with the impact that recognition of this may have upon public discourse regarding the historical Jesus. There is no evidence that Wright conceives of Christian epistemology as being able to exist alongside other worldviews in public discourse. Indeed, it seems as though Wright imagines that only shared worldviews can facilitate public (or indeed any) dialogue. He only mentions the post-Enlightenment worldview in his survey of the five senses of history. Where Wright does mention other worldviews (i.e., in his indictment of Frei as a quasi-totalitarian figure), there is no indication that people of these worldviews may contribute to public discourse without conformity to this all-encompassing post-Enlightenment metaphysics. Furthermore, Wright's distinction between public and private, with a Christian worldview relegated to the private sphere, evidences his indebtedness to a secular reasoning within which this distinction also plays a crucial role.

It is true that Frei's theory 'is always in danger of describing a closed epistemological circle, a fideism from within which everything can be seen clearly but which necessarily remains opaque to those outside' (21). What Wright fails to acknowledge is that there are *only* closed epistemological circles when it comes to the resurrection. If one has a Christian worldview that begins by taking the resurrection as a historical given, then one can either affirm the historicity of the resurrection (thus closing the epistemological circle) or deny it (thus undermining the epistemological foundations for such a claim and nullifying the conclusion). If one is of a non-Christian worldview that proceeds from another epistemological starting point, one can either deny the historicity of the resurrection (thus closing the epistemological circle) or affirming it (thus affirming it as the real foundation of epistemology and therefore undermining the epistemological foundations for such a claim and nullifying the conclusion). There is no neutral starting point regarding the resurrection. It is a *worldview-defining event*. One cannot pass judgement on the historicity regarding the resurrection without tacitly passing judgement on how various worldviews conceive of the resurrection. To dismiss the historicity of the resurrection is also to dismiss the Christian worldview that takes it as given. Since metaphysical frameworks (i.e., worldviews) proceed historiography, cyclical or self-contradictory epistemologies are unavoidable.

Wright himself seems to acknowledge this in his recent Gifford Lectures, wherein he writes, 'nobody asks questions about God and the world from a detached standpoint. A pretended objectivity is merely naïve.'[53] Even more explicitly in these lectures, he claims 'the resurrection of Jesus is presented in the New Testament as, more specifically, an event which brings its own ontology and epistemology with it.'[54] But Wright does not appear to consider it appropriate to incorporate this new ontology and epistemology into his historical methodology. To be clear, Wright does recognise some of the resurrection's potency when he remarks:

> The strange signposts we find in the present world [including the resurrection of Jesus], though in the dark of midnight they might seem to point elsewhere, or even to be some kind of sick joke, are after all true, if broken, signposts to the ultimate realities of God and the world.[55]

However, this conviction in 'the ultimate realities of God' does not directly impact upon his historiographical method, a method which remains decidedly free of reference to these self-same 'ultimate realities.' In other words, Wright end up in a position whereby his Christian worldview, proffered as a conclusion to his research, is reached and upheld by a series of methods predicated upon a secular worldview.

Let us consider, for example, Wright's conclusions regarding the resurrection. He takes as his starting point the early Christian belief that 'Jesus of Nazareth was bodily raised from the dead,' a belief which 'was at the centre of [early Christian] characteristic praxis, narrative.' The question is thus posed: 'what caused this belief in the resurrection of Jesus?' (685). In answering this question, he suggests there are 'two things which must be regarded as historically secure' (686). These are (1) the empty tomb, and (2) the resurrection appearances. Wright begins by examining the empty tomb.[56] Wright asserts the empty tomb would, on its own, not have been an unusual enough event to warrant belief in Jesus' resurrection but would have instead been viewed as the 'fairly common practice of grave-robbery' (688). Certainly, the disciples of Jesus were not expecting Jesus to be resurrected, prior to the Easter event and 'had the tomb been empty, with no other unusual occurrences, no one would have said that Jesus was the Messiah of the lord of the world' (689).

Similarly, the so-called resurrection appearances would not have led to belief in the bodily resurrection of Jesus, unless supplemented by other phenomena. Visions of the recently-deceased were not uncommon in antiquity, and never led to the belief that the person in question had been brought back from the dead.[57] Thus, the post-Easter experience of Jesus would have been highly unlikely to have led to the belief that Jesus had risen from the dead. As Wright notes:

> Precisely because such encounters were reasonably well known … they *could not possibly*, by themselves, have given rise to the belief that Jesus had been raised from the dead. They are a thoroughly *insufficient* condition for the early Christian belief. (690, emphases original).

Therefore, Wright concludes:

> It is thus comparatively straightforward to show that, by themselves, neither an empty tomb nor visual 'appearances'—however we categorize them—would be sufficient to generate the early Christian beliefs we have been studying … Neither, without the other, makes the sense that the early Christians believed they made … Bring them together, however, and they generate early Christian belief. (692)

The early belief in Jesus' resurrection is thus itself strong evidence for the historicity of the disappearance of Jesus' body (what Wright and others anachronistically refer to as 'the empty tomb') *and* of the so-called resurrection appearances. It follows, therefore, that both the disappearance of Jesus' body, and the post-Easter appearances of Jesus to his disciples, should be ascribed a high probability regarding their historicity:

> I conclude that the historian, of whatever persuasion, has no option but to affirm both the empty tomb and the 'meetings' with Jesus as 'historical events' in all senses we sketched in chapter 1 [of *RSG*]: they took place as real events; they were significant events; they are, in the normal sense required by historians, provable events; historians can and should write about them. We cannot account for early Christianity without them. (709)

Having established these two pieces of historical data, Wright seeks to ascertain the most plausible explanation for them. The best explanation available is that Jesus was bodily raised from the dead: 'if Jesus was raised, with … a "transphysical" body, both the same and yet in some mysterious way transformed, the two key pieces of evidence, the empty tomb and the "meetings" are explained. The arch fits the pillars exactly' (711). Other than the comments in the passage here quoted, Wright does not articulate the precise nuances of the phrase 'transphysical body.' However, Wright is frequently at pains to note Jesus' *bodily* resurrection (over against claims that Jesus was *spiritually* resurrected) since it is vital for his analysis of the so-called 'empty tomb.'

His conclusion—which he categorises as an '*inference to the best explanation*, which is one variety of "abduction"' (716, emphasis original)—is that all other explanations of these two pieces of data are ultimately problematic. Psychoanalytical approaches to the resurrection appearances do not account for the empty tomb; theories that the disciples stole Jesus' body do not account for the appearances, and so on. The least problematic (and therefore most plausible) explanation is that Jesus was bodily risen from the dead. Wright's argument may be summarised thus:

1. The texts of the New Testament betray an early belief in the resurrection of Jesus.
2. This belief can *only* be explained by *both* the disappearance of Jesus' body *and* experiences of him appearing to his disciples after his death.
3. Neither of these phenomena on their own would have prompted belief in Jesus' resurrection.
4. The combination of these two phenomena gives historians grounds to ascribe plausibility to the bodily resurrection of Jesus.

Aside from some minor technical points, I concur with Wright on points 1–3. Tracing the impact of Jesus' life through the beliefs of the earliest Christians as crystallised in the texts of the New Testament is a legitimate means of ascertaining historical knowledge and may be seen as a historical version of Gadamerian *Wirkungsgeschichte*. Rather, my issue with Wright's methodology is found in the way he moves from the evidence in point 3 (there was an empty tomb and resurrection appearances) to the conclusion in point 4 (therefore, Jesus was probably risen bodily from the dead). Here Wright's conclusions undermine the metaphysical framework within which his historical method is construed. Even if we grant Wright points 1–3, point 4 does not logically follow. To be more specific, Wright's secular framework for making historical judgements logically prohibits him from drawing the very conclusion found in point 4, since it is a decidedly *un*secular assertion. More importantly for my overall argument, it is in this manoeuvre that one may observe the fundamentally metaphysical nature of all historical judgements.

I have demonstrated, above, that Wright's methodology might be described as 'secular,' insofar as it is 'emptied of God, or of any reference to ultimate reality,'[58] to reiterate the language of Taylor. In other words, Wright begins his historical reconstruction from a place that does not allow the influence of religious metaphysics.

However, there can be no neutral historiography, insofar as all historiography is metaphysical and, therefore, impinges upon claims about the divine (even if that is the divine's non-existence or passivity regarding human affairs). Furthermore, Wright understands his method as 'the application of history to the same overall procedure as is used in the hard sciences,' without acknowledging the metaphysical and methodological biases inherent therein, as noted by Popper[59] and (from a more theological standpoint) Milbank.[60]

Wright's willingness to move freely beyond his critical realism framework is perhaps best evidenced in one startling and blunt passage, where he deals with the notoriously difficult pericope of Matt. 27.51–53, a pericope with numerous issues textually, theologically, and historically.[61] It reads:

> And behold, at that moment the curtain of the temple was torn in two from top to bottom. The earth shook, the rocks split, and the tombs broke open. The bodies of many holy people who had died were raised to life. They came out of the tombs after Jesus' resurrection and went into the holy city and appeared to many.

The theological symbolism here is rich, and the historical evidence for these events is scarce.[62] So, what does Wright make of this pericope? Seemingly casting aside his critical realism framework for a moment, he simply concludes that 'some stories are so odd that they may just have happened. This may be one of them' (636). Allison rightfully takes issue with this sentiment, noting that:

> These lame words lack all historical sense. They are pure apologetics, a product of the will to believe, and a prize illustration of theological predispositions moving an intelligent man to render an unintelligent verdict.[63]

The irony of Wright's work is that Lonergan, as we have seen, advanced critical realism as a *via media* between empiricism and idealism, both of which were said to fail the test of 'self-reversal,' whereby 'I quite spontaneously operate in one way, but laboriously theorize in another.'[64] This also applies to Wright's method: he acknowledges the transcendence of God and God's supremacy over history, and yet proceeds in a historical reconstruction that leaves no room for religious metaphysical presuppositions to influence his method. Wright himself notes:

> To say, as the early Christians did, that the tomb was empty, and that the 'meetings' with Jesus took place, because he had been bodily raised from the dead, seems to require the suspension of all our normal language about how we know things about the past. (710).

And yet he at no point acknowledges the fact that his own historical framework should be included in this methodological 'suspension.' Wright's conclusion is akin to suggesting 'my historical reconstruction of the resurrection undermines all secular historiography except my own.' Wright's historiographical worldview resists influence from religious metaphysical presuppositions; and yet his conclusion leads him to make metaphysical claims that fundamentally oppose this historiographical worldview.

It is worth noting briefly, also, what Wright's argument does *not* entail. Wright does not present his argument from within a secular historiographical worldview to show the *limitations* of that framework (and thus to reflect on whether a different framework might be better placed to make sense of the historical data under consideration). Instead, Wright concludes something rather different. While remaining within this secular historiographical worldview, Wright states the following, at the climax of his argument:

> The actual bodily resurrection of Jesus (not a mere resuscitation, but a transforming revivification) clearly provides a *sufficient* condition of the tomb being empty and the '[resurrection appearance] meetings' taking place. Nobody is likely to doubt that … My claim is stronger: that the bodily resurrection of Jesus provides a *necessary* condition for these things; in other words, that no other explanation could or would do. All the efforts to find alternative explanations fail, and they were bound to do so. (717, emphases original)

Wright is clear that a *necessary* condition constitutes 'something that has to be the case for the conclusion to follow: it is a necessary condition of my computer working properly that the house be connected to an electricity supply' (687). Wright does appear to leave open the possibility of alternative explanations for the phenomena of the empty tomb and resurrection appearances. But he does so in such a manner that reinforces the notion that Wright considers the bodily resurrection a *necessary condition* of these phenomena, asking:

> What alternative account can be offered which will explain the data just as well [as the bodily resurrection of Jesus], which can provide an alternative *sufficient* explanation for all the evidence and so challenge the right of the bodily resurrection to be regarded as the *necessary* one? (718, emphases original).

This 'stronger claim' about the *necessity* of Jesus' bodily resurrection from the dead is precisely the point at which Wright's argument comes unstuck. Rather than presenting the resurrection as a *sufficient* cause for the empty tomb and the resurrection appearances that raises questions of significance concerning secular historiography's ability to account for these phenomena, Wright goes a step further, and claims it to be a *necessary* cause also. But this claim is advanced apart from any meaningful reflection on what such a conclusion might mean for the very methods and framework by which the conclusion is reached; he fails to acknowledge that his conclusion explodes the methodology that precedes it. My contention here is similar to my contention with Dunn's position on the resurrection (cf. Chapter 8, §6). However, whereas Dunn correctly asserts that the resurrection was not merely one historical fact amongst others, but the starting point for perceiving reality as it really is (albeit a starting point from which Dunn does not examine his own historiographical worldview), this is not true of Wright. (More specifically, it is not true of Wright in *RSG*; more nuance is present in his recent *History and Eschatology*, but the implications of the resurrection upon historiography are not fully explored). For both Dunn and Wright, the resurrection remains something argued *for*, not argued *from*, even if Dunn correctly acknowledges that the historicity of the resurrection should prompt us to undertake the latter approach.

That early Christian *belief* in the resurrection contributed to interest in the historical Jesus is certainly beyond dispute.[65] However, to prevaricate about whether such belief is *warranted* goes beyond that which is permissible within his critical realist framework. As such, I disagree here with Licona who suggests historians might discuss the 'mere facticity' of so-called 'miraculous' events (here Licona speaks in broad terms rather than with regards to the resurrection specifically), without adjudicating on the *cause* of such events.[66] In other words, we might say Jesus healed blind people without speculating as to how. On some occasions this might be true, but with regards to the resurrection specifically, its facticity and its causation are impossible to tease apart and are impossible to adjudicate upon without concurrently making metaphysical claims about the person of Jesus of Nazareth.

Wright even doubles-down on this assertion of the historicity of Jesus' bodily resurrection in the aftermath of *RSG*. In response to four review essays on the book, Wright states

> I still believe, and nothing in these four essays remotely challenges this, that the best historical explanation for the rise of the multi-faceted phenomenon we know as early Christianity is the combination of an empty tomb and the sightings of Jesus himself bodily alive (though in a transformed, not merely resurrected body) for a month or so after his crucifixion; and that the best explanation for the empty tomb and the sightings is the proposal that Jesus was indeed full alive again and that his body had been transformed into what I have called a 'transphysical' state.[67]

Crucially, he makes clear again in this response that he seeks to operate in the historical-critical mode of enquiry dominant within historical Jesus research:

> *The Resurrection of the Son of God* is an attempt to … answer the question in the terms in which it has been put, that is, by means of a historical argument, while pointing on to the fact that full Christian faith is not a matter of history alone.[68]

Wright himself makes a similar distinction to Lonergan between what he calls 'positivism' and 'phenomenalism.'[69] In attempting to chart a *via media*, Wright employs what is essentially a secular metaphysics (particularised in the instance of a Lonerganian epistemology) to advance a hypothesis that God raised Jesus from the dead. If this hypothesis is correct, then it negates the very methodology Wright uses to come to this conclusion. In the words of Wright's muse, Meyer, 'you are not allowed to escape the consequences of cutting off the branch you are sitting on.'[70]

To Wright's credit, there are signs—even if still not an outright acknowledgement—in his recent Gifford Lectures that he is aware of having gone too far in *RSG*.[71] He notes that it is possible for the historian to 'defeat the defeaters' regarding the resurrection (i.e., to counteract arguments *against* the historicity of the resurrection). But crucially, he further notes that

> None of this ['defeating the defeaters'] in itself—to the disappointment of some, perhaps—is intended to serve as a knock-down argument for the historicity of Jesus' bodily resurrection … At this the discipline of history can have nothing more to say … it can lead us to the water, but it can't make us drink … the resurrection offers itself as the centre of a new kind of ontology, inviting a new kind of epistemology. (197–8)

Here, for the first time, Wright seems finally to have acknowledged what many have stressed previously, and what I have again asserted in this chapter, that the claim in *RSG* for the bodily resurrection of Jesus as a *necessary condition* of the phenomena of the empty tomb and the resurrection appearances simply moves irrevocably beyond the metaphysical confines of his critical realist method. Disappointingly, however, Wright is yet to state explicitly whether he still holds to the claim about the necessity of the resurrection in *RSG* in the aftermath this (apparent) shift in his position. It is difficult to see how the conclusion to *RSG*, cited above, can stand given what is said in *H&E* but, if Wright is cognisant of this, he is yet to vocalise with clarity this logical aporia underpinning his *Christian Origins and the Question of God* project.

And yet further confusion remains about Wright's project in the aftermath of *H&E*. Wright insists that Christian historians must not appeal to 'the worst kind of special pleading, the most blatant confession of "private knowing", a sheer subjectivity with no possible purchase on ordinary reality,' (188) speaking frequently in the lectures about the need for the Christian historian to engage in 'public scholarship.' As with many crucial terms in *H&E*, Wright is maddeningly unclear about what he means by this. Additionally, one wonders precisely to what 'ordinary reality' refers in the above quote. I say with all sincerity that I deeply appreciate Wright's willingness to think about and take seriously the issues he addresses in *H&E* and throughout his *Christian Origins* project. However, his lack of precision about the meaning of key terms and phrases obfuscates his argument to a considerable degree. This problem is also found regarding his 'epistemology of love' which, despite being central to his argument and aims in *H&E*, is never clearly defined or explained, to the point that the term is so vague to essentially become meaningless.

Presumably, in this context, Wright uses the term 'public' to suggest Christian historians should not engage in dialogue in such a manner that one must assent to Christian doctrine in order to participate. Here, Wright's argument in *H&E* is hampered by the text's basis on his Gifford Lectures, which must be posited as 'public discourse.' Facets of Wright's argument—like the aforementioned insistence that he is doing 'public scholarship,' his disagreements with (and misreadings of) Barth, and the rather bewildering connection to 'natural theology' (Wright's version of which looks nothing like any recognisable form of 'natural theology')—do appear 'shoehorned' into his argument to fit with the remit of the Gifford Lectures. One wonders: in a parallel universe where *H&E* was not first written as the Gifford Lectures, how different would the text and its argument be?

He states that 'telling the historically rooted story of Jesus *as the story of God* … can never collapse into the "in-talk" of those who have received a private "special revelation",' further noting that 'none of this is to imply that history itself can produce primary God-talk' (276, emphasis original). And yet, on the very next page (itself the final page of *H&E*), he notes (without further explanation or clarification!) that 'the power of the spirit … [is one of] the necessary conditions for … first order God-talk' (277). What Wright *seems* to be proposing is a dual-stage process whereby events are first assessed according to 'publicly-accessible' secular historiography, and then second given theological 'significance' in and through a separate theological process (his 'epistemology of love'), such that the latter *may* affirm the bodily resurrection of Jesus, while the former *may not*. (However, it bears repeating that Wright is not at all clear on this point.)

But all of this fails to consider what I have demonstrated earlier in this study, that *all* historiographical methods proceed from historiographical worldviews that are irrevocably and unavoidably *metaphysical* and, in the case at least of historiographical worldviews within which the historical Jesus is apprehended, *theological*. As such, Wright's first, 'purely historical' stage is *no less theological* than his second 'explicitly theological' stage in such a way that the former cannot inform the latter, since the latter takes as its foundation (amongst other things) the bodily resurrection and the work of the Spirit, both phenomena that are impossible to affirm and proceed from within the former stage. As Allison has written elsewhere:

> We should be more modest in our abilities. Robust confidence in our historical-critical conclusions is out of place … People's arguments regarding the origins of Christianity are unavoidably driven by large assumptions about the nature of the world, assumptions that cannot often if ever be the upshot of historical investigation … Wright's passionate belief in the traditional Christian confession was not the result of his historical researches but rather an article of faith that has informed his scholarly work from its inception.[72]

As such, while *H&E* sees, for the first time, Wright appearing to acknowledge the fulness of the metaphysical and theological implications of the resurrection of Jesus, and their impact upon historiography, Wright still does not fully apply these implications to his own methodology in thoroughgoing fashion. Such an application would, at the very least, involve Wright recanting claims about the necessity of the bodily resurrection in *RSG* and would ideally see Wright positing a single, unified historiographical method that explicitly takes the resurrection of Jesus as its starting point.

9.4 Conclusion

Wright criticises Schillebeeckx for failing to follow through on his promise to reject enlightenment historiographies (and rightly so),[73] and yet we might equally burden Wright with the same critique. In this chapter, I analysed the historical methodology of N.T. Wright's *Christian Origins and the Question of God* series, taken as paradigmatic (not *representative*) of modern historical approaches to Jesus, due to his acute awareness of historical methodology and interaction with the metaphysically potent subject of the resurrection. I examined the framework known as critical realism, in the form espoused by Lonergan, Meyer, and Wright himself. Using this as the entry point to assess Wright's broader historical method, I asserted that Wright's historiography might accurately be described as 'secular,' insofar as it refuses to incorporate any aspect of divine activity. I then turned to Wright's examination of the resurrection of Jesus where I examined the manner in which Wright moves from historical data (regarding the 'empty tomb, and the resurrection appearances') to the conclusion that Jesus was bodily risen from the dead. I claimed this is a move that Wright's secular critical realist methodology does not allow him to make, logically speaking, since it undermines his metaphysical historiographical foundation.

Having surveyed in the previous three chapters the 'Quest' for the historical Jesus in broad terms, including some of its key figureheads, I have sought to supplement that analysis with a detailed examination of one particular participant in the 'Quest': N.T. Wright. This macro- and micro-level analysis is intended to function concurrently, and to serve as collective warrant for the claim that the 'Quest' for the historical Jesus has operated with a set of historiographical worldviews that evidence a shared tendency not to allow religious metaphysical presuppositions influence within historiographical methodology. We might, I suggest, therefore describe the discipline as a 'secular' discipline, in accordance with the definition of 'secular' derived in Chapter 5 of the present study. All that is left is to discuss the implications of this claim for the discipline moving forward. It is to this task that I turn in the next and final chapter.

Notes

1 This chapter is a slightly revised version of my earlier article: Jonathan Rowlands, 'The Theological Lineage of N.T. Wright's Historical Method', *JTI* 16.1 (2022), 110–31.

2 Theresa Heilig and Christoph Heilig, 'Historical Methodology', in *God and the Faithfulness of Paul: A Critical Examination of the Pauline Theology of N.T. Wright*, ed. Christoph Heilig, J. Thomas Hewitt, and Michael F. Bird, WUNT II.413 (Tübingen: Mohr Siebeck, 2016), 115–50 (115–16).

3 S. Neill and N.T. Wright, *The Interpretation of the New Testament 1961–1986*, 2nd ed. (Oxford: Oxford University, 1988), 363, 379.

4 Thus far the series has considered hermeneutical and historical methodology (*NTPG*), the historical Jesus (*JVG*), the historicity of Jesus' resurrection (*RSG*), and Pauline theology (*PFG*).

5 Andreas Losch, 'Wright's Version of Critical Realism', in *God and the Faithfulness of Paul: A Critical Examination of the Pauline Theology of N.T. Wright*, ed. Christoph Heilig, J. Thomas Hewitt, and Michael F. Bird, WUNT II.413 (Tübingen: Mohr Siebeck, 2016), 101–14.

6 Bernard J.F. Lonergan, *Grace and Freedom: Operative Grace in the Thought of Thomas Aquinas* (Toronto, ON: University of Toronto, 2000); idem, *Verbum: Word and Idea in Aquinas* (Toronto, ON: University of Toronto, 1997).

7 See the comments in Bernard J.F. Lonergan, 'Insight Revisited', in *A Second Collection*, ed. William F.J. Ryan and Bernard J. Tyrrell (Philadelphia, PA: Westminster John Knox, 1974), 263–78 (268, 277).

8 Stanley E. Porter and Andrew W. Pitts, 'Critical Realism in Context: N. T. Wright's Historical Method and Analytic Epistemology', *JSHJ* 13.2–3 (2015), 276–306 (278).

9 Porter and Pitts, 'Critical Realism in Context', 289.

10 See the comments by Robert B. Stewart, *The Quest of the Hermeneutical Jesus: The Impact of Hermeneutics on the Jesus Research of John Dominic Crossan and N. T. Wright* (Lanham, MD: University Press of America, 2008), 77; Robert L. Webb, 'The Historical Enterprise and Historical Jesus Research', in *Key Events in the Life of the Historical Jesus*, ed. Darrell L. Bock and Robert L. Webb, WUNT, 247 (Tübingen: Mohr Siebeck, 2009), 9–94 (28 n.55).

11 Bernier, *Demise of Authenticity*, 5–6.

12 Porter and Pitts, 'Critical Realism in Context', 288.

13 Bernard J.F. Lonergan, *Insight: A Study of Human Understanding*, Collected Works of Bernard Lonergan, 3, 5th ed. (Toronto, ON: University of Toronto, 1992); idem, *Method in Theology* (New York: Herder & Herder, 1972).

14 On the confluences between Lonergan and Wittgenstein, see Christopher Sean Friel, 'Wittgenstein and Lonergan on Mathematical Wonder: Towards a Dialogue of Methods', *Modern Theology* 31.3 (2015), 469–87.

15 Lonergan, *Method in Theology*, 238–39.

16 Ibid., 9.

17 Ibid.

18 Ibid.

19 Ibid.

20 Ibid.

21 Jonathan Bernier, 'A Response to Porter and Pitts' "Wright's Critical Realism in Context"', *JSHJ* 14.2 (2016), 186–93 (187). However, see also Stanley E. Porter and Andrew W. Pitts, 'Has Jonathan Bernier Rescued Critical Realism?', *JSHJ* 14.3 (2016), 241–47 (esp. 242–43).

22 See, for example, the argument in Patrick Giddy, 'Why Theology Can and Should Be Taught at Secular Universities: Lonergan on Intellectual Conversion', *Journal of Philosophy of Education* 45.3 (2011), 527–43. Similarly, Hill claims Lonergan's critical realist approach might allow theology to flourish in a higher education context operative in the aftermath of the emergence of postmodernity. See Samuel Hill, 'Lonergan, Lyotard, and Lindbeck: Bringing *Method in Theology* into Dialogue with Postmodernity', *HeyJ* 58.6 (2017), 908–16.

23 Lonergan, *Method in Theology*, xii.

24 Nicholas Lash, 'In Defense of Lonergan's Critics', *New Blackfriars* 57.670 (1976), 124–26 (125).

25 Hugo Meynell, 'Taking A(nother) Look at Lonergan's Method'. *New Blackfriars* 90 (2009), 474–500 (476).

26 Avery Dulles, 'Book Review: *Method in Theology*', *Theological Studies* 33.3 (1972), 533–35 (555).
27 Patrick A. Sullivan, 'Theological Instruction and Faith Transmission: Lonergan's Method as Pedagogy Theology', *New Blackfriars* 95 (2014), 593–605 (599–600).
28 "Die theologische Methode bei Lonergan abstrahiert … von der ganz eigentümlichen einmaligen Bezogenheit auf die konkrete Person Jesu." See Karl Rahner, 'Kritische Bermerkungen zu B.J.F. Lonergan's Aufsatz: "Functional Specialities in Theology"', *Gregorianum* 51.3 (1970), 537–40 (538).
29 Anthony J. Kelly, 'Is Lonergan's *Method* Adequate to Christian Mystery?' *The Thomist* 39.3 (1975), 437–70 (441).
30 Terrence Reynolds, 'Method Divorced from Content in Theology? An Assessment of Lonergan's *Method in Theology*', *The Thomist* 55.2 (1991), 245–69 (268).
31 Aidan Nichols, *Scribe of the Kingdom: Essays on Theology and Culture*, 2 vols (London: Sheed & Ward, 1994), II.63.
32 Ben F. Meyer, *Reality and Illusion in New Testament Scholarship: A Primer in Critical Realist Hermeneutics* (Collegeville, MN: Liturgical Press, 1994), viii.
33 Donald L. Denton, *Historiography and Hermeneutics in Jesus Studies: An Examination of the Work of John Dominic Crossan and Ben F. Meyer*, JSNTSup, 262 (London: T&T Clark, 2004), 81.
34 Ben F. Meyer, *The Aims of Jesus*, repr. ed. with new introduction (Eugene, OR: Pickwick, 2002), 13.
35 Ibid., 14.
36 In addition to Meyer's method as outlined in *The Aims of Jesus*, see the discussion on Lonergan's critical realism in Ben F. Meyer, *Critical Realism and the New Testament* (Allison Park, PA: Pickwick, 1989), esp. 1–16.
37 Bernier, *The Quest for the Historical Jesus after the Demise of Authenticity*, 7.
38 Meyer, *Aims*, 14.
39 Ibid., 15.
40 Lonergan, *Method in Theology*, xi.
41 Wright, *PFG*, xviii.
42 A term he borrows from Bruce J. Malina and Jerome H. Neyrey, *Portraits of Paul: An Archaeology of Ancient Personality* (Louisville, KY: John Knox, 1996), ix–x, and ultimately Charles S. Peirce, *Science and Philosophy*, ed. Arthur W. Burks (Cambridge, MA: Harvard University, 1958), 89–164.
43 N.T. Wright, *NTPG*, 35. (emphases original)
44 Dunn, *Jesus Remembered.*
45 Denton; *Historiography*. See also his more recent article, 'Being Interpreted by the Parables: Critical Realism as Hermeneutical Epistemology', *JSHJ* 13.2–3 (2015), 232–54.
46 Scot McKnight, *Jesus and His Death: Historiography, the Historical Jesus, and Atonement Theory* (Waco, TX: Baylor University, 2005).
47 Bernier, *Demise of Authenticity*.
48 Stanley E. Porter and Andrew W. Pitts, 'Critical Realism in Context: N. T. Wright's Historical Method and Analytic Epistemology', *JSHJ* 13.2–3 (2015), 276–306. See the response from Jonathan Bernier, 'A Response to Porter and Pitts' "Wright's Critical Realism in Context"', *JSHJ* 14.2 (2016), 186–93, and the counter response: Stanley E. Porter and Andrew W. Pitts, 'Has Jonathan Bernier Rescued Critical Realism?', *JSHJ* 14.3 (2016), 241–47.
49 N.T. Wright, *RSG*, 11.
50 I am very grateful to Dr. Seth Heringer for his clarity and insight on this point.
51 Crossan, *Historical Jesus*, xxvii.
52 Especially Hans W. Frei, *The Identity of Jesus Christ, the Hermeneutical Bases of Dogmatic Theology* (Philadelphia, PA: Fortress, 1975); idem, *Theology and Narrative: Selected Essays* (New York: OUP, 1993).

53 N.T. Wright, *History and Eschatology: Jesus and the Promise of Natural Theology* (London: SPCK, 2019), 41.

54 Ibid., 187.

55 Ibid., 213.

56 Implicit in his analysis is a common modern assumption the tomb of Jesus was a single-use and single-occupancy tomb, whereas it is highly probable Jesus was buried in a tomb designed to house an entire family. On this point, it is especially telling that the phrase 'empty tomb' is absent in the NT texts, since Jesus' body might have been absent from the tomb without the tomb being empty. The standard treatment on Jewish family tombs in this period is Rachel Hachlili, *Jewish Funerary Customs, Practices and Rites in the Second Temple Period*, JSJS 94 (Leiden: Brill, 2005), esp. 235–310. Of course, even if the family tomb in question here is new (and thus 'empty' prior to Jesus' being interred), my point is simply that the 'emptiness' of the tomb *per se* is not the decisive issue here, but the presence (or lack thereof) of a specific person's body within that tomb).

57 The classic study on the topic remains Aniela Jaffe, *Apparitions: An Archetypal Approach to Death, Dreams, and Ghosts* (Irving, TX: Spring, 1979).

58 Taylor, *Secular Age*, 2.

59 Karl Popper, *Logik der Forschung: Zur Erkenntnistheorie der modernen Naturwissenschaf* (Tübingen: Mohr Siebeck, 1934).

60 Milbank, *Theology and Social Theory*; idem, *Beyond Secular Order*.

61 See Donald Senior, 'The Death of Jesus and the Resurrection of the Holy Ones (Mt 27:51-53)', *CBQ* 38.3 (1976), 312–29; David Hill, 'Matthew 27:51-53 in the Theology of the Evangelist', *IBS* 71.1 (1985), 76–87; Ronald D. Witherup, 'The Death of Jesus and the Rising of the Saints: Matthew 27:51-54 in Context', *SBLSP* (Atlanta, GA: Scholars, 1987), 26:574–85 (581–82); Ronald L. Troxel, 'Matt 27.51-4 Reconsidered: Its Role in the Passion Narrative, Meaning and Origin', *NTS* 48.1 (2002), 30–47; Kenneth L. Waters, Sr., 'Matthew 27:52-53 as Apocalyptic Apostrophe: Temporal-Spatial Collapse in the Gospel of Matthew', *JBL* 122.3 (2003), 489–515.

62 I cannot expound fully my interpretation of this passage here, especially given that it is only of secondary importance for the present purposes. Suffice it to say here, in a paper delivered at the Tyndale Fellowship Biblical Theology Conference, Cambridge, 5–7 July 2017, I asserted that the phrase τὴν ἁγίαν πόλιν in Matt. 4.5 and 27.53 is best understood as a reference to the heavenly Jerusalem, and thus builds upon the Matthean motif of 'heaven and earth' language, which has been identified by numerous scholars. See Gerhard Schneider, '"Im Himmel - auf Erden": Eine Perspektive matthäischer Theologie', in *Studien zum Matthäusevangelium: Festschrift für Wilhelm Pesch*, ed. Ludger Schenke (Stuttgart: Katholisches Bibelwerk, 1988), 285–97; Kari Syreeni, 'Between Heaven and Earth: On the Structure of Matthew's Symbolic Universe', *JSNT* 13.40 (1990), 3–13; Robert Foster, 'Why on Earth Use "Kingdom of Heaven"?: Matthew's Terminology Revisited', *NTS* 48.4 (2002), 487–99; Jonathan T. Pennington, *Heaven and Earth in the Gospel of Matthew*, NovTSup 126 (Leiden: Brill, 2007).

63 Allison, Jr., *Historical Christ*, 21.

64 Meyer, *Reality and Illusion*, 40.

65 See Larry W. Hurtado, 'Resurrection-Faith and the 'Historical' Jesus', *JSHJ* 11.1 (2013), 35–52.

66 Michael R. Licona, 'Historians and Miracle Claims', *JSHJ* 12.1–2 (2014), 106–29.

67 N.T. Wright, 'Resurrecting Old Arguments: Responding to Four Essays', *JSHJ* 3.2 (2005), 209–31 (210).

68 Wright, 'Resurrecting Old Arguments', 211–12.

69 Wright, *NTPG*, 32–35.

70 Meyer, *Reality and Illusion*, 41.

71 On Wright's *H&E*, I have benefitted greatly from conversation with Mitchell D. Mallary, whose doctoral thesis *Jesus, History, & Revelation: Analyzing the Impasse*

between Karl Barth and N. T. Wright (University of St. Andrews, 2022) was supervised by Wright himself and benefits greatly from private conversation with Wright. I eagerly await the publication of Mallary's thesis which, in numerous ways, explains Wright's position in *H&E* in greater clarity than Wright himself manages.

72 Dale C. Allison, Jr., 'Explaining the Resurrection: Conflicting Convictions', *JSHJ* 3.2 (2005), 117–33 (133).

73 Wright, *RSG*, 712–13 n. 78. See Edward Schillebeeckx, *Jezus, het verhall van een levende* (Bloemendaal: Nelissen, 1974); ET: *Jesus: An Experiment in Christology*, trans Hubert Hoskins (London: Collins, 1979).

10 Expanding the Boundaries of Historical Jesus Research

10.1 Introduction

Sarah Rollens has recently lamented that 'methodological reflection and theoretical rigor are routinely lacking in biblical studies, with some scholars even claiming that they "don't really use theories in their work."'[1] For example, the venerable Martin Hengel famously wrote: 'there is only *one* proper exegesis, namely, the one that does justice to the text (and its contexts).'[2] In this study I have argued that this methodological lacuna is none more apparent than with regards to the role of metaphysics in historical Jesus research. I have argued that engagement with metaphysics in historical Jesus research is logically unavoidable, and that recognition of this should serve as a clarion call for Jesus historians to reflect in depth upon the metaphysical foundations of their work, to make them explicit from the outset of their historical (re)construction(s).

In this chapter, I conclude by summarising my argument and discussing its implications, recognising that secular metaphysical presuppositions influencing modern academic historical Jesus research should result in a more generous view of what may be considered academically acceptable among participants within the 'Quest.'

10.2 Summary of This Study

In Chapter 1, I outlined the argument of my study and engaged with previous scholarship on the relationship between Christian theology and historical Jesus research. In so doing, I concluded more work was required on the subject since the core fundamental methodological problem within historical Jesus research had yet to be explicated in its fulness. I intimated that this problem was best discussed in relation to metaphysics, and best observed in relation to the role of worldviews in historical Jesus research.

In Chapters 2 and 3, I introduced the categories of metaphysics and worldview, respectively, defining the latter in relation to the former. By outlining the five 'pillars' of metaphysical philosophy—ontology, identity, space and time, causality, and modality—I defined metaphysics as *the study of reality, including its constituent parts and their relationships to one another*. This being the case, I

DOI: 10.4324/b23077-12

proceeded to examine the concept of worldview in the western philosophical tradition. Although it was coined by Kant to refer to our sensory perception of the external world, Fichte introduced the term to Schelling while at Jena, who subsequently reconceived of worldview as a cognitive (rather than sensory) term. From then on, worldview retained this cognitive sense as its primary referent. Dilthey, Jaspers, and Husserl began to probe the concept of worldview in greater depth and ultimately demonstrated that one's worldview is a wholly subjective means of apprehending the external world by constructing a metaphysical framework for philosophical reflection. Thus, these thinkers became increasingly frustrated by, and critical of, the perceived rise in *Weltanschauungsphilosophie*, which could never provide 'objective' insight into the nature of reality. This was compounded by the work of Heidegger and Wittgenstein, the former highlighting the inevitability of one's worldview impinging upon philosophical discourse, and the latter demonstrating its implicit metaphysical character. Thus, I concluded this chapter by defining a worldview as *a set of metaphysical presuppositions taken as given when assessing new information about the external world.*

In Chapter 4, I examined the role worldviews play in historical decision-making. I engaged with the work of three thinkers of varying traditions, on the nature of historical knowledge: Collingwood, Nietzsche, and Blondel. Each of these conceive of historiography as an inescapably subjective discipline, whereby the historical circumstances of the historian inform their assessment of the past, and where plausibility provides the key to assessing historical evidence. Plausibility is measured in direct correlation to one's worldview. In other words, something is more plausible the more it coheres with the given metaphysical presuppositions that comprise one's worldview. I employed Bayesian reasoning as just one test case in assessing historical evidence. Like all historiographical decision-making processes, Bayesian reasoning requires one makes plausibility judgements that comprise a baseline against which other plausibilities are then assessed. When critically assessing the plausibility of any historical data, one does so against the backdrop of other plausibilities which are assumed uncritically. These uncritical plausibilities, I argued, are one's historiographical worldview. Therefore, I concluded this chapter by claiming *all historiography is inescapably filtered through one's worldview.*

In the fifth chapter, I identified characteristics of secular scholarship by engaging with three contemporary sociological theories of secularisation as potential descriptors for scholarly research. The first of these theories defined secularism as the decline in religious belief. Although there are some figures to support this theory, it is problematic for three reasons. First, it is unclear how we measure religious belief, since precisely what constitutes a religion remains obfuscated, such that secular thought itself may be termed 'religious.' Second, even if one could define religion, declining figures would still be of limited use since they rely upon the presupposition that we may unquestioningly trust people's self-designation as religious (or not). Third, even if there was a basis for trust, the available figures appear to indicate that the 21st century will see an increase in religiously affiliated individuals, and a decline in the religiously unaffiliated.

The presence (or lack thereof) of religious belief, then, was not considered a helpful characterisation of secularism and, therefore, the religious beliefs (or lack thereof) of the participants in the 'Quest' for the historical Jesus was deemed to be unimportant in determining whether one may describe the discipline as secular.

The second theory of secularisation conceived of the phenomenon as the decline in religious authority. This theory posits that, while religious participation may fluctuate, religious institutions themselves no longer enjoy the same authority to engage in public discourse, thus characterising secularism. Although this theory was again not without its flaws, I argued it was a more helpful means of characterising secularism (and, thus, secular scholarship). Finally, I engaged with religio-economic critiques of secularisation theories which posit secularism as a self-limiting process, with religious institutions playing an important supply-side role in meeting the demands of those less powerful in society. Ultimately, these critiques had no bearing upon my argument, since they proceed from methodologically questionable presuppositions, and employ statistical analyses in support of their arguments in a manner that has been severely criticised. Therefore, I claimed we might describe secular societies as those in which religious institutions enjoy limited authority to engage in public discourse and, therefore, *secular scholarship might be understood as any scholarship which refuses to allow religious perspectives the authority to contribute to such issues.* If the 'Quest' for the historical Jesus is a secular discipline, therefore, it will evidence a tendency not to allow religious metaphysical presuppositions to contribute to its historical method.

In the second part of the study, I built upon the technical foundation constructed in the first part to enquire as to the historiographical worldviews operative in historical Jesus research. If historiography is inescapably conducted within a metaphysical framework (or, historiographical worldview), and a secular worldview comprises a series of positively construed metaphysical claims that result in the rejection of religious authority, then to what extent might it be accurate to describe modern historical Jesus research as secular? The answer to this question was split into two parts. In Chapters 6–8, I adopted a macro-level approach and claimed the 'Quest,' from Reimarus to the present day, possessed the characteristics of secular scholarship, as outlined in Chapter 5. By this I mean that it has consistently evidenced a tendency not to allow religious metaphysical presuppositions to contribute to the discipline.

In Chapter 9, I adopted a more detailed approach to the question of the secular nature of the 'Quest,' by examining the historical method of N.T. Wright. I traced Wright's method of critical realism back through the work of Meyer and Lonergan. I argued the resurrection is a worldview-defining event, insofar as one's conclusion regarding the historicity of the resurrection also spoke to the content of one's worldview. Despite Wright's claims to the contrary, through examining his methodology, I observed that his critical realist approach to history ultimately conformed to a secular worldview. I asserted these two chapters combined breadth and depth and provided me with warrant to claim modern academic historical Jesus research is a secular discipline.

10.3 Implications of This Study

The foregoing summary of my argument begs the question, 'why does it matter if historical Jesus research is predicated upon a secular historiographical worldview?' Even if I am right that secular metaphysical presuppositions are the gatekeepers of participation in the 'Quest,' why is this noteworthy? Stated in the most fundamental terms possible, this observation regarding the 'Quest' is significant because secularism (and secular metaphysics) is not a value-neutral framework. This point is best made in conversation with two thinkers briefly introduced here: John Milbank (and the Radical Orthodoxy movement), and Charles Taylor.

Milbank first rose to prominence following the publication of his first book,[3] *Theology and Social Theory*, in 1990. This work was followed by a sequel in 2013[4] and laid the groundwork for what would become known as the Radical Orthodoxy movement (hereafter RO; occasionally called the Cambridge School),[5] itself the subject of a great deal of critical interaction.[6] *Theology and Social Theory* caused something of a stir within Anglophone theology upon its publication. One reviewer wrote that 'John Milbank's sprawling, ambitious and intellectually rewarding book is in a class of its own,'[7] while another early responder concluded that:

> *Theology and Social Theory: Beyond Secular Reason* is an extended and brilliant exercise in despair. Insofar as this book has been received with something close to uncritical adulation in theological circles then it confirms the profound intellectual ghettoization and malaise of much Christian theology.[8]

Ostensibly concerned with delineating the enmeshment of theological and sociological discourses, Milbank's most important contribution lies in his insistence that Christian theology must break free of this harmful academic nexus if it is to truly flourish.

For Milbank and the RO movement, the secular is only possible following the development of the concept of univocity of being. In other words, secular reasoning and secular metaphysics itself is only possible because it proceeds from theological developments within the Christian tradition itself. To explain this involves tracing the debate as far back as Aquinas, a key influence upon RO. Indeed, it is significant that one of the first volumes to be published with the Radical Orthodoxy sensibility sought to re-evaluate the work of Aquinas to construct a framework for the theological discernment of 'truth.'[9]

In Thomistic thought analogy is the key to speaking about God. Finite creatures are entirely incapable of speaking about infinite and boundless divinity. Thus, when we speak of God, we employ language primarily designed to speak about creaturely realities, rather than their transcendent creator. For example, we might pick up a piece of cutlery and say, 'this is a good knife.' The word 'good' here might mean that it is good at the job for which it was designed; it may be strong, with a comfortable handle and a sharp blade. But if we were to say that God is good it cannot be meant in this same sense, since God is in no way the product of a designer but is wholly sufficient in himself. Thus, Aquinas highlights two modes of speech: equivocal and univocal. Equivocal speech uses the same words in entirely different senses. Oliver gives the following example: 'we might refer to "river bank" and "high street bank", thus using the word "bank" equivocally to the point where we might wonder if we are, in any meaningful sense, using the same word.'[10]

If we employ univocal speech, however, we use the same word in the same sense. For Aquinas, God-talk is neither equivocal (thereby making knowledge of God impossible) nor univocal (thereby obliterating the creature/creator divide). Instead, he proposes a third way of speaking: analogy. He writes:

> This way of using words lies somewhere between pure equivocation and simply univocity, for the word is neither used in the same sense, as with univocal usage, nor in totally different senses, as with equivocation. The several senses of a word used analogically signify different relations to some one thing, as 'health' in a complexion means a symptom of health in a man, and in a diet a cause of that health.[11]

The example of 'health' here is helpful: if we say a food is 'healthy,' we do not mean that it itself possesses health. Rather, we mean that the food is attributed health because it is the cause of health in others. When we speak analogically of God, therefore, it is in these terms. If we describe a person as 'good' it is in analogy to God's goodness: the person's 'goodness' is attributed to them because of their relationship to God. In Aquinas' own words: 'the word [good] means it is used primarily of God and derivatively of creatures, for what the word means—the perfection it signifies—flows from God to the creature.'[12]

For Milbank and others within RO, creatures therefore exist in participation in God's existence. Creatures are not sufficient beings capable of existence apart from God, but are only able to exist because God allows them the gift of participation in his own existence:

> Creatures, for Aquinas, beneath the levels of patterns of granted relative necessity and subsistence, are radically accidental. But not thereby, of course, accidents of the divine substance: rather they subsist by participation in it.[13]

However, following Aquinas, the concept of the analogy of being was fundamentally undone by John Duns Scotus (ca. 1265–1308) among others.[14] Rather than speaking of the analogy of being, Scotus instead recasts the Thomistic notion of participation and instead prefers to speak of the univocity of being. Whereas for Aquinas, creatures and the creator existed in a different manner to one another (there is an ontological difference), Scotus suggested (or, at least, was subsequently received as having suggested) that existence was a univocal category, that God and creation exist in the same way. This is significant because it posits an untraversable, infinite distance between God and creation. By conceiving of God and creation as sharing the same kind of existence, the univocity of being ensures creature and creator will always be estranged from one another. By contrast, only the analogy of being allows for genuine mediation and participation to occur: there is no infinity of sameness to overcome, only difference.

For Milbank and those within RO, it is this infinity of sameness that has paved the way for the distant deistic picture of God which is ultimately pushed out of the public sphere and relegated to a matter of private belief. Thus, as Milbank writes in the famous opening to *Theology and Social Theory*:

> Once, there was no 'secular.' And the secular was not latent, waiting to fill more space with the stream of the 'purely human', when the pressure of the sacred was relaxed … The secular as a domain had to be instituted or *imagined*, both in theory and in practice. This institution is not correctly grasped in merely negative terms as a desacralization … Received sociology altogether misses the positive institution of the secular.[15]

This metaphysical posturing found in certain medieval Christian theological traditions is what has paved the way for the birth of the secular: stated differently, secularism is the product of Christian theology askew. It is, in other words, little more than Christian heresy. Therefore, Milbank suggests that 'only theology can overcome metaphysics.'[16] It is for this reason that Milbank claims, 'if theology no longer seeks to position, qualify or criticize other discourses, then it is inevitable that these discourses will position theology';[17] only by resisting the demands placed upon theology by disciplines that proceed from secular metaphysical presumptions and presuppositions, can theology be truly free to be theology.

However, as Tonstad has recently argued, to frame interaction with other disciplines in terms of a power-struggle, in which theologians seek mastery over their colleagues in other disciplines, is implicitly to perpetuate the very claims about knowledge and the pursuit of knowledge that have endangered theological discourse in the first place. Rather, theologians are to be radically 'other' in their methods, compared to colleagues in these disciplines.[18] Milbank (and the RO movement more broadly) is right in his diagnosis of the theological origins of secular reasoning, and the cause for concern this should give theologians, but his thoughts on how theologians might best respond to these theological origins unhelpfully entrenches disciplinary divides and reinforces the very problems that have resulted in the current fragmentation of the university and marginalisation of theology (including New Testament studies and historical Jesus research). The implications of what has been discussed here will be outlined in more depth shortly (see below). However, suffice it to say for now that the work of Milbank and the RO movement allow us to see that secular metaphysical presuppositions are not devoid of theological content; they are *differently* theological, not *less* theological.

A similar argument has been made by Charles Taylor, whose work in many ways shares considerable overlap with the RO movement. The magnitude of Taylor's legacy is perhaps best demonstrated by the fact that not one, but two of his works might equally lay claim to be his *magnus opus*; both *Sources of the Self* and *A Secular Age* are landmark publications rich in insight. However, for present purposes, it is the latter of the two that will prove vital, although in many ways the two works seek to complement each other. Although not everyone has responded positively to the work,[19] based on the 1998–99 Gifford Lectures, *A Secular Age* has been described as a 'magnificent, epoch-making work,'[20] and has prompted interaction from a variety of conversation partners,[21] resulting in Taylor being awarded the Templeton Prize in 2007. *A Secular Age* is an extremely detailed and lengthy work (standing at 776 pages excluding notes, indices, and bibliography). Like Milbank and the RO movement, in *A Secular Age* Taylor also suggests that secularism has its origins within Christian theology. Although his reading of the emergence of secularism is slightly different from that of RO, this fundamental claim remains the same; Taylor's argument is 'in many ways highly consonant with the writings in the Radical Orthodoxy sphere.'[22]

Taylor intimates early on that he wishes to stray away from the history of ideas approach to secularism; he treats 'belief and un-belief, not as rival *theories*,' but rather as 'different kinds of lived experience involved in understanding your life in one way or the other … what it's like to live as a believer or an unbeliever.'[23] All people, regardless of their worldview, experience something that enriches their life:

> Somewhere, in some activity, or condition, lies a fulness, a richness; that is, in that place (activity or condition), life is fuller, richer, deeper, more worth while, more admirable, more what it should be … Perhaps this sense of fulness is something we just catch glimpses of from afar off … But sometimes there will be moments of experiences fulness, of joy and fulfilment, where we feel ourselves there.[24]

It is this focus on 'fulness' that 'allow[s] us to understand better belief and unbelief as lived conditions, not just as theories or sets of beliefs subscribed to.'[25] Taylor's efforts, then, turn towards describing this 'fulness' as understood within Christian and secular paradigms. 'For believers,' he writes, 'the account of the place of fulness requires reference to God, that is, to something beyond human life and/or nature,' whereas for those of a secular disposition 'the power to reach fulness is within,' whether that be reason, or the need to procreate.[26]

It is this framework of lived experience and the pursuit of fulness that provides the context for Taylor's study. But before he begins his study proper, he introduces another category—one which will be helpful for the present purposes—regarding the 'types' of belief, either 'naïve' or 'reflective.' In other words, all kinds of belief are either taken for granted ('naïve') or are the result of critical reflection ('reflective'). One reason for the emergence of secularism has been the shift from belief in God being a 'naïve,' unquestionable belief to a 'reflective,' optional one:

> This emerges as soon as we take account of the fact that all beliefs are held within a context or framework of the taken-for-granted, which usually remains tacit, and may even be unacknowledged by the agent because

> never formulated. This is what philosophers, influenced by Wittgenstein, Heidegger or Polanyi, have called the 'background' … The difference I've been talking about above is one of the whole background framework in which one believes or refuses to believe in God. The frameworks of yesterday and today are related as 'naïve' and 'reflective', because the latter has opened a question which had been foreclosed in the former by the unacknowledged shape of the background.[27]

Taylor's description of a 'background' is congruous with my conception of worldviews and historiographical worldview. Beliefs are formulated in relation to a series of given, pre-cognisant metaphysical presuppositions. Where 'new' beliefs or data challenge one of these tacitly held presuppositions, this paves the way for a 'naïve' (i.e., unchallenged) framework to be re-examined and opened up for critique. Taylor suggests the shift from belief in God as a common, 'naïve' worldview to an optional 'reflective' belief is what makes possible the conditions for the secular. In his own words, this may be described as a 'shift in background, or better the disruption of the earlier background.'[28] Or, as he states elsewhere:

> It is this shift in background … that I am calling the coming of a secular age … How did we move from a condition where, in Christendom, people lived naïvely within a theistic construal, to one in which we all shunt between two stances, in which everyone's construal shows up as such; and in which, moreover, unbelief[29] has become for many the major default option? This is the transformation that I want to describe, and perhaps also (very partially) explain in the following chapters.[30]

To begin his analysis of this transformation, Taylor begins by outlining a 'naïve' background (i.e., a worldview) that was once ubiquitous within Christendom, a worldview which may be characterised by three metaphysical presuppositions. (1) The cosmos was imagined to testify to the purpose and activity of the divine. Thus, natural events such as famine, floods, storms etc., were thought to be the result of divine purpose and activity. (2) Society itself (construed as 'polis, kingdom, church, or whatever'[31]), was conceived of as comprising something more than simply the result of human labour but which found its ultimate source in the divine. All facets of society and culture, then, find their foundation in God. (3) People viewed the world as 'enchanted'—which Taylor construes in opposition to the Weberian notion of disenchantment (*Entzauberung*)[32]—whereby it is thought that unseen forces, spirits, and divinities can and do interact in the realm of human affairs.

To say that certain societies have become secular, then, is to say that these three metaphysical presuppositions are no longer present in the worldview(s) operative within those societies. However, like Milbank before him, Taylor rejects the prevalent theory of secularisation as the retreat of religion from the public sphere: 'the rise of modernity isn't just a story of loss, of subtraction.'[33] Rather, the birth of the secular must be posited. Again, Taylor conceives of this positing of the secular in terms of 'fulness':

> Now the disappearance of these three modes of God's felt presence in our world, while it certainly facilitates this change, couldn't by itself bring it about. Because we can certainly go on experiencing fullness as a gift from God, even in a disenchanted world, a secular society, and a post-cosmic universe … And so the story I have to tell will relate not only how God's presence receded in these three dimensions; it also has to explain how something other than God could become the necessary objective poll of moral or spiritual aspiration, of 'fullness.'[34]

Over against meta-narratives that posit secularism as mere lack of reference to God, Taylor consistently demonstrates that the modern condition is comprised of various positively advanced alternatives to God. For example, where once the individual thought of themselves as susceptible to interference from unseen forces (Taylor calls this 'the porous self'), within modernity one imagines oneself to be free from such interference ('the buffered self'). However, 'it took more than disenchantment to produce the buffered self; it was also necessary to have confidence in our own powers of moral ordering.'[35]

Instead—and again in coherence with Milbank—Taylor identifies the impetus for secularisation as being birthed within Christendom itself. Specifically, the various developments that took place under the auspices of the reformation enabled the modern, secular self to be born. The 'confidence in our own powers of moral ordering' to which Taylor refers (above) stems from the emergence of 'the disciplined society.' Prior to the reformation movement, individuals within Christendom found themselves living in an 'age of anxiety,'[36] whereby society was characterised by conflict and insecurity, not least in the wake of the devastating wars of religion. Certainly, as Milbank and others have shown, these theological developments began long before the reformation, but Taylor is right to highlight the reformation as an important stepping-stone in the theological process of secularisation. Most recently, Silvianne Aspray's excellent work on Peter Vermigli has demonstrated that the reformation is not the vehicle for univocity of being that it is often portrayed as being. Rather, key reformation thinkers remained largely rooted in medieval participatory metaphysics; the reformation was certainly a stepping-stone on the road to secularisation, but not the decisive turning point that is sometimes claimed.[37]

Faced with societal unrest, those among the reformation movement 'held to a hyper-Augustinian position, according to which only a small minority were saved … [meaning] it would have to be that the Godly minority control things and keep them on the right track.'[38] For example, then, the Puritan movement sought to bring about this level of societal control by raising generation after generation of 'disciplined' Christians: 'these men are industrious, disciplined, do useful work, and above all can be relied upon … with such men, a safe, well-ordered society can be built.'[39] (A similar thesis is, of course, advocated by Weber in *Die protestantische Ethik*[40].) However, this programme of self-discipline was unexpectedly successful and (although Taylor rightfully warns that 'one mustn't exaggerate' the scope of these changes) produced 'a feeling that the powers of reconstruction had been successfully exercised, in which anthropocentrism could flourish, and the conditions were created at last in which a live option of exclusive humanism could emerge from the womb of history.'[41] Or, as Taylor notes elsewhere, 'disengaged discipline frames a new experience of the self as having a telos of autarky.'[42]

Until this point Taylor's analysis has been exclusively theoretical. As noted above, he is concerned with telling the story of the lived experienced of individuals, rather than outlining a history of ideas. Accordingly, he seeks to answer the question 'what exactly is involved, when a theory penetrates and transforms the social imaginary?'[43] In intimating the practical changes that these theoretical developments inaugurated, Taylor highlights three 'forms of social self-understanding' that emerge following the birth of the 'disciplined society.'[44] They are: (1) the economy, (2) the public sphere, and (3) democratic self-rule.

The 'economy' is understood in two ways, first as metaphor, then as telos. It is understood as a metaphor which mimics the (divinely inaugurated) enmeshed nature of human relationships which comprise a series of exchanges: 'humans are engaged in an exchange of services. The fundamental model seems to be what we have come to call an economy.'[45] And yet the economy possesses its own telos, distinct from the telos of humanity. Regarding the telos of the economic element of the new modern self-understanding, Taylor refers to Montchrétien who viewed economic flourishing as the end goal of society and advocates for the ruler to direct the manner in which economic growth contributes to the common good.[46]

The public sphere is understood as 'a common space in which the members of society are deemed to meet through a variety of media: print, electronic, and also face-to-face encounters; to discuss matters of common interest; and thus to be able to form a common mind about these.'[47] This sphere, which is later described as a 'meta topical agency,' is thought to exist completely independently of the political component of society and reinforces the disenchanted, reformation-inspired focus on the autonomy of humanity (both individually and corporately) to the degree that it has now become ubiquitous, 'so that we have trouble even recalling what it was like before' the inauguration of the public sphere.[48]

Finally, Taylor examines the practical changes that take place regarding democratic self-rule. Whereas the aforementioned theorical developments brought about practical changes that resulted in the construction of an economic system and a public sphere, here Taylor stresses that the practical changes in question involve 'a re-interpretation of a practice which already existed in the old dispensation.'[49] This is to say, nothing 'new' is created *per se*, but rather some pre-existing state is transmuted as a result of these theorical developments within Christendom.

In this case, the change in question concerns the nature of government, which is no longer viewed as a divinely inaugurated, top-down system of rule, but instead a bottom-up system stemming from the people themselves: 'the United States is a case in point … the American Revolution transformed into a full-fledged foundation of popular sovereignty, whereby the U.S. constitution is put in the mouth of "We, the people."'[50] Again, this practical change is brought about, ultimately, due to the theoretical developments of the reformation that stress the autonomy of humanity at the expense of a conception of our reliance upon transcendence.

These practical changes—driven by positively construed reformation ideology—ultimately result in a conception of the *polis* as an unmediated given, rather than a divinely inaugurated gift. This may be understood as the birth of the secular, wherein it is possible to engage in all aspects of life without encountering reference to God at any point:

> A purely secular time-understanding allows us to imagine society 'horizontally', unrelated to any 'high points', where the ordinary sequence of events touches higher time, and therefore without recognising any privileged persons or agencies—such as kings or priests—who stand and mediate at such alleged points … We have moved from a hierarchical order of personalized links to an impersonal egalitarian one; from a vertical world of mediated-access to horizontal, direct-access societies.[51]

Taylor concludes by comparing his approach to that of John Milbank and the RO movement. The main difference, according to Taylor (and later reinforced by Milbank himself[52]) is that whereas RO focusses on the history of ideas, Taylor is concerned with secularism 'as a mass phenomenon,' that influences the practices of individuals in society.[53] The basic premise however—that secularism and secular metaphysics is born out of Christian theology—remains the same. As with Milbank and the RO movement, Taylor demonstrates (albeit through different means and for different purposes) that secular reasoning finds its origins within the Christian theological tradition itself. Secularism is not merely the result of the removal of theological narratives from public life. Rather, it is itself a *different kind* of theological narrative, one whose content is no less theologically potent or significant than its 'religious' counterparts, just differently so.

Secular metaphysics is ultimately the result of distinct developments within Christian theology itself. It is not a neutral platform for historical enquiry into the person of Jesus, nor any other historical figure for that matter. To proceed uncritically to reconstruct the past from within a secular worldview, therefore, is to concurrently give assent to the theological developments that enabled secularism to emerge in the first instance. In other words, for New Testament studies and historical Jesus research to resist the influence of religious metaphysics is not to resist the introduction of theology into its discourse, but it is to give a *certain instance* of theological reasoning uncritically earned dominance within the discipline. It is not to reduce the amount of influence that theological presuppositions exert upon the discipline, but to see that influence manifest itself as a dominance residing solely within one narrow and specific form of theological presupposition.

Following the publication of George Marsden's work *The Soul of the American University*, one review noted:

> No doubt discrimination has occurred and will occur against the ostentatiously religious. But Marsden, who has certainly been generously rewarded in the academy, has little room to complain himself. In addition, I suspect the discrimination against Protestants is considerably less than it was against would-be atheist scholars in 1850. Someone who felt more strongly about these things than I do might urge, with some truth, that Christians have had their way with learning for almost 2000 years, and if they have not irrevocably lost a major battle, so much the worse for religious belief—it has had its time, and now its time is over.[54]

But this rhetoric fails to see that secularism is born out of the same 'religious belief' whose time is apparently over. In other words, the tendency towards a secular metaphysical framework within the 'Quest' for the historical Jesus does not circumvent the introduction of metaphysics into the discipline, but rather seeks to mask it. As Stevenson writes:

> Historical Jesus studies, as with historical biblical scholarship more broadly, tends to operate with Kantian or post-Kantian anti-metaphysical assumptions, such that for the most part scholars engaging in the 'quest' intentionally limit their investigations to the realm of the 'phenomenal'. The result, however, is not that metaphysical suppositions are removed from the inquiry. They continue to play a role but avoid critical investigation or justification.[55]

Or as Aspray notes elsewhere:

> Metaphysics cannot, by definition, be an entirely extraneous endeavour to theological reasoning. All reasoning—and especially theological reasoning—involves fundamental assumptions about the nature of being, knowledge and language, and ultimately about how the transcendent relates (or does not relate) to the immanent. These assumptions, however, are metaphysical in nature.[56]

In short, then, it is significant that modern academic historical Jesus research operates within a secular metaphysical framework because this framework severely limits who can participate in the discipline *and* what the discipline is able to say about the person of Jesus. As researchers of the historical Jesus, we ought to allow participants of the 'Quest' to engage with the subject from a greater variety of metaphysical frameworks, rather than affording secular metaphysics priority within the discourse. Blondel notes in concluding *Histoire et dogme*:

> It can no longer be held that the part which [Christian belief] plays in the inner life of each Christian is simply a matter of individual psychology; as

> long as it is not clearly realised that in addition to dogmatic theology and exegesis there is a knowledge, a real science of action, capable of extracting, for the benefit of an experimental and progressive theology, the lessons which life draws from history, there will always be recurrent conflicts or interferences or mutual ostracism.[57]

As I have stated at various points in this study, that historical Jesus research has operated under the influence of a dominant secular (and therefore *theological*) metaphysics should not be met with calls to abandon the endeavour. Rather, the discipline ought to be open to exploring the possibility of historiographical approaches that proceed from *differently theological* metaphysical frameworks. This claim is carefully worded; secular metaphysical presuppositions are not *less* theological than (what I have called in this study) religious metaphysical presuppositions. The work of Milbank and the RO movement, as well as Taylor, have highlighted the theological origins of secular metaphysics. Therefore, to call for the inclusion within historical Jesus research of other historiographical worldviews that proceed from other metaphysical presuppositions is not to introduce theology into the discipline. Rather, it is to add greater variety and diversity to the theological presuppositions that are always already at play within it.

In the introduction to this study, I briefly addressed the question of categorising my argument. Here, at its conclusion, I reiterate my stance that the present study is best understood as a work of New Testament studies (broadly construed) and historical Jesus research (in particular). While I have drawn heavily from sociologists, philosophers, and theologians to make my case, this has been done to demonstrate that theological metaphysics inescapably lies hidden at the very heart of the 'Quest' for the historical Jesus. There simply can be no historiographical worldview that does not build upon an assumed theological metaphysics. The question before us is not *whether* we allow theological metaphysics a say in the discipline, but *which* theological metaphysics we allow a say, and how we mediate discussion between historians of different and/or competing metaphysical frameworks.

The Jesus of history and the Christ of faith are not quite so distinct as Kähler and (the early) Troeltsch thought. Rather, there is no divide between the Jesus of history and the Christ of faith. To speak of the Jesus of history is always already and concurrently to speak of *a* Christ of faith, since history and historiography are themselves terms inescapably and irrevocably burdened with the heavy weight of implicit metaphysical and theological import. The only questions left for the 'Quest' for the historical Jesus is *whose* faith is permitted to serve as gatekeeper for the discipline's pre-methodological foundations? *Which* metaphysical and theological presuppositions are to be considered an acceptable foundation for enquiry into the historical Jesus? *What* tradition is to be allowed its Christ of faith to enmesh uncritically with its Jesus of history, under the auspices of academic acceptability?

To this end, recognition of the theological metaphysics already operative in the 'Quest' for the historical Jesus should prompt the discipline to reflect upon the boundaries of what it considers to be academically acceptable historiography.

This, I suggest, ought to involve not the revocation of what has gone before. I do not wish to argue that secular approaches to the historical Jesus ought to be discontinued; such endeavours offer genuinely vital insights into the historical Jesus with which scholars of all traditions might benefit from interacting. However, recognition of the inherently metaphysical and theological nature of the discipline should entail an openness to historiographical approaches that proceed from other metaphysical frameworks.

10.4 Opportunities for Further Research

But the above begs the question: what shape might these other frameworks take? In what methods might they be made manifest? It is not possible here to answer these questions fully. In the first instance, I do not believe it is appropriate for me to speak to the content of anyone's worldview except my own and, perhaps, scholars within my own tradition, through mutual dialogue. I cannot offer suggestions regarding the shape of Buddhist or atheist historiography, for example. I instead offer some tentative suggestions regarding Christian historiography. Even then, what follows is only a series of suggestions and avenues for potential further research, not pronouncements.

In the introduction to this study, when surveying previous scholarship on the notion of theologically sensitive, or faith-informed historiography, I noted that Deines and Heringer both offer suggestions regarding the characteristics of such historiographies.[58] Here, I would like first to combine these two sets of suggestions (which are highly consonant with one another anyway), and second, to build upon them to enquire as to the characteristics of *Christian* historiography in particular. In *Acts of God in History*, Deines suggests characteristics of a 'theologically-motivated historiography,' to use his terminology. For Deines, a historical method that incorporates divine agency into its historical reconstruction must be:

10.4.1 Critical

This term is invoked by Deines, who means two things by this. First, it should distinguish between truth and falsity regarding the past. Second, it must be open to criticism: any historical method that does not allow others (including those outside its metaphysical and/or theological tradition) to comment upon it should not be deemed academically acceptable. Heringer's language of historiography as a two-level process is helpful here, too: to retain a critical element, theologically sensitive historiography must wrestle with the complicated relationship between (1) pure historical facts and (2) the narratives invoked to make sense of those facts. History (in the sense of writing or writing about history) comprises both facts and narrative; history is neither pure fact nor pure narrative. Drawing on Irenaeus, Heringer highlights the importance of a critical approach to both:

> A Christian approach to history will recognize that both the selection of events and the narrative constructed are done according to a hypothesis. At least for

> Irenaeus, the Christian hypothesis should be the world as described by the Rule of Truth/Faith and recapitulated in Jesus. This hypothesis, however, runs contrary to the naturalism of the historical method. Before one piece of evidence has been examined, these two positions are already engaged in an intractable struggle. Thus, the conflict will not be decided on the level of historical evidence, but on the level of narratives, hypotheses and social imaginaries.[59]

In distinguishing between fact and narrative, one is able to highlight more openly the theologically informed aspects of one's historical reconstruction. Thus, a theologically sensitive historiography must remain critical of the past (in the sense of able to distinguish between true and false claims about the past), while simultaneously remaining openly critical of itself. A sharp and explicit distinction between fact and narrative in theologically sensitive accounts of the past serves as a helpful part of fulfilling these requirements.

10.4.2 Coherent

Again, Deines' intention is twofold. First, a historical method must be coherent in the sense that the fundamental presuppositions from within which one approaches the past (what I have described as a worldview) should produce a disposition whereby these presuppositions may also be used to assess historical evidence. In other words, one's worldview may not preclude the possibility of studying the past. Second, it must be coherent in the sense that it can explain all the available historical evidence without any exceptions or gaps.

10.4.3 Rational and Describable

Here I have conflated the third and fourth of Deines' suggested characteristics of theologically sensitive historiography. Any claims made upon the basis of a historical method must have the potential to be universally true [*Universalisierbarkeit*]. By this he means that it must be translatable, understandable, and capable of producing meaning in other contexts, societies, cultures, and time periods; others must be able to understand a historical method or a historical claim, even if they do not agree with it.

This raises a further question, one I cannot answer fully here: how do scholars of competing historiographical worldviews engage in meaningful dialogue with one another? Any historiographical method that proceeds from a theologically sensitive worldview must be open to critique from scholars both within and outside of similar worldviews. Thus, a necessary task concurrent with constructing a theologically sensitive historiographical method is to reflect on the nature of inter-worldview dialogue within the academy. An increase in the plurality of metaphysical frameworks operative within historical Jesus research must, therefore, go hand in hand with a commitment to robust methodological reflection upon inter-framework dialogue if the discipline is to avoid ghettoisation along religious and/or denominational fault lines.

10.4.4 Comprehensive

Deines' conception of comprehensiveness is distinct from the second sense of 'coherent,' as described above. Instead, comprehensiveness here means that, as well as advancing certain historical claims, a historical method must allow scholars to be self-reflective and examine the presuppositions that have allowed (or even encouraged) them to make these claims in the first place. In other words, it must be capable of deep, critical self-examination on a foundational level.

This might also be one means by which inter-worldview dialogue may take place. By assessing the internal consistency and comprehensiveness of the historical reconstruction of the metaphysical and/or religious 'other,' it is possible for meaningful dialogue to take place that traverses metaphysical boundaries without either party being forced to make fundamental concessions regarding their own worldview. In other words, internal consistency and comprehensiveness might serve as two entry points into meaningful dialogue between historians of competing worldviews.

10.4.5 Pluralist

A historical method must reject movements towards methodological totalitarianism and instead encourage views that emerge from other perspectives. If a historical method does not allow for others to engage with the same evidence from a different perspective, it should not be viewed as academically acceptable. A concurrent commitment of theologically sensitive historiography would be what Heringer calls a 'rejection of neutrality (and objectivity).'[60] A genuinely pluralist guild of historical Jesus researchers must accept the metaphysically posited foundations of all historiographical methodologies, including traditional, secular historical-critical method. As Heringer writes, neutrality is a systemic impossibility, insofar as historiographical methodology is concerned:

> A 'proper' methodology cannot solve these problems, for bias is built into the very structure of history [i.e., historiography] itself. An appeal to reality will also not bring neutrality nor objectivity, for to think so, one would have to assume that we have access to the past itself: both the events and the stories … [But] there is no True Narrative that properly tells the story of the world.

Theologically sensitive historiography, as with secular historiography, must contend with its own metaphysical provisionality in a way that does not exclude historical reconstructions undertaken within other metaphysical frameworks. Anything less would be tantamount to academic totalitarianism. Attempts—implicit or explicit—to posit one's own metaphysical framework as a neutral or objective framework within which all historiography may or must be undertaken must therefore be brought to light and highlighted as the power move that it is.

These criteria would all be true of a Christian historiography, to be sure. Moreover, to my mind they do not go far enough: a historiographical approach could conform to all these criteria and still not be 'theologically-motivated' (in general), let alone Christian (in particular). Heringer rightfully notes in his fifth suggested characteristic of theologically sensitive historiography that 'for Christians, the historical method as currently practiced needs to be abandoned and replaced with an explicitly Christian historical approach.'[61] However, as I noted in the introduction to this study, Deines' criteria underwhelm if one seeks an authentically Christian historiographical method; what Deines describes in his work is good scholarship, but not necessarily or particularly Christian scholarship. This should not be a surprise to us since Deines' aim is to suggest some characteristics that theologically motivated historiography must demonstrate if it is to meet the rigorous standards of academic acceptability. However, it raises the further question of what else we might say about the potential shape of theologically motivated historiography.

Within the possibilities that emerge from the notion of such historiography, genuinely Christian historiography will be markedly different from historical methods arising from other metaphysical frameworks. It will not proceed from the same foundations, nor operate in the same manner as, say, a Hindu or Jewish historiography. To the same degree that these are different religions (i.e., different worldviews comprised of metaphysical frameworks), so too will they naturally produce different means of apprehending the past. Accordingly, the following additional criteria might characterise Christian historical Jesus research specifically (the numbering continuing from above). It is worth noting here also that the *order* of these suggestions is not intentionally important here. I am not suggesting, for example, that Christian theology or historiography *must* be Christocentric *before* it should be trinitarian, in any sense.

10.4.6 Christological

If Christian historiography is to be a genuine alternative to its secular counterpart, it must be Christological. In other words, it must place Christology as central to its methodology and it must reject the desire to treat Jesus as primarily an object of study, and treat Jesus as *one who speaks, even the one who is the very speech of God*, rather than just one about whom things are spoken. Writing to critique Lonergan's theological methodology (discussed in Chapter 9 of this study) McGregor writes, 'the essential reason Lonergan's method is not valid is because it is theistic rather than Christic… It is not sufficient for a theological method to be "theological." It must also be "Christological."'[62]

While most academic disciplines treat their subject matter as an object, this cannot be true of Christian theology. Therefore, it cannot be true of a genuinely Christian historiographical method. God is 'Being Itself'; *Ipsum Esse* to use the language of Aquinas.[63] God does not possess existence as an attribute,[64] but He is to be identified with existence.

The notion of *Ipsum Esse* finds its roots in the biblical narrative. Specifically, when Moses encounters YHWH in the burning bush, who says: 'I am who I am …

thus you shall say to the Israelites, "I am has sent me to you"' (Exod. 3.14). When speaking about a being who is Being Itself in this manner, we cannot approach Him as though He were simply one object among many within the world. The Christian faith contends that in Jesus the second person of the triune God who is Being Itself became manifest in human flesh. One of the aims of Christian scholarship should be to allow Jesus to speak through the scholar, as much as the scholar speaks about Jesus. This may not work itself out practically in the form of any methods *per se*, but instead is to be manifest as a general scholarly disposition among Christian historians as scholars who listen first and speak second.

10.4.7 Trinitarian

While Christian historiography must be Christological, it is no paradox to also say that it must affirm Sonderegger's cry that 'not all is Christology!'[65] Sonderegger's systematic project seeks to push back against overly trinitarian theology that neglects the study of God in God's self (*Qui sit et quid sit Deus*). Ironically, this primacy of trinitarianism can be traced to Rahner, who lamented the lack of trinitarian dogmatics amidst contemporary speculation that focussed almost exclusively on the doctrine of the one God. Recall, for example, his famous claim: 'should the doctrine of the Trinity have to be dropped as false, the major part of religious literature could well remain virtually unchanged.'[66] The situation has come full-circle in less than half a century! Although Rahner's quote is often mis-used, or at times even abused, in service of legitimising studies on the Trinity—Rahner himself had as his target here a scholastic form of Catholic theology that he and others in the *Nouvelle théologie* movement sought to repudiate—the point stands that Christology, theology, and the Trinity must be thought together in a properly ordered Christian historiographical project.

Christian scholarship, in approaching Jesus as both fully human and fully divine, should acknowledge that this divinity speaks to the divine who is triune in nature. This is to say, one of the features that will distinguish Christian scholarship from other theologically sensitive scholarship is the belief in the specific God who is three-in-one and one-in-three. The doctrine of the Trinity is an indissoluble aspect of the Christian understanding of God. Reflection upon the nature of the Trinity is significant for historiography since it introduces the categories of the Immanent Trinity (God in God's self, the 'inner life' of the Trinity, as it were) and the Economic Trinity ('the being of God in relation with [hu]man[s] and his world' as one theologian puts it[67]). It is this second sense of the Trinity with which we as historians are concerned. Although theologians such as Karl Rahner might disagree—'the "economic" Trinity is the "immanent" Trinity and the "immanent" Trinity is the "economic" Trinity,' he famously argues[68]—it is this distinction that some theologians would fight to preserve.[69]

Although Pannenberg[70] and Weber[71] trace the distinction back to Augustus Urlsperger (1728–1806), Moltmann[72] and Berkouwer[73] (among others) have articulated an implicit use of the distinction throughout church history, showing it to be a fundamental element of Christian doctrine. All this is to say that while it is important that a historical method must speak of the trinitarian God of the Bible to be authentically Christian, it must also be careful not to move too quickly from making historical claims that speak of the Economic Trinity to making claims about the Immanent Trinity without proper theological and metaphysical warrant.

10.4.8 Cruciform

By this I mean it must take Jesus' death and resurrection as historical truths from the outset. Any historical project that denies the historicity of the resurrection cannot be described as genuinely Christian. As Richard Hays argues:

> On the issue of the resurrection, many preachers and New Testament scholars are unwitting partisans of the Sadducees. Because they deny the truth of Scripture's proclamation that God raised Jesus from the dead—or waffle about it—they leave the church in a state of uncertainty, lacking confidence in its mission, knowing neither the Scriptures nor the power of God.[74]

This means that Christian historians may have little to say about the historicity of the resurrection. This is because, as discussed in the ninth chapter of this study, the resurrection of Jesus is a worldview-defining event, in that one's opinion of it informs which worldview one operates within. Since, logically speaking, historiography is undertaken after the formation of a worldview, a decision must be made as to the operative power one affords to the resurrection before one's historical reconstruction may take place. 'God is' as Jenson famously wrote, 'whoever raised Jesus from the dead, having before raised Israel from Egypt.'[75] This magisterial sentence from Robert Jenson highlights[76] that when one speaks of the Christian God, one refers to this God in particular. To engage in Christian historiography, therefore, is to engage in historiography in light of this God's resurrection of Jesus. It cannot engage in historiography apart from the God who 'raised Jesus from the dead, having before raised Israel from Egypt.'

In practice, this means that statements regarding the historicity of the resurrection will be meaningless, in terms of formal logic. If—as we saw with N.T. Wright in Chapter 9—one begins from a non-Christian worldview (understood as any worldview that does not accept the central beliefs of orthodox Christianity, including the historicity of the resurrection) and attempts to affirm the historicity of the resurrection, this conclusion gives assent to a worldview which contains metaphysical claims contrary to those with which the historian began. In other words, the conclusion undermines the premise, and the entire argument collapses in on itself into meaninglessness. On the other hand, if one begins from a Christian perspective, this necessarily involves a belief in the historicity of the resurrection. As such, any attempts to advance an argument in favour of the historicity of the resurrection will merely be restating this foundational presupposition. It will be a tautology, in other words, again resulting in meaninglessness. If a historical method is to be genuinely Christian, then, the historicity of the resurrection cannot simply be one discussion point among others, as one might discuss Jesus' parables for example. It is vital to—gives life to—the Christian faith. As such, it must be the starting point from which one undertakes historical reconstruction. Much in the same way that scripture is 'read backwards,' so too must the life and ministry of the historical Jesus be reconstructed backwards, considering and proceeding from the conviction that He was raised from the dead.

One might object to this criterion and respond by questioning the validity of assuming the historicity of one aspect of Jesus' life to inform our study of other aspects. However, to this I would point out precedents set by Jesus historians operating within a secular milieu. As just one example, when probing possible avenues of enquiry for a potential fourth 'Quest' for the historical Jesus, Ernst Baasland suggests we focus upon Jesus' desires and motives. Any reconstruction of Jesus' motives, he argues, must be able to explain certain *events* in Jesus' life. These include Jesus' death, the cleansing of the temple, his meals with different social groups, his miracles, his teaching, his baptism by John, and his relationship with the synagogue.[77] In other words, Baasland suggests we take for granted some information about these elements of Jesus' life (including the fact that they happened in the first place) and use them as points of reference when discussing Jesus' motives. What I propose is that it is to operate in a similar manner, taking as fundamental the death and resurrection of Jesus, and reconstructing his life and teaching.

This does not mean that Christian historians cannot engage with debates surrounding the resurrection at all. It is entirely possible for a Christian historian to point out internal inconsistencies in the way historians of other historiographical worldviews approach the issue. In other words, a Christian historian may approach the work of a non-Christian and highlight claims that are inconsistent or problematic even if one adopts the historiographical worldview of the other historian. (Likewise, non-Christian historians may, of course, engage with Christian historiography in the same manner.) For example, following Leon Festinger's work in the 1950's, some have suggested that early belief in the resurrection is the result of cognitive dissonance, that Jesus' disciples refused to believe he had died and so concocted the notion of the resurrection.[78] Festinger, for example, remarks on how an individual might continue to smoke despite being fully cognisant of the health risks this entails.[79]

Before I move on to the next criterion, note too that this need not involve giving assent to the notion of Jesus' *bodily* resurrection from the dead. To be clear, it is my conviction that Jesus' resurrection was a physical one; Jesus' bodily resurrection to my mind makes the most sense of the theologies of the New Testament. However, I am aware that there are many Christians who instead conceive of Jesus' resurrection in purely *spiritual* terms. (Note, for example, my engagement with the work of Edward Schillebeeckx in §6 of Chapter 7). Although I think this position is very problematic both in the way in which it requires us to read the texts of the New Testament and in the implications this has for Christian theology more broadly, I also do not think it is my place to ordain this position as 'un-Christian.' Thus, I suggest Christian historiography begin from a place of affirming Jesus' death and resurrection in the most fundamental terms possible.

As Williams remarks, belief in the resurrection 'is the minimum we need to say to ensure some sort of continuity between the New Testament and our own theologizing about Easter.'[80]

10.4.9 Scriptural

Since the texts of the New Testament are simultaneously a key source of information pertaining to the historical Jesus and a constituent part of the Scriptures of the Christian faith, Christian historiography must be grounded upon a solid doctrine of the ontology of Scripture (i.e., what Scripture is). It simply will not suffice to make lazy appeals to the authority of Scripture to support the veracity of claims made therein about the historical Jesus. Equally, it will not do to prioritise the canonical texts over noncanonical texts insofar as they are engaged as historical documents (and on this point Crossley is correct to highlight this tendency in aspects of Wright's work[81]). Here John Webster's work on Scripture as sanctified is vital.[82]

I cannot fully do justice to Webster's work here, but central to his ontology of Scripture is the notion of Scripture as sanctified. For Webster, sanctification is 'the act of God the Holy Spirit in hallowing creaturely processes, employing them in the service of the taking form of revelation within the history of the creation.'[83] Webster notes that an ontological view of Scripture as sanctified

> needs to draw heavily upon the resources of the theology of the Spirit of the Risen Christ as the free, active self-presence of the triune God in creation, sanctifying creaturely realities for the divine service and, more specifically, inspiring the biblical writings.[84]

Crucially, this 'free, active self-presence' which sanctifies creaturely realities such as the texts of Scripture, does so in a manner that does not obliterate their creatureliness. The act of Scripture being 'elected, shaped and preserved to undertake a role in the economy of salvation' by the Spirit, 'is not simply occasional or punctiliar, an act from above which arrests and overwhelms the creaturely reality, employs it, and then puts it to one side.'[85]

Instead, 'sanctification is thus not the extraction of creaturely reality from its creatureliness, but the annexing and ordering of its course so that it may fittingly assist in that work which is proper to God.'[86] As such, while Scripture is not *merely* human text, the creatureliness of the text can never be irradicated from a proper ontology of those Scriptures which are to be examined in the course of historical enquiry: 'it is *as*—not *despite*—the creaturely realities that they are that they serve God.'[87] Such an ontology of Scripture retains the creatureliness of the texts of the New Testament (thus allowing—even requiring—engagement with them on a historical level) while simultaneously affirming their authority as creaturely texts that God has chosen to sanctify as part of the divine economy.

Proper recognition of Scripture as sanctified is crucial for Christian historiography, for three reasons. First, it guards against lazy and uncritical appeals to the authority of Scripture as historically determinative for matters pertaining to the person of Jesus of Nazareth. Second, it allows (even encourages) the Christian historian to incorporate the evidence of noncanonical sources of knowledge of the historical Jesus. Third, it untethers the authority and witness of Scripture *qua* Scripture from the findings of enquiry into the historical person of Jesus.

10.4.10 Eschatological

Genuinely Christian historiography must also be of an eschatological outlook. In less technical terms, it must be hopeful; it must, as Heringer rightly notes, be considerate of 'the interconnectedness of past, present, and future.'[88] To speak of the past in genuinely Christian terms is to speak of it with reference to the God who is both One and Three, the second person of whom took on human flesh to reconcile creation to its creator. Thus, any Christian historiography must proceed in part from robust theology of creation that culminates in its renewal at the turning point of the age to come.

In other words, Christian scholarly reflection upon the past should be marked by recognition that creation is not as it ought to be, that it awaits eschatological renewal 'with eager longing … groaning in labor pains,' as Paul writes (Rom. 8.19–22). To my mind, the most promising means by which this might be accomplished would be the construction of a Christian historiographical method informed by an eschatologically oriented theology of creation, that encompasses both the act of creation, and creation *qua* creation.

10.4.11 Prayerful

If Christian scholarship is to be marked by a belief in a God who is triune, and who wilfully died on our behalf and was resurrected, then Christian scholarship must also be informed by communion and communication with this same God. This is to say, it must be prayerful scholarship. Or, more accurately, scholarship undertaken by prayerful men and women. As Simeon Zahl has recently demonstrated, a fully rounded account of the work of the Holy Spirit must take seriously the nature of Christian experience (not only in the role of prayer, but at least inclusive of it).[89] In other words, then, even if there is no mention of prayer in the written output of Christian historians, these historians ought to be men and women formed and shaped by communion with the triune God who 'raised Jesus from death, having before raised Israel out of Egypt,' to echo again Jenson's language.[90] This is perhaps not a characteristic of Christian historiography *per se*, but of the Christian historian at least.

I will not be prescriptive here regarding the nature of prayer itself, nor of Christian experience. As Zahl notes, there is great danger in such an approach:

> Overspecification of the experiential shape of the Spirit's work can also risk doing a kind of violence to enormously complex and multivalent Christian experiences—a life-changing conversion, for example—by attempting to

reduce them to a few simple emotional and motivational effects that are empirically available.[91]

However, suffice it to say here that prayerful Christian scholarship must exhibit a conception of being influenced by ongoing dialogue with God. As von Balthasar writes, 'prayer is a conversation between God and the soul, and secondly, a particular language is spoken: God's language. Prayer is dialogue, not man's monologue before God.'[92] One may hold to this proposition without prescribing the particularities of prayerful praxis. However, regardless of how one applies prayer in one's scholarship, it must be present in a genuinely Christian historiography. As Sonderegger writes in the first volume of her systematic theology:

> So in the end, we must say that a doctrine of God cannot but take the wings of prayer. There is no study, no examination nor understanding, without a heart seared by intercession, by repentance, by worship and praise … This is the proper dogmatic for of the doctrine of God: the intellect, bent down, glorified, in prayer.[93]

Elsewhere, Coakley has spoken of the need for a *théologie totale* (or theology *in via*) which takes seriously 'an insistence on the ascetical practice of contemplation' which, she notes, 'cannot be undertaken *at all* without close attention to prayer.'[94] She writes that:

> Theology involves not merely the *metaphysical* task of adumbrating a vision of God, the world, and humanity, but simultaneously the *epistemological* task of cleansing, reordering, and redirecting the apparatus of one's own thinking, desiring, and seeing.[95]

In other words, Christian theology—and therefore Christian historiography—involves not only making claims about God, but also allowing God to speak to oneself, to be a vital part of the epistemological process. This seems to take Christian historiography beyond Deines' claim that theologically motivated historical methods must be *critical*, in the sense of encouraging criticism from others. Introducing prayer into the methodology of Christian historiography seems instinctively to preclude criticism of this kind. I am aware that, for some, I tread here on perilously thin academic ice (if the ice has not already cracked). How does one open up one's inner prayer life to criticism in a meaningful way? How does one stop prayer from being used as a *force majeure* whereby others are compelled to accept something because it is the result of apparently prayerful revelation?

To be clear, I am not advocating for the centrality of prayer on *epistemological* grounds, but on *formational* grounds. As Webster notes, 'prayer is not to be thought of functionally or instrumentally. It is not a means to an end.'[96] Prayer is not to be understood as a source of historical knowledge as though God might reveal to the pray-er how things really were; Berdyaev's infamous footnote—'this was once revealed to me in a dream'[97]—would have no place in the kind of

Christian historiography I propose. However, prayer must be central to such an endeavour because prayer is one of the key acts through which the Christian is sanctified and conformed to the image of Christ. Christian historiography must take seriously the formational work of God in the life of the historian and, therefore, must take seriously prayer as one crucial cite of such formational work.

These above criteria are advanced here not as an end to discussion regarding the form of Christian historiography. They are simply suggestions and, while I think in each case they are reasonable ones to make, they remain suggestions nonetheless. These criteria are envisioned as being the beginning of an ongoing dialogue regarding the shape that a genuinely Christian historiography might take. Stevenson summarises the notion well, writing:

> The point is not that a Christian historian will possess only naïve credulity when it comes to studying Jesus. Rather, hard-won nuanced and clearly expressed philosophical and theological understandings of the world should be brought to bear on all areas of knowledge, especially in the field of history.[98]

By offering these suggested criteria here, I invite others to engage with them, to critique them, to refine them, and to add to them.

10.5 Concluding Remarks

In this study I have examined, at a very fundamental level, the way in which we make claims about the historical Jesus, and have demonstrated that apprehending the historical Jesus, as with any historical discipline, requires the historian to engage with metaphysics, even if this is only done implicitly and/or unsystematically. In addition to this, I have made the following two points: (1) that modern academic historical Jesus research has largely been conformed to a secular metaphysical framework, and (2) that secular metaphysics is itself a positively construed metaphysical framework, and not a neutral residue left over following the withdrawal of religion. I have further suggested that recognition of these two points should prompt New Testament studies and historical Jesus research to reflect more deeply on its metaphysical (and theological) foundation and to permit the inclusion of approaches that proceed from other historiographical worldviews. These worldviews, I have suggested, should be seen as differently theological, not less theological; exclusion of other historiographical worldviews does not inculcate New Testament studies and historical Jesus research from theology, but rather it uncritically and implicitly gives dominance to one specific and certain type of theological and metaphysical foundation.

Recognition of these facts should not lead to the total abandonment of secular historiography and the installation of another historiographical worldview in its place. If all historiography is necessarily metaphysical, as I have claimed, then as long as one historiographical worldview enjoys imposed dominance within the 'Quest,' or even supposed dominance, then this will continue to be problematic, regardless of which historiographical worldview enjoys dominance. The reader should not construe the argument I have advanced in this monograph, then, as a call for change *per se*. Rather, it is a call for expansion. If the academy is to be a place of genuine plurality, academic acceptability must be expanded so that it may allow scholars of other (non-secular) worldviews to partake in the 'Quest,' without their work being relegated to a lower tier of scholarly standards. In an effort to contribute to this task, in the final chapter of this study, therefore, I have begun to think about what shape(s) a genuinely Christian historiographical worldview might take, while recognising the need for more sustained research to be undertaken on this matter.

In many ways, therefore, this study raises more questions than it has answered. There is still much work that would need to be done to construct historical-critical methods that do not conform to a secular worldview. However, I hope that my argument here adds legitimacy and support to the endeavours of scholars who wish to take up this work in the future. To speak of the metaphysics of historical Jesus research is not to introduce a 'new' category into the 'Quest.' Nor is it to apply inappropriately a theological framework to the historical-critical methodologies of New Testament studies. Rather, it is to recognise that these methodologies themselves are already and inescapably theological. It is this recognition of what has lain dormant and implicit within the 'Quest' for the historical Jesus that will allow the discipline to expand, and to flourish.

Notes

1 Sarah E. Rollens, 'Socialscapes and Abstractions: An Appraisal of Richard A. Horsley's Theorizing of Antiquity', *JSHJ* 18.2 (2020), 101–23 (102).

2 "Es gibt nur *eine* sachgemäße Exegese, nämlich diejenige, die dem Text (und seinen Kontexten) Gerecht wird." Martin Hengel, 'Eine junge theologische Disziplin in der Krise', in *Theologische, historische und biographische Skizzen: Kleine Schriften VII*, ed. Claus-Jürgen Thornton, WUNT 253 (Tübingen: Mohr Siebeck, 2010), 279–91 (283).

3 Milbank's PhD thesis on Vico was actually published after *Theology and Social Theory* as John Milbank, *The Religious Dimension in the Thought of Giambattista Vico*, Studies in the History of Philosophy 23, 2 vols (Lewiston, NY: E. Mellon, 1991–92).

4 Milbank, *Beyond Secular Order*.

5 Most importantly, see *Radical Orthodoxy: A New Theology*, ed. John Milbank, Catherine Pickstock, and Graham Ward (London: Routledge, 1999); *The Radical Orthodoxy Reader*, ed. John Milbank and Simon Oliver (London: Routledge, 2009).

6 See the helpful article by David F. Ford, 'Radical Orthodoxy and the Future of British Theology', *SJT* 54.3 (2001), 385–404. In addition, the 21st Century has seen a number of monographs and edited volumes which seek to interact with RO with varying degrees of sympathy. See, Wayne J. Hankey and Douglas Hedley (eds), *Deconstructing Radical Orthodoxy: Postmodern Theology, Rhetoric and Truth* (Aldershot: Ashgate, 2005); Rosemary Radford Reuther and Marion Grau (eds), *Interpreting the Postmodern: Responses to 'Radical Orthodoxy'* (New York: T&T Clark, 2006); Lisa Isherwood and Marko Zlomislić (eds), *The Poverty of Radical Orthodoxy*, Postmodern Ethics, 3 (Eugene, OR: Pickwick, 2012); Daniel P. Horan, *Postmodernity and Univocity: A Critical Account of Radical Orthodoxy and John Duns Scotus* (Minneapolis, MN: Fortress, 2014).

7 Oliver O'Donovan, '*Theology and Social Theory: Beyond Secular Reason* by John Milbank', *Studies in Christian Ethics* 5.1 (1992), 80.
8 Richard H. Roberts, 'Transcendental Sociology? A Critique of John Milbank's *Theology and Social Theory: Beyond Secular Reason*', *SJT* 46.4 (1993), 527–35 (535).
9 John Milbank and Catherine Pickstock, *Truth in Aquinas*, Radical Orthodoxy (London: Routledge, 2001).
10 Simon Oliver, 'Introducing Radical Orthodoxy: From Participation to Late Modernity', in *The Radical Orthodoxy Reader*, ed. John Milbank and Simon Oliver (London: Routledge, 2009), 3–27 (14).
11 Thomas Aquinas, *Summa Theologiae: Latin Text and English Translation with Introductions, Notes, Appendices, and Glossaries* (London: Blackfriars, 1964), 1a.13.5.
12 Aquinas, *ST*, 1a.13.7.
13 Milbank and Pickstock, *Truth in Aquinas*, 51. This reading of Aquinas on the accident of creation is also crucial to Pickstock's claim that eucharistic transubstantiation is a re-enacting of the grace-gift of creation. See Catherine Pickstock, *After Writing: On the Liturgical Consummation of Philosophy*, Challenges in Contemporary Theology (Oxford: Blackwell, 1998), esp. 259–66.
14 One caricature of RO suggests they unnecessarily present Scotus as the 'villain' of mediaeval theology. It is true that RO has placed a great deal of emphasis of Scotus' conception of univocity, perhaps even to the point of misread Scotus himself. However, to say that RO lays the blame solely at the feet of Scotus would be an equally misguided reading of the relevant texts.
15 Milbank, *Theology and Social Theory*, 9.
16 This is the title of the second chapter of John Milbank, *The Word Made Strange: Theology, Language, Culture* (Oxford: Blackwell, 1997).
17 Milbank, *Theology and Social Theory*, 1.
18 Linn Marie Tonstad, '(Un)wise Theologians: Systematic Theology in the University', *IJST* 22.4 (2020), 494–511. I have made a similar argument concerning New Testament studies, that challenges faced by the discipline are not overcome by embracing the presuppositions from which these challenges emerge, but by being a discipline that is radically 'other' to, say, history, or classics, by embracing the unique metaphysical potency that its subject matter contains. See further, Jonathan Rowlands, 'Reception History, Theological Interpretation, and the Future of New Testament Studies', *JTI* 13.2 (2019), 147–67.
19 One reviewer, for example, writes "its size is preposterous," and it is "poorly proofread," that "Taylor's scholarship leaves something to be desired," and "displays a shocking partiality in its approach." See Charles Larmore, 'How Much Can We Stand?', *The New Republic*, 9 April 2008, https://newrepublic.com/article/63415/how-much-can-we-stand.
20 John Milbank, 'A Closer Walk on the Wild Side: Some Comments on Charles Taylor's *A Secular Age*', *Studies in Christian Ethics* 22.1 (2009), 89–104 (89). This review has also been reprinted as John Milbank, 'A Closer Walk on the Wild Side', in *Varieties of Secularism in a Secular Age*, ed. Michael Warner, Jonathan Vanantwerpen, and Craig Calhoun (Cambridge, MA: Harvard University, 2010), 54–82. In the 2010 version of the text, the above quote appears on p. 54.
21 See, for example, James K.A. Smith, *How (Not) to Be Secular: Reading Charles Taylor* (Grand Rapids, MI: Eerdmans, 2014) and the important recent volume *Our Secular Age: Ten Years of Reading and Applying Charles Taylor*, ed. Collin Hansen (Deerfield, IL: The Gospel Coalition, 2017).
22 Oliver, 'Introduction', 4.
23 Taylor, *A Secular Age*, 4, 5. (Emphasis original). Taylor's reference to 'un-belief' is one that I myself would be wary of, not least because, as Milbank has shown, adhering to a secular worldview is to believe in a positively construed metaphysical framework, to the same extent as adhering to a Christian worldview would be. Accordingly,

I will refer to secularism and its cognates rather than using Taylor's terminology of 'un-belief.'

24 Ibid., 5.
25 Ibid., 8.
26 Ibid.
27 Ibid., 13.
28 Ibid.
29 Again, I highlight my objection to Taylor's use of the term 'unbelief' here since secularism is itself a belief system. However, insofar as Taylor means that "'belief in secular reasoning' has become for the many the major default option," I am in agreement.
30 Taylor, *A Secular Age*, 14.
31 Ibid., 25.
32 The concept of Entzauberung is developed by Weber in (among other works) the 1919 lecture "Wissenschaft als Beruf," available as Max Weber, 'Science as Vocation', in *The Vocation Lectures*, ed. David S. Owen and Tracy B. Strong, trans. Rodney Livingstone (Indianapolis, IN: Hackett Pub, 2004). See also the study by Hartmut Lehmann, *Die Entzauberung der Welt: Studien zu Themen von Max Weber* (Göttingen: Wallstein, 2009).
33 Taylor, *A Secular Age*, 26.
34 Ibid.
35 Ibid., 27.
36 Taylor explicitly borrows this term from Jean Delumeau, *Le Péché et la Peur* (Paris: Fayard, 1978).
37 See Silvianne Aspray, *Metaphysics in the Reformation: The Case of Peter Martyr Vermilgi* (Oxford: OUP, 2021).
38 Taylor, *A Secular Age*, 105.
39 Ibid., 106.
40 Originally published as a series of essays in 1904–5, the original German text is available as Max Weber, 'Die protestantische Ethik und der Geitst des Kapitalismus', in *Gesammelte Aufsätze zur Religionssoziologie 1* (Tübingen: Mohr Siebeck, 1920), 17–206.
41 Taylor, *A Secular Age*, 130.
42 Ibid., 138.
43 Ibid., 175.
44 Ibid., 176.
45 Ibid., 177.
46 Although Taylor never explicitly quotes from Montchrétien, one suspects he is alluding to the 1615 treatise *Traicté de l'œconomie politique*, a critical edition of which is available as Antoine de Montchrestien, *Traicté de l'œconomie politique*, ed. François Billacois, Les classiques de la pensée politique, 16 (Genève: Librairie Droz, 1999).
47 Taylor, *A Secular Age*, 185.
48 Ibid., 196.
49 Ibid., 196.
50 Ibid., 197.
51 Ibid., 209.
52 Milbank, 'Closer Walk', 100.
53 Taylor, *A Secular Age*, 775.
54 Kuklick, 'Review', 84.
55 Stevenson, 'Self-Understanding', 303.
56 Silvianne Aspray, 'A Complex Legacy: Louis Bouyer and the Metaphysics of the Reformation', *Modern Theology* 34.1 (2018), 3–22 (9).
57 Blondel, *History and Dogma*, 287.
58 Deines, *Acts of God*, 24–26; Heringer, *Uniting History and Theology*, 179–210.
59 Heringer, *Uniting History and Theology*, 185–86.

60 Heringer, *Uniting History and Theology*, 186–95.
61 Ibid., 208.
62 Peter John McGregor, 'Is Lonergan's Method Theological?', *Radical Orthodoxy: Theology, Philosophy, Politics* 5.1 (2019), 61–99 (98).
63 Aquinas, *Summa Theologiae*, 1a.13.5.
64 The very concept of applying 'attributes' to God is problematic, as recently argued by Janet Martin Soskice, 'Being and Love: Schleiermacher, Aquinas and Augustine', *Modern Theology* 34.4 (2018), 480–91. Herein Soskice engages Schleiermacher's claim that love is a divine attribute: "only love and no other divine attribute can be equated with God in this fashion" (Friedrich Schleiermacher, *Christian Faith: A New Translation and Critical Edition*, ed. Catherine L. Kelsey and Terrence N. Tice, trans. Terrence N. Tice, Catherine L. Kelsey, and Edwina Lawler (Louisville, KY: Westminster John Knox, 2016), §167). Instead, she suggests it is more helpful to think of divine *names* rather than divine attributes, which allows us to speak of the most fundamental qualities of God without reducing them to predicates. Similarly, in the same issue of *Modern Theology*, Behr argues that 'Father' should be properly considered a name of God, rather than something attributed to him, since that more accurately conveys the sense meant by the phrase 'God the Father' (John Behr, '"One God Father Almighty"', *Modern Theology* 34.3 (2018), 320–30).
65 Katherine Sonderegger, *Systematic Theology: Volume 1, The Doctrine of God* (Minneapolis, MN: Fortress, 2015), xvii.
66 Karl Rahner, *The Trinity*, trans. Joseph Donceel (Tunbridge Wells: Burns & Oates, 1970), 11.
67 Eberhard Jüngel, *God as the Mystery of the World: On the Foundation of the Theology and the Crucified One in the Dispute between Theism and Atheism*, trans. Darrell L. Guder (Grand Rapids, MI: Eerdmans, 1983), 346.
68 Rahner, *The Trinity*, 22. A helpful introduction to Rahner's doctrine of the Trinity is David Rohrer Budiash, 'Fundamental Theology for the Trinity: Karl Rahner's Contribution', *HeyJ* 57.6 (2016), 917–34.
69 See Seung Goo Lee, 'The Relationship between the Ontological Trinity and the Economic Trinity', *Journal of Reformed Theology* 3.1 (2009), 90–107.
70 Wolfhart Pannenberg and Geoffrey W. Bromiley, *Systematic Theology* (Grand Rapids, MI: Eerdmans, 1991), 291 n.111.
71 Otto Weber and Darrell L. Guder, *Foundations of Dogmatics* (Grand Rapids, MI: Eerdmans, 1981), I.388 n. 124.
72 Jürgen Moltmann, *The Crucified God*, trans. R.A. Wilson and John Bowden (London: SCM, 1974), 151; idem, *The Trinity and the Kingdom: The Doctrine of God*, trans. Margaret Kohl (London: SCM, 1981), 235.
73 G.C. Berkouwer, *A Half Century of Theology: Movements and Motives*, ed. & trans. Lewis Smedes (Grand Rapids, MI: Eerdmans, 1977), 259.
74 Richard B. Hays, 'Reading Scripture in the Light of the Resurrection', in *The Art of Reading Scripture*, ed. Ellen F. Davis and Richard B. Hays (Grand Rapids, MI: Eerdmans, 2003), 216–38 (216).
75 Robert W. Jenson, *Systematic Theology, vol. 1: The Triune God* (New York: OUP, 1997), 63.
76 This statement is, of course, about much more than Jesus' resurrection and reflects the importance Jenson placed upon God as *the God of Israel* in his theology. See Andrew W. Nicol, *Exodus and Resurrection: The God of Israel in the Theology of Robert W. Jenson*, Emerging Scholars (Minneapolis, MN: Fortress, 2016). Pp. 1–20 serves as a helpful introduction to the issue.
77 Baasland, 'Fourth Quest?', I:49.
78 Leon Festinger, Henry Riecken, and Stanley Schachter, *When Prophecy Fails: A Social and Psychological Study of a Modern Group that Predicted the Destruction of the World* (Minneapolis, MN: University of Minnesota, 1956); Leon Festinger, *A Theory*

of Cognitive Dissonance (Stanford, CA: Stanford University, 1957). See, also, Hugh Jackson, 'The Resurrection Belief of the Earliest Church: A Response to the Failure of Prophecy?', *JR* 55.4 (1975), 415–25.
79 Festinger, *Cognitive Dissonance*, 5.
80 Rowan Williams, *Resurrection: Interpreting the Easter Gospel* (London: Darton, Longman and Todd, 1982), 93.
81 James Crossley, 'Against the Historical Plausibility of the Empty Tomb Story and Bodily Resurrection of Jesus', *JSHJ* 3.2 (2005), 171–86.
82 John Webster, *Holy Scripture: A Dogmatic Sketch* (Current Issues in Theology: Cambridge: CUP, 2003).
83 Ibid., 17–18.
84 Ibid., 18.
85 Ibid., 26.
86 Ibid., 26–27.
87 Ibid., 28.
88 Heringer, *Uniting History and Theology*, 195 (cf., 195–201).
89 Simeon Zahl, *The Holy Spirit and Christian Experience* (Oxford: OUP, 2020).
90 Jenson, *Systematic Theology*, vol. 1, 63.
91 Zahl, *Holy Spirit*, 79.
92 Hans Urs von Balthasar, *Prayer* (San Francisco, CA: Ignatius, 1986), 14.
93 Sonderegger, *Systematic Theology: Volume 1*, xxi.
94 Sarah Coakley, *God, Sexuality and the Self: An Essay 'On the Trinity'* (Cambridge: Cambridge University Press, 2013), 83, 27. (emphasis mine)
95 Ibid., 20. (emphases original)
96 John Webster, *The Culture of Theology* (Grand Rapids, MI: Baker, 2019), 143.
97 Nicolas Berdyaev, *The Divine and the Human* (London: Geoffrey Bles, 1949), 6 n.1.
98 Stevenson, 'Self-Understanding', 307.

Bibliography

Adams, R. M. 'Time and Thisness'. In *Midwest Studies in Philosophy*, edited by P. French, T. Uehling, and H. Wettstein, xi:315–30. Minneapolis, MN: University of Minnesota, 1986.

Allison, Jr., Dale C. *The Resurrection of Jesus: Apologetics, Polemics, History*. London: T&T Clark, 2021.

———. 'How to Marginalize the Traditional Criteria of Authenticity'. In *Handbook for the Study of the Historical Jesus*, edited by Tom Holmén and Stanley Porter, 1:3–30. Leiden: Brill, 2011.

———. *Constructing Jesus: Memory, Imagination, and History*. Grand Rapids, MI: Baker Academic, 2010.

———. *The Historical Christ and the Theological Jesus*. Grand Rapids, MI: William B. Eerdmans, 2009.

———. 'Explaining the Resurrection: Conflicting Convictions'. *Journal for the Study of the Historical Jesus* 3.2 (2005a), 117–33.

———. *Resurrecting Jesus: The Earliest Christian tradition and its Interpreters*. New York: T&T Clark, 2005b.

———. 'The Secularizing of the Historical Jesus'. *Perspectives in Religious Studies* 27.2 (2000), 135–51.

———. *Jesus of Nazareth: Millenarian Prophet*. Philadelphia, PA: Fortress, 1998.

Alter, Robert. *The Art of Biblical Narrative*. New York: Basic Books, 1981.

Alvis, Jason W. 'How to Overcome the World: Henry, Heidegger, and the Post-Secular'. *International Journal of Philosophical Studies* 24.5 (2016), 663–84.

Ameriks, Karl. *Kant and the Historical Turn: Philosophy as Critical Interpretation*. Oxford: Oxford University, 2006.

Anonymous. 'Von Interpolationen im Evangelium Matthaei'. In *Repertorium für biblische und morgenlandische Literature 9*, edited by J.G. Eichhorn. Leipzig: Weidmann, 1781.

Anscombe, G.E.M. *An Introduction to Wittgenstein's Tractatus*. London: Hutchinson, 1971.

Aquinas, Thomas. *Summa Theologiae: Latin Text and English Translation with Introductions, Notes, Appendices, and Glossaries*. London: Blackfriars, 1964.

Ariew, Roger, ed. *G. W. Leibniz and Samuel Clarke: Correspondence*. Indianapolis, IN: Hackett, 2000.

Arnal, William E. *The Symbolic Jesus: Historical Scholarship, Judaism and the Construction of Contemporary Identity*. Religion in Culture. London: Equinox, 2005.

Asad, Talal. *Formations of the Secular: Christianity, Islam, Modernity. Cultural Memory in the Present*. Stanford, CA: Stanford University, 2003.

Aspray, Silvianne. *Metaphysics in the Reformation: The Case of Peter Martyr Vermigli*. Oxford: Oxford University Press, 2021.

———. 'A Complex Legacy: Louis Bouyer and the Metaphysics of the Reformation'. *Modern Theology* 34.1 (2018), 3–22.
Augustine of Hippo. *De Civitate Dei*. Edited and translated by P.G. Walsh. Oxford: Oxbow Books, 2005.
Avalos, Hector. *The End of Biblical Studies*. Amherst, NY: Prometheus Books, 2007.
Ayer, A.J. *Language, Truth, and Logic*. Oxford: Oxford University, 1936.
Azzouni, Jody. 'On "On What There Is"'. *Pacific Philosophical Quarterly* 79.1 (1998), 1–18.
Baader, Franz von. *Vorlesnungen über speculative Dogmatik*. Stuttgart: Cotta, 1828.
Baasland, Ernst. 'Forth Quest? What Did Jesus Really Want?' In *Handbook for the Study of the Historical Jesus*, edited by Tom Holmén and Stanley Porter, 1:31–56. Leiden: Brill, 2011.
Backhaus, Knut. 'Echoes from the Wilderness: The Historical John the Baptist'. In *Handbook for the Study of the Historical Jesus*, edited by Tom Holmén and Stanley Porter, 2: 1747–85. Leiden: Brill, 2011.
Bacon, Francis. *Novum Organum and Associated Texts*. Edited by Graham Rees. The Instauratio Magna, II. Oxford: Clarendon, 2004.
Badiou, Alain. *Being and Event*. Translated by Oliver Feltham. London: Continuum, 2005.
———. *L'Être et l'Événement. L'Ordre philosophique*. Paris: Seuil, 1988.
Bahr, Lynne Moss. 'The 'Temporal Turn' in New Testament Studies'. *Currents in Biblical Research* 18.3 (2020), 268–79.
———. *'The Time is Fulfilled': Jesus's Apocalypticism in the Context of Continental Philosophy*. LNTS 596. London: T&T Clark, 2019.
Baird, William. *History of New Testament Research*. 3 Vols. Minneapolis, MN: Fortress, 1992–2013.
Barbour, R.S. *Traditio-Historical Criticism of the Gospels*. Studies in Creative Criticism 4. London: SPCK, 1972.
Barcan, Ruth C. 'The Identity of Individuals in a Strict Functional Calculus of Second Order'. *The Journal of Symbolic Logic* 12.1 (1947), 12–15.
———. 'The Deduction Theorem in a Functional Calculus of First Order Based on Strict Implication'. *The Journal of Symbolic Logic* 11.4 (1946a), 115–18.
———. 'A Functional Calculus of First Order Based on Strict Implication'. *The Journal of Symbolic Logic* 11.1 (1946b), 1–16.
Barclay, John M. G. *Paul & the Gift*. Grand Rapids, MI: Eerdmans, 2015.
Barner, Wilfred, Klaus Beans, Helmuth Kiesel, Arno Schilson, Jürgen Stenzel, Gunter E. Grimm, and Conrad Wiedemann, eds. *Gotthold Ephraim Lessing Werke und Briefe*. 12 vols. Bibliothek Deutscher Klassiker. Frankfurt am Main: Deutscher Klassiker, 1989.
Barnett, Paul W. *Jesus and the Logic of History*. New Studies in Biblical Theology 3. Downers Grove, IL: IVP, 1997.
Bartholomew, Craig G. *The God Who Acts in History: The Significance of Sinai*. Grand Rapids, MI: Eerdmans, 2019.
Bauckham, Richard. *Jesus and the Eyewitnesses: The Gospels as Eyewitness Testimony*. 2nd ed. Grand Rapids, MI: Eerdmans, 2017.
Beard, T. Randolph, Robert B. Ekelund, George S. Ford, and Ben Gaskins. 'Secularism, Religion, and Political Choice in the United States'. *Politics and Religion* 6.4 (2013), 753–77.
Becker, Gary S. *The Economics of Crime*. Richmond, VA: Federal Reserve Bank of Richmond, 1995.

———. 'Nobel Lecture: The Economic Way of Looking at Behaviour'. *Journal of Political Economy* 101.3 (1993), 385–409.
———. 'Pressure Groups and Political Behaviour'. In *Capitalism and Democracy: Schumpeter Revisited*, edited by R. D. Coe, 120–46. Notre Dame, IL: University of Notre Dame, 1985a.
———. 'Public Policies, Pressure Groups, and Dead Weight Costs'. *Journal of Public Economics* 28.3 (1985b), 329–47.
———. *A Treatise on the Family*. Cambridge, MA: Harvard University, 1981.
———. 'A Theory of Marriage: Part II'. *Journal of Political Economy* 82.2 (1974), 11–26.
———. 'A Theory of Marriage: Part I'. *Journal of Political Economy* 81.4 (1973), 813–46.
———. *Human Capital: A Theoretical and Empirical Analysis, with Special Reference to Education*. New York: National Bureau of Economic Research, 1964.
———. *The Economics of Discrimination*. Chicago, IL: University of Chicago, 1957.
Becker, Gary S., William H. J. Hubbard, and Kevin M. Murphy. 'Explaining the Worldwide Boom in Higher Education of Women'. *Journal of Human Capital* 4.3 (2010a). 201–41.
———. 'The Market for College Graduates and the Worldwide Boom in Higher Education of Women'. *American Economic Review* 100.3 (2010b), 229–33.
Becker, Jürgen. 'The Search for Jesus' Special Profile'. In *Handbook for the Study of the Historical Jesus*, edited by Tom Holmén and Stanley Porter, 1:57–89. Leiden: Brill, 2011.
Beeck, F. J. van. 'The Quest of the Historical Jesus: Origins, Achievements, and the Specter of Diminishing Returns'. In *Jesus and Faith: A Conversation on the Work of John Dominic Crossan*, edited by Jeffrey Carlson and Robert A. Ludwig, 83–99. Maryknoll, NY: Orbis, 1994.
Behr, John. '"One God Father Almighty"'. *Modern Theology* 34.3 (2018), 320–30.
Beiser, Frederick. 'Fichte and the French Revolution'. In *The Cambridge Companion to Fichte*, edited by David James and Günter Zöller, 38–64. Cambridge: Cambridge University, 2016.
Bell, Richard H. 'The Resurrection Appearances in 1 Corinthians 15'. In *Epiphanies of the Divine in the Septuagint and the New Testament*, edited by Roland Deines and Mark Wreford. Tübingen: Mohr Siebeck, forthcoming.
Bennett, Karen. 'Composition, Colocation, and Metaontology'. In *Metametaphysics: New Essays on the Foundations of Ontology*, edited by David Chalmers, David Manley, and Ryan Wasserman, 38–76. Oxford: Clarendon, 2009.
Berdyaev, Nicolas. *The Divine and The Human*. London: Geoffrey Bles, 1949.
Berg, Herbert, and Sarah Rollens, 'The Historical Muḥammad and the Historical Jesus: A Comparison of Scholarly Reinventions and Reinterpretations'. *Studies in Religion* 37.2 (2008), 271–92.
Berkouwer, G. C. *A Half Century of Theology: Movements and Motives*. Edited and translated by Lewis Smedes. Grand Rapids, MI: Eerdmans, 1977.
Bermejo-Rubio, Fernando. 'Theses on the Nature of the *Leben-Jesu-Forschung*: A Proposal for a Paradigm Shift in Understanding the Quest'. *Journal for the Study of the Historical Jesus* 17.1–2 (2019), 1–34.
———. 'The Fiction of the 'Three Quests': An Argument for Dismantling a Dubious Historiographical Paradigm'. *Journal for the Study of the Historical Jesus* 7.3 (2009), 211–53.
———. 'Historiografía, exégesis e ideología. La ficción contemporánea de las 'tres búsquedas' del Jesús histórico (II)'. *Revista Catalana de Teología* 31.1 (2006), 53–114.

———. 'Historiografía, exégesis e ideología. La ficción contemporánea de las 'tres búsquedas' del Jesús histórico (I)'. *Revista Catalana de Teología* 30.2 (2005), 349–406.

Bernardi, Peter J. *Maurice Blondel, Social Catholicism, and Action Française: The Clash over the Church's Role in Society during the Modernist Era*. Washington, DC: The Catholic University of America, 2009.

Bernier, Jonathan. 'A Response to Porter and Pitts' "Wright's Critical Realism in Context"'. *Journal for the Study of the Historical Jesus* 14.2 (2016a), 186–93.

———. *The Quest for the Historical Jesus after the Demise of Authenticity: Toward a Critical Realist Philosophy of History in Jesus Studies*. LNTS 540. London: Bloomsbury, 2016b.

Bigelow, John. 'Presentism and Properties'. *Philosophical Perspectives* 10.1 (1996), 35–52.

Bilde, Per. 'Can It Be Justified to Talk about Scholarly Progress in the History of Modern Jesus Research since Reimarus?' In *The Mission of Jesus: Second Nordic Symposium on the Historical Jesus, Lund, 7–10 October 2012*, edited by Samuel Byrskog and Tobias Hägerland, 5–24. WUNT II 391. Tübingen: Mohr Siebeck, 2015.

Birch, Jonathan C. P. 'Revolutionary Contexts for the Quest: Jesus in the Rhetoric and Methods of Early Modern Intellectual History'. *Journal for the Study of the Historical Jesus* 17.1–2 (2019), 35–80.

———. 'Reimarus and the Religious Enlightenment: His Apologetic Project'. *Expository Times* 129.6 (2018), 245–53.

Bird, Graham. *The Revolutionary Kant: A Commentary on the* Critique of Pure Reason. Chicago, IL: Open Court, 2006.

Bird, Michael F. *Jesus the Eternal Son: Answering Adoptionist Christology*. Grand Rapids, MI: Eerdmans, 2017.

Black, Max. *A Companion to Wittgensetin's Tractatus*. Ithaca, NY: Cornell University, 1964.

Blau, Judith R., Kenneth C. Land, and Kent Redding. 'The Expansion of Religious Affiliation: An Explanation of the Growth of Church Participation in the United States, 1850–1930'. *Social Science Research* 21.4 (1992), 329–52.

Bloch, Marc. *La société féodale. L'Évolution de l'humanité*. Paris: Albin Michel, 1939.

Blondel, Eric. *Nietzsche: The Body and Culture: Philosophy as a Philological Genealogy*. Translated by Seán Hand. London: Athlone, 1991.

Blondel, Maurice. *The Letter on Apologetics & History and Dogma*. Translated by Alexander Dru and Illtyd Trethowan. Ressourcement: Retrieval and Renewal in Catholic Thought. Edinburgh: T&T Clark, 1994.

———. *Histoire et dogme: les lacunes philosophiques de l'exégèse moderne*. Impr.: Libraire de Montligeon, 1904.

———. *L'Action: Essai d'une critique de la vie et d'une science de la pratique*. Paris: Alcan, 1893.

Bock, Darrell L., and J. Ed Komoszewski, eds. *Jesus, Skepticism and the Problem of History: Criteria and Context in the Study of Cristian Origins*. Grand Rapids, MI: Zondervan, 2019.

Bock, Darrell L., and Robert L. Webb. 'Introduction to Key Events and Actions in the Life of the Historical Jesus'. In *Key Events in the Life of the Historical Jesus: A Collaborative Exploration of Context and Coherence*, edited by Darrell L. Bock and Robert L. Webb, 1–8. WUNT 247. Tübingen: Mohr Siebeck, 2009.

Bond, Helen. *The First Biography of Jesus: Genre and Meaning in Mark's Gospel*. Grand Rapids, MI: Eerdmans, 2020.

———. *The Historical Jesus: A Guide for the Perplexed.* London: Bloomsbury, 2012.

Borg, Marcus J. 'A Renaissance in Jesus Studies'. *Theology Today* 45.3 (1988), 280–92.

Bormann, Lukas. '"Auch unter politischen Gesichtspunkten sehr sorgfältig ausgewählt": Die ersten deutschen Mitglieder der Studiorum Novi Testamenti Societas (SNTS) 1937-1946'. *New Testament Studies* 58.3 (2012), 416–452.

Bornkamm, Günther. *Jesus of Nazareth.* Translated by Irene McLuskey, Fraser McLuskey, and James M. Robinson. London: Hodder & Stoughton, 1960.

———. *Jesus von Nazareth.* Kohlhammer Urban-Taschenbücher 19. Stuttgart: Kohlhammer, 1956.

Briggs, Richard S. 'History and Hermeneutics. By Murray A. Rae'. *The Heythrop Journal* 50.1 (2008), 123–4.

Broad, C. D. *Scientific Thought.* New York: Harcourt, 1927.

Broadhead, Edwin K. 'Implicit Christology and the Historical Jesus'. In *Handbook for the Study of the Historical Jesus*, edited by Tom Holmén and Stanley Porter, 2:1169–82. Leiden: Brill, 2011.

Brown, Colin. 'The Quest of the Unhistorical Jesus and the Quest of the Historical Jesus'. In *Handbook for the Study of the Historical Jesus*, edited by Tom Holmén and Stanley Porter2:855–86. Leiden: Brill, 2011.

———. *Jesus in European Protestant Thought, 1778–1860.* Grand Rapids, MI: Baker Academic, 1988.

Brown, Raymond E. *An Introduction to the New Testament.* New York: Doubleday, 1996.

———. 'Church Pronouncements'. In *The New Jerome Biblical Commentary*, edited by Raymond E. Brown, Joseph A. Fitzmyer, and Roland E. Murphy, 1167. Englewood Cliffs, NJ: Prentice-Hall, 1993.

Bruce, Steve. 'Defining Religion: A Practical Response'. *Revue Internationale de Sociologie* 21.1 (2011a), 107–20.

———. *Secularization: In Defense of an Unfashionable Theory.* Oxford: Oxford University, 2011b.

———. *God Is Dead: Secularization in the West. Religion and Spirituality in the Modern World.* Oxford: Blackwell, 2002.

———. *Choice and Religion: A Critique of Rational Choice.* Oxford: Oxford University, 1999.

Bryant, Joseph M. 'Cost-Benefit Accounting and the Piety Business: Is *Homo Religiosus*, at Bottom, a *Homo Economicus*?' *Method and Theory in the Study of Religion* 12.1–4 (2000), 520–48.

Buckley, Philip. 'Phenomenology as Soteriology: Husserl and the Call for '*Erneuerung*' in the 1920s'. *Modern Theology* 35.1 (2019), 5–22.

Budiash, David Rohrer. 'Fundamental Theology for the Trinity: Karl Rahner's Contribution'. *The Heythrop Journal* 57.6 (2016), 917–34.

Bultmann, Rudolf. *The New Testament and Mythology and Other Basic Writings.* Translated by Schubert Miles Ogden. Philadelphia, PA: Fortress, 1984.

———. *Jesus.* Berlin: Deutsche Bibliothek, 1926.

Burkitt, F. Crawford. 'Johannes Weiss: In Memoriam'. *Harvard Theological Review* 8.3 (1915), 291–97.

Cabantous, Laure, and Jean-Pascal Gond. 'The Resistible Rise of Bayesian Thinking in Management: Historical Lessons from Decision Analysis'. *Journal of Management* 41.2 (2015), 441–71.

Callicott, J. Baird. 'The Worldview Concept and Aldo Leopold's Project of 'World View' Remediation'. *Journal for the Study of Religion, Nature, and Culture* 5.4 (2011), 510–28.

Carleton Paget, James. 'Albert Schweitzer and the Jews'. *Harvard Theological Review* 107.3 (2014), 363–98.

———. 'Albert Schweitzer and Africa'. *Journal of Religion in Africa* 42.3 (2012), 277–316.

———. 'Albert Schweitzer and Adolf von Harnack: An Unlikely Alliance'. *Zeitschrift Für Kirchengeschichte* 122.2–3 (2011a), 257–87.

———. 'Schweitzer and Paul'. *Journal for the Study of the New Testament* 33.3 (2011b), 223–56.

———. 'Theologians in Context: Albert Schweitzer'. *Journal of Ecclesiastical History* 62.1 (2011c), 116–31.

———. 'Albert Schweitzer's Second Edition of *The Quest of the Historical Jesus*'. *Bulletin of the John Rylands Library* 88.1 (2006), 3–39.

———. 'Quests for the Historical Jesus'. In *The Cambridge Companion to Jesus*, edited by Markus Bockmuehl, 138–55. Cambridge: Cambridge University, 2001.

Carnap, Rudolf. 'Empiricism, Semantics, and Ontology'. In *Meaning and Necessity: A Study in Semantics and Modal Logic*, 2nd ed., 205–21. Chicago, IL: University of Chicago, 1956.

———. *Philosophy and Logical Syntax*. Psyche Miniatures General Series 70. London: Kegan Paul, 1935.

———. *Logische Syntax der Sprache*. Berlin: Julius Springer, 1934.

———. *Scheinprobleme in der Philosophie: Das Fremdpsychische Und der Realismusstreit*. Berlin: Weltkreis, 1928.

Carr, David. *Interpreting Husserl: Critical and Comparative Studies*. Boston, MA: Martinus Nijhoff, 1987.

———. *Phenomenology and the Problem of History: A Study of Husserl's Transcendental Philosophy*. Evanston, IL: Northwestern University, 1974.

———. 'Husserl's Problematic Concept of the Life-World'. *American Philosophical Quarterly* 7.4 (1970), 331–39.

Casey, Maurice. *Jesus: Evidence and Argument or Mythicist Myths?* London: T&T Clark, 2014.

———. *Jesus of Nazareth: An Independent Historian's Account of His Life and Teaching*. London: T&T Clark, 2000.

———. 'Some Anti-Semitic Assumptions in the "Theological Dictionary of the New Testament"'. *Novum Testamentum* 41.3 (1999), 280–91.

Cassirer, Ernst. *Kant's Life and Thought*. Translated by James Haden. New Haven, CT: Yale University, 1981.

Chamberlain, H. S. *The Foundations of the Nineteenth Century*. Translated by J. Lees. 2 vols. London ; New York: Lane; Bodley Head, 1910.

———. *Die Grundlagen des neunzehnten Jahrhunderts*. 2 vols. München: Bruckmann, 1899.

Charlesworth, James H. 'The Historical Jesus: How to Ask Questions and Remain Inquisitive'. In *Handbook for the Study of the Historical Jesus*, edited by Tom Holmén and Stanley Porter, 1:91–128. Leiden: Brill, 2011.

———. 'The Historical Jesus in the Fourth Gospel: A Paradigm Shift'. *Journal for the Study of the Historical Jesus* 8.1 (2010), 3–46.

———. *Jesus within Judaism: New Light from Exciting Archaeological Evidence*. London: SPCK, 1989.

Chaves, Mark. 'Secularization as Declining Religious Authority'. *Social Forces* 72.3 (1994), 749–74.

Chaves, Mark, and Philip S. Gorski. 'Religious Pluralism and Religious Participation'. *Annual Review of Sociology* 27.1 (2001), 261–81.

Chisholm, Roderick M. 'Referring to Things That No Longer Exist'. *Philosophical Perspectives* 4.1 (1990), 545–56.

Clarke, Samuel. *A Collection of Papers, Which Passed Between the Late Learned Mr. Leibniz, and Dr. Clarke, in the Years 1715 and 1716*. London: James Knapton, 1717.

Coakley, Sarah. *God, Sexuality and the Self: An Essay 'On the Trinity'*. Cambridge: Cambridge University Press, 2013.

Collingwood, R.G. *Essays in the Philosophy of History*. Edited by W. Debbins. Austin, TX: University of Texas, 1965.

———. *The Idea of History*. Oxford: Clarendon, 1946.

———. *An Autobiography*. Oxford: Oxford University, 1939.

———. 'Are History and Science Different Kinds of Knowledge?' *Mind* 31.124 (1922), 443–51.

Conant, James. 'The Method of the *Tractatus*'. In *From Frege to Wittgenstein: Perspectives on Early Analytical Philosophy*, edited by Erich H. Reck. Oxford: Oxford University, 2002.

———. 'Kierkegaard, Wittgenstein, and Nonsense'. In *Pursuits of Reason*, edited by Ted Cohen, Paul Guyer, and Hilary Putnam. Lubbock, TX: Texas Tech University, 1993.

———. 'The Search for Logically Alien Thought: Descartes, Kant, Frege, and the *Tractatus*'. *Philosophical Topics* 20.1 (1991), 115–80.

———. 'Must We Show What We Cannot Say?' In *The Senses of Stanley Cavell*, edited by R. Flemming and M. Payne, 242–83. Lewisburg, PA: Bucknell University, 1989.

Crager, Adam. 'Three Ones and Aristotle's *Metaphysics*'. *Metaphysics* 1.1 (2018), 110–34.

Crick, Francis. *The Astonishing Hypothesis: The Scientific Search for the Soul*. London: Simon & Schuster, 1994.

Crisp, Thomas M. 'Presentism'. In *The Oxford Handbook of Metaphysics*, edited by Michael J. Loux and Dean W. Zimmerman, 211–45. Oxford: Oxford University, 2003.

Crook, Zeba A. 'Collective Memory Distortion and the Quest for the Historical Jesus'. *Journal for the Study of the Historical Jesus* 11.1 (2013), 53–76.

Crossan, John Dominic. *A Long Way from Tipperary: A Memoir*. New York: HarperCollins, 2000.

———. *Jesus: A Revolutionary Biography*. San Francisco, CA: HarperCollins, 1994.

———. *The Historical Jesus: The Life of a Mediterranean Jewish Peasant*. New York: HarperCollins, 1991.

Crossley, James G. 'The Next Quest for the Historical Jesus'. *Journal for the Study of the Historical Jesus* 19.3 (2021), 261–64.

———. 'Review of *The Pope and Jesus of Nazareth: Christ, Scripture and the Church*, Edited by Adrian Pabst and Angus Paddison'. *Relegere* 1.1 (2011), 188–95.

Cunningham, Conor. *Genealogy of Nihilism: Philosophy of Nothing and the Difference of Theology. Radical Orthodoxy*. London; New York: Routledge, 2002.

Dale, A.I. 'Bayes or Laplace? An Examination of the Origin and Early Applications of Bayes' Theorem'. *Archive for History of Exact Science* 27.1 (1982), 23–47.

Dawes, Gregory W. *The Historical Jesus Question: The Challenge of History to Religious Authority*. Louisville, KY: Westminster John Knox Press, 2001.

Day, Mark. *The Philosophy of History: An Introduction*. London: Continuum, 2008.

Day, Mark, and Gregory Radick. 'Historiographic Evidence and Confirmation'. In *A Companion to the Philosophy of History and Historiography*, edited by Aviezer Tucker, 87–97. BCP. Oxford: Blackwell, 2009.

Deacy, Christopher. *Christmas as Religion: Rethinking Santa, the Secular, and the Sacred*. New York: Oxford University, 2016.

Deines, Roland. *Acts of God in History: Studies Towards Recovering a Theological Historiography*. Edited by Christoph Ochs and Peter Watts. WUNT 317. Tübingen: Mohr Siebeck, 2013.

———. 'Jesus and the Jewish Traditions of His Time'. *Early Christianity* 1.3 (2010), 344–71.

———. 'Can the "Real" Jesus Be Identified with the Historical Jesus? A Review of the Pope's Challenge to Biblical Scholarship and the Various Reactions It Provoked'. *Didaskalia* 39.1 (2009), 11–46.

Deines, Roland, Volker Leppin, and Karl-Wilhelm Niebuhr, eds. *Walter Grundmann: Ein Neutestamentler im Dritten Reich*. Arbeiten zur Kirchen- und Theologiegeschichte, Band 21. Leipzig: Evangelische Verlagsanstalt, 2007.

Deleuze, Gilles. *Difference and Repetition*. Translated by Paul Patton. New York: Columbia University, 1994.

Delumeau, Jean. *Le Péché et la Peur*. Paris: Fayard, 1978.

Denton, Donald L. 'Being Interpreted By the Parables: Critical Realism as Hermeneutical Epistemology'. *Journal for the Study of the Historical Jesus* 13.2–3 (2015), 232–54.

———. *Historiography and Hermeneutics in Jesus Studies: An Examination of the Work of John Dominic Crossan and Ben F. Meyer*. JSNTSup 262. London: T&T Clark, 2004.

Derrida, Jacques. *Given Time, Vol. 1: Counterfeit Money*. Translated by P. Kamuf. Chicago, IL: University of Chicago, 1992.

———. *De l'esprit: Heidegger et la question*. Paris: Editions Galilée, 1987.

———. *De la grammatologie*. Paris: Minuit, 1967a.

———. *La Voix et le Phénomène*. Paris: PUF, 1967b.

———. *L'écriture et la différence*. Paris: Seuil, 1967c.

Descartes, René. *Discours de la Méthode Pour bien conduire sa raison, et chercher la vérité dans les sciences*. Leiden: Ian Maire, 1637.

DeWitt, Richard. *Worldviews: An Introduction to the History and PhilSci*. 3rd ed. Oxford: Wiley-Blackwell, 2018.

Diamond, Cora. 'Ethics, Imagination and the Method of Wittgenstein's *Tractatus*'. In *Bilder Der Philosophie*, edited by R. Heinrich and H. Vetter, 55–90. Wiener Reihe 5. Vienna: Oldenbourg, 1991.

———. 'Rules: Looking in the Right Place'. In *Wittgenstein: Attention to Particulars*, edited by D.Z. Phillips and P. Winch, 12–34. Basingstoke: Palgrave MacMillan, 1989.

———. 'Throwing Away the Ladder'. *Philosophy* 63.243 (1988), 5–27.

Dilthey, Wilhelm. *Dilthey's Philosophy of Existence: Introduction to Weltanschauunglehre*. Translated by William Kluback and Martin Weinbaum. New York: Bookman Associates, 1957.

Dobbelaere, Karel. 'The Secularization of Society? Some Methodological Suggestions'. In *Secularization and Fundamentalism Reconsidered*, edited by Jeffrey K. Hadden and Anson Shupe, 27–43. New York: Paragon House, 1989.

———. 'Secularization, Pillarization, Religious Involvement, and Religious Change in the Low Countries'. In *World Catholicism in Transition*, edited by Thomas M. Gannon, 80–115. New York: MacMillan, 1988.
———. 'Some Trends in European Sociology of Religion: The Secularization Debate'. *Sociology of Religion* 48.2 (1987), 107–37.
———. 'Secularization Theories and Sociological Paradigms: A Reformulation of the Private-Public Dichotomy and the Problem of Societal Integration'. *Sociology of Relgion* 46.4 (1985), 377–87.
———. 'Secularization: A Multi-Dimensional Concept'. *Current Sociology* 29.2 (1981), 1–216.
Dodd, C. H. *The Parables of the Kingdom*. London: Nisbet & Co., 1935.
Downing, F. Gerald. *Cynics and Christian Origins*. Edinburgh: T&T Clark, 1992.
Drescher, Hans-Georg. *Ernst Troeltsch: Leben und Werk*. Göttingen: Vandenhoeck & Ruprecht, 1991.
Droogers, André, and Anton van Harskamp, eds. *Methods for the Study of Religious Change: From Religious Studies to Worldview Studies*. Sheffield: Equinox, 2014.
Dru, Alexander, trans. *The Journals of Kierkegaard*. London: Oxford University Press, 1938.
Dulles, Avery. 'Book Review: *Method in Theology*'. *Theological Studies* 33.3 (1972), 553–5.
Dungan, David. 'Albert Schweitzer's Disillusionment with the Historical Reconstruction of the Life of Jesus'. *Perkins (School of Theology) Journal* 29.1 (1976), 27–48.
Dunn, James D. G. *The Oral Gospel Tradition*. Grand Rapids, MI: Eerdmans, 2013.
———. 'Remembering Jesus: How the Quest of the Historical Jesus Lost Its Way'. In *Handbook for the Study of the Historical Jesus*, edited by Tom Holmén and Stanley Porter, 1:183–205. Leiden: Brill, 2011.
———. *The New Perspective on Paul: Collected Essays*. WUNT 185. Tübingen: Mohr Siebeck, 2005.
———. *Christianity in the Making*. 3 vols. Grand Rapids, MI: Eerdmans, 2003–15.
———. *Christology in the Making: An Inquiry into the Origins of the Doctrine of the Incarnation*. 2nd ed. London: SCM, 1989.
———. *Baptism in the Holy Spirit: A Re-Examination of the New Testament Teaching on the Gift of the Spirit in Relation to Pentecostalism Today*. Studies in Biblical Theology Second Series 15. London: SCM, 1970.
Ebeling, Gerhard. *Theology and Proclamation: A Discussion with Rudolf Bultmann*. Edited by John Riches. London: Collins, 1966.
Edwards, James R. *Between the Swastika and the Sickle: The Life, Disappearance, and Execution of Ernst Lohmeyer*. Grand Rapids, MI: Eerdmans, 2019.
Egerton, Karl. 'Getting off the Inwagen: A Critique of Quinean Metaontology'. *Journal for the History of Analytical Philosophy* 4.6 (2016), 1–22.
Ehrman, Bart D. *How Jesus Became God: The Exaltation of a Jewish Preacher from Galilee*. New York: HarperOne, 2014.
Eichhorn, J.G. *Einleitung in das Neue Testament*. 2nd ed. Leipzig: Weidmann, 1820.
Eklund, Matti. 'Carnap and Ontological Pluralism'. In *Metametaphysics: New Essays on the Foundations of Ontology*, edited by David Chalmers, David Manley, and Ryan Wasserman, 130–56. Oxford: Clarendon, 2009.
———. 'The Picture of Reality as an Amorphous Lump'. In *Contemporary Debates in Metaphysics*, edited by Theodore Sider, John Hawthorne, and Dean W. Zimmerman, 382–96. Malden, MA: Blackwell, 2008.

———. 'Neo-Fregean Ontology'. *Philosophical Perspectives* 20.1 (2006), 95–121.

Entwistle, David N. *Integrative Approaches to Psychology and Christianity: An Introduction to Worldview Issues, Philosophical Foundations, and Models of Integration*. 3rd ed. Eugene, OR: Cascade, 2015.

Eribon, Didier. *Michel Foucault*. Translated by Betsy Wing. Cambridge, MA: Harvard University, 1991.

Ermarth, Michael. *William Dilthey: The Critique of Historical Reason*. Chicago, IL: University of Chicago, 1978.

Eschenmayer, Carl A. *Der Ischariotismus unserer Tage: Eine Zugabe zu dem Werke: Das Leben Jesu von Strauß*. Tübingen: Fues, 1835.

Escudero, Jesús Adrián. 'Heidegger's *Black Notebooks* and the Question of Anti-Semitism'. *Gatherings: The Heidegger Circle Annual* 5.1 (2015), 21–49.

Farías, Víctor. *Heidegger and Nazism*. Translated by Joseph Margolis and Tom Rockmore. Philadelphia, PA: Temple University, 1989.

———. *Heidegger et le nazisme*. Paris: Verdier, 1987.

Feldman, Fred. 'Leibniz and "Leibniz" Law'. *The Philosophical Review* 79.4 (1970), 510–22.

Ferda, Tucker S. Daniel Frayer-Griggs, and Nathan C. Johnson. 'Introduction'. In *"To Recover What Has Been Lost": Essays on Eschatology, Intertextuality, and Reception History in Honor of Dale C. Allison Jr.*, edited by Tucker S. Ferda, Daniel Frayer-Griggs, and Nathan C. Johnson, 1–11. NovTSup 183. Leiden: Brill, 2021.

Festinger, Leon. *A Theory of Cognitive Dissonance*. Stanford, CA: Stanford University, 1957.

Festinger, Leon, Henry Riecken, and Stanley Schachter. *When Prophecy Fails: A Social and Psychological Study of a Modern Group That Predicted the Destruction of the World*. Minneapolis, MN: University of Minnesota, 1956.

Fichte, Johann Gottlieb. *Versuch einer Critik aller Offenbarung. Zweite Auflage*. Königsberg: Hartungschen Buchhandlung, 1793.

Fiebig, P. *Neues Testament und Nationalsozialismus. Drei Üniversitätsvorlesungen über Führerprinzip - Rassenfrage - Kampf. Schriften der Deutschen Christen*. Dresden: Deutsch-christliche Verlag, 1935.

———. *Das Vaterunser. Ursprung, Sinn und Bedeutung des christlichen Hauptgebetes*. BFChT 30. Gütersloh: Bertelsmann, 1927.

———. *Jesu Bergpredigt. Rabbinische Texte zum Verständnis der Bergpredigt, ins Deutsche übersetzt, in ihren Ursprachen dargeboten und mit Erläuterungen und Lesarten versehen*. FRLANT NF 20. Göttingen: Vandenhoeck & Ruprecht, 1924.

———. *Die Gleichnisreden Jesu im Lichte der rabbinischen Gleichnisse des neutestamentlichen Zeitalters*. Tübingen: J. C. B. Mohr, 1912.

———. *Altjüdische Gleichnisse und die Gleichnisse Jesu*. Tübingen: J. C. B. Mohr, 1904.

———. *Der Menschensohn: Jesu Selbstbezeichnung*. Tübingen: J. C. B. Mohr, 1901.

Fienberg, Stephen E. 'The Early Statistical Years: 1947–1967. A Conversation with Howard Raiffa'. *Statistical Science* 23.1 (2008), 136–49.

———. 'When Did Bayesian Inference Become 'Bayesian'?' *Baysian Analysis* 1.1 (2006), 1–40.

Finetti, Bruno de. 'Probabilism: A Critical Essay on the Theory of Probability and on the Value of Science'. *Erkenntnis* 31.2–3 (1989), 169–223.

Finke, Roger. 'An Unsecular America'. In *Religion and Modernization: Sociologists and Historians Debate the Secularization Thesis*, edited by Steve Bruce, 145–69. Oxford: Oxford University, 1992.

Finke, Roger, and Laurence A. Iannaccone. 'Supply-Side Explanations for Religious Change'. *Annals of the American Academy of Political and Social Science* 527.1 (1993), 27–39.

Finke, Roger, and Rodney Stark. *The Churching of America, 1776–1990: Winners and Losers in Our Religious Economy*. New Brunswick, NJ: Rutgers University, 1992.

———. 'Religious Economies and Sacred Canopies: Religious Mobilization in American Cities, 1906'. *American Sociological Review* 53.1 (1988), 41–49.

Fish, Stanley. *Doing What Comes Naturally: Change, Rhetoric and the Practice of Theory in Literary and Legal Studies*. Oxford: Clarendon, 1989.

———. *Is There a Text in This Class? The Authority of Interpretive Communities*. Cambridge, MA: Harvard University, 1980.

Fisher, R.A. *Statistical Methods for Research Workers*. Edinburgh: Oliver and Boyd, 1925.

———. 'Frequency Distribution of the Values of the Correlation Coefficient in Samples from an Indefinitely Large Population'. *Biometrika* 10.4 (1915), 507–21.

Flusser, David. *Jesus: The Sage from Galilee*. 2nd augmented ed. Jerusalem: Magnes; The Hebrew University, 1998.

Ford, David F. 'Radical Orthodoxy and the Future of British Theology'. *Scottish Journal of Theology* 54.3 (2001), 385–404.

Foster, Paul. 'Book Review: Collected Writings of Roland Deines: C. Ochs and P. Watts (Eds), Roland Deines - *Acts of God in History*'. *Expository Times* 126.5 (2015), 255.

Foster, Robert. 'Why on Earth Use 'Kingdom of Heaven'?: Matthew's Terminology Revisited'. *New Testament Studies* 48.4 (2002), 487–99.

Foucault, Michel. *L'archéologie du savoir*. Paris: Gallimard, 1969.

———. *Les mots et les choses: Une archéologie des sciences humaines*. Paris: Gallimard, 1966.

———. *Naissance de la clinique*. Paris: PUF, 1963.

———. *Folie et déraison: Histoire de la folie à l'âge classique*. Paris: Plon, 1961.

Frei, Hans W. *Theology and Narrative: Selected Essays*. New York: Oxford University, 1993.

———. *The Identity of Jesus Christ, the Hermeneutical Bases of Dogmatic Theology*. Philadelphia, PA: Fortress, 1975.

———. *The Eclipse of Biblical Narrative: A Study in Eighteenth and Nineteenth Century Hermeneutics*. New Haven, CT: Yale University, 1974.

Friedland, Roger, and Robert R. Alford. 'Bringing Society Back In: Symbols, Practices, and Institutional Contradictions'. In *The New Institutionalism in Organizational Analysis*, edited by Walter W. Powell and Paul J. DiMaggio. Chicago, IL: University of Chicago, 1991.

Friel, Christopher Sean. Wittgenstein and Lonergan on Mathematical Wonder: Towards a Dialogue of Methods. *Modern Theology* 31.3 (2015), 469–87.

Froese, Paul, and Steven Pfaff. 'Replete and Desolate Markets: Poland, East Germany, and the New Religious Paradigm'. *Social Forces* 80.2 (2001), 481–507.

Frogel, Shai. 'Descartes: Truth and Self-Deception'. *Philosophy* 91.1 (2016), 93–108.

Fuller, Reginald H. 'Review: Rediscovering the Teaching of Jesus, by Norman Perrin'. *Theology Today* 24.3 (1967), 412–14.

Funk, Robert W. *The Poetics of Biblical Narrative*. Sonoma, CL: Polebridge, 1988.

Funk, Robert W., Bernard B. Scott, and James R. Butts, eds. *The Parables of the Jesus: Red Letter Edition*. Sonoma, CL: Polebridge, 1988.

Gadamer, Hans-Georg. *Truth and Method*. Translated by Joel Weinsheimer and Donald Marshall. 2nd rev. ed. London: Continuum, 2004.
———. *Wahrheit und Methode*. Tübingen: J. C. B. Mohr (Paul Siebeck), 1960.
Gathercole, Simon. '"Sins" in Paul'. *New Testament Studies* 64.2 (2018), 143–61.
———. *Defending Substitution: An Essay on Atonement in Paul*. Grand Rapids, MI: Baker Academic, 2015.
Gerdmar, A. *Roots of Theological Anti-Semitism: German Biblical Interpretation and the Jews, from Herder and Semler to Kittel and Bultmann*. SJHC 20. Leiden: Brill, 2009.
Giambrone, Anthony. 'Schweitzer, Lagrange, and the German Roots of Historical Jesus Research'. *Journal for the Study of the Historical Jesus* 17.1–2 (2019), 121–44.
Giddy, Patrick. 'Why Theology Can and Should be Taught at Secular Universities: Lonergan on Intellectual Conversion'. *Journal of Philosophy of Education* 45.3 (2011), 527–43.
Gill, Mary Louise. 'Aristotle's *Metaphysics* Reconsidered'. *Journal of the History of Philosophy* 43.3 (2005), 223–51.
Gill, Robin, C. Kirk Hadaway, and Penny Long Marler. 'Is Religious Belief Declining in Britain?' *Journal for the Scientific Study of Religion* 37.3 (1998), 507–16.
Given, Mark D. '2019.03.23. Heilig, Hidden Criticism?' *Review of Bibilcal Literature*, 2019. http://rblnewsletter.blogspot.com/2019/03/20190323-heilig-hidden-criticism.html.
Goldfarb, Warren. 'Metaphysics and Nonsense: On Cora Diamond's *The Realistic Spirit*'. *Journal of Philosophical Research* 22.1 (1997), 57–73.
Goodchild, Philip. *Theology of Money*. London: SCM, 2007.
———. *Capitalism and Religion: The Price of Piety*. London: Routledge, 2002.
Graham, Daniel W. *Aristotle's Two Systems*. Oxford: Clarendon, 1987.
Gribetz, Sarit Kattan, and Lynn Kaye. 'The Temporal Turn in Ancient Judaism and Jewish Studies'. *Currents in Biblical Research* 17.3 (2019), 332–95.
Griesbach, Johann Jakob. *Commentatio qua Marci Evangelium Totum e Matthaei et Lucae Commentariis Decerptum Esse Monstratur*. Jena: Officina Stranckmannio-Fickelscherria, 1790.
Groetsch, Ulrich. *Hermann Samuel Reimarus (1694–1768): Classicist, Hebraist, Enlightenment Radical in Disguise*. Brill's Studies in Intellectual History 237. Leiden: Brill, 2015.
Grotius, Hugo. *The Law of War and Peace*. Translated by Francis W. Kelsey et al. Indianapolis, IN: Bobbs-Merrill, 1925.
Grumett, David. 'Review: *Maurice Blondel: A Philosophical Life* by Olivia Blanchette'. *The Thomist* 27.4 (2011), 708–12.
Grünbaum, Adolf. *Philosophical Problems of Space and Time*. New York: Alfred A. Knopf, 1963.
Grundmann, Walter. *Jesus der Galiläer und das Judentum*. Leipzig: Wigand, 1940.
———. *Die Entjudung des religiösen Lebens als Aufgabe deutsche Theologie und Kirche*. Weimar: Verlag Deutsche Christen, 1939.
Guigenbert, C. *Jesus*. Translated by S. H. Hooke. London: Kegan Paul, 1935.
———. *Jésus*. Paris: Renaissance du Livre, 1933.
Guyer, Paul. *Kant. Routledge Philosophers*. London: Routledge, 2006.
Habermas, Jürgen. 'Work and Weltanschauung: The Heidegger Controversy from a German Perspective'. Translated by John McCumber. *Critical Inquiry* 15.2 (1989), 431–56.
Hachlili, Rachel. *Jewish Funerary Customs, Practices and Rites in the Second Temple Period*. JSJS 94. Leiden: Brill, 2005.

Hacker, P.M.S. *Wittgenstein's Place in Twentieth-Century Analytic Philosophy*. Oxford: Blackwell, 1996.

———. *Insight and Illusion: Themes in the Philosophy of Wittgenstein*. Oxford: Clarendon, 1972.

Hacking, Ian. *The Emergence of Probability: A Philosophical Study of Early Ideas about Probability, Induction and Statistical Inference*. Cambridge: Cambridge University, 1975.

Hadden, Jeffrey K. 'Toward Desacralizing Secularization Theory'. *Social Forces* 65.3 (1987), 587–611.

Hägerland, Tobias. 'The Future of Criteria in Historical Jesus Research'. *Journal for the Study of the Historical Jesus* 13.1 (2013), 43–65.

Hagner, Donald A. 'The Jesus Quest and Jewish-Christian Relations'. In *Handbook for the Study of the Historical Jesus*, edited by Tom Holmén and Stanley Porter, 2:1055–77. Leiden: Brill, 2011.

Halphen, Louis. *Johdatus historiantutkimukseen. Alkuteos Introduction à l'histoire. Suom. Eino E. Suolahti*. Historiallinen kirjasto, XIV. Helsinki: WSOY, 1951.

Hankey, Wayne J., and Douglas Hedley, eds. *Deconstructing Radical Orthodoxy: Postmodern Theology, Rhetoric and Truth*. Aldershot: Ashgate, 2005.

Hannay, Alastair. *Kierkegaard: A Biography*. Cambridge: Cambridge University, 2001.

Hansen, Collin, ed. *Our Secular Age: Ten Years of Reading and Applying Charles Taylor*. Deerfield, IL: The Gospel Coalition, 2017.

Harney, Hanns Ludwig. *Bayesian Inference: Data Evaluation and Decisions*. 2nd ed. Basel: Springer, 2016.

Harris, Ruth. 'Schweitzer and Africa'. *The Historical Journal* 59.4 (2016), 1107–32.

Hart, David Bentley. *The New Testament: A Translation*. New Haven, CT: Yale University, 2017.

———. *The Beauty of the Infinite: The Aesthetics of Christian Truth*. Grand Rapids, MI: Eerdmans, 2003.

Hart, Patrick. *A Prolegomenon to the Study of Paul*. SMTSR 15. Leiden: Brill, 2020.

Hartog, Paul. 'Blondel Remembered: His Philosophical Analysis of the 'Quest for the Historical Jesus''. *Themelios* 33.1 (2008), 5–15.

Haskell, John D. 'Hugo Grotius in the Contemporary Memory of International Law: Secularism, Liberalism, and the Politics of Restatement and Denial'. *Emory International Law Review* 25.1 (2011), 269–98.

Hauerwas, Stanley, and L. Gregory Jones, eds. *Why Narrative? Readings in Narrative Theology*. Grand Rapids, MI: Eerdmans, 1989.

Hawthorne, John. 'Identity'. In *The Oxford Handbook of Metaphysics*, edited by Michael J. Loux and Dean W. Zimmerman, 99–130. Oxford: Oxford University, 2003.

Hays, Richard B. 'Reading Scripture in the Light of the Resurrection'. In *The Art of Reading Scripture*, edited by Ellen F. Davis and Richard B. Hays, 216–38. Grand Rapids, MI: Eerdmans, 2003.

Head, Peter M. 'The Nazi Quest for an Aryan Jesus'. *Journal for the Study of the Historical Jesus* 2.1 (2004), 55–89.

Headlam, A.C. *The Life and Teaching of Jesus the Christ*. London: Murray, 1923.

Hegel, G.F.W. *The Difference Between Fichte's and Schelling's System of Philosophy*. Translated by H. S. Harris and Walter Cerf. Albany, NY: State of University of New York Press, 1977.

———. *The Phenomenology of Mind*. Translated by J. B. Baillie. 2nd ed. London: George Allen and Unwin, 1961.

———. *The Philosophy of History*. Translated by J. Sibree. Chicago, IL: Encyclopaedia Britannica, 1952.

Heidegger, Martin. *The Basic Problems of Phenomenology*. Translated by Albert Hofstadter. Studies in Phenomenology and Existential Philosophy. Bloomington, IN: Indiana University, 1982.

———. 'Anmerkungen zu Karl Jaspers' *Psychologie der Weltanschauung*'. In *Wegmarken*, edited by F.-W. von Herrmann, 1–44. Gesamtausgabe 9. Frankfurt: Klostermann, 1976.

Heilig, Christoph. *Hidden Criticism? The Methodology and Plausibility of the Search for a Counter-Imperial Subtext in Paul*. WUNT II 392. Tübingen: Mohr Siebeck, 2015 (repr. Minneapolis, MN: Fortress, 2017).

———. 'What Bayesian Reasoning Can and Can't Do for Biblical Research'. *Zürich New Testament Blog* (blog), 27 March 2019. https://www.uzh.ch/blog/theologie-nt/2019/03/27/what-bayesian-reasoning-can-and-cant-do-for-biblical-research/?fbclid=IwAR1yI8Xy2Y15OnGcPKkTuKomR1I69E5KZPS8d3whGEEm4tpYyzQqGDBPCR4.

Heilig, Theresa, and Christoph Heilig. 'Historical Methodology'. In *God and the Faithfulness of Paul: A Critical Examination of the Pauline Theology of N.T. Wright*, edited by Christoph Heilig, J. Thomas Hewitt, and Michael F. Bird, 115–50. WUNT II 413. Tübingen: Mohr Siebeck, 2016.

Heller, Mark. 'Varieties of Four Dimensionalism'. *Australasian Journal of Philosophy* 71.1 (1993). 47–59.

———. *The Ontology of Physical Objects*. Cambridge: Cambridge University, 1990.

Hengel, Martin. 'Eine junge theologische Disziplin in der Krise'. In *Theologische, historische und biographische Skizzen: Kleine Schriften VII*, edited by Claus-Jürgen Thornton, 279–91. WUNT 253. Tübingen: Mohr Siebeck, 2010.

———. 'Der Alte Und Der Neue 'Schürer''. *Journal of Semitic Studies* 35.1 (1990), 19–72.

———. *The Son of God: The Origin of Christology and the History of Jewish Hellenistic Religion*. Philadelphia, PA: Fortress, 1976.

Henry, Michel. *I Am the Truth: Toward a Philosophy of Christianity*. Stanford, CA: Stanford University, 2003.

Heringer, Seth. *Uniting History and Theology: A Theological Critique of the Historical Method*. Lanham, MD: Lexington/Fortress, 2018.

———. 'Forgetting the Power of Leaven: The Historical Method in Recent New Testament Theology'. *Scottish Journal of Theology* 67.1 (2014), 85–104.

Heschel, Susannah. *The Aryan Jesus: Christian Theologians and the Bible in Nazi Germany*. Princeton, NJ: Princeton Univeristy, 2008.

Hill, David. 'Matthew 27:51–53 in the Theology of the Evangelist'. *Irish Biblical Studies* 7.1 (1985), 76–87.

Hill, Samuel. 'Lonergan, Lyotard, and Lindbeck: Bringing *Method in Theology* into dialogue with Postmodernity'. *The Heythrop Journal* 58.6 (2017), 908–16.

Hinchliff, Mark. 'A Defense of Presentism in a Relativistic Setting'. *Philosophy of Science* 67.3 (2000), 575–86.

———. 'The Puzzle of Change'. *Philosophical Perspectives* 10.1 (1996), 119–36.

Hirsch, Eli. 'Physical-Object Ontology, Verbal Disputes, and Common Sense'. *Philosophy and Phenomenological Research* 70.1 (2005), 67–98.

———. 'Against Revisionary Ontology'. *Philosophical Topics* 30.1 (2002a), 103–28.

———. 'Quantifier Variance and Realism'. *Philosophical Issues* 12.1 (2002b), 51–73.

Höffe, Otfried. *Immanuel Kant*. Translated by Marshall Farrier. Albany, NY: State of University of New York, 1994.

Hofweber, Thomas. 'A Puzzle About Ontology'. *Noûs* 39.2 (2005), 256–83.

Holmén, Tom. 'Authenticity Criteria'. In *Encyclopedia of the Historical Jesus*, edited by Craig A. Evans, 43–54. New York: Routledge, 2010.

Holmes, Arthur. 'Phenomenology and the Relativity of World-Views'. *Personalist* 48.3 (1967), 328–44.

Holtzmann, Heinrich Julius. *Die synoptischen Evangelien: ihr Ursprung und geschichtlicher Charakter*. Leipzig: Wilhelm Engelmann, 1863.

Holyoake, G.J. *English Secularism: A Confession of Belief.* Chicago, IL: Open Court, 1896.

Hooker, M. D. 'On Using the Wrong Tool'. *Theology* 75.629 (1972). 570–81.

———. 'Christology and Methodology'. *New Testament Studies* 17.4 (1971), 480–87.

Horan, Daniel P. *Postmodernity and Univocity: A Critical Account of Radical Orthodoxy and John Duns Scotus*. Minneapolis, MN: Fortress, 2014.

Horsley, Richard A. *Jesus and Magic: Freeing the Gospel Stories from Modern Misconceptions*. Eugene, OR: Cascade, 2014.

———. *Jesus and the Politics of Roman Palestine*. Columbia, TN: University of South Carolina, 2013.

———. *Jesus in Context: Power, People, and Performance*. Minneapolis, MN: Fortress, 2008.

———. *Jesus and Empire: The Kingdom of God and the New World Disorder*. Minneapolis, MN: Fortress, 2003.

———. *Jesus and the Spiral of Violence: Popular Jewish Resistance in Roman Palestine*. San Francisco, CA: Harper & Row, 1987.

Hout, Michael, and Andrew M. Greeley. 'The Center Doesn't Hold: Church Attendance in the United States, 1940–1984'. *American Sociological Review* 52.3 (1987), 325–45.

Hughes, G. E., and M. J. Cresswell. *An Introduction to Modal Logic*. London: Methuen, 1968.

Hume, David. *Of Miracles*. La Salle, IL: Open Court, 1985.

———. *Philosophical Essays Concerning Human Understanding*. London: A. Millar, 1748.

Hurtado, Larry W. *How on Earth Did Jesus Become a God? Historical Questions about Earliest Devotion to Jesus*. Grand Rapids, MI: Eerdmans, 2005.

———. *Lord Jesus Christ: Devotion to Jesus in Earliest Christianity*. Grand Rapids, MI: Eerdmans, 2003.

———. *One God, One Lord: Early Christian Devotion and Ancient Jewish Monotheism*. London: SCM, 1988.

Husserl, Edmund. 'Philosophy as Rigorous Science'. In *The New Yearbook for Phenomenology and Phenomenological Philosophy*, edited by Burt Hopkins and Steven Crowell, translated by Marcus Brainard, II:249–95. London: Routledge, 2002.

———. *The Crisis of European Sciences and Transcendental Phenomenology: An Introduction to Phenomenological Philosophy*. Edited and translated by David Carr. Northwestern University Studies in Phenomenology and Existential Philosophy. Evanston, IL: Northwestern University, 1970.

———. *Die Krisis der europäischen Wissenschaften und die transzendentale Phänomenologie*. Edited by Walter Biemel. Gesammelte Werke, VI. The Hague: Martinus Nijhoff, 1954.

———. 'Philosophie als strenge Wissenschaft'. *Logos. Internationale Zeitschrift für Philosophie der Kultur* 1 (November 1910), 289–341.

Husserl, Edmund, and Wilhelm Dilthey. 'The Dilthey-Husserl Correspondance'. In *Husserl: Shorter Works*, edited by Peter McCormick and Frederick A. Elliston. Notre Dame, IL: University of Notre Dame, 1981.

Hyppolite, Jean. *Genesis and Structure of Hegel's Phenomenology of Spirit.* Translated by Samuel Cherniak and John Heckman. Northwestern University Studies in Phenomenology and Existential Philosophy. Evanston, IL: Northwestern University, 1974.

Iannaccone, Laurence A. 'The Consequences of Religious Market Structure: Adam Smith and the Economics of Religion'. *Rationality and Society* 3.2 (1991), 156–77.

Inwagen, Peter van. 'Being, Existence, and Ontological Commitment'. In *Metametaphysics: New Essays on the Foundations of Ontology*, edited by David Chalmers, David Manley, and Ryan Wasserman, 472–506. Oxford: Clarendon, 2009.

Isaacs, Marie E. *Sacred Space: An Approach to the Theology of the Epistle to the Hebrews.* JSNTSup 73. Sheffield: JSOT, 1992.

Iser, Wolfgang. 'Interaction between Text and Reader'. In *The Reader in the Text: Essays on Audience and Interpretation*, edited by Susan R. Suleiman and Inge Crosman, 106–19. Princeton, NJ: Princeton University, 1980.

———. *The Act of Reading: A Theory of Aesthetic Response*. London: Routledge and Kegan Paul, 1978.

———. *The Implied Reader: Patterns of Communication in Prose Fiction from Bunyan to Beckett.* London: John Hopkins University, 1974.

Isherwood, Lisa, and Marko Zlomislić, eds. *The Poverty of Radical Orthodoxy.* Postmodern Ethics 3. Eugene, OR: Pickwick, 2012.

Israel, Jonathan. 'The Philosophical Context of Hermann Samuel Reimarus' Radical Bible Criticism'. In *Between Philology and Radical Enlightenment: Herman Samuel Reimarus (1694–1768)*, edited by Martin Mulsow, 183–200. Brill's Studies in Intellectual History 203. Leiden: Brill, 2011.

Jackson, Frank. 'Leibniz's Law and the Philosophy of the Mind'. *Proceedings of the Aristotelian Society* 112.3 (2012), 269–83.

———. 'On the Metaphysical Implications of Some Epistemological Commonplaces'. In *From Truth to Reality: New Essays in Logic and Metaphysics*, edited by Heather Dyke, 99–111. London: Routledge, 2009.

Jackson, Hugh. 'The Resurrection Belief of the Earliest Church: A Response to the Failure of Prophecy?' *JRThe Journal of Religion* 55.4 (1975), 415–25.

Jaeger, Werner Wilhelm. *Aristotle: Fundamentals of the History of His Development.* Translated by Richard Robinson. Oxford: Oxford University, 1948.

———. *Aristoteles: Grundlegung einer Geschichte seiner Entwicklung*. Berlin: Weidmann, 1923.

———. *Studien zur Entstehungsgeschichte der Metaphysik des Aristoteles*. Berlin: Weidmann, 1912.

Jaffe, Aniela. *Apparitions: An Archetypal Approach to Death, Dreams, and Ghosts*. Irving, TX: Spring, 1979.

Jaspers, Karl. *Philosophical Autobiography*. edited by Paul Arthur Schlipp, 5–94. Library of Living Philosophers. La Salle, IL: Open Court, 1981.

———. *Psychologie der Weltanschauungen*. Berlin: Springer, 1919.

Jelen, Ted G. *Sacred Markets, Sacred Canopies: Essays on Religious Markets and Religious Pluralism*. Lanham, MD: Rowman & Littlefield, 2002.

Jenkins, Scott. 'Nietzsche's Use of Monumental History'. *Journal of Nietzsche Studies* 45.2 (2014), 169–81.

Jenson, Robert W. *Systematic Theology, Vol. 1: The Triune God*. New York: Oxford University Press, 1997.

Jeremias, Joachim. *Die Abendmahlsworte Jesu*. Göttingen: Vandenhoeck & Ruprecht, 1949.

———. *Die Gleichnisse Jesu*. Zürich: Zwingli Verlag, 1947.

Johnson, Luke Timothy. 'Review of Joseph Ratzinger, *Jesus of Nazareth: From the Baptism in the Jordan to the Transfiguration*'. *Modern Theology* 24.2 (2008), 318–20.

Johnson, Robert L. 'Review: *The Soul of the American University: From Protestant Establishment to Established Nonbelief* by George M. Marsden'. *Theology Today* 52.3 (1995), 430–32.

Jüngel, Eberhard. *God as the Mystery of the World: On the Foundation of the Theology and the Crucified One in the Dispute between Theism and Atheism*. Translated by Darrell L. Guder. Grand Rapids, MI: Eerdmans, 1983.

Kähler, Martin. *The So-Called Historical Jesus and the Historical Biblical Christ*. Edited and translated by Carl E. Braaten. Philadelphia, PA: Fortress, 1964.

———. *Der sogenannte historische Jesus und der geschichtliche biblische Christus*. Munich: Kaiser, 1892 (repr. Berlin: Berlin University, 2013).

Kankaanniemi, Matti. 'Mission as Reaction: Exhausted Jesus at the Well of Sychar'. In *The Mission of Jesus: Second Nordic Symposium on the Historical Jesus, Lund, 7–10 October 2012*, edited by Samuel Byrskog and Tobias Hägerland, 161–76. WUNT II 391. Tübingen: Mohr Siebeck, 2015.

Kant, Immanuel. *Critique of Pure Reason*. Translated by Norman Kemp Smith. Rev. 2nd ed. Basingstoke: Palgrave MacMillan, 2007.

———. *Kritik der Urteilskraft*. Edited by Karl Vorländer. Fünfte Auflage. Der philosophischen Bibliothek 39. Leipzig: Felix Meiner, 1922.

———. *Critik der reinen Vernunft*. Riga: Johann Friedrich Hartknock, 1781.

Käsemann, Ernst. *Essays on New Testament Themes*. London: SCM, 1964.

———. 'Das Problem des historischen Jesus'. *Zeitschrift für Theologie und Kirche* 51.2 (1954), 125–53.

Kaye, Bruce N. 'D. F. Strauss and the European Theological Tradition: 'Der Ischariotismus Unsere Tag'?' *The Journal of Religious History* 17.2 (1992), 172–93.

Keck, Leander E. *A Future for the Historical Jesus*. Nashville, TN: Abingdon, 1971.

———. 'Bornkamm's *Jesus of Nazareth* Revisited'. *The Journal of Religion* 49.1 (1969), 1–17.

Keene, Edward. *Beyond the Anarchical Society: Grotius, Colonialism and Order in World Politics*. Cambridge: Cambridge University, 2002.

Keener, Craig S. *Christobiography: Memory, History, and the Reliability of the Gospels*. Grand Rapids, MI: Eerdmans, 2019.

———. *Miracles: The Credibility of the New Testament Accounts*. 2 vols. Grand Rapids, MI: Baker Academic, 2011.

Keiling, Tobias. 'Heidegger's *Black Notebooks* and the Logic of a History of Being'. *Research in Phenomenology* 47.3 (2017), 406–28.

Keith, Chris. *Jesus Against the Scribal Elite: The Origins of the Conflict*. Grand Rapids, MI: Baker Academic, 2014.

———. *Jesus' Literacy: Scribal Culture and the Teacher from Galilee*. LNTS 413. London: T&T Clark, 2011a.

———. 'Memory and Authenticity: Jesus Tradition and What Really Happened'. *Zeitschrift für die Neutestamentliche Wissenschaft und Kunde der Älteren Kirche* 102.2 (2011b), 155–77.

Keith, Chris, and Anthony Le Donne, eds. *Jesus, Criteria, and the Demise of Authenticity*. London: T&T Clark, 2012.

Kierkegaard, Søren. *Af en endnu Levendes Papirer. Om Begrebet Ironi*. Edited by Niels Jørgen Cappelørn, Joakim Garff, and Johnny Kondrup. Søren Kierkegaards Skrifter 1. København: Gad, 1997.

———. *Practice in Christianity*. Edited and translated by Howard V. Hong and Edna H. Hong. Princeton, NJ: Princeton University, 1991.

King, Richard H. *Arendt and America*. Chicago, IL: The University of Chicago Press, 2015.

Kingsbury, Benedict, and Adam Roberts. 'Introduction: Grotian Thought in International Relations'. In *Hugo Grotius and International Relations*, edited by Hedley Bulls, Benedict Kingsbury, and Adam Roberts, 1–64. Oxford: Oxford University, 1990.

Kirk, Alan. *Memory and the Jesus Tradition*. The Reception of Jesus in the First Three Centuries 2. London: Bloomsbury, 2018.

Kirkeby, Ole Fogh. *Selvet sker. Bevidsthedens begivenhed*. København: Samfundslitteratur, 2008.

———. *Skønheden sker: Begivenhedens æstetik*. København: Samfundslitteratur, 2007.

———. *Eventum Tantum: Begivenhedens ethos*. København: Samfundslitteratur, 2005.

Kisiel, Theodore. 'Heidegger's Gesamtausgabe: An International Scandal of Scholarship'. *Philosophy Today* 39.1 (1995), 3–15.

———. *The Genesis of Heidegger's 'Being and Time'*. Berkeley, CA: University of California, 1993.

Klein, Dietrich. *Hermann Samuel Reimarus (1694–1768): Das theologische Werk. Beiträge zur historischen Theologie 145*. Tübingen: Mohr Siebeck, 2009.

Kloppenborg, John S. 'Sources, Methods and Discursive Locations in the Quest of the Historical Jesus'. In *Handbook for the Study of the Historical Jesus*, edited by Tom Holmén and Stanley Porter, 1:241–90. Leiden: Brill, 2011.

———. 'Review: Meier, John P., *A Marginal Jew: Rethinking the Historical Jesus* Volume III: Companions and Competitors'. *Biblical Interpretation* 12.2 (2004), 211–15.

Kovacs, George. 'Philosophy as Primordial Science in Heidegger's Courses of 1919'. In *Reading Heidegger from the Start: Essays in His Earliest Thought*, edited by Theodore Kisiel and John van Buren, 91–108. SUNY Series in Contemporary Continental Philosophy. Albany, NY: State of University of New York, 1994.

Kuhn, Thomas S. *The Structure of Scientific Revolutions. International Encyclopedia of Unified Science*. Chicago, IL: University of Chicago, 1962.

Kuklick, Bruce. 'Review: George M. Marsden, *The Soul of the American University: From Protestant Establishment to Established Nonbelief*'. *Method and Theory in the Study of Religion* 8.1 (1996), 79–84.

Kümmel, Werner Georg. *The New Testament: The History of the Investigation of its Problems* translated by S. McLean Gilmour and Howard C. Kee. London: SCM, 1973.

Laas, Oliver. 'Toward Truthlikeness in Historiography'. *European Journal of Pragmatism and American Philosophy* 8.2 (2016), 1–29.

Lacan, Jacques. 'Le symbolique, l'imaginaire et le réel'. *Bulletin de l'Association Freudienne* 1.1 (1982), 4–13.

Land, Kenneth C., Glenn Deane, and Judith R. Blau. 'Religious Pluralism and Church Membership: A Spatial Diffusion Model'. *American Sociological Review* 56.2 (1991), 237–49.

Laplace, Pierre-Simon. 'Mémoire sur la probabilité des causes par les événements'. In *Œuvres complète de Laplace*, 8:27–65. Paris: Gauthier-Villars, 1878.

Larmore, Charles. 'How Much Can We Stand?' *The New Republic*, 9 April 2008. https://newrepublic.com/article/63415/how-much-can-we-stand.

Lash, Nicholas. 'In Defense of Lonergan's Critics'. *New Blackfriars* 57.670 (1976), 124–6.

Latour, Bruno. *We Have Never Been Modern*. Translated by Catherine Porter. Cambridge, MA: Harvard University, 1993.

———. *Nous n'avons Jamais Été Modernes: Essai d'anthropologie Symétrique*. Paris: La Découverte, 1991.

Lawler, Edwina G. *David Friedrich Strauss and His Critics: The Life of Jesus Debate in Early Nineteenth-Century German Journals*. New York: Peter Lang, 1986.

Le Donne, Anthony. 'The Third Quest in Retrospect'. *Journal for the Study of the Historical Jesus* 14.1 (2016), 1–5.

———. *The Historiographical Jesus: Memory, Typology, and the Son of David*. Waco, TX: Baylor University, 2005.

Lechner, Frank J. 'The Case against Secularization: A Rebuttal'. *Social Forces* 69.4 (1991), 1103–19.

Lee, Seung Goo. 'The Relationship between the Ontological Trinity and the Economic Trinity'. *Journal of Reformed Theology* 3.1 (2009), 90–107.

Lehmann, Hartmut. *Die Entzauberung der Welt: Studien zu Themen von Max Weber*. Göttingen: Wallstein, 2009.

LePoidevin, Robin. *Change, Cause, and Contradiction*. New York: St. Martin's, 1991.

Lessing, G.E. *Fragments from Reimarus Consisting of Brief Critical Remarks on the Object of Jesus and His Disciples as Seen in the New Testament*. Edited and translated by Charles Voysey. London: Williams and Nogate, 1879.

Levine, Peter. *Nietzsche and the Modern Crisis of the Humanities*. Albany, NY: State of University of New York, 1995.

Lewis, Clarence Irving. *A Survey of Symbolic Logic*. Berkeley, CA: University of California, 1918.

———. '*The Place of Intuition in Knowledge*'. Ph.D. diss., Harvard University, 1910.

Lewis, Clarence Irving, and Cooper Harold Langford. *Symbolic Logic*. New York: Dover Publications, 1932.

Lewis, David. *On the Plurality of Worlds*. Oxford: Blackwell, 1986.

———. 'Counterparts of Persons and Their Bodies'. *Journal of Philosophy* 68.7 (1971), 203–11.

———. 'General Semantics'. *Synthese* 22.1 (1970), 18–67.

———. 'Counterpart Theory and Quantified Modal Logic'. *Journal of Philosophy* 65.5 (1968), 113–26.

Lichtenberger, Hermann. "Karl Georg Kuhn (1906–1976): Two Academic Careers in Germany," in *Protestant Bible Scholarship: Antisemitism, Philosemitism and Anti-Judaism*, edited by Arjen F. Bakker, René Bloch, Yael Fisch, Paula Fredriksen, and Hindy Najman, 1–23. JSJS 200; Leiden: Brill, 2022.

Lindley, Dennis V. 'A Statistical Paradox'. *Biometrika* 44.1–2 (1957), 187–92.

———. 'Statistical Inference'. *Journal of the Royal Statistical Society. Series B (Methodological)* 15.1 (1953), 30–76.

Lohse, Bernhard. *Martin Luther's Theology: Its Historical and Systematic Development*. Translated by Roy A. Harrisville. Edinburgh: T&T Clark, 1999.

Lonergan, Bernard J. F. *Grace and Freedom: Operative Grace in the Thought of Thomas Aquinas*. Collected Works of Bernard Lonergan 1. Toronto, ON: University of Toronto, 2000.

———. *Verbum: Word and Idea in Aquinas*. Collected Works of Bernard Lonergan 2. Toronto, ON: University of Toronto, 1997.

———. *Insight: A Study of Human Understanding*. 5th ed. Collected Works of Bernard Lonergan 3. Toronto, ON: University of Toronto, 1992.

———. 'Insight Revisited'. In *A Second Collection*, edited by William F. J. Ryan and Bernard J. Tyrrell, 263–78. Philadelphia, PA: Westminster John Knox, 1974.

———. *Method in Theology*. New York: Herder & Herder, 1972.

Losch, Andreas. 'Wright's Version of Critical Realism'. In *God and the Faithfulness of Paul: A Critical Examination of the Pauline Theology of N.T. Wright*, edited by Christoph Heilig, J. Thomas Hewitt, and Michael F. Bird, 101–514. WUNT II.413. Tübingen: Mohr Siebeck, 2016.

Loux, Michael J., and Dean W. Zimmerman. 'Introduction'. In *The Oxford Handbook of Metaphysics*, edited by Michael J. Loux and Dean W. Zimmerman, 1–7. Oxford: Oxford University, 2003.

Lubac, Henri de. *A Brief Catechesis on Nature and Grace*. Translated by Richard Arnandez. San Francisco, CA: Ignatius, 1984.

Lüdemann, Gerd. *Jesus after 2000 Years: What He Really Said and Did*. London: SCM, 2000.

———. *Jesus nach 2000 Jahren. Was er wirklich sagte und tat*. Lüneburg: zu Klampen, 2000.

Ludwig, Frieder. 'Football, Culture and Religion: Varieties of Interaction'. *Studies in World Christianity* 21.3 (2015), 201–22.

Luther, Martin. 'Temporal Authority: To What Extent It Should Be Obeyed'. In *Luther's Works*, edited by Walther I. Brandt and Helmut T. Lehmann 45: The Christian in Society II:77–133. Philadelphia, PA: Fortress, 1962.

Lycan, William G. 'Materialism and Leibniz's Law'. *The Monist* 56.2 (1972), 276–87.

Lyon, Robert W. 'Jesus: A Revolutionary Biography. By John Dominic Crossan'. *Journal of Church and State* 37.3 (1995), 660.

Lyotard, Jean-François. *Heidegger et 'les juifs'*. Paris: Débats, 1988.

———. *The Post-Modern Condition: A Report on Knowledge*. Translated by Geoff Bennington and Brian Massumi. Manchester: Manchester University, 1984.

———. *La condition postmoderne: rapport sur le savoir*. Paris: Minuit, 1979.

MacAskill, Grant. *The New Testament and Intellectual Humility*. Oxford: Oxford University, 2019.

———. 'Christian Scriptures and the Formation of Intellectual Humility'. *Journal of Psychology and Theology* 46.4 (2018), 243–52.

MacDonald, Nathan. 'Review: *Hermann Samuel Reimarus (1694–1768): Classicist, Hebraist, Enlightenment Radical in Disguise*. By Ulrich Groetsch'. *Journal of Theological Studies* 68.1 (2017), 412–13.

Macey, David. *The Lives of Michel Foucault*. London: Hutchinson, 1993.

MacIntyre, Alasdair. *After Virtue: A Study in Moral Theology*. 2nd ed. Notre Dame, IL: Notre Dame University, 1985.

Mack, Burton L. *A Myth of Innocence: Mark and Christian Origins*. Philadelphia, PA: Fortress, 1988.

Mackie, J. L. *The Cement of the Universe: A Study of Causation*. Oxford: Oxford University, 1980.

Madges, William. 'D. F. Strauss in Retrospect: His Reception among Roman Catholics'. *The Heythrop Journal* 30.3 (1989), 273–92.

———. *The Core of Christian Faith: D. F. Strauss and His Catholic Critics*. Theology and Religion 38. Paris: Peter Lang, 1987.

Magidor, Ofra. 'Arguments by Leibniz' Law in Metaphysics'. *Philosophy Compass* 6.3 (2011), 180–95.

Malan, Gert J. 'Mythology, Weltanschauung, Symbolic Universe and States of Consciousness'. *HTS Teologiese Studies* 72.1 (2016), 1–8.

Malcolm, Norman. *Nothing Is Hidden: Wittgenstein's Criticism of His Early Thought*. Oxford: Blackwell, 1986.

Malina, Bruce J., and Jerome H. Neyrey. *Portraits of Paul: An Archaeology of Ancient Personality*. Louisville, KY: John Knox, 1996.

Manley, David. 'Introduction: A Guided Tour of Metametaphysics'. In *Metametaphysics: New Essays on the Foundations of Ontology*, edited by David Chalmers, David Manley, and Ryan Wasserman, 1–37. Oxford: Clarendon, 2009.

Manson, T. W. *The Teaching of Jesus: Studies of Its Form and Content*. Cambridge: Cambridge University, 1931.

Marino, Stefano. *Aesthetics, Metaphysics, Language: Essays on Heidegger and Gadamer*. Newcastle upon Tyne: Cambridge Scholars, 2015.

Marius, Richard. *Martin Luther: The Christian between God and Death*. Cambridge, MA: Belknap Press, 1999.

Marsden, George M. *A Short Life of Jonathan Edwards*. Grand Rapids, MI: Eerdmans, 2008.

———. *Jonathan Edwards: A Life*. New Haven, CT: Yale University, 2003.

———. *The Outrageous Idea of Christian Scholarship*. New York: Oxford University Press, 1998.

———. *The Soul of the American University: From Protestant Establishment to Established Nonbelief*. New York: Oxford University, 1994.

Marsh, Clive. 'Review: John P. Meier, *A Marginal Jew Volume III: Companions and Competitors*'. *Journal for the Study of the New Testament* 26.3 (2004), 374–76.

———. 'Quests of the Historical Jesus in New Historicist Perspective'. *Biblical Interpretation* 5.4 (1997), 403–37.

Mauss, Marcel. *The Gift: The Form and Reason for Exchange in Archaic Societies*. London: Routledge, 2002.

———. *Essai sur le don in sociologie et anthropologie*. Paris: Universitairs de France, 1950.

McCormack, Bruce Lindley. *The Humility of the Eternal Son: Reformed Kenoticism and the Repair of Chalcedon*. Cambridge: Cambridge University Press, 2021.

McCoubrey, Hilaire. 'Natural Law, Religion and the Development of International Law'. In *Religion and International Law*, edited by Mark W. Janis and Carolyn Evans, 177–90. The Hague: Martinus Nijhoff, 1999.

McDonough, Sean M. *Christ as Creator: Origins of a New Testament Doctrine*. Oxford: Oxford University Press, 2009.

McGaughey, Douglas R. 'On D.F. Strauß and the 1839 Revolution in Zurich'. Http://Www.Chora-Strangers.Org/Files/Chora/Mcgaughey_1994.Pdf (blog), 1994. Accessed 30 June 2018.

McGinn, Marie. 'Between Metaphysics and Nonsense: Elucidation in Wittgenstein's *Tractatus*'. *Philosophical Quarterly* 49.197 (1999), 491–513.

McGrayne, Sharon Bertsch. *The Theory That Would Not Die: How Bayes' Rule Cracked the Enigma Code, Hunted Down Russian Submarines, and Emerged Triumphant from Two Centuries of Controversy*. New Haven, CT: Yale University, 2012.

McGregor, Peter John. 'Is Lonergan's Method Theological?'. *Radical Orthodoxy: Theology, Philosophy, Politics* 5.1 (2019), 61–99.

McKee, Rob Austin, and C. Chet Miller. 'Institutionalizing Bayesianism within the Organizational Sciences: A Practical Guide Featuring Comments from Eminent Scholars'. *Journal of Management* 41.2 (2015), 471–90.

McKinnon, Alastair. *Fundamental Polyglot Konkordans til Kierkegaards Samlede Værker*. Leiden: Brill, 1971.

McKnight, Scot. *Jesus and His Death: Historiography, the Historical Jesus, and Atonement Theory*. Waco, TX: Baylor University, 2005.

Meier, Helmut G. '*"Weltanschauung": Studien zu einer Geschichte und Theorie des Begriffs*'. Ph.D. diss., Westfälischen Wilhelms-Universität zu Münster, 1967.

Meier, John P. 'Basic Methodology in the Quest for the Historical Jesus'. In *Handbook for the Study of the Historical Jesus*, edited by Tom Holmén and Stanley Porter, 1:291–331. Leiden: Brill, 2011.

———. *A Marginal Jew: Rethinking the Historical Jesus*. 5 vols. AYB. New York: Doubleday, 1991–2016.

Mellor, D. H. *Real Time II*. London: Routledge, 1998.

———. *Real Time*. Cambridge: Cambridge University, 1981.

Merleau-Ponty, Maurice. *Phenomenolgie de la perception*. Paris: PUF, 1945.

Merricks, Trenton. 'Persistence, Parts, and Presentism'. *Noûs* 33.3 (1996), 421–38.

———. 'On the Incompatibility of Enduring and Perduring Entities'. *Mind* 104.415 (1995), 512–31.

———. 'Endurance and Indiscernibility'. *Journal of Philosophy* 91.4 (1994), 165–84.

Meyer, Ben F. *The Aims of Jesus*. Repr. ed. with new introduction. Eugene, OR: Pickwick, 2002.

———. *Reality and Illusion in New Testament Scholarship: A Primer in Critical Realist Hermeneutics*. Collegeville, MN: Liturgical Press, 1994.

———. 'Some Consequences of Birger Gerhardsson's Account of the Origins of the Gospel Tradition'. In *Jesus and the Oral Gospel Traditon*, edited by Henry Wansbrough, 424–40. JSNTSup 64. Sheffield: Sheffield Academic, 1991.

———. *Critical Realism and the New Testament*. Allison Park, PA: Pickwick, 1989.

Meynell, Hugo. 'Taking A(nother) Look at Lonergan's Method'. *New Blackfriars* 90 (2009), 474–500.

Milbank, John. *The Gift Exchanged: The Gift in Religion*. Oxford: Blackwell, 2017.

———. *Beyond Secular Order: The Representation of Being and the Representation of the People. Illuminations: Theory and Religion*. Oxford: Blackwell, 2013.

———. 'A Closer Walk on the Wild Side: Some Comments on Charles Taylor's *A Secular Age*'. *Studies in Christian Ethics* 22.1 (2009), 89–104 (repr. in *Varieties of Secularism in a Secular Age*, edited by Michael Warner, Jonathan Vanantwerpen, and Craig Calhoun, 54–82. Cambridge, MA: Harvard University, 2010).

———. *Theology and Social Theory: Beyond Secular Reason*. 2nd ed. Oxford: Blackwell, 2006.

———. *Being Reconciled: Ontology and Pardon*. Radical Orthodoxy. London: Routledge, 2003.

———. *The Word Made Strange: Theology, Language, Culture*. Oxford: Blackwell, 1997.

———. 'Can a Gift Be Given? Prolegomena to a Future Trinitarian Metaphysic'. *Modern Theology* 11.1 (1995), 119–61.

———. *The Religious Dimension in the Thought of Giambattista Vico. 2 vols. Studies in the History of Philosophy 23*. Lewiston, NY: E. Mellon, 1991.

Milbank, John, and Simon Oliver, eds. *The Radical Orthodoxy Reader*. London: Routledge, 2009.

Milbank, John, and Catherine Pickstock. *Truth in Aquinas*. Radical Orthodoxy. London: Routledge, 2001.

Milbank, John, Catherine Pickstock, and Graham Ward, eds. *Radical Orthodoxy: A New Theology*. London: Routledge, 1999.

Miller, James. *The Passion of Michel Foucault*. New York: Simon & Schuster, 1993.

Mirvish, Adrian. 'The Presuppositions of Husserl's Presuppositionless Philosophy'. *Journal of the British Society for Phenomenology* 26.2 (1995), 147–70.

Moffitt, David M. '"If Another Priest Arises": Jesus' Resurrection and the High Priestly Christology of Hebrews'. In *A Cloud of Witnesses: The Theology of Hebrews in Its Ancient Context*, edited by Richard Bauckham, Daniel Driver, Trevor Hart, and Nathan MacDonald, 68–79. LNTS 387. London: T&T Clark, 2008 (repr. in *The Letter to the Hebrews: Critical Readings*, edited by Scott D. Mackie, 124–35. Critical Readings in Biblical Studies. London: T&T Clark, 2018).

Moller, Hilde Brekke. *The Vermes Quest: The Significance of Geza Vermes for Jesus Research*. LNTS 576. London: T&T Clark, 2017.

Moltmann, Jürgen. *The Trinity and the Kingdom: The Doctrine of God*. Translated by Margaret Kohl. London: SCM, 1981.

———. *The Crucified God*. Translated by R. A. Wilson and John Bowden. London: SCM, 1974.

Montchrestien, Antoine de. *Traicté de l'œconomie politique*. Edited by François Billacois. Les classiques de la pensée politique 16. Genève: Librairie Droz, 1999.

Morgan, Robert. 'Reimarus, Schweitzer, and Modern Theology'. *Expository Times* 129.6 (2018), 254–64.

———. 'Pope Benedict's Jesus: Joseph Ratzinger/Pope Benedict XVI, *Jesus of Nazareth*'. *Expository Times* 119.6 (2008), 282–83.

Naugle, David K. *Worldview: The History of a Concept*. Grand Rapids, MI: Eerdmans, 2002.

Neill, S., and N. T. Wright. *The Interpretation of the New Testament 1961-1986*. 2nd ed. Oxford: Oxford University, 1988.

Nerlich, Graham. 'Space-Time Substantivalism'. In *The Oxford Handbook of Metaphysics*, edited by Michael J. Loux and Dean W. Zimmerman, 281–314. Oxford: Oxford University, 2003.

Ney, Alyssa. *Metaphysics: An Introduction*. London: Routledge, 2014.

Nicol, Andrew W. *Exodus and Resurrection: The God of Israel in The Theology of Robert W. Jenson*. Emerging Scholars. Minneapolis, MN: Fortress, 2016.

Niebergall, Friedrich. 'Über Die Absolutheit Des Christentums'. *Studien Des Rheinischen Predigervereins* 4 (1898).

Niebuhr, Karl-Wilhelm. 'Welchen Jesus predigen wir? Überlegungen im Anschluss an Martin Kähler'. *Sacra Scripta* 10.2 (2011), 123–42.

Nietzsche, Friedrich. *Untimely Meditations*. Edited by Daniel Breazeale, translated by R. J. Hollingdale. Cambridge: Cambridge University, 1997.

———. *Sämtliche Werke: Kritische Studienausgabe in 15 Bänden*. Edited by Giorgio Colli and Mazzino Montinari. Berlin: de Gruyter, 1980.

———. *The Will to Power: An Attempted Transvaluation of All Values*. 3rd edition, translated by Anthony M. Ludovici. London: T. N. Foulis, 1914.

———. *Menschliches, Allzumenschliches. Ein Buch für freie Geister. Neue Ausgabe mit einer einführenden Vorrede*. 2 vols. Leipzig: E.W. Fritzsch, 1886.

Norris, Pippa, and Ronald Ingelhart. *Secular and Sacred: Religion and Politics Worldwide*. Cambridge: Cambridge University, 2004.

O'Brien, David J. 'Review: *The Soul of the American University: From Protestant Establishment to Established Nonbelief* by George M. Marsden'. *The Catholic Historical Review* 82.2 (1996), 305–7.

O'Donovan, Oliver. 'Theology and Social Theory: Beyond Secular Reason by John Milbank'. *Studies in Christian Ethics* 5.1 (1992), 80–86.

Oliver, Simon. *Philosophy, God and Motion.* Radical Orthodoxy. London: Routledge, 2013.

———. 'Introducing Radical Orthodoxy: From Participation to Late Modernity'. In *The Radical Orthodoxy Reader*, edited by John Milbank and Simon Oliver, 3–27. London: Routledge, 2009.

Olson, Daniel V. A. 'Religious Pluralism and US Church Membership: A Reassessment'. *Sociology of Religion* 60.2 (1999), 149–73.

———. 'Religious Pluralism in Contemporary U.S. Counties'. *American Sociological Review* 63.5 (1998), 759–61.

Oman, Charles. *On the Writing of History*. London: Methuen, 1939.

Orr, James. *The Christian View of God and the World.* Grand Rapids, MI: Kregel, 1989.

———. *English Deism: Its Roots and Its Fruits*. Grand Rapids, MI: Eerdmans, 1934.

Ott, Hugo. *Martin Heidegger: A Political Life*. London: HarperCollins, 1993.

———. *Martin Heidegger: Unterwegs zur seiner Biographie*. Frankfurt: Campus, 1988.

Owen, G. E. L. 'The Platonism of Aristotle'. In *Logic, Science, and Dialectic: Collected Papers in Greek Philosophy*, edited by M. C. Nussbaum, 200–220. London: Duckworth, 1986.

———. 'The Platonism of Aristotle'. *Proceedings of the British Academy* 50.1 (1965), 125–50.

Owen, Henry. *Observations on the Four Gospels; Tending Chiefly to Ascertain the Time of Their Publication, and to Illustrate the Form and Manner of Their Composition.* London: Payne, 1764.

Pabst, Adrian, and Angus Paddison, eds. *The Pope and Jesus of Nazareth: Christ, Scripture and the Church.* Veritas. London: SCM, 2009.

Paci, Enzo. *The Function of the Sciences and the Meaning of Man*. Translated by Paul Piccone and James E. Hansen. Northwestern University Studies in Phenomenology and Existential Philosophy. Evanston, IL: Northwestern University, 1972.

Paddison, Angus. 'Theological Interpretation and the Bible as Public Text'. *Journal of Theological Interpretation* 8.2 (2014), 175–92.

———. *Scripture: A Very Theological Proposal*. London: T&T Clark, 2013.

Palu, Ma'afu. *Jesus and Time: An Interpretation of Mark 1:15.* LNTS 468. London: T&T Clark, 2012.

Pals, Daniel L. *The Victorian 'Lives' of Jesus.* Trinity University Monograph Series in Religion 7. San Antonio, TX: Trinity University, 1982.

Pannenberg, Wolfhart. *Systematic Theology*. Translated by Geoffrey W. Bromiley. Grand Rapids, MI: Eerdmans, 1991.

Parla, Taha, Andrew Davison, and Janet R. Jakobsen. 'Secularism and Laicism in Turkey'. In *Secularisms*, 58–75. Social Text Books. Durham, NC: Duke University, 2008.

Parsons, Talcott. *Societies: Evolutionary and Comparative Perspectives*. Englewood Cliffs, NJ: Prentice-Hall, 1966.

Patterson, Stephen J. 'Bultmann's Jesus in America'. In *"To Recover What Has Been Lost": Essays on Eschatology, Intertextuality, and Reception History in Honor of Dale C. Allison Jr.*, edited by Tucker S. Ferda, Daniel Frayer-Griggs, and Nathan C. Johnson 405–28. NovTSup 183. Leiden: Brill, 2021.

Peirce, Charles S. *Science and Philosophy*. Edited by Arthur W. Burks. Collected Papers, vol. 7. Cambridge, MA: Harvard University, 1958.

Peltonen, Matti. 'The Method of Clues and History Theory'. In *Historical Knowledge: In Quest of Theory, Method and Evidence*, edited by Susanna Fellman and Marjatta Rahikainen, 45–76. Newcastle upon Tyne: Cambridge Scholars, 2012.

Pennington, Jonathan T. *Heaven and Earth in the Gospel of Matthew*. NovTSup 126. Leiden: Brill, 2007.

Peramatzis, Michail. 'Metaphysics A.7, 988b16-21: Artistotle's Conclusion About His Predecessors on Causes'. *Philosophical Inquiry* 41.2–3 (2017), 55–65.

Perrin, Norman. *Rediscovering the Teaching of Jesus*. London: SCM, 1967.

Pickstock, Catherine. 'Duns Scotus: His Historical and Contemporary Significance'. *Modern Theology* 21.4 (2005), 543–74.

———. *After Writing: On the Liturgical Consummation of Philosophy*. Challenges in Contemporary Theology. Oxford: Blackwell, 1998.

Pitre, Brant. *Jesus and the Last Supper*. Grand Rapids, MI: Eerdmans, 2015.

Plutarch. 'Theseus'. In *Lives, Volume I: Theseus and Romulus. Lycurgus and Numa. Solon and Publicola*, translated by Bernadotte Perrin. Loeb Classical Library 46. Cambridge, MA: Harvard University, 1914.

Popper, Karl. *Logik der Forschung: Zur Erkenntnistheorie der modernen Naturwissenschaf*. Tübingen: Mohr Siebeck, 1934.

Porter, Stanley E. *The Criteria for Authenticity in Historical-Jesus Research*. Sheffield: Sheffield Academic, 2000.

Porter, Stanley E., and Andrew W. Pitts. 'Has Jonathan Bernier Rescued Critical Realism?' *Journal for the Study of the Historical Jesus* 14.3 (2016), 241–47.

———. 'Critical Realism in Context: N. T. Wright's Historical Method and Analytic Epistemology'. *Journal for the Study of the Historical Jesus* 13.2–3 (2015), 276–306.

Postow, B.C. 'Husserl's Failure to Establish a Presuppositionless Science'. *The Southern Journal of Philosophy* 14.2 (1976), 179–88.

Poulsom, Martin G. 'Schillebeeckx and the *Sensus Fidelium*'. *New Blackfriars* 98.1074 (2017), 203–17.

———. *The Dialectics of Creation: Creation and the Creator in Edward Schillebeeckx and David Burrell*. London: T&T Clark, 2014.

Powell, Mark A. *Jesus as a Figure in History*. Louisville, KY: Westminster John Knox, 1998.

Prideaux, Sue. *I Am Dynamite! A Life of Friedrich Nietzsche*. London: Faber & Faber, 2018.

Prior, A. N. 'Some Free Thinking about Time'. In *Logic and Reality: Essays on the Legacy of Arthur Prior*, edited by B. J. Copeland, 47–51. Oxford: Oxford University, 1996.

———. 'The Notion of the Present'. *Studium Generale* 23.3 (1970), 245–48.

———. *Papers on Time and Tense*. London: Oxford University, 1968.

———. *Past. Present, and Future*. Oxford: Clarendon, 1967.

———. 'Thank Goodness That's Over'. *Philosophy* 34.1 (1959), 12–17.

———. *Time and Modality*. Oxford: Oxford University, 1957.

Putnam, Hilary. *Ethics without Ontology*. Cambridge: Harvard University, 2004.

———. *Words and Life*. edited by James Conant. Cambridge, MA: Harvard University, 1994.

Quine, W.V.O. 'On What There Is'. *The Review of Metaphysics* 2.5 (1948), 21–38.

Rae, Murray A. *History and Hermeneutics*. London: T&T Clark, 2005.

———. 'The Forgetfulness of Historical-Talkative Remembrance in Kierkegaard's 'Practice in Christianity''. In *International Kierkegaard Commentary: Practice in Christianity*, edited by Robert L. Perkins, 69–94. Macon, GA: Mercer University, 2004.

Räisänen, Heikki. *Beyond New Testament Theology: A Story and a Programme*. 2nd edition. London: SCM, 2000.

Rahikainen, Marjatta, and Susanna Fellman. 'Introduction'. In *Historical Knowledge: In Quest of Theory, Method and Evidence*, edited by Susanna Fellman and Marjatta Rahikainen, 1–3. Newcastle upon Tyne: Cambridge Scholars, 2012.

———. 'On Historical Writing and Evidence'. In *Historical Knowledge: In Quest of Theory, Method and Evidence*, edited by Susanna Fellman and Marjatta Rahikainen, 5–44. Newcastle upon Tyne: Cambridge Scholars, 2012.

Rahner, Karl. 'Kritische Bermerkungen zu B.J.F. Lonergan's Aufsatz: 'Functional Specialities in Theology'. *Gregorianum* 51.3 (1970), 537–40.

———. *The Trinity*. Translated by Joseph Donceel. Tunbridge Wells: Burns & Oates, 1970.

Raiffa, Howard. *Decision Analysis*. Reading, MA: Addison Wesley, 1968.

Raiffa, Howard, and Robert O. Schlaifer. *Applied Statistical Decision Theory*. Cambridge, MA: Harvard University, 1961.

Rakić, Nataša. 'Past, Present, Future, and Special Relativity'. *British Journal for the Philosophy of Science* 48.2 (1997), 257–80.

Ramsey, Frank P. *The Foundations of Mathematics and Other Logical Essays*. London: Kegan Paul, 1931.

———. 'Critical Notice of L. Wittgenstein's *Tractatus Logico-Philosophicus*'. *Mind* 32.128 (1923), 465–78.

Ratzinger, Joseph. *Jesus of Nazareth: From the Baptism in the Jordan to the Transfiguration*. London: Bloomsbury, 2007.

Re Manning, Russell, ed. *The Cambridge Companion to Paul Tillich*. Cambridge: Cambridge University, 2009.

Rea, Michael C. 'Four-Dimensionalism'. In *The Oxford Handbook of Metaphysics*, edited by Michael J. Louw and Dean W. Zimmerman, 246–80. Oxford: Oxford University, 2003.

Reardon, Bernard M.G. 'Review of Maurice Blondel, *The Letter on Apologetics and History and Dogma*'. *Expository Times* 107.1 (1995), 29.

Rectenwald, Michael. *Nineteenth-Century British Secularism. Histories of the Sacred and the Secular, 1700–2000*. Basingstoke: Palgrave MacMillan, 2016.

Reed-Downing, Teresa. 'Husserl's Presuppositionless Philosophy'. *Research in Phenomenology* 20.1 (1990), 136–51.

Reimarus, Hermann Samuel. *Apologie oder Schutzschrift für die vernünftigen Verehrer Gottes*. Edited by Gerhard Alexander. 2 vols. Hamburg: Insel, 1972.

Reuther, Rosemary Radford, and Marion Grau, eds. *Interpreting the Postmodern: Responses to 'Radical Orthodoxy'*. New York: T&T Clark, 2006.

Reynolds, Terrence. 'Method Divorced from Content in Theology? An Assessment of Lonergan's *Method in Theology*'. *The Thomist* 55.2 (1991), 245–69.

Ricketts, Thomas. 'Pictures, Logic, and the Limits of Sense in Wittgenstein's *Tractatus*'. In *The Cambridge Companion to Wittgenstein*, edited by Hans D. Sluga and David G. Stern, 59–99. Cambridge: Cambridge University, 1996.

Ricœur, Paul. *Time and Narrative*. Translated by Robert Czerny, Kathleen McLaughlin, and David Pellauer. 3 vols. Chicago, IL: Chicago University, 1984.

Rist, John M. *The Mind of Aristotle: A Study of Philosophical Growth*. Toronto, ON: University of Toronto, 1989.

Roberts, Richard H. 'Transcendental Sociology? A Critique of John Milbank's *Theology and Social Theory Beyond Secular Reason*'. *Scottish Journal of Theology* 46.4 (1993), 527–35.

Rockmore, Tom. 'Philosophy or Weltanschauung? Heidegger on Hönigswald'. *History of Philosophy Quarterly* 16.1 (1999), 97–115.

Rodríquez, Rafael. *Structuring Early Christian Memory: Jesus in Tradition, Performance, and Text.* LNTS 407. London: T&T Clark, 2010.

Roesenthal, Jerome. 'Voltaire's Philosophy of History'. *Journal of the History of Ideas* 16.2 (1955), 151–78.

Rollens, Sarah E. 'Socialscapes and Abstractions: An Appraisal of Richard A. Horsley's Theorizing of Antiquity'. *Journal for the Study of the Historical Jesus* 18.2 (2020). 101–23.

Rorty, Richard. *Philosophy and the Mirror of Nature*. Princeton, NJ: Princeton University, 1979.

Rowe, C. Kavin. 'What if it were True? Why Study the New Testament'. *New Testament Studies* 68.2 (2022), 144–55.

Rowlands, Jonathan. 'The Theological Lineage of N.T. Wright's Historical Method'. *Journal of Theological Interpretation* 16.1 (2022), 110–31.

———. 'Reception History, Theological Interpretation, and the Future of New Testament Studies'. *Journal of Theological Interpretation* 13.2 (2019), 147–67.

———. 'Jesus and the Wings of YHWH: Bird Imagery in the Lament Over Jerusalem (Matt. 23.37–39; Luke 13.34–35'. *Novum Testamentum* 61.2 (2019), 115–36.

Russell, Bertrand. 'On the Experience of Time'. *The Monist* 25.2 (1915), 212–33.

Ryan, Jordan J. 'The Historian's Craft and the Future of Historical Jesus Research: Engaging Brant Pitre's Jesus and the Last Supper as a Work of History'. *Journal for the Study of the Historical Jesus* 15.1 (2017), 60–87.

———. 'Jesus at the Crossroads of Inference and Imagination: The Relevance of R.G. Collingwood's Philosophy of History for Current Methodological Discussions in Historical Jesus Research'. *Journal for the Study of the Historical Jesus* 13.1 (2015), 66–89.

Sajó, András. 'Preliminaries to a Concept of Constitutional Secularism'. *International Journal of Constitutional Law* 6.3–4 (2008), 605–29.

Sanday, William. *The Life of Christ in Recent Research.* New York: Oxford University, 1907.

Sanders, E.P. *Jesus and Judaism*. London: SCM, 1985.

———. *Paul and Palestinian Judaism: A Comparison of Patterns of Religion.* London: SCM, 1977.

Sarna, Jan W. 'On Some Presuppositions of Husserl's 'Presuppositionless' Philosophy'. *Analecta Husserliana* 27 (1989), 239–50.

Savage, Leonard J. *The Foundations of Statistics*. Oxford: John Wiley & Sons, 1954 (2d rev. ed. New York: Dover Publications, 1972).

Scanlon, John. 'The Manifold Meanings of 'Life World' in Husserl's Crisis'. *American Catholic Philosophical Quarterly* 66.2 (1992), 229–39.

Schacht, Richard. 'Nietzsche and the Method of Philosophy'. In *Nietzsche as Affirmative Thinker: Papers Presented at the Fifth Jerusalem Philosophical Encounter, April 1983*, edited by Yirmiyahu Yovel, 1–19. Martinus Nijhoff Philosophical Library 13. Dordrecht: Springer, 1986.

———. 'Nietzsche on Philosophy, Interpretation and Truth'. *Noûs* 18.1 (1984), 75–85.

Schaffer, Jonathan. 'On What Grounds What'. In *Metametaphysics: New Essays on the Foundations of Ontology*, edited by David Chalmers, David Manley, and Ryan Wasserman, 347–83. Oxford: Clarendon, 2009.

Schillebeeckx, Edward. 'The Problem of the Infallibility of the Church's Office'. In *The Language of Faith: Essays on Jesus, Theology and the Church*, translated by Smith, 55–69. London: SCM, 1995.

———. *Jesus in Our Western Culture: Mysticism, Ethic and Politics*. Translated by John Bowden. London: SCM, 1987.

———. *Jesus: An Experiment in Christology*. Translated by Hubert Hoskins. London: Collins, 1979.

———. *Jezus, het verhaal van een levende*. Bloemendaal: Nelissen, 1974.

Schlaifer, Robert O. *Probability and Statistics for Business Decisions*. New York: McGraw-Hill, 1959.

Schleiermacher, Friedrich. *Christian Faith: A New Translation and Critical Edition*. Edited by Catherine L. Kelsey and Terrence N. Tice. Translated by Terrence N. Tice, Catherine L. Kelsey, and Edwina Lawler. 2 vols. Louisville, KY: Westminster John Knox, 2016.

———. *The Life of Jesus*. Translated by S. MacLean Gilmour. Lives of Jesus Series. Philadelphia, PA: Fortress, 1975.

Schnackenburg, Rudolf. *Jesus in the Gospels: A Biblical Christology*. Translated by O. C. Dean Jr. Louisville, KY: Westminster John Knox, 1995.

Schneider, Gerhard. '"Im Himmel - auf Erden": Eine Perspektive matthäischer Theologie'. In *Studien zum Matthäusevangelium: Festschrift für Wilhelm Pesch*, edited by Ludger Schenke, 285–97. Stuttgart: Katholisches Bibelwerk, 1988.

Schnieder, Benjamin. ''By Leibniz's Law': Remarks on a Fallacy'. *Philosophical Quarterly* 56.222 (2006), 39–54.

Schoof, Ted, ed. *The Schillebeeckx Case*. New Haven, CT: Paulist, 1984.

Schoot, Rens van de, David Kaplan, Jaap Denissen, Jens B. Asendorpf, Franz J. Neyer, and Marcel A.G. van Aken. 'A Gentle Introduction to Bayesian Analysis: Applications to Developmental Research'. *Child Development* 85.3 (2014), 842–60.

Schüssler Fiorenza, Elisabeth. 'Jesus and the Politics of Interpretation'. *Harvard Theological Review* 90.4 (1997), 343–58.

Schwartz, Seth. *Were the Jews a Mediterranean Society?* Princeton, NJ: Princeton University, 2010.

Schweitzer, Albert. *The Quest of the Historical Jesus*. Translated by W. Montgomery. Mineola, NY: Dover, 2005.

———. *The Psychiatric Study of Jesus: Exposition and Criticism*. Translated by Charles R. Joy. Boston, MA: Beacon, 1948.

———. *Die psychiatrische Beurteilung Jesu. Darstellung und Kritik*. Tübingen: J. C. B. Mohr, 1913.

———. *Von Reimarus zu Wrede: eine Geschichte der Leben-Jesu-Forschung*. Tübingen: J. C. B. Mohr, 1906.

Scott, E. F. 'Recent Lives of Jesus'. *Harvard theological Review* 27.1 (1934), 1–31.

Senior, Donald. 'The Death of Jesus and the Resurrection of the Holy Ones (Mt 27:51-53)'. *Catholic Bible Quarterly* 38.3 (1976), 312–29.

Shiner, Larry. 'The Concept of Secularization in Empirical Research'. *Journal for the Scientific Study of Religion* 6.2 (1967), 207–20.

Sidelle, Alan. 'Is There a True Metaphysics of Material Objects?' *Noûs* 36.1 (2002), 118–45.

Sider, Theodore. *Writing the Book of the World*. Oxford: Clarendon, 2011.

———. 'Ontological Realism'. In *Metametaphysics: New Essays on the Foundations of Ontology*, edited by David Chalmers, David Manley, and Ryan Wasserman. Oxford: Clarendon, 2009.

———. 'Reductive Theories of Modality'. In *The Oxford Handbook of Metaphysics*, edited by Michael J. Loux and Dean W. Zimmerman, 180–208. Oxford: Oxford University, 2003.

———. *Four-Dimensionalism*. Oxford: Oxford University, 2001.

———. 'Four-Dimensionalism'. *The Philosophical Review* 106.2 (1997), 197–231.

Simons, John. 'Maurice Blondel: Philosophy and Christianity'. *Canadian Journal of Theology* 13.4 (1967), 241–53.

Simons, Peter. 'Events'. In *The Oxford Handbook of Metaphysics*, edited by Michael J. Loux and Dean W. Zimmerman, 357–85. Oxford: Oxford University, 2003.

Simut, Ramona. 'Edward Schillebeeckx's Position on the Resurrection and the Time Test: What Is Resurrection Today?' *Journal for the Study of Religions and Ideologies* 16.48 (2017), 16–30.

Sire, James W. *Naming the Elephant: Worldview as a Concept*. 2nd ed. Downers Grove, IL: IVP, 2015.

Skinner, Quentin. *The Foundations of Modern Political Thought*. 2 vols. Cambridge: Cambridge University, 1978.

Smart, J. J. C. *Philosophy and Scientific Realism*. London: Routledge and Kegan Paul, 1963.

Smith, James K. A. *How (Not) to Be Secular: Reading Charles Taylor*. Grand Rapids, MI: Eerdmans, 2014.

Smith, R.B. 'R.G. Collingwood's Definition of Historical Knowledge'. *History of European Ideas* 33.3 (2007), 350–71.

Sonderegger, Katherine. *Systematic Theology: Volume 1, The Doctrine of God*. Minneapolis, MN: Fortress, 2015.

Soskice, Janet Martin. 'Being and Love: Schleiermacher, Aquinas and Augustine'. *Modern Theology* 34.4 (2018), 480–91.

Stanton, Graham N. *The Gospels and Jesus*. 2nd ed. Oxford: Oxford University, 2002.

Stark, Rodney. 'German and German-American Religiousness'. *Journal for the Scientific Study of Religion* 36.2 (1997), 182–93.

———. 'Secularization, R.I.P.'. *Sociology of Religion* 60.3 (1990), 249–73.

Stark, Rodney, and William Sims Bainbridge. *A Theory of Religion*. New York: Peter Lang, 1987.

Stark, Rodney, and Laurence A. Iannaccone. 'Sociology of Religion'. In *The Encyclopedia of Sociology*, edited by Edgar F. Borgatta and Marie L. Borgatta 4:2029–37. New York: MacMillan, 1992.

Stephenson, John R. 'The Two Governments and the Two Kingdoms in Luther's Thought'. *Scottish Journal of Theology* 34.4 (1981), 321–37.

Stevenson, Austin. 'The Self-Understanding of Jesus: A Metaphysical Reading of Historical Jesus Studies'. *Scottish Journal of Theology* 72.3 (2019), 291–307.

Stewart, Robert B. *The Quest of the Hermeneutical Jesus: The Impact of Hermeneutics on the Jesus Research of John Dominic Crossan and N. T. Wright*. Lanham, MD: University Press of America, 2008.

Strauss, D. F. *In Defense of My Life of Jesus against the Hegelians*. Translated by Marilyn Chapin Massey. Hamden, CT: Archon, 1983.

———. *The Christ of Faith and the Jesus of History: A Critique of Schleiermacher's Life of Jesus*. Translated by Leander E. Keck. Lives of Jesus Series. Philadelphia, PA: Fortress, 1977.

———. *Herman Samuel Reimarus und seine Schutzschrift für die vernünftigen Verehrer Gottes*. Leipzig: Brodhauß, 1862.

———. *The Life of Jesus: Critically Examined.* 2 vols. London: Chapman, 1846.

———. *Das Leben Jesu, kritisch bearbeitet.* 2 vols. Tübingen: C. F. Osiander, 1835.

Streeter, B. H. *The Four Gospels: A Study of Origins*. London: MacMillan, 1924.

Strong, Tracey B. 'Review of Heidegger and Nazism. By Victor Farias'. *American Political Science Review* 84.3 (1990), 962–64.

Sullivan, Patrick A. 'Theological Instruction and Faith Transmission: Lonergan's Method as Pedagogy Theology'. *New Blackfriars* 95 (2014), 593–605.

Svenungsson, Jayne. 'Introduction: Heidegger and Theology after the Black Notebooks'. In *Heidegger's Black Notebooks and the Future of Theology*, edited by Mårtin Björk and Jayne Svenungsson, 1–22. Cham: Springer Nature, 2017.

Swinburne, Richard, ed. *Bayes's Theorem.* PBA 113. Oxford: Oxford University, 2002.

Syreeni, Kari. 'Between Heaven and Earth: On the Structure of Matthew's Symbolic Universe'. *Journal for the Study of the New Testament* 13.40 (1990), 3–13.

Tanner, Kathryn. *Christianity and the New Spirit of Capitalism.* New Haven, CT: Yale University, 2019.

Taylor, Charles. *A Secular Age*. Cambridge, MA: Belknap Press, 2007.

———. 'Modes of Secularism'. In *Secularism and Its Critics*, edited by Rajeev Bhargava. Delhi: Oxford University, 1998.

———. *Sources of the Self: The Making of the Modern Identity*. Cambridge, MA: Harvard University, 1989.

Thalos, Mariam. *Without Hierarchies: The Scale Freedom of the Universe*. Oxford: Oxford University, 2013.

Thate, Michael J. *Remembrance of Things Past? Albert Schweitzer, the Anxiety of Influence, and the Untidy Jesus of Markan Memory.* WUNT II 351. Tübingen: Mohr Siebeck, 2013.

Theissen, Gerd. *The Shadow of the Galilean: The Quest of the Historical Jesus in Narrative Form.* Minneapolis, MN: Fortress, 1986.

Theissen, Gerd, and Annette Merz. *The Historical Jesus: A Comprehensive Guide.* Minneapolis, MN: Fortress Press, 1998.

Theissen, Gerd, and Dagmar Winter. *The Quest for the Plausible Jesus: The Question of Criteria.* Translated by M. Eugene Boring. Louisville, KY: Westminster John Knox, 2002.

Thiselton, Anthony C. *Hermeneutics of Doctrine*. Grand Rapids, MI: Eerdmans, 2007.

Thomasson, Amie L. 'Existence Questions'. *Philosophical Studies* 141.1 (2008), 63–78.

———. *Ordinary Objects*. New York: Oxford University, 2007.

Thompson, Daniel Speed. *The Language of Dissent: Edward Schillebeeckx on the Crisis of Authority in the Catholic Church.* Notre Dame, IL: University of Notre Dame, 2003.

Tonstad, Linn Marie. '(Un)wise Theologians: Systematic Theology in the University'. *International Journal of Systematic Theology* 22.4 (2020), 494–511.

Tooley, Michael. 'Causation and Supervenience'. In *The Oxford Handbook of Metaphysics*, edited by Michael J. Loux and Dean W. Zimmerman, 386–434. Oxford: Oxford University, 2003.

———. *Time, Tense, and Causation*. Oxford: Clarendon, 1997.

Troeltsch, Ernst. 'Historical and Dogmatic Method in Theology'. In *Religion in History*, edited by J. L. Adams and W. F. Bense, 11–32. Minneapolis, MN: Fortress Press, 1991.

———. *The Absoluteness of Christianity and the History of Religions*. Translated by David Reid. London: SCM, 1971.

———. *Der Historismus und seine Probleme*. Tübingen: Mohr Siebeck, 1922a.

———. 'Die Krisis des Historismus'. *Die neue Rundschau* 33.1 (1922b), 572–90.

———. *Zur Religiösen Lage, Religionsphilosophie Und Ethik*. 2nd ed. Gesammelte Schriften, II. Tübingen: Mohr Siebeck, 1922c.

———. *Die Absolutheit des Christentums und die Religionsgeschichte: Vortrag gehalten auf der Versammlund der Freunde der Christlichen Welt zu Mühlacker am 3. Oktober 1901*. Tübingen: J. C. B. Mohr (Paul Siebeck), 1902.

Troxel, Ronald L. 'Matt 27.51–4 Reconsidered: Its Role in the Passion Narrative, Meaning and Origin'. *New Testament Studies* 48.1 (2002), 30–47.

Tschannen, Oliver. 'The Secularization Paradigm: A Systematization'. *Journal for the Scientific Study of Religion* 30.4 (1991), 395–415.

Tucker, Aviezer. *Our Knowledge of the Past: A Philosophy of Historiography*. Cambridge: Cambridge University, 2008.

Turner, Bryan S. *Religion and Social Theory*. 2nd ed. New York: City University of New York, 1991.

Twining, William. 'R.G. Collingwood's Autobiography: One Reader's Response'. *Journal of Law and Society* 25.4 (1998), 603–20.

Tyrrell, George. *Christianity at the Cross-Roads*. London: Longmans, Green and Co., 1909.

Vanhoye, Albert. *The Letter to the Hebrews: A New Commentary*. Mahwah, NJ: Paulist Press, 2015.

Vermes, Géza. *The Religion of Jesus the Jew*. London: SCM, 1993.

———. *Jesus and the World of Judaism*. London: SCM, 1983.

———. *Jesus the Jew: A Historian's Reading of the Gospels*. Minneapolis, MN: Fortress Press, 1973.

Voas, David. 'The Rise and Fall of Fuzzy Fidelity in Europe'. *European Sociological Review* 25.2 (2009), 155–68.

Voigt, Friedemann, ed. *Ernst Troeltsch Lesebuch: Ausgewählte Texte*. UTB 2452. Tübingen: Mohr Siebeck, 2003.

von Balthasar, Hans Urs. *Prayer*. San Francisco, CA: Ignatius, 1986.

Voltaire. *Essai sur les mœurs et l'esprit des nations et sur les principaux faits de l'histoire depuis Charlemagne jusqu'à Louis XIII*. Edited by Bruno Bernard, John Renwick, Nicholas Cronk, and Janet Godden. Vol. 21–27. Œuvres complètes de Voltaire. Oxford: The Voltaire Foundation, 2009.

Wamba-dia-Wamba, Ernest. 'How Is Historical Knowledge Recognized?' *History in Africa* 13 (1986), 331–44.

Waters, Sr., L. Kenneth. 'Matthew 27:52–53 as Apocalyptic Apostrophe: Temporal-Spatial Collapse in the Gospel of Matthew'. *Journal of Biblical Literature* 122.3 (2003), 489–515.

Weaver, Walter P. *The Historical Jesus in the Twentieth Century: 1900–1950*. Harrisburg, PA: Trinity International, 1999.

Webb, Eugene. *Worldview and Mind: Religious Thought and Psychological Development*. The Eric Voegelin Institute Series in Political Philosophy. Columbia, TN: University of Missouri, 2009.

Webb, Robert L. 'The Historical Enterprise and Historical Jesus Research'. In *Key Events in the Life of the Historical Jesus*, edited by Darrell L. Bock and Robert L. Webb, 9–94. WUNT 247. Tübingen: Mohr Siebeck, 2009.

Weber, Max. 'Science as Vocation'. In *The Vocation Lectures*, edited by David S. Owen and Tracy B. Strong, translated by Rodney Livingstone. Indianapolis, IN: Hackett Pub, 2004.

———. *Wirtschaft and Gesellschaft*. Tübingen: J. C. B. Mohr (Paul Siebeck), 1922.

———. 'Die protestantische Ethik und der Geitst des Kapitalismus'. In *Gesammelte Aufsätze zur Religionssoziologie*, 1:17–206. Tübingen: Mohr Siebeck, 1920.

Weber, Otto, and Darrell L. Guder. *Foundations of Dogmatics*. Vol. I. Grand Rapids, MI: Eerdmans, 1981.

Webster, John. *The Culture of Theology*. Grand Rapids, MI: Baker, 2019.

———. *Holy Scripture: A Dogmatic Sketch*. Current Issues in Theology; Cambridge: Cambridge University Press, 2003.

Weiss, Johannes. *Die Predigt Jesu vom Reiche Gottes*. Göttingen: Vandenhoeck & Ruprecht, 1892.

Weisse, Christian Hermann. *Die evangelische Geschichte, kritisch und philosophisch bearbeitet*. Leipzig: Breitkopf und Hartel, 1838.

Wenell, Karen J. *Jesus and Land: Sacred and Social Space in Second Temple Judaism*. LNTS 334. London: T&T Clark, 2007.

White, Hayden. *Tropics of Discourse: Essays in Cultural Criticism*. Baltimore, MD: John Hopkins, 1978.

———. *Metahistory: The Historical Imagination in Nineteenth-Century Europe*. Baltimore, MD: John Hopkins University, 1973.

Widder, Nathan. 'John Duns Scotus'. In *Deleuze's Philosophical Lineage*, edited by Graham Jones and Jon Roffe, 27–43. Edinburgh: Edinburgh University, 2009.

Williams, Donald C. 'The Myth of Passage'. *Journal of Philosophy* 48.15 (1951), 457–72.

Williams, Rowan. *Resurrection: Interpreting the Easter Gospel*. London: Darton, Longman and Todd, 1982.

Wilson, Bryan. 'Secularization: The Inherited Model'. In *The Sacred in a Secular Age*, edited by Phillip E. Hammond, 9–20. Berkeley, CA: University of California, 1985.

———. *Religion in Sociological Perspective*. Oxford: Oxford University, 1982.

———. 'The Return of the Sacred'. *Journal for the Scientific Study of Religion* 18.3 (1979), 268–80.

———. *Contemporary Transformations of Religion*. Oxford: Oxford University, 1976.

Witherington III, Ben. *The Jesus Quest: The Third Search for the Jew of Nazareth*. Carlisle: Paternoster, 1995.

Witherup, Ronald D. 'The Death of Jesus and the Rising of the Saints: Matthew 27:51–54 in Context'. In *Society of Biblical Literature Seminar Papers* 26, 574–85. Atlanta, GA: Scholars, 1987.

Wittgenstein, Ludwig. *Philosophical Investigations*. Translated by G.E.M. Anscombe. London: MacMillan, 1953.

———. *Tractatus Logico-Philosophicus*. London: Kegan Paul, 1922.

———. 'Logisch-Philosophische Abhandlung'. Edited by Wilhelm Ostwald. *Annalen Der Naturphilosophie* 14 (1921), 184–262.

Wolfe, Judith. 'The Eschatological Turn in German Philosophy'. *Modern Theology* 35.1 (2019), 55–70.

Wood, Allen W. *Kant*. Blackwell Great Minds. Oxford: Blackwell, 2005.

Wrede, William. *Das Messiasgeheimnis in den Evangelien: Zugleich ein Beitrag zum Verständnis des Markusevangeliums*. Göttingen: Vandenhoeck & Ruprecht, 1901.

Wright, N. T. *History and Eschatology: Jesus and the Promise of Natural Theology*. London: SPCK, 2019.

———. *Paul and the Faithfulness of God*. London: SPCK, 2013.

———. *The Resurrection of the Son of God*. London: SPCK, 2003.

———. *Jesus and the Victory of God*. London: SPCK, 1996.

———. 'Jesus, Quest for the Historical'in *The Anchor Bible Dictionary: Volume 3*, edited by David Noel Freedman, 3:796–802. 3 vols. New York: Doubleday, 1992a.

———. *The New Testament and the People of God*. London: SPCK, 1992b.

Wright, Stephen. 'The Leibniz's Law Problem (For Stage Theory)'. *Metaphysica* 11.2 (2010), 137–51.

Yablo, Stephen. 'A Priority and Existence'. In *New Essays on the* A Priori, edited by P. Boghossian and C. Peacocke, 197–228. Oxford: Oxford University, 2000.

———. 'Does Ontology Rest on a Mistake?' *Aristotelian Society Supplement* 72.1 (1998), 229–83.

Young, Lawrence A., ed. *Rational Choice Theory and Religion*. London: Routledge, 1997.

Zahl, Simeon. *The Holy Spirit and Christian Experience*. Oxford: OUP, 2020.

Zeilicovici, David. 'Temporal Becoming Minus the Moving-Now'. *Noûs* 23.4 (1989), 505–24.

Zimmerman, Dean. 'Chisholm on the Essences of Events'. In *The Philosophy of Roderick M. Chisholm*, edited by L. E. Hahn, 73–100. Chicago, IL: Open Court, 1997.

Zimmerman, Dean W. 'Temporary Intrinsics and Presentism'. In *Metaphysics: The Big Questions*, edited by Dean W. Zimmerman and Peter van Inwagen, 206–20. Cambridge, MA: Basil Blackwell, 1998.

———. 'Persistence and Presentism'. *Philosophical Papera* 25.2 (1996), 115–26.

Žižek, Slavoj. *Event.* Philosophy in Transit. London: Penguin, 2014.

———. *The Ticklish Subject*: *The Absent Centre of Political Ontology*. London and New York: Verso, 1999.

Zöller, Günter. 'Introduction'. In *The Cambridge Companion to Fichte*, edited by David James and Günter Zöller, 1–6. Cambridge: Cambridge University, 2016.

Zuckerman, Phil. *The Nonreligious: Understanding Secular People and Societies*. Oxford: Oxford University, 2016.

Zyphur, Michael J., and Frederick L. Oswald. 'Bayesian Estimation and Inference: A User's Guide'. *Journal of Management* 41.2 (2015), 390–420.

Zyphur, Michael J., Frederick L. Oswald, and Deborah E. Rupp. 'Rendezvous Overdue: Bayes Analysis Meets Organizational Research'. *Journal of Management* 41.2 (2014), 387–89.

Author Index

Allison, Jr., Dale C. 98, 133, 143, 156–59, 180, 184
Alvis, Jason W. 63
Ankersmit, Frank 19
Aquinas, Thomas 44n19, 193–94, 206, 215n13
Arnal, William E. 134
Asad, Talal 96, 98
Aspray, Silvianne 198, 201
Augustine of Hippo 110n4, 198
Avalos, Hector 13, 25n11
Ayer, A. J. 10, 41–42

Baasland, Ernst 145n64, 160, 209
Backhaus, Knut 121
Bacon, Francis 41
Badiou, Alain 38
Bainbridge, William Sims 103–7
Baird, William 120, 121, 126
Balthasar, Hans Urs von 47n51, 212
Barbour, Ian 167
Barcan, Ruth C. 39
Barclay, John M. G. 107, 114n80
Barthes, Roland 18
Bartholomew, Craig G. 25n12
Becker, Gary S. 104, 109
Behr, John 217
Beiser, Frederick 52
Berdyaev, Nicholas 212
Berg, Herbert 23, 88
Berkouwer, G. C. 207
Bermejo-Rubio, Fernando 119, 159–60
Bernier, Jonathan 168, 169, 172, 174
Bilde, Per 119
Birch, Jonathan C. P. 118, 119
Bloch, Marc 74
Blondel, Eric 57
Blondel, Maurice 47n51, 73, 78–82, 89, 140, 191, 201–2
Bock, Darrell L. 160
Bond, Helen 45n28, 118
Borg, Marcus J. 146
Bormann, Lukas 134
Bornkamm, Günther 138–39
Briggs, Richard S. 13
Brown, Colin 120
Brown, Raymond E. 14
Bruce, Steve 107, 109
Buckley, Philip 59
Bultmann, Rudolf 5, 13, 123, 133, 135–37, 139, 141

Carleton Paget, James 118–19
Carnap, Rudolf 31–32, 41–42
Carr, David 60
Casey, Maurice 134, 147
Chamberlain, H. S. 134, 135
Charlesworth, James H. 147
Chaves, Mark 100–103, 108
Clark, Samuel 36
Coakley, Sarah 212
Collingwood, R. G. 73–76, 81, 89, 191
Crick, Francis 82
Crossan, John Dominic 98, 149–52, 175
Crossley, James G. 14, 23, 210
Cullmann, Oscar 13

Danto, Arthur 18
Deines, Roland 5, 16–17, 20, 124, 146, 148, 203–6, 212
Denton, Donald L. 171, 174
Derrida Jacques 62, 72, 107
Descartes, René 12, 81
Dilthey, Wilhelm 55–56, 58–59, 65, 191
Dobbelaere, Karel 102
Dodd, C. H. 133
Dulles, Avery 170
Dunn, James D. G. 118, 139, 154–57, 159–60, 174, 182

Ebeling, Gerhard 7
Eschenmayer, Carl A. 121

Farías, Victor 62
Feldman, Fred 34
Festinger, Leon 209
Fichte, Johann Gottlieb 52–53, 64, 191
Fiebig, P. 134
Finetti, Bruno de 84
Finke, Roger 103, 108
Fish, Stanley 10
Fisher, R. A. 83
Flusser, David 147
Foucault, Michel 77
Frei, Hans W. 18–19, 176–77
Funk, Robert W. 149–50, 166, 167

Gadamer, Hans-Georg 60, 139, 154, 179
Goodchild, Philip 104
Gorski, Philip S. 108
Grotius, Hugo 95
Grundmann, Walter 134–35

Habermas, Jürgen 62
Halphen, Louis 74
Hart, David Bentley 30, 150
Hart, Patrick 4
Hartog, Paul 78
Hays, Richard B. 208
Head, Peter M. 134
Headlam, A. C. 133
Hegel, G. F. W. 53–54, 56, 58, 61, 63, 65, 72
Heidegger, Martin 52, 53, 62–65, 71, 136, 191, 197
Heilig, Christoph 84–85
Hengel, Martin 159–60, 190
Henry, Michel 79, 81, 88
Heringer, Seth 17–19, 20, 203–6, 211
Heschel, Susannah 134
Holyoake, G. J. 85
Hooker, M. D. 160
Horsley, Richard A. 147
Hume, David 37–38, 41, 42, 120, 155
Husserl, Edmund 58–65, 191

Iannaccone, Laurence A. 103–4
Inwagen, Peter van 31–33
Iser, Wolfgang 10

Jaeger, Werner Wilhelm 31
Jaspers, Karl 60–63, 65, 191
Jenson, Robert W. 208, 211
Jeremias, Joachim 133
Johnson, Luke Timothy 14

Kähler, Martin 6–9, 13, 18–20, 118, 123–27, 137–38, 202
Kant, Immanuel 21, 36, 41, 51–53, 56–59, 64, 126, 168, 173, 191, 201
Käsemann, Ernst 13, 123, 137–38
Kaye, Bruce N. 122
Keck, Leander E. 138, 146
Kierkegaard, Søren 54–55, 65
King, Richard H. 62
Kirkeby, Ole Fogh 38
Kuhn, Karl Georg 133
Kuhn, Thomas S. 10, 74
Kümmel, Werner Georg 121

Laas, Oliver 82–83
Laplace, Pierre-Simon 85
Lash, Nicholas 170
Latour, Bruno 101
Le Donne, Anthony 72
Lechner, Frank J. 101–2
Leibniz, G. W. 34, 36, 39–40
Lessing, G. E. 13, 119
Lewis, Clarence Irving 39
Lewis, David 40
Licona, Michael R. 182
Lindley, Dennis V. 84
Lonergan, Bernard J. F. 167–74, 180, 182, 183, 185, 192, 206
Losch, Andreas 167
Loux, Michael J. 42
Lubac, Henri de 78
Lüdemann, Gerd 147
Luther, Martin 95
Lyon, Robert W. 150
Lyotard, Jean-Françoise 10, 62, 72

MacDonald, Nathan 119
Malan, Gert J. 51
Marsden, George 9–12, 20, 201
Marsh, Clive 134
Mauss, Marcel 107
McCormack, Bruce Lindley 42
McGregor, Peter John 206
McKnight, Scott 174
Meier, John P. 152–53, 159
Merleau-Ponty, Maurice 63
Meyer, Ben F. 167–68, 171–72, 174, 183, 185, 192
Meynell, Hugo 170
Milbank, John 5, 107, 180, 193–98, 200, 202
Moltmann, Jürgen 207
Montchrestien, Antoine de 199
Morgan, Robert 14

Naugle, David K. 52, 55, 58, 59
Nerlich, Graham 35
Niebergall, Friedrich 125
Nietzsche, Friedrich 56–57, 65, 73, 75–78, 81, 89, 191

Oliver, Simon 36, 194
Olson, Daniel V. A. 108
Oman, Charles 74
Orr, James 57
Ott, Hugo 62
Owen, G. E. L. 31

Paci, Enzo 59
Paddison, Angus 6, 24
Palu, Ma'afu 36
Pannenberg, Wolfhart 13, 18, 19, 207
Perrin, Norman 148, 152, 160
Pitre, Brant 72, 85, 160
Pitts, Andrew W. 168, 174
Plutarch 34
Popper, Karl 180
Porter, Stanley E. 168, 174
Powell, Mark A. 146
Prior, A. N. 39

Quine, W. V. O. 31–33

Rae, Murray A. 12–14, 20
Rahner, Karl 170, 207
Raiffa, Howard 84
Räisänen, Heikki 9
Ramsey, Frank P. 84
Ratzinger, Joseph 14–16, 20, 148
Reimarus, Hermann Samuel 13, 118–21, 123, 125, 127, 155, 161, 192
Reynolds, Terrence 171
Roesenthal, Jerome 90
Rollens, Sarah E. 23, 190
Rorty, Richard 10, 72
Russell, Bertrand 42
Ryan, Jordan J. 160

Sanders, E. P. 72, 146, 148–49, 152, 157, 160
Sarna, Jan W. 60
Savage, Leonard J. 84
Schacht, Richard 57
Schillebeeckx, Edward 118, 139–42, 185, 209
Schlaifer, Robert O. 84
Schleiermacher, Friedrich 122–23
Schnackenburg, Rudolf 14
Schüssler Fiorenza, Elisabeth 3
Schwartz, Seth 107
Schweitzer, Albert 118–21, 125–27, 133, 136
Scott, E. F. 133
Scotus, John Duns 44n19, 194–95
Shiner, Larry 96
Sider, Theodore 39, 40
Simons, Peter 37
Simut, Ramona 139
Sire, James W. 56
Skinner, Quentin 74
Sonderegger, Katherine 207, 212
Stark, Rodney 103–8
Stevenson, Austin 25n12, 133, 201, 213
Strauss, D. F. 121–23, 125–27
Streeter, B. H. 133
Sullivan, Patrick A. 170

Tanner, Kathryn 104
Taylor, Charles 5, 56, 95–96, 101, 180, 193, 195–200, 202
Thate, Michael J. 125
Theissen, Gerd 72, 147
Thiselton, Anthony C. 33
Tonstad, Linn Marie 21, 195
Tooley, Michael 37, 47
Troeltsch, Ernst 7–9, 18–20, 123–25, 127, 138, 202
Tschannen, Oliver 101
Turner, Bryan S. 101

Vermes, Géza 146–49
Voltaire 72–73

Weaver, Walter P. 133
Webb, Eugene 60
Webb, Robert L. 160
Weber, Max 102–3, 197–98
Webster, John 210–12
Weiss, Johannes 125
White, Hayden 10, 18, 72
Williams, Rowan 210
Wilson, Bryan 100, 102
Winter, Dagmar 72
Witherington III, Ben 148, 149
Wittgenstein, Ludwig 41–42, 64, 65, 168, 191, 197
Wrede, William 126
Wright, N. T. 13, 18–19, 22, 50, 83, 87, 98, 102, 117, 133, 146–47, 162, 166–68, 172–85, 192, 208, 210

Zahl, Simeon 211–12
Zimmerman, Dean W. 42
Žižek, Slavoj 38

Subject Index

analogy of being 193–95
anti-Semitism *see* Nazi Germany
Aryan *see* Nazi Germany

Bayes' theorem 83–89, 191

causality 37–39, 42–43, 182, 190
change *see* identity
Christ of faith, the 6–7, 14, 20, 122–27, 138, 152, 202
compensators 104–9
contemplation *see* prayer
creation 13, 44n19, 53, 194, 210, 211
criteria of authenticity 140–41, 158, 160
critical realism 18, 160, 161, 166–75, 180, 182, 183, 185

Deism 13, 100, 120, 122, 123, 129n23, 148, 155, 173, 195

Enlightenment, the 5, 6, 10, 18, 20, 56, 72, 118, 120–21, 124, 126–27, 175–76, 185
event(s) 37–38, 73–75, 79, 81–85, 89, 175–78, 182, 184, 209
existentialism 63, 126, 136

hermeneutics 12, 15, 154–56, 171

identity 34–35, 39, 42–43, 82, 89, 106, 146, 173, 190
imagination 74–75, 81, 157

miracles 38, 120, 127, 155, 209
modal logic 39–40, 81

narrative 4, 10, 19, 50, 72, 74, 200, 203–4
Nazi Germany 62, 134–36
Nouvelle théologie 47n51, 78, 207

objectivity 5, 61, 151, 177, 205
ontology 31–34, 42, 63, 80, 177, 210

perception 50–53, 168, 173
phenomenology 59–60, 63, 80
plausibility 72–73, 81–89, 156, 158, 160, 179
prayer 211–13
probability *see* plausibility

Radical Orthodoxy 25n7, 45n19, 193–96
reformation, the 198–200
resurrection 5, 13, 139, 155–56, 158–59, 175–85, 208–10
rewards (economic) 104–8

scripture 14, 210–11
sense *see* perception
space 35–37
supernatural *see* miracles

temporality 35–37
Trinity, the 35, 207–8

univocity of being 44n19, 193–95

Wirkungsgeschichte 139, 154–56, 179